THE NOTION OF *DIṬṬHI* IN THERAVĀDA BUDDHISM

The notion of 'view' or 'opinion' (*diṭṭhi*) as an obstacle to 'seeing things as they are' is a central concept in Buddhist thought. This book considers the two ways in which the notion of views is usually understood. Are we to understand right-view as a correction of wrong-views (the opposition understanding), or is the aim of the Buddhist path the overcoming of all views, even right-view (the no-views understanding)? This book argues that neither approach is correct. Instead, it suggests that the early texts do not understand right-view as a correction of wrong-view, but as a detached order of seeing, completely different from the attitude of holding to any view, wrong or right. Claiming that by the term 'right-view' we should understand an order of seeing which transcends all views, this work is a valuable addition to the study of Buddhist philosophy.

Paul Fuller is a Religious Studies graduate from the University of Edinburgh. He holds an MA and a PhD from the University of Bristol and is currently teaching Buddhist Studies at Webster University, Thailand.

ROUTLEDGECURZON CRITICAL STUDIES IN BUDDHISM

General Editors:
Charles S. Prebish and Damien Keown

RoutledgeCurzon Critical Studies in Buddhism is a comprehensive study of the Buddhist tradition. The series explores this complex and extensive tradition from a variety of perspectives, using a range of different methodologies.

The series is diverse in its focus, including historical studies, textual translations and commentaries, sociological investigations, bibliographical studies and considerations of religious practice as an expression of Buddhism's integral religiosity. It also presents materials on modern intellectual historical studies, including the role of Buddhist thought and scholarship in a contemporary, critical context and in the light of current social issues. The series is expansive and imaginative in scope, spanning more than two and a half millennia of Buddhist history. It is receptive to all research works that inform and advance our knowledge and understanding of the Buddhist tradition.

THE REFLEXIVE NATURE OF AWARENESS
Paul Williams

ALTRUISM AND REALITY
Paul Williams

BUDDHISM AND HUMAN RIGHTS
Edited by Damien Keown, Charles Prebish, Wayne Husted

WOMEN IN THE FOOTSTEPS OF THE BUDDHA
Kathryn R. Blackstone

THE RESONANCE OF EMPTINESS
Gay Watson

IMAGING WISDOM
Jacob N. Kinnard

PAIN AND ITS ENDING
Carol S. Anderson

EMPTINESS APPRAISED
David F. Burton

THE SOUND OF LIBERATING TRUTH
Edited by Sallie B. King and Paul O. Ingram

BUDDHIST THEOLOGY
Edited by Roger R. Jackson and John J. Makransky

THE GLORIOUS DEEDS OF PURNA
Joel Tatelman

EARLY BUDDHISM – A NEW APPROACH
Sue Hamilton

CONTEMPRORARY BUDDHIST ETHICS
Edited by Damien Keown

INNOVATIVE BUDDHIST WOMEN
Edited by Karma Lekshe Tsomo

TEACHING BUDDHISM IN THE WEST
Edited by V. S. Hori, R. P. Hayes and J. M. Shields

SELF, REALITY AND REASON IN TIBETAN PHILOSOPHY
Thupten Jinpa

IN DEFENSA OF DHARMA
Tessa J. Bartholomeusz

BUDDHIST PHENOMENOLOGY
Dan Lusthaus

RELIGIOUS MOTIVATION AND THE ORIGINS OF BUDDHISM
Torkel Brekke

DEVELOPMENTS IN AUSTRALIAN BUDDHISM
Michelle Spuler

ZEN WAR STORIES
Brian Victoria

THE BUDDHIST UNCONSCIOUS
William S. Waldron

INDIAN BUDDHIST THEORIES OF PERSONS
James Duerlinger

ACTION DHARMA
Edited by Christopher Queen, Charles Prebish and Damien Keown

TIBETAN AND ZEN BUDDHISM IN BRITAIN
David N. Kay

THE CONCEPT OF THE BUDDHA
Guang Xing

THE PHILOSOPHY OF DESIRE IN THE BUDDHIST PALI CANON
David Webster

THE NOTION OF *DIṬṬHI* IN THERAVĀDA BUDDHISM
Paul Fuller

The following titles are published in association with the *Oxford Centre for Buddhist Studies*

Oxford Centre for Buddhist Studies
a project of The Society for the Wider Understanding of the Buddhist Tradition

The *Oxford Centre for Buddhist Studies* conducts and promotes rigorous teaching and research into all forms of the Buddhist tradition.

EARLY BUDDHIST METAPHYSICS
Noa Ronkin

MIPHAM'S DIALECTICS AND THE DEBATES ON EMPTINESS
Karma Phuntso

THE NOTION OF *DIṬṬHI* IN THERAVĀDA BUDDHISM

The point of view

Paul Fuller

RoutledgeCurzon
Taylor & Francis Group
LONDON AND NEW YORK

First published 2005
by RoutledgeCurzon
2 Park Square, Milton Park, Abingdon, Oxon OX14 4RN

Simultaneously published in the USA and Canada
by RoutledgeCurzon
711 Third Avenue, New York, NY 10017

RoutledgeCurzon is an imprint of the Taylor & Francis Group

First issued in paperback 2012

Typeset in Times by
HWA Text and Data Management, Tunbridge Wells

British Library Cataloguing in Publication Data
A catalogue record for this book is available from the British Library

Library of Congress Cataloging in Publication Data
A catalog record for this book has been requested

ISBN 978-0-415-34293-3 (hbk)
ISBN 978-0-415-65049-6 (pbk)

DEDICATED TO THE MEMORY OF MY SISTER

DEBBIE

1962–1998

I closed my eyes to see you no more
I closed my eyes to cry
Because I saw you no more

(Paul Eluard)

CONTENTS

PREFACE

I grew up in a small town, a town that it is best to leave – I left – this book is a direct result of my leaving. A number of people helped. I thank my family, each of whom understood, in their own ways, what I was doing. The vehicle that got me away was Buddhism (and, more generally, education, and in a different way, music). I am grateful to all those who encouraged me in the past.

Once away, I was very lucky to study with Paul Dundas in Edinburgh. It was Paul who first noticed my interest in the study of religion, and who first suggested that I should continue studying, which I did, in Bristol. There, Rupert Gethin was an understanding supervisor. One particular article he wrote on *diṭṭhi* explains very clearly what I have attempted to argue in this book. I have a suspicion that I am merely expanding on these ideas.

At certain times, at bad times, we need friends, and my friends at such a time were Theo Bertram, Samantha Grant, Louise Nelstrop and Adam Rounce. The way they acted will always stay with me and I will never forget their kindness and understanding. I wrote this book in Bristol where I could wish for no greater company than Carl Dolan and Tim Saunders. Also in Bristol, David Webster and I finished our doctorates at the same time, I thank him for some great nights sharing all that was happening.

I began this preface by saying how I wanted to get away from where I was. If I have learned anything from Buddhism it is that we cannot escape from where we are, for there is nothing ultimately wrong with the world, but with the way we grasp things. In order to discover this, we need to find a different way of seeing things. Without my very good friend Les Billingham, I would never have began to think and to explore such ideas. Few greater gifts can be given than the one he gave to me.

I recently met and married the person that you only meet once in life. I love her with all my heart. She truly is my inspiration, my best friend and the person who knows my heart. I cannot thank my love, or ever use words that express what I feel for her.

As I write, we are in Thailand and my wife and our unborn child are sleeping in the bed nearby. That they are both happy, I can wish no more. Peaceful dreams my loves.

ACKNOWLEDGEMENTS

I am happy to acknowledge the assistance of the British Academy (now the AHRB) for funding all my postgraduate research. I also express my gratitude to Dawn Collins, Oliver Cooper and Adam Rounce for proof reading the original thesis. More recently my good friend Justin Meiland was kind enough to read through the entire manuscript for which I am profoundly grateful. Justin corrected much of the Pāli, but the mistakes that remain are my own. Pascale Engelmajer also read through the thesis, then the manuscript, more often than she can perhaps care to remember. The whole book has benefited greatly through these careful readings.

The examiners of the original PhD thesis, of which this book is a revised version, were Sue Hamilton and Paul Williams. I thank both Sue and Paul for their honesty and help in making me think coherently about my ideas.

Teaching has been an amazing experience for me. I would prefer to see myself as a teacher above all the things that go with having conducted any research. This book owes much to my first students who listened, questioned, and helped me to explain what I understand about Buddhism.

ABBREVIATIONS

A	Aṅguttara-nikāya
As	Atthasālinī (Dhammasaṅgaṇi-aṭṭhakathā)
D	Dīgha-nikāya
Dhp	Dhammapada
Dhp-a	Dhammapadaṭṭhakathā
Dhs	Dhammasaṅgaṇi
J	Jātaka
Kv	Katthāvatthu
Kv-a	Pañcappakaraṇaṭṭhakathā (Katthāvatthu-aṭṭhakathā)
M	Majjhima-nikāya
Mhv	Mahāvaṃsa
Mil	Milindapañha
Mp	Manorathapūraṇī (Aṅguttara-nikāya-aṭṭhakathā)
Nett	Nettippakaraṇa
Nidd I	Mahāniddesa
P	Pāli
Paṭis	Paṭisambhidāmagga
Paṭṭh	Paṭṭhāna
Paṭṭh-a	Pañcappakaraṇa-aṭṭhakathā (Paṭṭhāna-aṭṭhakathā)
PED	Pāli–English Dictionary
Peṭ	Peṭakopadesa
Ps	Papañcasūdanī (Majjhima-nikāya-aṭṭhakathā)
PTS	Pāli Text Society
Pugg	Puggalapaññatti
S	Saṃyutta-nikāya
Skt	Sanskrit
Sn	Suttanipāta
Spk	Sāratthappakāsinī (Saṃyutta-nikāya-aṭṭhakathā)
Sv	Sumaṅgalavilāsinī (Dīgha-nikāya aṭṭhakathā)
Tikap	Tikapaṭṭhāna
Ud	Udāna
Ud-a	Udānaaṭṭhakathā
Vibh	Vibhaṅga
Vibh-a	Sammohavinodanī
Vin	Vinayapiṭaka
Vism	Visuddhimagga

INTRODUCTION

The notion of 'view' or 'opinion' (*diṭṭhi*) as an obstacle to 'seeing things as they are' (*yathābhūtadassana*) is a central concept in Buddhist thought. In the study of *diṭṭhi* there is a dilemma. Early Buddhist texts talk about it as 'wrong' (*micchā*) and 'right' (*sammā*). The aim of the path is the cultivation of 'right-view' (*sammā-diṭṭhi*) and the abandoning of 'wrong-views' (*micchā-diṭṭhi*).[1] I shall refer to this as the opposition understanding of views, i.e. right-view stands in opposition to, or corrects, wrong-views. It is generally assumed that this is by far the most usual understanding of *diṭṭhi* found within the Nikāyas. However, there is also a tradition of Buddhist thought evident in some *Sutta-nipāta* verses (the *Aṭṭhakavagga* and, to a lesser extent, the *Pārāyanavagga*), and certain *suttas* from the Nikāyas, that equates 'right-view' with 'no-view' at all. The aim of the Buddhist path is here seen as the overcoming of all views, even right-view.[2] Views, if held with attachment, are wrong-views. Just as objects of the senses are a hindrance, so all views and opinions, both 'wrong' and 'right' and even 'knowledge' (*ñāṇa*), are rejected as the means towards the goal of complete non-attachment. The aim of the path is not the cultivation of right-view and the abandoning of wrong-views but the relinquishment of all views, wrong or right. I shall refer to this as the no-views understanding of views.

On the face of it, these understandings are somewhat different. However, it is my argument that the difference is apparent. I will suggest that the early texts do not understand right-views as a correction of wrong-view, but as a detached order of seeing, completely different from the attitude of holding to any view, wrong or right. Right-view is not a doctrine, a correct proposition, as I think the opposition theory implies, but the correct knowledge of doctrine. Right-view is practised, not adopted or believed in. By this I mean that it is the correct attitude towards the Buddha's teachings, towards the *dhamma*. A correct knowledge of doctrine should not involve attachment. A true statement, if it is an object of attachment, is *micchā-diṭṭhi*, even though it is still true. Wrong-view is a form of greed and attachment, right-view the cessation of greed and attachment. Right-view signifies the cessation of craving, not the rejection of *all* views. Consequently, neither the opposition understanding, nor the no-views understanding gives a proper explanation of the notion of *diṭṭhi*. I will argue that there are not in fact two tendencies found within the early texts and that the attainment of right-view and the practising of no-view amount to the same thing. In other words, to say that one has right-view is to say that one has no-view. The consequence of achieving right-view is that one does not hold *any* views. The aim of the path is the transcendence of all views.Why is there such a strong focus upon the notion of *diṭṭhi* within early Buddhism? Views entail mental rigidity and are potential objects of attachment. Buddhism teaches that one should not indulge in objects of sensual desire, and in a sense, Buddhist philosophy is a warning against becoming attached to objects of cognition. In the same way that the Buddha is said to have passed beyond attachment to sensual desire, he is also said to have 'passed beyond' (*samatikkanta*) the 'bondage, tie, greed, obsession, acceptance, attachment and lust of view' (*diṭṭhi-rāga-abhivinivesa-vinibandha-paligedha-pariyuṭṭhānajjhosāna*, A I 66). Although such assertions as the four truths may counter the philosophical views of other schools, I would argue that for them to be *sammā-diṭṭhi*, for them to be right, they could not themselves be views at all. It is in this way that they are right-views. They may counter incorrect propositions, but they are not intended to be 'correct' propositions in the usual sense of the term. They are right, *sammā*, precisely because they cannot be an object of attachment. Though they are termed *diṭṭhi*, it is precisely because they do not share the unwholesome aspects of *micchā-diṭṭhi* that they are termed *sammā-diṭṭhi*. The four truths may then correct and counter views, but as propositions, they are not intended to be held as *micchā-diṭṭhi* are held, but to reflect a detached form of cognition. It is right-view, *sammā-diṭṭhi*, which implies this different order of seeing.

The opposition understanding

What are wrong and right-views? First, wrong-view is the denial of *kamma*, the denial that actions have consequences. Right-view is the affirmation of *kamma*, the affirmation that actions have consequences. Second, wrong-views are views about the self. The self is held either to exist eternally (*sassata-diṭṭhi*) or to be annihilated (*uccheda-diṭṭhi*). The right-view which corrects these wrong-views is either the knowledge of suffering, its arising, cessation, and the way to its cessation, i.e. knowledge of the four truths; or the knowledge of the arising and cessation of one or all of the twelve links of 'dependent-origination' (*paṭicca-samuppāda*), seeing the conditioned nature of all phenomena. There is a positive doctrinal statement here, a *sammā-diṭṭhi*. In the opposition understanding a right-view *corrects* a wrong-view. Right-view is the opposite of wrong-view. Other terms such as 'accomplishment in view' (*diṭṭhi-sampadā*), 'accomplished in view' (*diṭṭhi-sampanna*), and 'purification of view' (*diṭṭhi-visuddhi*), stress the importance of right-view. All these terms suggest an attitude to views that places right-view above wrong-view as a superior doctrine. Right-view is something that one should strive to attain. The holder of right-view has knowledge of a certain aspect of Buddhist doctrine. These terms suggest a definite approach to the notion of *diṭṭhi*, one in which right-views are cultivated and wrong-views abandoned. Such terms emphasise a different path structure to that of rejecting all views. Some views *are* beneficial.

The no-views understanding

The no-views understanding, the strategy to negate all *diṭṭhi* even if, in theory, they express what is 'true', is found primarily in the *Aṭṭhakavagga* and the *Pārāyanavagga* of the *Sutta-nipāta.*[3] Richard Gombrich has argued that to state that the Buddha 'has no viewpoint [. . .] at all' is an 'extreme position', found only in the *Aṭṭhakavagga* and the *Pārāyanavagga.*[4] The no-views understanding has been termed 'Proto-Mādhyamika' by Luis Gómez.[5] Richard Hayes has used the term 'doxastic minimalism' to describe this understanding within Buddhist thought.[6] As is well-known, the Nāgārjuna of the *Mūlamādhyamakakārikā* also displayed an explicit awareness of the danger of holding to any view, wrong or right.

The *Aṭṭhakavagga* itself strikes one as practical in nature. In the *Aṭṭhakavagga* there are, apparently, no 'four truths', no 'eightfold path', no 'dependent-origination', the content of right-view, but constantly and persistently the practice of turning away from all ideas of wrong and right, pure or impure, higher or lower, is advised. A typical verse illustrates this:

> An involved person is indeed involved in dispute(s) in respect of doctrines (but) how, about what, could one dispute with one who is not involved? He has taken up or laid down nothing. He has shaken off all views in this world.[7]

These themes are repeated continuously in the *Aṭṭhakavagga*. We find it said that the brahmin should 'not fall back on any view' (*diṭṭhi* [...] *pacceti kiñci*, Sn 800) or 'adopt a view' (*diṭṭhim anādiyānaṃ*, Sn 802). Both 'knowledge' (*ñāṇa*) and *diṭṭhi* come in for equal criticism. The ideas of 'correct' or 'incorrect' knowledge or views are, in the final analysis, irrelevant for the *Aṭṭhakavagga*. The psychological destructiveness of 'craving' (*taṇhā*) and 'attachment' (*upādāna*) invalidates the possible metaphysical validity of any standpoint. Views, for the *Aṭṭhakavagga*, are not essentially cognitive mistakes but, through being expressions of attachment, give rise to what ought not to be done. All views, in this interpretation, whether they assert what is or is not, whether they are right or wrong, express what is 'unwholesome' (*akusala*). Holding any proposition involves a subtle attachment. Luis Gómez has commented on the procedure of the *Aṭṭhakavagga* towards Buddhist doctrine:

> The Aṭṭha's doctrine [...] is a 'no-doctrine' in the sense that someone who accepts this doctrine is expected to have an attitude with respect to it which is precisely the contrary of what we normally expect from someone

> who espouses a theory. And this is not the philosophical silence of skepticism nor the methodological bracketing of the phenomenologist. It is the simple fact that to be practically consistent, a theory of the silencing of the moorings of apperception must be self-abrogating. Thus, the theory is incomplete without the practice because theory cannot silence itself by itself. It must culminate in a practice which will bring its consummation by consuming it.[8]

We find then one understanding in which right-view is to be adopted and wrong-views abandoned and another understanding in which all views, if held with attachment, are wrong. Of particular interest is how far the no-views understanding of the *Aṭṭhakavagga* is implicit in the treatment of *diṭṭhi* in other parts of the Nikāyas. For example, is not the relinquishing of all bases, all truth claims, a necessary consequence of what, in one understanding, constitutes 'knowledge' in the Nikāyas, namely the means between the two extremes of identity and difference, negation and affirmation, denial and assertion? How, in fact, is the middle-way asserted: is it possible to express a right-view that is not held with attachment? The two extremes that right-view must avoid are termed *uccheda-diṭṭhi*, the view of annihilation, and *sassata-diṭṭhi*, the view of eternalism. How can there be a view, a *sammā-diṭṭhi*, that expresses the position (if this is the correct term) between these two extremes? For example, Paul J. Griffiths has argued that the Buddhist tradition wanted to express a proposition but not a view,[9] a subject I will treat in more detail below. One way of stating the distinction between the non-attachment to all views and the adoption of right-view and the rejection of wrong-view is as follows: one path structure holds that, by necessity, there can be no positive assertion, no cataphasis. Right-view should not replace wrong-view–no *view* is the 'right-view'. The other path structure states that there can be a right-view, a *sammā-diṭṭhi*, that is of such a nature that it expresses what is both doctrinally true and is of value. This second path structure gives validity to *sammā-diṭṭhi*. The apophasis of no-views is itself a hindrance.[10] It denies the means towards the goal. Right-view, *sammā-diṭṭhi*, agrees with the *dhamma* and is a valid means towards the goal of *nibbāna*, *micchā-diṭṭhi* disagrees with doctrine and destroys the path.

Recent studies of the notion of *diṭṭhi*

I would like to consider the notion of *diṭṭhi* as considered in some modern academic studies. I will take as my starting point the analysis of *diṭṭhi* by Steven Collins. Collins bases his analysis of views on the twofold model which I have just outlined. First, there is a distinction between wrong-views and right-views (the opposition understanding). For example, theories of self are replaced by the theory of impersonal elements (*dhammas*),[11] this being correct doctrine. He further divides this opposition understanding into three categories. The first he terms 'pro-attitude': *sammā-diṭṭhi* is opposed to *micchā-diṭṭhi* by the holder of right-view 'having a correct attitude to one's social and religious duties, in the light of the belief system of *karma* and *saṃsāra*'.[12] Collins holds that there is nothing specifically Buddhist about such an attitude. His second category is 'acquaintance with Buddhist doctrine'. This is the first stage of the noble eightfold path. It consists of knowledge of such Buddhist doctrines as the four truths and dependent-origination. This 'involves only an initial knowledge of Buddhist teaching, an ability to identify correctly certain key doctrines'.[13] His third category, taken from the *Mahācattārīsaka-sutta*, explains *sammā-diṭṭhi* as 'wisdom' (*paññā*).[14] He describes right-view at this stage as 'liberating insight'. This consists of the investigation of *dhammas* in such practices as meditation.[15]

The second way of analysing views is that of 'no-views' (what I have termed the no-views understanding).[16] Collins devotes an entire chapter to this way of understanding views. He suggests that, at a certain stage of the path, all views are classified according to the degree of attachment with which they are held:

> The dichotomy between right and wrong-views is replaced [...] by a continuum, along which all conceptual standpoints and cognitive acts are graded according to the degree to which they are held or performed with attachment'.[17]

Views are appraised 'in relation to the single affective dimension of "attachment"'.[18] Views are something to which we become attached. They give rise to confusion and are opposed to calm and stillness. The idea that this proliferation of conceptuality, or acts of cognition, are potential hindrances, has been important throughout Buddhist thought. In his study of *papañca* Ñāṇananda has highlighted the role of *diṭṭhi* as an aspect of 'mental proliferation'. The notion of *papañca* is described by Ñāṇananda as 'the inveterate tendency towards proliferation in the realm of ideation'.[19] The *dhamma*, as Buddhist doctrine, may be defined in the opposite terms. It tends towards a cessation of craving and attachment.[20] In one sense, Ñāṇananda holds that the Buddhist path may be explained as 'a path of non-proliferation' (*nippapañcapatha*, A III 211).[21] The aim of *sammā-diṭṭhi*, of the *dhamma*, 'is to purge the mind of all views inclusive of itself'.[22] This aspect of wrong-view, as being symptomatic of mental proliferation in the cognitive process, has also been suggested by Sue Hamilton. She argues that views in general are expressed within the conceptual framework of existence and non-existence and 'within the conceptual framework of manifoldness and permanence'.[23] In a sense, any position is an erroneous position, precisely because it is a position.[24] Any position can give rise to craving. As I stated above, *sammā-diṭṭhi* must be an expression of the path between the two extremes of *uccheda* and *sassata-diṭṭhi*.

A number of related points have been made by Carol Anderson about the notion of *diṭṭhi*. As she states, on the evidence of the *suttas*, *sammā-diṭṭhi* is not simply to be 'positively regarded' but 'fully developed, practised and learned'.[25] She believes that, in the study of religion, experience has been divided into action and cognition and that this has distorted our understanding. Following the observations made by Mary Douglas, she holds that we should look for the underlying structure of the whole human experience, the religious life, to explain what may appear anomalous to scholars who separate the cognitive and affective.[26] The notion of *sammā-diṭṭhi*, which may initially be understood as propositional, to which intellectual assent is given, is closely associated with action and behaviour. In considering the relationship between right-view, propositions and action, Anderson states that:

> As *sammā-diṭṭhi*, propositions initially require intellectual agreement. But beyond that, developing a familiarity with the teachings and knowing them as liberation involves more than the mind. In turn, the Theravāda canon demonstrates that views are efficacious in and of themselves, influencing one's actions and success along the path.[27]

Anderson arrives at these conclusions by considering the nature of *sammā-diṭṭhi* in several ways. First, she argues that right-view is similar to doctrine in that it contains propositions that express the central claims of a religious community.[28] Second, right-view and doctrine are similar in that the learning of the proposition expressed by right-view involves the practice of 'proper conduct', which, in the Buddhist context, involves the generation of *kamma*. Third, Anderson states that 'intellectual assent' to right-view is required in the Buddhist tradition. All three of these aspects of right-view make it comparable to doctrine. However, she argues that *sammā-diṭṭhi* and doctrine are not comparable in that 'right view actuates religious transformation when learned as a component of the path'.[29]

Anderson makes two important points. The first is that *sammā-diṭṭhi* is involved in, and intrinsically related to, action. In the Nikāyas this would imply a type of view called 'mundane right-view' (*lokiya-sammā-diṭṭhi*), which is involved in the accumulation of merit and the production of *kamma*.[30] Anderson's other suggestion, that the adoption of right-view 'actuates religious transformation' is also important because it would fit with the Nikāya description of 'supramundane right-view' (*lokuttara-sammā-diṭṭhi*), which is explained as *paññā*.[31] This implies that, as a component of the path, *sammā-diṭṭhi* is effective in the transformation of the cognitive processes of the person who holds the view. This religious transformation possibly implies the role of *sammā-diṭṭhi* in activating non-attachment from all cognitive acts. Right-view, in this understanding, is not so much a right doctrine that is opposed to wrong doctrine, but part of the correct attitude, or right practice, commensurate with the Buddhist path. In fact, it is the correct attitude towards knowledge, towards doctrine. A similar understanding of the nature of right-view is proposed by John Ross Carter. In a discussion of the four truths, he makes the suggestion that a better understanding of the term *sammā* would be 'proper'. He proposes this to diverge from an understanding of *sammā* and *micchā* as wrong and right truth claims. In Carter's understanding, *sammā-diṭṭhi* is 'right' or 'proper', as being appropriate to the overcoming of craving and ignorance (*taṇhā* and *avijjā*).[32] It is the affective nature of a view which causes it to be classified as wrong or right. In this understanding, a wrong-view is wrong because it is 'unwholesome' (*akusala*), whereas a right-view is right because it is 'wholesome' (*kusala*).

This leads away from an understanding of *micchā-diṭṭhi* as a wrong proposition and *sammā-diṭṭhi* as a right proposition.

The notion of *diṭṭhi* has less to do with truth and falsehood, than with craving and its cessation. This idea is important to my argument against both the opposition and no-views understandings. Both understandings are based upon a misinterpretation of *diṭṭhi*. Rupert Gethin suggests that the propositional understanding of views is similar to an understanding of *sammā-diṭṭhi* according to the categories of 'pro-attitude' and 'acquaintance with Buddhist doctrine'.[33] Views, as propositions, stand in opposition to other views. Right-view 'corrects' wrong-views. But this is not, argues Gethin, how the early Abhidhamma understood the notion of *sammā-diṭṭhi*:

> When the *Dhammasaṅgaṇi* states that right-view occurs as a mental-concomitant of ordinary, sense sphere, skilful consciousness – a kind of consciousness that the commentaries suggest might occur when we give a gift, or turn away from harming a living creature or taking what is not given, or perform some other meritorious and auspicious action – it is not suggesting the occurrence of a dispositional attitude towards propositions of Buddhist teachings, nor acquaintance with basic Buddhist doctrine, nor even a theoretical understanding of Buddhist doctrine. Rather we must take it at face value; the *Dhammasaṅgaṇi* is claiming that at the time of the occurrence of that consciousness some kind of direct awareness of the nature of suffering, its arising, its cessation, and the path leading to its cessation occurs.[34]

I will argue that the aim of right-view is the eradication of all mental rigidity and cognitive attachment. The content of right-view is the knowledge of the cessation of craving and attachment.

These are some of the issues involved in understanding the opposition between *micchā-diṭṭhi* and *sammā-diṭṭhi*. As I have suggested, the usual understanding of these notions, as a simple opposition between wrong and right doctrines, may be misleading, but it is still the prevalent understanding. The no-views understanding, only thought to be found in a few isolated passages, is suggestive of the proper understanding of the notion of views. By this I mean that the transcendence of views has some of the characteristics of the practising of no-views, but to realise this different order of seeing, one *must* achieve right-view.

Three ideas shape my argument: the idea that views should be understood as knowledge of doctrine, the relationship between 'is' and 'ought', and the relationship between propositions and ways of seeing.

Knowledge of doctrine

I argued above that right-view is not a correct proposition in opposition to an incorrect proposition. I think that it is more helpful to understand right-view as correct knowledge of doctrine, i.e. as an attitude free from craving and attachment. As mentioned above, in her study of the four truths, Carol Anderson equates the notion of *diṭṭhi* with doctrine. I think this severely distorts her understanding of the notion of *diṭṭhi*. The notion of doctrine would be better understood as the *dhamma*, while the notion of *diṭṭhi* would better be understood as knowledge of the *dhamma*. Right-view is right knowledge of the *dhamma*, wrong-view is wrong knowledge of the *dhamma*. To put this another way, right-view is a true knowledge of things as they are, as they should be understood for the cessation of *dukkha*; wrong-view is a false knowledge of things as they are, which binds one to *dukkha*.

Two points support the idea that views should be understood as knowledge of doctrine. First, right-view and wrong-view are concerned with a correct and incorrect grasp of the teachings. It is clear that there can be attachment to the *dhamma*, and this constitutes wrong-view. Wrong-view is a wrong grasp of the teachings, right-view is a correct grasp of the teachings. It is an understanding free from craving. However, I am not arguing for a pragmatic understanding of Buddhism. The simile of the raft (M I 134–5) suggests that the teachings should not be grasped, not that the teachings are only of pragmatic value: the *dhamma* is both true and of value. As I shall set out below, I do not think that the Buddha's teachings should be understood only as value statements: they are true and of value.

This is related to my second point, that wrong-view is a craving and greed for doctrine, whether that doctrine is wrong or right. Right-view is the cessation of craving for doctrine. It is a form of wisdom. This point is clear from the fact that views in general are regarded as a form of greed in the Nikāyas. The notions of ignorance (*avijjā*) and wrong-view (or any view) are distinguished in the Nikāyas. Wrong-view is primarily a form of greed, while ignorance is primarily a form of delusion. Though their definitions do overlap, it is helpful to understand *diṭṭhi* as a wrong grasp of knowledge, not ignorance itself. It can be argued that wrong-views are the grasping aspect of ignorance, whereas right-view is that aspect of wisdom which does not crave, which is free from greed and attachment.

In terms of my overall argument, these points are important. The understanding of views as correct and incorrect knowledge of doctrine has far-reaching implications for the two understandings of views that I have outlined. First, the opposition understanding is challenged because there is not an opposition between wrong-view and right-view as incorrect and correct truth claims but an opposition between craving and the cessation of craving. Second, the rejection of all views is not being advised, but the abandoning of craving and attachment to views. It is not the validity of 'seeing things as they are' which is being rejected, but the greed for that way of apprehending things. The early texts do not reject knowledge, but attachment to knowledge.

Is/ought

In *After Virtue*, Alasdair MacIntyre has suggested that a dichotomy between 'is' and 'ought', between fact and value, is a modern phenomenon. Indeed, MacIntyre argues that, until modern times, the distinction between 'is' and 'ought' was not made.[35] Western thought may then make a distinction between thought and action, between fact and value, that was not made in India. This point has been made by Paul Williams:

> In the Indian context it would have been axiomatic that liberation comes from discerning how things actually are, the true nature of things. That seeing things how they are has soteriological benefits would have been expected, and is just another way of articulating the 'is' and 'ought' dimension of Indian Dharma. The 'ought' (pragmatic benefit) is never cut adrift from the 'is' (cognitive factual truth). Otherwise it would follow that the Buddha might be able to benefit beings (and thus bring them to enlightenment) even without seeing things the way they really are at all. And that is not Buddhism.[36]

The uncoupling of the categories of 'is' and 'ought' is usually traced to Hume. Since Hume, it has been questioned whether we can derive statements of value from statements of fact. Hume argued the following:

> In every system of morality, which I have hitherto met with, I have always remarked, that the author proceeds for some time in the ordinary way of reasoning, and establishes the being of a God, or makes observations concerning human affairs; when of a sudden I am surprised to find, that instead of the usual copulations of propositions, *is*, and *is not*, I meet with no proposition that is not connected with an *ought*, or an *ought not*. This change is imperceptible; but is, however, of the last consequence. For as this *ought*, or *ought not*, expresses some new relation or affirmation, it is necessary that it should be observed and explained; and at the same time that a reason should be given, for what seems altogether inconceivable, how this new relation can be a deduction from others, which are entirely different from it. But as authors do not commonly use this precaution, I shall presume to recommend it to readers; and am persuaded, that this small attention would subvert all the vulgar systems of morality, and let us see, that the distinction of vice and virtue is not founded merely on the relation of objects, nor is perceived by reason.[37]

Hume is arguing that a statement of fact, how things are, 'cannot provide a logical basis for morality'.[38] In other words, we cannot derive what is of value from apprehending the true nature of things. However, as Paul Williams suggests, such a dichotomy may never have existed in India. It does, moreover, greatly alter our understanding of certain statements if the distinction between 'is' and 'ought' is not made. One set of statements that do not make such a distinction is right-view, which expresses both fact and value. As I have argued, right-view is both an 'is' and an 'ought' statement.

First, it is clear that without the distinction between 'is' and 'ought', statements of fact are also statements of value. This means that seeing things as they are is also soteriologically transformative. In the context of Buddhist soteriology, this is usually stated in terms of craving and ignorance being overcome by calm and insight. It is important to reflect upon what is being suggested by the interaction of calm and insight. Early Buddhist soteriology is both descriptive and prescriptive. These two methods are not mutually exclusive. What is of value is based upon seeing things in a certain way: it is based upon insight into the way things are. In the early Pāli canon, what we crave is inseparable from what we know, and what we know inseparable from what we crave. One of the conclusions we can draw from such an understanding is that thought affects action and action affects thought. This process is very clear if we look at the notion of *diṭṭhi*. With the adoption of wrong-view an unwholesome course of action follows; with the adoption of right-view a wholesome course of action follows. Our understanding of how things are affects how we act. One of the reasons to adopt right-view and reject wrong-views is because right-view produces this wholesome course of action. It produces the cessation of craving. The reason for this, the early texts suggest, is that it is based upon a true description of reality. Through combining the notions of 'is' and 'ought' *diṭṭhi* encompasses a number of factors: the cognitive and affective; the descriptive and prescriptive; fact and value. The affective nature of things is not separate from what is cognitive. The conclusion that we may reach is that insight into the way things are has a transformative effect and that categories that we may normally separate are intrinsically bound and inseparable factors on the Buddhist path. By not separating the 'is' from the 'ought', the early texts are making an important point. This is that ignorance and craving are inseparable in producing unwholesome action and in turning away from the way things really are. In a similar way, the cessation of craving is caused by seeing things as they are.

Two theories may be proposed as to the nature of seeing things as they are. These are the strong and the weak theories.[39] The strong theory would hold that statements of the way things are are not, in fact, statements of the way things are, but are value statements. Much of Buddhist discourse should be understood as evaluative and prescriptive. Their value is based upon their transformative effect. When the texts speak of seeing things as they are, we should not understand this literally. Such statements produce the cessation of craving, therefore they are true. The weak theory holds that statements of the way things are are, quite literally, statements of the way things are. Further, seeing things as they are produces a radical change in one's actions. Apprehending things in a particular way is transformative. The strong theory emphasises the 'ought', the weak theory the 'is' and the 'ought'. It is the weak theory that I am arguing for in this book. As I have suggested, the 'is' cannot be divorced from the 'ought' without undermining the purpose of Buddhist doctrine. The seeing of things as they are is a statement of fact and value.

The lack of a distinction between the categories of 'is' and 'ought' is important for understanding the notion of *diṭṭhi*. Wrong-view sees things as they are not, and seeing things in such a way has an effect which is detrimental, it produces what ought not to be done: 'is not' produces an 'ought not'. Seeing things in such a way is not simply a cognitive mistake which can be corrected by its opposite. It is a profound form of delusion. In the same way, right-view is an insight into the way things really are and this insight is intimately bound up with what has value. Wrong-view is wrong because it is a form of greed based upon not seeing things as they are. Right-view is right because it is an apprehension of things as they are which is transformative. It is the cessation of greed and craving. Wrong-view does not see *dukkha*, its arising, cessation and the way to its cessation, whereas right-view does apprehend this process: what is and ought to be done.

Wrong-view is neither a wrong proposition requiring correction – the adoption of right-view; nor is it entirely a form of craving requiring rejection – the practising of no-views. It combines both what is untrue and harmful. On the other hand, right-view is not the adoption of a correct doctrine and the rejection of an incorrect doctrine; nor is it the rejection of knowledge – the abandoning of all views. The realisation of the way things are is itself the cessation of craving. It combines the notions of 'is' and 'ought' and in so doing reflects both 'what is' and what has ultimate value.

Propositions and ways of seeing

I would finally like to consider an important aspect of the nature of Buddhist doctrines. In what sense are they to be considered propositions? The question is important as it relates to whether wrong-views are to be corrected or transcended by right-view. To hold that there is no rebirth can be *corrected* by the proposition that there is rebirth. Similarly, the view that actions do not have consequences can be corrected by the view that actions do have consequences. However, as I will suggest, it is not by holding the view 'actions have consequences' that one achieves right-view. For holding to the view 'actions have consequences' has a consequence: the unwholesome consequence of being attached to a view, even a 'right-view' (cf., the *Pāṭali-sutta* at S IV 340–58 discussed in Chapter 5). Right-view is not realised when one holds the view 'actions have consequences' but when one acts in a certain way, usually explained as practising the 'ten wholesome courses of action' (*dasa kusala-kammapathā*, which I will discuss in Chapter 2). Acting in such a way is an expression of right-view. As I have said, right-view is practised, not adopted or believed in. There are also the views about the self. Are we justified in saying that this is corrected by the view of not-self? I do not think we are for the reasons that I will give in this book. In a similar way the annihilationist and eternalist-views are not corrected by the view of dependent-origination or the four truths. For, in a sense, it is difficult to describe the opposite proposition to the four truths or to dependent-origination.[40] This difficulty may inform us of something specific about the notion of *diṭṭhi*. This is that at a certain stage of the Buddhist path any position (*sassata/uccheda-diṭṭhi*) is 'corrected' by no-position, for there is a transcendence of all views.

Although he is arguing that early Buddhist thought itself misunderstood the nature of some of its doctrines, Luis Gómez makes a valuable point in stating that:

> Much of early Buddhist philosophy could be thought of as a vain attempt at reinterpreting the doctrine of detachment in terms of metaphysical formulas. To this purpose, the concept of non-self – no doubt very old, but lacking in metaphysical denotation in its early history – was to fit perfectly. The fundamental question should have been whether any discursive structure could adequately express a doctrine of complete detachment, which often underlined the importance of transcending all forms of speech, of breaking the bonds of conceptualisation. But there can be no doubt about the fact that most Buddhists understood the non-self doctrine literally and considered detachment rather as the corollary of non-self, not conversely.[41]

Gómez is suggesting that Buddhist doctrine proposes detachment from theorising. The doctrine of 'not-self' (*anattā*) does not propose the view 'there is no self', but the idea that we should not be attached to the notion of a self. Attachment is the problem, not whether there is or is not a self. Gómez is highlighting the problem of the possibility of there being any right-view which can express the *dhamma*: a view which can have knowledge of doctrines, without being attached to those doctrines. How can any proposition, even a 'correct' proposition, not become an object of attachment, and so become incorrect? All views are potential manifestations of craving. It is not so much views that are the problem but attachment to them. Gómez is suggesting that the problem is that of overcoming attachment. This is of primary importance. Right-view should reflect this. The right-view which has knowledge of *anattā* is a manifestation of non-attachment.

In a discussion of the nature of *nirvāṇa*, Paul J. Griffiths has considered the problems involved in a proposition that is not intended to state a position, that is not intended to become a view. It can propose (for example, a course of action), but must not be susceptible to craving and attachment. He discusses the dilemma faced by the Buddhist who states that 'all views about *nirvāṇa* are false' having to concede that this is false, because, 'all views about *nirvāṇa* are false'. Stated differently, Griffiths is considering the dilemma that 'all views are false' is a false view, because, 'all views are false'. Griffiths claims that the Buddhists use a method of the following kind:

> The most common [method] in Buddhist texts is to say that this view – all views about Nirvana (or in some schools about anything at all) are false – is not itself a view but (something like) a metalinguistic and

> metaphilosophical pointer to the truth, which, naturally, transcends all verbalization. If this move is to work – and ultimately I don't think it can – we need some fairly tight criteria for what 'views' are and why such things as the proposition 'all views are false' isn't one. Such criteria are not usually given in Buddhist texts. If an attempt were made to generate some criteria which would exclude 'all views are false', the probable result would be to empty such statements of all philosophical power. Suppose we suggest as a necessary (and possibly sufficient) condition for any proposition P to be considered a 'view' that P and its contradictory cannot both be true; if the proposition 'all views are false' isn't a view given this condition, then it's hard to know what it is or why anyone would want to assert it or even what it would mean to assert it. Can one assert a proposition P which does not logically exclude not-P?[42]

Griffiths is suggesting simply that the Buddhist position is that 'all views are false', and that this cannot be true – because 'all views are false'. But for Buddhist texts the statement 'all views are false' is not in fact a view – hence the negation of views is not itself a view.[43] In Theravāda Buddhism it is implicit that 'all views are false' if they are held with attachment. All views are false, even right-view, if they become an object of greed and attachment. The Theravāda Abhidhamma, in its discussion of views, is primarily concerned with *micchā diṭṭhi*. As I have said, right-view is equated with 'wisdom'. In a very real sense *micchā-diṭṭhi* and *sammā-diṭṭhi*, though both 'views', are of an entirely different nature. Views, whether they express correct or incorrect propositions, are all potential objects of attachment. As Rupert Gethin has suggested, 'even so-called "right-views" can be "views" (*diṭṭhi*) in so far as they can become fixed and the objects of attachment'.[44] The Buddhist view, *sammā-diṭṭhi*, is not meant to express a position because, as Gethin suggests, 'right-view should not be understood as a view itself, but as freedom from all views'.[45] I will not argue that the *dhamma*, Buddhist doctrine, does not make metaphysical claims, as I think that this would be a severe distortion of Buddhism, but that the correct knowledge of those doctrines should not involve attachment. A true statement, if it is an object of attachment, is *micchā-diṭṭhi*, even though it is still true.[46]

The three ideas I have introduced are related. First, I have suggested that *diṭṭhi* are not doctrines, but knowledge of doctrines. The notion of *diṭṭhi* relates to *how* we know doctrines. Second, I have suggested that Buddhist discourse does not distinguish between 'is' and 'ought' and that right-view should be understood as a statement of fact *and* value. I have argued that when the Buddhist texts claim that the aim of the path is to 'see things as they are' such statements should be taken quite literally: things *are* seen as they are, and apprehending things in this way is transformative. Seeing things in such a way combines the notions of 'is' and 'ought'. Finally, I have questioned whether views should be understood in a propositional sense. Right-view is not the opposite of wrong-view. I have argued this in order to suggest that right-view is not a correction of wrong-view but a different order of seeing.

1

THE CONTENT OF WRONG-VIEW

This chapter gives a comprehensive account of the various views that are explicitly stated to be wrong-views (*micchā-diṭṭhi*) in the four primary Nikāyas. In the first place this chapter aims to answer the question: what views are classified as wrong-views? The term *diṭṭhi* (Skt. *dṛṣṭi*) indicates a way of seeing. The word 'view' translates the term well. Wrong-views are a fixed way of seeing, a specific view of the way things are. I will consider *micchā-diṭṭhi* under two broad categories: first, there are views that deny *kamma*, that deny that actions have consequences; second, there are views about the self.[1]

In the Nikāyas we find attempts to classify and summarise wrong-views, most notably in the *Brahmajāla-sutta* (D I 1-46) and the *Diṭṭhi-saṃyutta* (S III 201-24) and, in undertaking this task, I am, to an extent, following in the footsteps of the early Abhidhamma. For example, the *Vibhaṅga* gives a list of some 115 wrong-views,[2] mostly drawn from the Nikāyas. I will use the *Vibhaṅga* summary as an entry point into the Nikāyas, as it is a convenient summary of those views classified as wrong-views.

A terminological issue must be considered first as the views classified in the *Vibhaṅga* as wrong-views are not consistently, or in some cases not at all, referred to as wrong-views in the Nikāyas. Indeed, the term *micchā-diṭṭhi* does not occur at all in the *Brahmajāla-sutta*. The *sutta* uses the term 'basis for views' (*diṭṭhiṭṭhāna*), to refer to the 62 views which it considers. In the Nikāyas the term *vāda* ('doctrine', 'theory' or 'school') is often used to refer to wrong-views. However, using the *Vibhaṅga* summary, I have classified as wrong-views only those views specifically called *micchā-diṭṭhi* in one or more places, in addition to the views that appear in the *Brahmajāla-sutta* or the *Diṭṭhi-saṃyutta*.

The *Khuddhaka-vatthu* of the *Vibhaṅga* gives the names and details of many *micchā-diṭṭhi*. There are:

> The 'becoming-view' (*bhava-diṭṭhi*), which holds that the self and the world will arise again (*bhavissati attā ca loko cā ti*, Vibh 358).[3]
>
> The 'non-becoming view' (*vibhava-diṭṭhi*), which holds that the self and the world will not be again (*na bhavissati attā ca loko cā ti*, ibid.).

The 'eternalist-view' (*sassata-diṭṭhi*), which holds that the self and the world are eternal (*sassato attā ca loko cā ti*, ibid.).

The 'annihilationist-view' (*uccheda-diṭṭhi*), which holds that the self and the world will cease (*ucchijjissati attā ca loko cā ti*, ibid.).

The 'finite-view' (*antavā-diṭṭhi*), which holds that the self and the world are finite (*antavā attā ca loko cā ti*, ibid.).

The 'infinite-view' (*anantavā-diṭṭhi*), which holds the opposite (*anantavā attā ca loko cā ti*, Vibh 359).

The 'ultimate-beginning-view' (*pubbantānudiṭṭhi*), concerning the ultimate beginning of beings, ibid.[4]

The 'ultimate-end-view' (*aparantānudiṭṭhi*), concerning the ultimate end of beings (*aparantaṃ ārabbha*, ibid.).

The 'identity-view' (*sakkāya-diṭṭhi*, Vibh 364).

The 'self-view' (*attānudiṭṭhi*, Vibh 368). The same view as *sakkāya-diṭṭhi*.

The 'gratification-view' (*assāda-diṭṭhi*), which holds that there is no fault in sense pleasures (*natthi kāmesu doso*, ibid.).

The 'four wrong-views' (*catasso diṭṭhiyo*): the first arises firmly as the truth that 'pleasure and pain are produced by themselves'; the second that 'pleasure and pain are produced by another cause'; the third that 'pleasure and pain are produced by themselves and by another cause'; the fourth that 'pleasure and pain are not produced by themselves, or by another cause, but arise without cause'.[5]

The 'six wrong-views' (*cha diṭṭhiyiyo*): the view that arises firmly as the truth that 'I have a self'; or 'I do not have a self'; or 'by the self I perceive what is self'; or 'by the self I perceive what is not self'; or 'by what is not self I perceive what is not self'; or 'it is this self of mine that speaks and feels and experiences for a long time here and there the results of good and destructive actions; this (self) is not born and never came to be; this (self) is not born and never will come to be; this (self) is permanent, everlasting, eternal, not subject to change' (Vibh 382).[6]

The 'seven wrong-views' (*satta diṭṭhiyo*, Vibh 383û5). These are the same views as the seven *uccheda-diṭṭhi* from the *Brahmajāla-sutta*.

The 'wrong view that has ten bases' (*dasavatthukā micchā-diṭṭhi*, Vibh 392). This is 'the view of nihilism' (*natthika-diṭṭhi*) that I will consider below.

The 'wrong-view' (*micchā-diṭṭhi*, ibid.). The same view as the preceding view.[7]

The 'extremist view that has ten bases' (*dasavatthukā antaggāhikā diṭṭhi*, ibid.). These are the ten unanswered questions (*avyākata*).[8]

The sixty-two wrong-views that were spoken of by the Buddha in the *Brahmajāla* exposition (*dvāsaṭṭhi diṭṭhigatāni brahmajāle veyyākaraṇe vuttāni bhagavatā*). These are the 'four eternalistic theories' (*cattāro sassata-vādā*); 'four partial eternalistic theories' (*cattāro ekaccasassatikā*); 'four finite and infinite theories' (*cattāro antānantikā*); 'four eel-wriggling theories' (*cattaro amarāvikkhepikā*); 'two theories (of occurrences) arising without a cause' (*dve adhiccasamuppannikā*); 'sixteen theories of having apperception' (*soḷasa saññī -vādā*);[9] 'eight theories of having non-apperception' (*aṭṭha asaññī-vādā*); 'eight theories of neither apperception nor-non-apperception' (*aṭṭha nevasaññī-nāsaññī-vādā*); 'seven annihilationist theories' (*satta uccheda-vādā*); 'five theories on *nibbāna* in the present existence' (*pañca diṭṭha-dhamma-nibbāna-vādā*, Vibh 400).

PART ONE: VIEWS THAT DENY THAT ACTIONS HAVE CONSEQUENCES

I will begin with the views of the 'six teachers' from the *Sāmaññaphala-sutta* (D I 47–86).[10] These views deny that actions have consequences, they deny the law of *kamma*. The group of six views are well-known throughout Buddhism as a whole, as the extant Pāli, Tibetan and Chinese sources show.[11] In the *Sāmaññaphala-sutta* each are given as the view of a certain teacher:

View 1: The view of nihilism (*natthika-diṭṭhi*): Ajita Kesakambalī

View 2: The view of non-doing (*akiriya-diṭṭhi*): Purāṇa Kassapa

View 3: The view of non-causality (*ahetu-diṭṭhi*): Makkhali Gosāla

View 4: The view of Pakudha Kaccāyana

View 5: The view of Nigaṇṭha Nātaputta

View 6: The view of Sañjaya Belaṭṭhiputta

The view of nihilism (*natthika-diṭṭhi*)

The view of nihilism is the following:

> Nothing is given, nothing offered, nothing sacrificed; there is no fruit or result of good and bad actions; no this world, no other world; no mother, no father; no beings who are reborn spontaneously; no good and virtuous recluses and brahmins in the world who have themselves realised by direct knowledge and declare this world and the other world.
>
> The person is composed of the four great elements; when he dies, earth returns and goes back to the element of earth, water returns and goes back to the element of water, fire returns and goes back to the element of fire, wind returns and goes back to the element of wind, while the senses disappear into space. [Four] men with the bier as a fifth take up

> the corpse, the funeral orations last as far as the burning ground, his bones are a dull white, his offerings end in ashes. They are fools who teach alms-giving. The doctrine of affirmation (*atthika-vāda*) is empty and false banter. Fools and wise alike are destroyed and perish at the breaking up of the body, they do not exist after death.[12]

Three versions of this formula are found: the first is this one from the *Sāmaññaphala-sutta* (D I 47–86) at D I 55 where the view is attributed to Ajita Kesakambalī.[13] A shorter version is often used which consists of the first paragraph.[14] In the *Vibhaṇga* classification this is the 'wrong-view that has ten bases' (*dasavatthukā micchā-diṭṭhi*), also simply called 'wrong-view'(*micchā-diṭṭhi*). A third version, which is very short, consists of the following: 'There is no other world, there are no spontaneously born beings, there is no fruit or result of good and bad actions.'[15]

The early Pāli canon seems to have understood the view of nihilism quite literally as the view that 'there is not'. Actions do not have consequences. There is no point in giving to others. There is no path to purity. There are no enlightened beings. There is no cessation of *dukkha*. The *Dhammasaṅgaṇi* uses the phrase 'non-accomplishment in view' (*diṭṭhi-vipatti*) to refer to the view of nihilism and 'accomplishment in view' (*diṭṭhi-sampadā*) to refer to the opposite view, the right-view which affirms that 'there is what is given', etc.[16] This right-view shall be referred to as 'the view of affirmation' (*atthika-diṭṭhi*). According to the *Dhammasaṅgaṇi*, all wrong-views are non-accomplishment in view, and all right-views are accomplishment in view.[17] Right-views are fortunate views, and wrong-views are unfortunate views.[18] Holding that actions have consequences has an effect on the mind of the one who holds this view. Buddhaghosa explains why it is better to have the view of affirmation than the view of nihilism, which may be summarised: accomplishment in view is opposed to attachment to view. For this reason it is accomplishment in view.[19] He also explains that whereas we know we can give to others, some grasp the idea that there is no fruit and result of these actions.[20] Our actions do produce consequences, and this is what this view-holder primarily denies. Indeed the view of nihilism is sometimes used to explain attachment. For example, the *Vibhaṇga* considers four attachments (*upādānas*): 'attachment to sensuality', 'attachment to view', 'attachment to precepts and vows' and 'attachment to the theory of self' (*kāmupādānaṃ, diṭṭhupādānaṃ, sīlabbatupādānaṃ, attavādupādānaṃ*). The attachment of wrong view is explained, first, as the view of nihilism, then it is stated that all wrong-views constitute attachment to view (*sabbāpi micchā-diṭṭhi diṭṭhupādānaṃ*).[21] All wrong-views are a form of greed and attachment.

Wrong-views are then opposed to right-view in the sense that right-view, the view of affirmation, is closer to non-attachment. One should practise right-view because it promotes a certain course of action, and in practising right-view there is the realisation of the nature of non-greed, non-hatred and non-delusion (*alobha, adosa, amoha*). To deny that actions have consequences is then, in a certain way, an expression of greed, hatred and delusion. Wrong-view prevents the very first stage of the path from being realised, the beginning of the transformation of action which eventually will lead to insight.

There has been some scholarly debate on the nature of the view of nihilism. Jayatilleke holds that the doctrine as a whole is based upon the epistemological motive that 'perception' (*pratyakṣa)* alone is the only valid means of knowledge.[22] Since perception is the only valid means of knowledge, 'higher perception' *(abhiññā)* is denied.

The view of nihilism claims that the person is composed of the 'four great elements', hence there is no self. Morality has no value.[23] The view that 'actions have consequences' (the right-view of affirmation) is denied because this law cannot be known by 'perception'. It cannot be known by any 'valid means of knowledge' (Skt. *pramāṇa),* hence it does not exist. It is generally held that this type of thinking reflects the views of the Lokāyata/Cārvāka schools, or so-called 'Indian Materialism',[24] and there are Lokāyata doctrines which may be compared to the view of nihilism. For example, the doctrine of *yadṛcchā-vāda* denies cause and effect and proposes that all relationships are an accident. The Lokāyata doctrine of *svabhāva-vāda* holds that things operate without a cause, and change according to their 'own nature'. Similarly, Tucci argues the following:

> This *svabhāva-vāda* [posits] the negation of the karma theory [...] it maintains that everything which happens on earth is only the effect of various combinations of material elements; human effort is useless [...] everything happens *svabhāvena,* according to the various combinations of the four elements which constitute the body of everything.[25]

According to Warder, the doctrine of *svabhāva-vāda* could then have been used to replace the theory of *kamma.*[26]

Tucci holds that the essential part of the view of nihilism is the phrase 'no fruit or result of good and bad actions' (*n' atthi sukaṭādukkaṭānaṁ kammānaṃ phalaṃ vipāko*), and that this is in fact the central idea of Indian Materialism.[27] He also thinks that if the view of nihilism was derived from real existing doctrines, this would help explain the parallel with Jain sources.[28] The main point made by these scholars is that the view of nihilism denies that actions have consequences.

The view of nihilism runs contrary to the experiential and empirical nature of early Buddhist thought. Actions are held to shape the conduct of body, speech and mind. As I suggested in the Introduction to this book, the notions of 'is' and 'ought' cannot be divorced from each other. To know how things are we must act in a wholesome way; to act in a wholesome way we must have insight into how things are. This process must begin with the transformation of action. The view of nihilism denies the possibility of transformation. It is a view that produces an unwholesome course of action and it is a wrong-view.

The view of non-doing (*akiriya-diṭṭhi*)

The wrong-view of nihilism primarily denies that actions have consequences. The second wrong-view also denies that actions have consequences and is described as 'the view of non-doing' (*akiriya-diṭṭhi*):

> When one acts or makes others act, when one mutilates or makes others mutilate, when one tortures or makes others inflict torture, when one inflicts sorrow or makes others inflict sorrow, when one oppresses or makes others inflict oppression, when one intimidates or makes others inflict intimidation, when one kills living beings, takes what is not given, breaks into houses, plunders wealth, commits burglary, ambushes highways, seduces another's wife, utters falsehood – no wrong is done by the doer. If, with a razor-rimmed wheel, one were to make the living beings on this earth into one mass of flesh, into one heap of flesh, because of this there would be no wrong and no outcome of wrong. If one were to go along the south bank of the Ganges killing and slaughtering, mutilating and making others mutilate, torturing and making others torture, because of this there would be no wrong and no outcome of wrong. If one were to go along the north bank of the Ganges giving gifts and making others give gifts, making offerings and making others make offerings, because of this there would be no merit and outcome of merit. From giving, from taming oneself, from restraint, from speaking truth, there is no merit and no outcome of merit.[29]

This view denies morality by denying that action has meaning. To call someone an *akiriya-vāda* appears to have been a term of disparagement, used by the different traditions. For example, the Jains called Buddhists *akiriya-vādins*, because of the Buddhist denial of self: 'The *akiriya-vādins* who deny karma, do not admit that the action (of the self is transmitted to) the future moments.'[30] As Gómez has suggested, a *kiriya-vādin* is one who believes in the law of *kamma*, that 'some kind of action or human effort [...] would lead to release from *saṃsāra*' whereas an *akiriya-vādin* held that our actions have no consequences.[31]

The view of non-causality *(ahetu-diṭṭhi)*

The third wrong-view, which is occasionally found together with the view of nihilism and the view of non-doing is the following:

> There is no cause or condition for the defilement of beings; beings are defiled without cause or condition. There is no cause or condition for the purification of beings; beings are purified without cause or condition. There is no self-power or other-power, there is no power in humans, no strength or force, no vigour or exertion. All beings, all living things, all creatures, all that lives is without control, without power or strength they

experience the fixed course of pleasure and pain through the six kinds of rebirth.

There are one million four hundred thousand principle sorts of birth, and six thousand others and again six hundred. There are five hundred kinds of *kamma*, or five kinds, and three kinds, and half *kamma*, sixty-two paths, sixty-two intermediary aeons, six classes of humans, eight stages of human progress, four thousand nine hundred occupations, four thousand nine hundred wanderers, four thousand nine hundred abodes of *nāgas*, two thousand sentient existences, three thousand hells, thirty-six places covered with dust, seven classes of rebirth as sentient beings, seven as insentient beings, and seven as beings 'freed from bonds', seven grades of *devas*, men and demons (*pisāca*), seven lakes, seven great and seven small protuberances, seven great and seven small abysses, seven great and seven small dreams, eight million four hundred thousand aeons during which fools and wise run on and circle round till they make an end of suffering. There is no question of bringing unripe *kamma* to fruition, nor of exhausting *kamma* already ripened, by virtuous conduct, by vows, by penance, or by chastity. That cannot be done. *Saṃsāra* is measured as with a bushel, with its joy and sorrow and its appointed end. It can neither be lessened nor increased, nor is there any excess or deficiency of it. Just as a ball of thread will, when thrown, unwind to its full length, so fool and wise alike will take their course, and make an end of sorrow.[32]

I shall refer to this *micchā-diṭṭhi* as 'the view of non-causality' (*ahetu-diṭṭhi*). In the *Sāmaññaphala-sutta* this view is also described as 'purification through *saṃsāra*' (*saṃsāra-suddhiṃ*). This may have been a familiar term for Ājīvika ideas. It contains the well-known Ājīvika notion of 'destiny' (*niyati*). Pande notes that this could reflect a central tenet of Ājīvika soteriology, 'the unalterable working out of a coiled up necessity'.[33] This notion is reflected in the last phrase of the view in which *saṃsāra* is compared to a ball of thread which, when thrown, will unwind naturally to its full length. In a similar fashion, fools and the wise are heading towards an end to sorrow, towards purification (*visuddhi*).[34]

I have now considered three wrong-views, the view of nihilism, the view of non-doing and the view of non-causality, which each deny that actions have consequences in their different ways. In the *suttas*, which will be discussed in Chapter 2, these three wrong-views are often found together, as I have said. These views are wrong because by denying the importance of action, they lead away from what is wholesome. Action can produce both what is unwholesome and wholesome. In characterising suffering as being caused by both craving and ignorance the *suttas* are suggesting that a course of unwholesome action increases both craving and a lack of knowledge. These views, then, not only increase unwholesome action but also craving and ignorance. In this way, they lead away from the true state of things.

The view of Pakudha Kaccāyana

The fourth wrong-view is the following:

> The seven elementary categories are neither made nor ordered, neither caused nor constructed; they are barren, as firm as mountains, as stable as pillars. They neither move nor develop; they do not injure one another, and one has no effect on joy, or on the sorrow, or on the joy and sorrow of another. What are the seven? The elementary category of the earth, of water, of fire, and of air, and joy and sorrow, with life as the seventh. [...] No man slays or causes to slay, hears or causes to hear, knows or causes to know. Even if a man cleaves another's head with a sharp sword, he does not take life, for the sword-cut passes between the seven elements.[35]

This view is attributed in the *Sāmaññaphala-sutta* to Pakudha Kaccāyana.[36] In the *Sāmaññaphala-sutta,* unlike most of the other views, it is not given a name, the text simply states that when Pakudha Kaccāyana was asked the fruits of the homeless life he 'answered with something quite different' (*aññena aññaṃ vyākāsi,* D I 56). A wrong-view appears in the *Diṭṭhi-saṃyutta* at S III 211 and is called the 'great view' (*mahādiṭṭhena).* This view consists of the first half of Pakudha's view, as found in the *Sāmaññaphala-sutta,* with some differences.[37]

Bhikkhu Bodhi refers to this view as 'the doctrine of seven bodies'.[38] Basham describes Pakudha's view as 'fantastic atomism', a 'Parmenidean doctrine of immobility'[39] and 'Eleatic atomism'.[40] Jayatilleke prefers to call it 'proto-Vaiśeṣika Realism'.[41]

I would like to consider the view of Pakudha with two other wrong-views, the first from the *Diṭṭhi-saṃyutta* and the second (group of four) from the *Brahmajāla-sutta*. The first is from the *Diṭṭhi-saṃyutta*:

> The winds do not blow, the rivers do not flow, pregnant women do not give birth, the moon and sun do not rise and set, but stand as stable as a pillar.[42]

This view is simply given the name 'wind' (*vātam*). This formula is called a *diṭṭhi,* and is introduced as such. Bhikkhu Bodhi notes that the commentarial definition of *vātam* is 'untrue representation' (*lesa*): although the wind appears to blow and the sun and moon appear to rise, they are an untrue representation of wind (*vata-lesa*), sun and moon.[43]

In the *Brahmajāla-sutta* four 'eternalist-views' (*sassata-diṭṭhi*) are found. As they are similar to the view of Pakudha and the *Diṭṭhi-saṃyutta* view, all four views can be summarised here in the following way:

> The self and the world are eternal, barren, steadfast as a mountain peak, standing firm like a pillar. And though these beings roam and wander (through the round of existence), pass away and re-arise, yet the self and the world remain the same just like eternity itself.[44]

I have given three views: that of Pakudha Kaccāyana, the view from the *Diṭṭhi-saṃyutta* called *vātam* and the four eternalist-views from the *Brahmajāla-sutta* (understanding the four eternalist-views as one wrong-view). All these wrong-views share at least part of the following: 'barren, as firm as a mountain, as stable as a pillar' (*vañjho kūṭaṭṭho esikaṭṭhāyiṭṭhito*). These *micchā-diṭṭhi* deny motion and change. They may contain speculations of a similar nature to the late Jain/Ājīvika *avicalita-nityatvam*, 'unchanging permanence'.[45] Jayatilleke believes that the simplest way of understanding these views is to regard them as expressions of the most prevalent doctrine of this period: that the real is being.[46] If the real is being, then all movement and change is unreal. All three views deny, again, that actions have consequences, but in a different way to the nature of the denial proposed by the views of nihilism, non-doing and non-causality. Instead of simply denying the law of *kamma*, they deny any effect of actions, even denying that action itself exists. This appears to be an extreme version of the denial of action proposed in the first three views.

The view of Nigaṇṭha Nātaputta

The fifth *micchā-diṭṭhi* found in the *Sāmaññaphala-sutta* is usually understood as being the view of the Jains:

> A Nigaṇṭha is bound by a fourfold restraint. What four? He is curbed by all curbs, enclosed by all curbs, cleared by all curbs, and claimed by all curbs. And as far as a Nigaṇṭha is bound by this fourfold restraint, thus the Nigaṇṭha is called self-protected, self-controlled, self-established.[47]

This view, in the *Sāmaññaphala-sutta,* is called the 'fourfold restraint' (*cātu-yāma-saṃvaraṃ*, D I 58). This is a difficult passage. In fact, to classify it as a type of *micchā-diṭṭhi* is problematic. The view appears to be a parody of Jain practice, not an expression of a view-point, a *micchā-diṭṭhi.* Basham calls the passage 'obscure'.[48] Rhys Davids attributes the difficulty of this passage to the idea that it is intended to be an ironical imitation of the Jains' way of talking.[49] The phrase 'curbed by all curbs, enclosed by all curbs, cleared by all curbs, and claimed by all curbs' (*sabba-vārī-vārito, sabba-vārī-yuto ca sabba-vārī-dhuto ca, sabba-vārī-phuṭṭho ca*), may involve a pun on the word *vāri,* which can mean 'water' or 'restraint/curb'.[50] Following Walshe, the passage is perhaps meant to parody one free from bonds, and yet bound by the bonds of restraint, bound by the very restraints that are meant to bring freedom.[51] Its classification as a wrong-view is perhaps due to the fact that it denies what is wholesome: the practice of the Buddhist path.

The view of Sañjaya Belaṭṭhiputta and the endless equivocators

The sixth wrong-view is that of Sañjaya Belaṭṭhiputta. On being asked the fruits of the homeless life, he answered in the following way:

> If you ask me: 'Is there another world?' – if I thought there is another world, I would declare that there is. I do not take it thus, I do not say it is true, I do not say it is otherwise, I do not say it is not so, I do not say it is not not so.
>
> Similarly, when asked any of the following questions, he resorts to the same evasive statements and to endless equivocation:
>
> 'Is there no world beyond?' 'Is it that there both is and is not a world beyond?' 'Is it that there neither is nor is not a world beyond?' 'Are there beings spontaneously reborn?' 'Are there no beings spontaneously reborn?' 'Is it that there both are and are not beings spontaneously reborn?' 'Is it that there neither are nor are not beings spontaneously reborn?' 'Is there fruit and result of good and bad actions?' 'Is there no fruit and result of good and bad actions?' 'Is it that there both is and is not fruit and result of good and bad actions?' 'Is it that there neither is nor is not fruit and result of good and bad actions?' 'Does the Tathāgata exist after death?' 'Does the Tathāgata not exist after death?' 'Does the Tathāgata both exist and not exist after death?' 'Does the Tathāgata neither exist nor not exist after death?'[52]

In the *Sāmaññaphala-sutta* this formula is, as I have indicated, attributed to Sañjaya Belaṭṭhiputta. These views are not given a name. The *sutta* states that when Sañjaya Belaṭṭhiputta was asked the fruits of the homeless life he 'replied by equivocating' (*vikkhepaṃ vyākāsi,* D I 57). In the *Brahmajāla-sutta* are found the wrong-views of the 'four endless equivocators' (*cattāro amarā-vikkhepikā*) which are very similar to the wrong-view of Sañjaya Belaṭṭhiputta. I have given these in Appendix 1. These are the views of those who avoid answering questions. In general the endless equivocators held that there was a 'moral danger' (*antarayo*) in making truth claims. The moral danger perceived was worry or remorse (*vighāto).* Jayatilleke has noted a 'superficial similarity' between these ideas and those of the Buddha.[53] Some have found in this an expression of a spiritual path.[54] Though the view of Sañjaya Belaṭṭhiputta does not express this sense of despondency with debate and the making of truth claims, it is in this context that I think the view should be considered.

I have now described a number of wrong-views. I suggested at the outset that these views are, to a greater or lesser extent, views that deny that actions have consequences. They are views which deny the law of *kamma.* These views deny what is of value, so they are wrong-views. However, I think there is something more at stake than this. In the *Sāmaññaphala-sutta* King Ajātasattu asks each of the six teachers to 'point to such a reward visible here and now as a fruit of the homeless life'.[55] In the same way that the Buddha refuses to answer certain questions, the six teachers appear to be unwilling to answer questions about the nature of action and the effects of actions; and in the same way that the Buddha refuses to answer questions of an ontological nature, so the six teachers, in a sense, will only answer questions of an ontological nature. In the *Sāmaññaphala-sutta* the Buddha's answer to King Ajātasattu suggests that action influences the realisation of knowledge (D I 62–85). His answer suggests the interplay of conduct and knowledge, the answers of the six teachers deny this, hence they are wrong-views.

Wrong-view or right-view?

Before moving onto the next group of views, I would like to consider a rather unusual view by way of introduction to the second half of this chapter. This view appears occasionally in the Nikāyas. I cannot equate this with any of the headings from the *Vibhaṅga*. It is the following:

> He has this view:
> 'I might not be,
> And it might not be for me;
> I will not be,
> [and] it will not be for me.'
> That annihilationist-view is an activity (a volitional formation).[56]

In the *Diṭṭhi-saṃyutta* at S III 200 and the *Diṭṭhi-vagga* at S III 182 this view is called 'and it might not be for me' (*no ca me siyā*). Interestingly, for a wrong-view, at A V 63 this *micchā-diṭṭhi* is called the 'highest of outside views' (*etadaggaṃ bāhirakānaṃ diṭṭhigatānaṃ*). The verse, infrequent in the Nikāyas, is then slightly ambiguous. Of some interest is its comparison to an earlier verse in the *Saṃyutta-nikāya*:

> There the Blessed One uttered this inspired utterance:
> 'It might not be, and it might not be for me;
> It will not be,
> [and] it will not be for me.'[57]

It is said that by resolving (*adhimuccamāno*) in this way a *bhikkhu* can cut the lower fetters, a reference to eradication of the five lower fetters that signifies one is an *anāgāmin*, a non-returner. The verse also occurs in the *Āneñjasappāya-sutta* (M II 261–6) at M II 264–5, with the phrase added, 'what exists, what has come to be, that I am abandoning' (*yad atthi yaṃ bhūtaṃ taṃ pajahāmi*).[58] It is said that there are two possible outcomes for the *bhikkhu* practising according to this view. The first outcome is that the *bhikkhu* will attain equanimity. However, the *bhikkhu* may become attached to and dependent upon that equanimity. The *sutta* states that in such a case the *bhikkhu* is clinging to the base of neither-apperception-nor-non-apperception (M II 265). The *sutta* explains that this is the 'best [object of] attachment' (*upādānaseṭṭhaṃ*, M II 265). The second outcome of practising according to this view is that, obtaining equanimity, the *bhikkhu* does not become attached to that equanimity, and that 'who is without attachment attains *nibbāna*' (*anupādāno* [...] *parinibbāyati*, M II 265). It seems clear that the *sutta* is describing how a view can have a negative or positive outcome, according to how the view is held. This suggests that the nature of knowledge is such that the effect that the view has on the holder of it is of some importance in its epistemological validity.

We find two changes of inflection between the annihilationist-view and the Buddha's 'inspired utterance' (*udāna*).[59] This changes the first-person verbs to third-person, making them contrary to the *dhamma*, or in accord with it. As Bhikkhu Bodhi suggests: 'The change of person shifts the stress from the view of self implicit in the annihilationist-view ("I will be annihilated") to an impersonal perspective that harmonises with the *anattā* doctrine'.[60] The commentarial interpretation on the negative *uccheda-diṭṭhi* at S III 99 is the following:

> *If I were not, it would not be for me* means (*ti*): If I were not (*sace ahaṃ na bhaveyyaṃ*), neither would there be my belongings (*mama patikkhāro*). Or else: If in my past there had not been *kammic* formation (*kammābhi saṃkhāro*), now there would not be for me these five aggregates.
>
> *I will not be* (*and*) *it will not be for me* means (*ti*): I will now so strive that there will not be any *kammic* formation of mine producing the aggregates in the future. When that is absent, there will be for me no future rebirth.[61]

The annihilationist-view identifies with, and is attached to, the five *khandhas*. One who is attached does not see things as they are. Seeing according to the 'inspired utterance' is to see in a different way. One not attached to the *khandhas* has a different order of seeing. As Bhikkhu Bodhi suggests: 'the world presented by them [the *khandhas*] will be terminated.'[62] The world presented by the *khandhas* is the world presented by attachment, by *micchā-diṭṭhi*. It is the world as seen according to attachment, characterised in the Nikāyas as the *khandhas*, which, in many respects, is an explanation of wrong-view. There is nothing wrong with the *khandhas* as such, but once there is identification with them, the perception of the world 'as it is' is distorted. I will return to this point in Chapter 5 with a discussion of the *Nikkhepa-kaṇḍaṃ* of the *Dhammasaṅgaṇi*.

This discussion leads to a consideration of the views classified as wrong that are primarily views of self based upon attachment to the *khandhas*.

PART TWO: VIEWS OF SELF

In the second half of this chapter I will consider views about the nature of the self. These wrong-views may be described as views that deny that attachments have consequences, in order to explain them as a cognitive and affective mistake. Though it may at first be assumed that views that deny the law of *kamma* and views about the self are different in nature, I would like to suggest that they share certain important characteristics. The most important of these is that they lead away from certain actions that are considered wholesome on the Buddhist path. They lead away from calm and insight, and towards craving and ignorance. In this sense a view that denies that our actions have consequences and a view that holds that there is (or is not) a self are both forms of *taṇhā* and *avijjā*: they deny what is and what ought to be done. It should be stressed that a view is not right which states 'there is no self'. This is as much a form of greed and attachment as one that states 'there is a self'. It is part of my argument that wrong-views are a wrong knowledge of doctrine, and by this I mean a wrong grasp of the teachings, of Buddhist doctrine, the *dhamma*. The view of annihilationism (*uccheda-diṭṭhi*) denies the existence of a self. The view of eternalism (*sassata-diṭṭhi*) posits the existence of a self. They are both forms of greed and attachment. These ideas are expressed by the view known as *sakkāya-diṭṭhi*.

Identity-view (*sakkāya-diṭṭhi*)

I translate *sakkāya-diṭṭhi* 'identity-view' and follow Bhikkhu Bodhi in this translation.[63] Collins translates *sakkāya-diṭṭhi* as 'personality belief',[64] Gethin as 'the view that the individual exists'.[65] I think that the term implies an 'identification' with the *khandhas*. The identity-view does not see things as they are, and this produces craving and attachment. The opposite to the identity-view is the non-identity-view, the non-craving-view, namely, right-view. The role of *sakkāya-diṭṭhi* in giving rise to other views is stressed in the Nikāyas. For example, in the *Dutiya isidatta-sutta* (S IV 285–8) at S IV 287, it is stated that when there is *sakkāya-diṭṭhi*, the ten 'unanswered questions' (*avyākata*) and the 62 views of the *Brahmajāla-sutta* come to be.[66] According to the *Peṭakopadesa*, *sakkāya-diṭṭhi* is the footing for all wrong-views.[67] The implication is that *sakkāya-diṭṭhi* is the first view out of which all other views come.

All, or part, of the following formula is common throughout the Nikāyas. The following is from the *Cūḷavedalla-sutta* (M I 299–305):

> How [...] does the identity-view come to be? Here [...] an untaught ordinary person, who has no regard for the noble ones and is unskilled and undisciplined in their *dhamma*, who has no regard for true men and is unskilled and undisciplined in the *dhamma*, regards form as self, or self as possessed of form, or form as in self, or self as in form. He regards feeling as self, or self as possessed of feeling, or feeling as in self, or self as in feeling. He regards apperception as self, or self as possessed of apperception, or apperception as in self, or self as in apperception. He regards volitional formations as self, or self as possessed of volitional formations, or volitional formations as in self, or self as in volitional

formations. He regards consciousness as self, or self as possessed of consciousness, or consciousness as in self, or self as in consciousness.[68]

The *Paṭisambhidāmagga* calls these views 'adherence through views about self' (*attānudiṭṭhi-abhinivesa*, Ps I 143). They are a conviction, a grasping after the self. Wrong-views are a matter of both craving and ignorance, a kind of adherence or conviction (*abhinivesa*), which cling and misinterpret.[69] I will return to a consideration of this in Chapter 3 on the function of wrong-view. At this point I wish to suggest that wrong-view is often caused by attachment to one or all of the *khandhas*.

The *Paṭisambhidāmagga* classifies *sakkāya-diṭṭhi* into two groups. To regard any of the *khandhas* as self is an *uccheda-diṭṭhi*. So there are five *uccheda-diṭṭhi*. To regard the self as possessed of any of the *khandhas*, or the *khandhas* as in self, or self as in the *khandhas*, are *sassata-diṭṭhi*. So there are fifteen *sassata-diṭṭhi*.[70]

Five uccheda-diṭṭhi

1. He regards form as self (*rūpaṃ attato samanupassati*)
2. He regards feeling as self (*vedanaṃ attato samanupassati*)
3. He regards apperception as self (*saññaṃ attato samanupassati*)
4. He regards volitional formations as self (*saṃkhāre attato samanupassati*)
5. He regards consciousness as self (*viññāṇaṃ attato samanupassati*)

Fifteen sassata-diṭṭhi

1-3. Self as possessed of form, or form as in self, or self as in form (*rūpavantaṃ vā attānaṃ, attani vā rūpaṃ, rupasmim vā attānaṃ*)

4–6. Self as possessed of feeling, or feeling as in self, or self as in feeling (*vedanāvantaṃ vā attānaṃ, attani vā vedanaṃ, vedanāya vā attānaṃ*)

7–9. Self as possessed of apperception, or apperception as in self, or self as in apperception (*saññāvantam vā attānaṃ, attani vā saññaṃ, saññāya vā attānaṃ*)

10–12. Self as possessed of volitional formations, or volitional formations as in self, or self as in volitional formations (*saṃkhāravantam vā attānaṃ, attani vā saṃkhāre, saṃkhāresu vā attānaṃ*)

13–15. Self as possessed of consciousness, or consciousness as in self, or self as in consciousness (*viññāṇavantaṃ vā attānaṃ, attani vā viññāṇaṃ, viññāṇasmiṃ vā attānaṃ*)

The *Nettippakaraṇa* uses the *uccheda* and *sassata-diṭṭhi* classifications to suggest that *uccheda-diṭṭhi* are based upon some form of delusion (*moha*), while *sassata-diṭṭhi* are based upon a form of craving (*taṇhā*). It does this by suggesting that one of 'view-temperament' (*diṭṭhi-carita*) approaches the *khandhas* as self, while one of 'craving temperament' (*taṇhā-carita*) approaches the self as possessing the *khandhas*, the *khandhas* as in self, or self as in the *khandhas*.[71] This suggests an interplay of craving and ignorance in hindering the attainment of knowledge.

One final point of significance is the simple numerical consideration that in one of the most prominent group of wrong-views according to the most basic classification, *uccheda* and *sassata-diṭṭhi*, a considerable majority of *micchā-diṭṭhi* are based upon a wrong grasp, on craving, not on a wrong understanding, on ignorance.

Miscellaneous destructive views

A certain group of wrong-views are given as the view of a named *bhikkhu, brahmin* or some other individual. Though not all these views are based upon the self or attachment to the *khandhas* I would like to consider them as a group at this point. These views are always introduced by the phrase, 'a destructive view arose' (*pāpakāṃ diṭṭhi-gataṃ uppannaṃ hoti*) to the named individual.[72] The first view is that of Ariṭṭha:

> Now on that occasion a destructive view had arisen in *bhikkhu* Ariṭṭha: 'As I understand the *dhamma* taught by the Fortunate One those things called obstructions by the Fortunate One are not able to obstruct one who practises them.'[73]

This wrong-view denies that the way one acts will affect the practising of the Buddhist path. In the Vinaya (Vin IV 134–5) the view that 'there is no fault in sense pleasures' *(n' atthi kāmesu doso)* is called 'a gratification-view' (*assāda-diṭṭhi*, Vibh 368).[74] This is the type of view expressed by Ariṭṭha: one can engage in sensual pleasure, and this will not be a hindrance on the spiritual path. This view found its way into the *Pāṭimokkha* as the sixty-eighth rule entailing expiation (*suddhapācittiyā*).[75] This view is one of 24 'stumbling blocks' (*antarāyikā*) found in the Vinaya (Vin I 93–4, II 271). Stumbling blocks are something causing an obstacle or an impediment. The view itself occurs in the Vinaya where we find Ariṭṭha given an 'act of suspension' (*ukkhepanīya-kammaṃ*, Vin II 27) for holding the view.[76] The idea appears to be that this act of suspension is carried out on Ariṭṭha for 'not seeing an offence' (*āpattiyā adassane*). Ariṭṭha has 'fallen away from (right)-view' (*diṭṭhi-vipattiyā*, Vin II 22) and so needs to be suspended from the order.[77]

I would like to consider briefly how holding wrong-views was seen as an offence (*āpatti*), which could result in an act of suspension in the Vinaya. A passage appears (Vin I 97–8) which describes how a *bhikkhu* can be suspended for not seeing an offence,[78] not making amends for an offence,[79] or not giving up a wrong-view.[80] If the *bhikkhu* sees the offence, makes amends for it, and gives up the wrong-view he may become a full part of the order again. However, there is a chance of the suspension being re-implemented if there is not a constant acknowledgement of the offence.[81]

Other passages explain how a *bhikkhu* could be variously accused of holding wrong-view. Holding wrong-view is an offence that should be seen (*āpatti daṭṭhabbā*, presumably implying that it is acknowledged). It is an offence for which amends should be made (*āpatti paṭikātabbā*), and the destructive view given up (*pāpikā diṭṭhi paṭinissajjetā*, Vin I 325). Other *bhikkhus* could ask the *bhikkhu* holding the view to give up his wrong-view, but the accused *bhikkhu* could claim that he does not hold a wrong-view. If, subsequently, the order suspends the *bhikkhu* for not giving up the wrong-view, this would not be a legally valid act (*adhammakamma*), as the *bhikkhu* had not held a wrong-view.[82] Alternatively, there could be a wrong-view that should be given up, and the offending *bhikkhu* could acknowledge this. Then, if the order suspends him for not giving up the wrong-view, this would not be a legally valid act (Vin I 323). Finally, there could be a wrong-view that should be given up, but the *bhikkhu* refuses to give it up, so the other *bhikkhus* suspend him for not giving up the wrong-view. This would be a legally valid act (Vin I 324). This is precisely the fate of Ariṭṭha, who refuses to give up his wrong-view: he is given a (formal) act of suspension (*ukkhepaniya-kammaṃ*), and is also not allowed to eat with the order for not giving up his wrong-view.[83] The point of these passages appears to be that if a wrong-view is taken up, it is an offence that should be seen, made amends for, and the view should be given up (*adassane vā appaṭikamme vā appaṭinissagge vā*, Vin I 325).

The view of *bhikkhu* Sāti:

> Now on that occasion a destructive view had arisen in *bhikkhu* Sāti: 'As I understand the *dhamma* taught by the Fortunate One, it is the same consciousness that runs and wanders through *saṃsāra,* not another.'[84]

Sāti posits an enduring entity, namely consciousness (*viññāṇa)*, which transmigrates. K.R. Norman has suggested that Sāti is recollecting a teaching similar to that found in the *Bṛhadāraṇyaka Upaniṣad* that consciousness (Skt. *vijñāna*) transmigrates.[85] Richard Gombrich has noted that both Ariṭṭha's view and Sāti's view, the former ethical/moral, to do with practice, the latter philosophical/ intellectual, to do with doctrine, are treated in a similar fashion in the Nikāya*s*, as being objects of craving.[86]

The view of Brahmā Baka:

> Now on that occasion a destructive view had arisen in Brahmā Baka: 'This is permanent, this lasts forever, this is constant, this is eternal, this is total, this is not subject to cessation; for this is neither born nor ages, nor dies, nor fades away, nor reappears, and beyond there is no cessation.'[87]

The view of Brahmā Baka expresses, in a simple understanding, a Brahmanic notion of 'being' and 'permanence', what in other contexts is likely to be called an eternalist-view.

The view of *bhikkhu* Yamaka:

> Now on that occasion a destructive view had arisen in *bhikkhu* Yamaka: 'Thus do I understand the *dhamma* taught by the Fortunate One: In so far as a *bhikkhu* has destroyed the corruptions (*āsavas*), he is broken up and dies when the body is broken up, he becomes not after death.'[88]

The view of Yamaka posits a notion of a 'being' which is destroyed upon reaching *nibbāna*. This should be understood as an annihilationist-view (*uccheda-diṭṭhi*).

A destructive view:

> A destructive view had arisen: 'No recluse or brahmin can come here [to this heavenly realm].'[89]

This wrong-view possibly expresses the idea that Brahmā, as the highest of the gods, is the controller of all things. Because of this certain cosmological realms are not accessible to all. For Buddhism this is a wrong-view.

A wrong-view about class:

> Once [....] when seven brahmin seers were dwelling in leaf huts in the forest, the following destructive view arose in them: 'Brahmins are the highest class, those of any other class are inferior; brahmins are the fairest class, those of any other class are dark; only brahmins are purified, not non-brahmins; brahmins alone are the sons of Brahmā, the offspring of Brahmā, born of his mouth, born of Brahmā, created by Brahmā, heirs of Brahmā'.[90]

The final wrong-view in this section is one that proposes that brahmins are the highest class (Skt. *varṇa*) and others are inferior. This formula appears several times in the *Assalāyana-sutta* (M II 147–57), but only on this occasion is it introduced as being a type of wrong-view.

All these views are then characterised as destructive views. They destroy the Buddhist path. In destroying discipline, how the holder of the view acts, they hinder the cleansing of body, speech and mind. I regard this as essential to an understanding of the notion of both wrong-view and right-view. Wrong-view increases greed, hatred and delusion, right-view achieves the cessation of greed, hatred and delusion.

The six bases for views (*diṭṭhi-ṭṭhāna*)

I will now consider six views from the *Alagaddūpama-sutta*. The text tells us that these *diṭṭhi* are 'bases for views' (*diṭṭhi-ṭṭhāna*). The commentary states that *diṭṭhi-ṭṭhāna* are themselves *micchā-diṭṭhi* which give rise to other *micchā-diṭṭhi*.[91] The *Brahmajāla-sutta* repeatedly states that all of its sixty-two views are *diṭṭhi-ṭṭhāna*.[92] K.R. Norman interprets all six views as 'wrong-views'[93] and

Richard Gombrich also translates *diṭṭhi-ṭṭhānā* as 'wrong-views'.[94] The formula is the following:

> *Bhikkhus*, there are these six bases for views. What are the six? Here, *bhikkhus*, an untaught ordinary person, who has no regard for the noble ones and is unskilled and undisciplined in their *dhamma*, who has no regard for true men and is unskilled and undisciplined in their *dhamma*:
> View 1: Regards form thus: 'This is mine, this I am, this is my self.'
> View 2: Regards feeling thus: 'This is mine, this I am, this is my self.'
> View 3: Regards apperception thus: 'This is mine, this I am, this is my self.'
> View 4: Regards volitional formations thus: 'This is mine, this I am, this is my self.'
> View 5: Regards what is seen, heard, thought, cognized, encountered, sought, mentally pondered thus: 'This is mine, this I am, this is my self.'
> View 6: And this basis for views, namely, 'This is self, this the world; after death I shall be permanent, everlasting, eternal, not subject to change; I shall endure and last as long as eternity' – this too he regards thus: 'This is mine, this I am, this is my self.[95]

Four of these views are different ways of 'regarding' (*samanupassati*) four of the *khandhas*. It is interesting that in the fifth view the *khandha* of consciousness does not appear but the view is based upon what is seen, heard, thought and cognized, etc. I think this is perhaps suggesting something about the *khandhas* and the nature of wrong-view in general.[96] This is that the notion of the *khandhas* and the ideas of what is seen, heard, thought and cognized, are, in a sense, interchangeable. In other words, wrong-views are based upon anything that they are attached to, upon anything that they identify with. This regarding, or forming a view about the *khandhas*, is very important for an understanding of what wrong-view is. The same idea was found in the formula for *sakkāya-diṭṭhi*, the views based upon identifying with the *khandhas*. It is clear that attachment to the *khandhas* (to the idea of a self) is a prominent cause of wrong-view.

Two important articles have appeared in recent years which shed some light on these views. K.R. Norman, in an article primarily on *attā,* has used these views, and other parts of the *Alagaddūpama-sutta*, to argue, contrary to some earlier scholars, that the Nikāyas were aware not only of the individual *ātman* but of the world-*ātman*.[97] This can be found in the phrase of the sixth *diṭṭhi, so loko so attā* which, he argues, points to the oneness of the individual and world-*attā*, so familiar and central to Upaniṣadic thought.[98] According to him, there may even be 'verbal echoes' of the Upaniṣads in the sixth wrong-view, for example *Chandogya Upaniṣad* III 3–4: *eṣa me ātmā* (taking *ātman* to be the equivalent of *brahman).* The phrase repeated throughout this formula *eso 'ham asmi* is, Norman argues, the famous 'that is you' (*tat tvam asi*) from the perspective of the first person, the realisation instead of the famous *Chāndogya Upaniṣad* instruction.[99]

As to the fifth *diṭṭhi*, it was Jayatilleke who first argued that this view has clear similarities to a passage which appears twice in the *Bṛhadāraṇyaka Upaniṣad* (2, 4, 5 and 4, 5, 6).[100] In these passages it is taught that the *ātman* should be seen (*draṣṭavyaḥ*), learnt of (*śrotavyaḥ*), conceived of (*mantavyaḥ*) and rationally understood (*nididhyāsitavyaḥ*).[101] As Jayatilleke points out, the *Alagaddūpama-sutta* knows of these ways of knowing, *diṭṭhaṃ sutaṃ mutaṃ viññātaṃ* (the *Alagaddūpama-sutta*, adding *pattaṃ*), and to identify with what is seen, heard, thought of or cognized, is described as a hindrance. Gombrich summarises all these arguments:

> The fifth wrong-view is to identify with what has been *diṭṭham sutaṃ mataṃ viññātaṃ*. What exactly is that? The answer is at *Bṛhadāraṇyaka* 4, 5, 6: *ātmani khalv* are *dṛṣṭe śrute mate vijñāte idaṃ sarvaṃ viditaṃ*. So here is the form of the microcosm-macrocosm equivalence to which the Buddha is alluding; and we can further see that his fifth wrong-view is Yājñavalkya's realisation of that identity in life, and his sixth wrong-view the making real that identity at death. But, says the Buddha, that is something which does not exist (*asat*).[102]

The verse to which Gombrich *et al.* are referring is the following:

> You see […] it is one's self (*ātman*) which one should see and hear, and on which one should reflect and concentrate. For when one has seen and heard one's self, when one has reflected and concentrated on one's self, one knows this whole world.[103]

To identify with what is seen or heard, thought or cognized is perhaps another way of stating that there is attachment to the *khandhas* and what is impermanent. It is to be attached to *dukkha*. In replacing the fifth *khandha* with the statement that the view arises based on what is seen, heard, thought or cognized, etc., the view in the *Alagaddūpama-sutta* is suggesting that wrong-view is an expression of *dukkha* itself. As I will suggest in my consideration of the *Aṭṭhakavagga* in Chapter 6, it is constantly stated that one should not be attached to what is seen, heard, thought and cognized. Wrong-views arise through attachment to the *khandhas*, through what is formed and constructed. To overcome this attachment there is needed both a course of action and insight into the process of the arising and cessation of *dukkha*. The seeing of *dukkha* (what is), leads to a radical change of one's actions (what ought to be done). As I suggested in my consideration of wrong-views that deny that actions have consequences, these views are wrong because they deny that action leads to knowledge.

Six wrong-views from the *Sabbāsava-sutta*

The next group of views about the self are found in the *Sabbāsava-sutta* (M I 6–12). These views are introduced by the statement that they are all a product of 'reflecting inappropriately' (*ayoniso manasikāra*).[104] I understand this in the way that I have described, as an expression of craving and ignorance. There is inappropriate reflecting when such questions arise as: 'Was I in the past? What was I in the past?' There is inappropriate reflecting when such questions are asked about the present and the future:

> To one reflecting inappropriately in this way one of six views occurs. The view:
> View 1: 'I have a self' arises firmly as the truth.
> View 2: 'I do not have a self' arises firmly as the truth.
> View 3: 'By the self I perceive what is self' arises firmly as the truth.
> View 4: 'By the self I perceive what is not self' arises firmly as the truth.
> View 5: 'By what is not self I perceive what is not self' arises firmly as the truth.
> View 6: 'It is this self of mine that speaks and feels and experiences here and there the result of good and destructive actions; but this self of mine is permanent, everlasting, eternal, not subject to change, and it will endure and last forever.'[105]

First, as can be seen, each of these views is said to 'arise as true and established' (*saccato thetato diṭṭhi uppajjati*). As I am suggesting, if things are not seen as they are, if one reflects inappropriately, the course of action undertaken will be an unwholesome course of action. It will be based upon attachment. Second, I do not consider the content of the propositions classified as *micchā-diṭṭhi* and *sammā-diṭṭhi* to be the only factor which makes them wrong or right. The problem that Buddhism wishes to address is *dukkha*. This being so, it is interested in *dukkha*, its arising, cessation and the way to its cessation. Seeing this is what constitutes 'knowledge' (*ñāṇa*). Knowledge and *sammā-diṭṭhi* are explained as 'knowledge concerning suffering' (*dukkhe ñāṇaṃ*),[106] and *sammā-diṭṭhi* is explained as having four names beginning with 'knowledge regarding suffering'.[107] These views from the *Sabbāsava-sutta* do not concern *dukkha*, hence they are wrong. They are not views about *dukkha*, its arising, cessation and the way to its cessation, the only valid content of a right-view. As I will discuss below, the commentaries analyse views in the following way: right-view always has two roots, 'non-greed' (*alobha*) and 'non-hate' (*adosa*, Ps I 205), wrong-view has greed and delusion as roots (Ps I 203). This takes us back to my first point: views become 'true and established'. They are an attachment which leads to an unwholesome course of action and so to ignorance. I mentioned above that certain *sassata-diṭṭhi* are described as volitional formations (*saṃkhāra*). They are part of the process of mental proliferation or manifoldness.[108] Whereas the Buddhist path, led by *sammā-diṭṭhi*, 'makes cessation its object'.[109] The point I wish to introduce at this stage is that *micchā-diṭṭhi* is a manifoldness (*papañca*) and a volitional formation: it is mental proliferation. In a very definite sense it can be argued that this is why certain views are classified as *miccha-diṭṭhi*: because they make for cognitive activity, they increase attachment and craving. A view that does the opposite to this, which makes for cessation, for a lessening and calming, is called *sammā-diṭṭhi*.

Acceptance of a view as a result of reflection *(diṭṭhi-nijjhānakhanti)*

In this chapter I am attempting to classify all the views described as wrong in the Nikāyas. However, it is important that we do not get lost in the details and attempt to understand what particular philosophical position each *micchā-diṭṭhi* is expressing. The Pāli canon is thorough in its classification. However, its classification should not divert us from the reasons for it. The canon enumerates many *micchā-diṭṭhi*. Forming a view is *micchā-diṭṭhi*. Any view is, I would argue, *micchā-diṭṭhi*. Wrong-views make judgements, about the self and the world, about the *khandhas*. The wrong-views found in the *Sabbāsava-sutta* that I have just considered are an example of this tendency. They are an expression of attachment and craving, of *dukkha* itself. Wrong-views should be understood as expressions of greed and attachment, and this is why they are classified as wrong. This makes them invalid means of knowledge and it is this aspect of wrong-views which I would now like to consider.

I would like to examine how the Nikāyas understand the notion of views as part of a list of ten (or sometimes five) means of knowledge. Usually these means of knowledge are invalidated due to their being the product of greed and attachment, but this is not always the case. Before considering these ten means of knowledge I will classify another groups of views which occasionally provide the context in which the means of knowledge are found. These are the following 16 views:

> Views 1–8*:* The self and the world are eternal (only this is true, anything else is wrong, repeated after each view); the self and the world are not eternal; eternal and not eternal; neither eternal nor not eternal; finite; infinite; both finite and infinite; neither finite nor infinite.
>
> Views 9–16: The self and the world are appercipient of unity (only this is true, anything else is wrong, repeated after each view); the self and the world are appercipient of diversity; appercipient of the limited; appercipient of the immeasurable; [experience] exclusively pleasure; [experience] exclusively pain; [experience] both pleasure and pain; [experience] neither pleasure nor pain.[110]

After the sixteen views in the *Pañcattaya-sutta* it is stated that it is impossible for one to realise the truth that these views proclaim. For the truth of the view to be realised, the *sutta* explains, would depend upon:

Faith (*saddhā*);
Approval (*ruci*);
Oral tradition (*anussava*);
Reasoned cogitation (*ākāraparivitakka*);
Acceptance of a view as a result of reflection (*diṭṭhi-nijjhānakkhanti*).[111]

Apart from these means of knowledge, the view holder will not have 'clear and personal knowledge'.[112] Even any 'fragmentary knowledge' (*ñāṇabhāgamattam eva*) that the view-holder has, the *sutta* explains as 'attachment' (*upādāna*). Attachment is then explained as 'conditioned and gross' (*saṃkhataṃ oḷārikaṃ*) and there should be cessation of this.[113] This is what the Buddha knows: attachment and its cessation, presumably this is what constitutes 'personal knowledge' (*paccattaṃ ñāṇaṃ*). Views (and the other four means of knowledge) are clearly being evaluated, in part, due to the effect that the means of knowledge has. How will a means of knowledge influence the conduct of the person who uses it? This issue has been considered by Walpola Rahula. In *What the Buddha Taught*, Rahula cites the *Kālama-sutta* (A I 188–93) as expressing an essential point of the Buddha's teaching. Stated simply this is the following: those seeking freedom from suffering should know for themselves what is 'wholesome' (*kusala*) and 'unwholesome' (*akusala*) and not rely on other things to achieve the end of *dukkha*. This simple piece of advice Rahula called 'unique in the history of religions'.[114]

In the *sutta* the Kālamas explain to the Buddha that the recluses and brahmins who come to Kesaputta proclaim their own doctrine (*vāda*) but abuse the doctrines of others.[115] They go on to say that they have 'doubt and wavering' (*kaṅkhā* [...] *vicikicchā*, A I 189) as to which recluses and brahmins are speaking truth and which are speaking falsehood (*saccaṃ āha, ko musā*, ibid.).[116] The Buddha replies that they may well doubt, they may well waver, but it is on a doubtful point that wavering arises.[117] The Buddha explains that they should not be misled by:

Report/oral tradition (*anussavena*);
Tradition (*paramparāya*);
Hearsay (*itikirāya*);
Not by proficiency in the collections (*piṭakasampadānena*);
Logic (*takkahetu*);
Inference (*nayahetu*);
Reasoned cogitation (*ākāraparivitakkena*);
Acceptance of a view as a result of reflection (*diṭṭhi-nijjhānakkhantiyā*);
Not because it fits becoming (*bhabbarūpatāya*);
Out of respect for a recluse (*samaṇo no garū*).[118]

The Buddha explains what they should understand:

When you know for yourselves: These things are unwholesome, these things are blameworthy, these things are censured by the wise; these things, when performed and undertaken, conduce to loss and sorrow – then reject them.[119]

The Buddha explains why he makes this statement: the ten incorrect means of knowledge are rooted in greed, hatred and delusion (*lobha, dosa, moha*). The reason for this is based on the Kālamas' earlier statement that the recluses and brahmins proclaim their own doctrines and abuse the doctrines of others.[120] The aim of the *dhamma* is to overcome what is unwholesome. As the conduct of the recluses and brahmins does not suggest that their teachings are achieving this, the Buddha takes them as wrong teachings. The Buddha explains this: with the arising of greed, hatred and delusion there is 'loss' (*ahitāya*) not 'profit' (*hitāya*, A I 189). Losing control of their minds, those overcome by greed, hatred and delusion kill living beings, take what is not given, commit adultery, tell lies and get others to do the same.[121] All these things are 'unwholesome' (*akusala*) not 'wholesome' (*kusala*), 'blameworthy' (*sāvajja*) not 'blameless' (*anavajja*), 'censured by the wise' (*viññū-garahita*), and when undertaken conduce to 'loss and sorrow' (*ahitāya dukkhāya*, A I 190). It is for this reason that a person should not be misled by the ten incorrect means of knowledge, for they are unwholesome.[122] They should not be depended upon. They are incorrect means of knowledge precisely because they are unwholesome. The person should know what is wholesome, blameless, praised by the wise, and what, when undertaken, conduces to profit and happiness.[123] Freedom from greed, hatred and delusion produces 'states' (*dhammā*) that are wholesome, blameless, praised by the wise and, when performed, conduce to happiness (A I 190–1).[124] As I have suggested, right-view leads to wholesome action, wrong-view leads to unwholesome action.

Though the ten means of knowledge are rejected in the *Kālama-sutta* there are occurrences in which some of them are valid or correct means of knowledge. In the *Pañcattaya-sutta* it was stated that the five do not lead to 'clear and personal knowledge' and that even any fragmentary knowledge that they give will be a form of attachment. In the *Cankī-sutta* (M II 164–77) the original five means of knowledge are again found (faith, approval, oral tradition, reasoned cogitation and acceptance of a view as a result of reflection). However, in the *Cankī-sutta* the five are said to have two possible outcomes.[125] Something may be fully accepted out of faith, approval, oral tradition, reasoned cogitation and acceptance of a view as a result of reflection, yet be 'empty, hollow and false' (*rittaṃ, tucchaṃ, musā*). However, something else may not be fully accepted out of faith, approval, oral tradition, reasoned cogitation and acceptance of a view as a result of reflection, yet it may be 'factual, true and unmistaken' (*bhūtaṃ, tucchaṃ, anaññathā*).[126]

The *sutta* considers how one 'preserves truth' (*saccānurakkhana*, M II 171). It explains that the person does not come to the definite conclusion that, 'only this is true, anything else is wrong' based on one of the five, but preserves truth when he says 'my faith is thus', etc., 'my acceptance of a view as a result of reflection is thus'.[127] This is how the five means of knowledge may have two different outcomes. The knowledge gained may be the same through one of the means of knowledge, but the attitude one has towards that knowledge is different. As I suggested above, it is perhaps misleading to look at all of the *micchā-diṭṭhi* found in the Nikāyas and attempt to understand the philosophical and metaphysical position which they posit. In the *Kālama-sutta* it is because the views of the various teachers, based upon the ten means of knowledge, do not lead to what is wholesome, which makes them incorrect means of knowledge. In the *Cankī-sutta* it is by becoming attached to the object of knowledge, by holding that it is 'true', that the knowledge itself loses its value. The *sutta* is positing a non-attached means of gaining knowledge.

If there is 'acceptance of a view as a result of reflection', this is likely to involve holding onto a specific view with the thought, 'only this is true, anything else is wrong'. However, as I will explain in the next chapter, right-view entails a knowledge of doctrine free from craving. It is an expression of non-greed, non-hatred and non-delusion; whereas wrong-view is an expression of greed, hatred and delusion. The notion of wrong-view describes a type of greed for knowledge. It is a false means of attaining knowledge. Things cannot be known 'as they are' with a mind corrupted by greed. It is this, in part, which the notion of wrong-view describes.

The *Cankī-sutta* finally explains how there is 'discovery of truth' (*saccānubodho*, M II 171). A *bhikkhu* should be found who has no states (*dhammā*) based on greed, hatred and delusion; who has a mind which is not obsessed by these *dhammas* (*dhammehi pariyādinnacitto*, M II 172–3); who does not claim to know and see, while not knowing and seeing,[128] and does not cause others to act in a harmful way.[129] This *bhikkhu*, who is not obsessed by greed, hatred and delusion, teaches a *dhamma* that is 'profound, hard to see and hard to understand, unattainable by mere reasoning, subtle, to be experienced by the wise'.[130] Such a *dhamma* as this cannot be taught by someone affected by greed, hatred and delusion.[131] In that *bhikkhu* who is purified from states of delusion (*visuddhaṃ mohanīyehi*) confidence can be placed. The *dhamma* can be heard from him and memorised (*sutvā dhammaṃ dhāreti*). The person examines the meaning of the teaching and, having examined the meaning, 'gains a reflective acceptance of the teaching' (*atthaṃ upaparikkhato dhammā nijjhānaṃ khamanti*, M II 173). This leads to 'scrutiny' (*tuleti*) of things.[132] With much effort, 'with the body he realises the ultimate truth and sees it by penetrating it with wisdom'.[133] In this way there is discovery of truth.[134] The *sutta* then states how it is in the 'repetition, development and cultivation of those same *dhammas* that there is final arrival at truth'.[135]

These *suttas* are clearly explaining a method by which early Buddhist epistemology is made valid. They are describing what a correct means of knowledge is. In a sense, a correct means of knowledge is the reflective acceptance of the *dhamma* from a trusted teacher. But in order to gain knowledge there needs to be some transformation of the conduct and thought of the person who seeks this knowledge. This is in order to realise 'clear and personal knowledge'. As I will argue in the next chapter, the gaining of knowledge requires the transformation of acts of body, speech and mind. Action is intimately bound up with knowledge. This is why the *suttas* reject views that deny *kamma* or posit a self. They both lead to action based upon greed and attachment.

Views of the unanswered (*avyākata*) type

Certain views are used in the Nikāyas as characteristic of the notion of wrong-view. One set of views that serves this purpose is the *avyākata*. I would like to continue with the idea at this point that views are not so much condemned as wrong because of what they propose, but because of the influence that the view has on its holder. As I have suggested, the means of gaining knowledge is intimately bound up with the way one acts and, as I will go on to argue, the way one acts is intimately bound up with the knowledge that one has. There is no major difference between the view that denies that actions have consequences, and those that posit a self (attachment to the *khandhas*, or to what is seen, heard, thought and cognized, or to one of the ten means of knowledge). They all produce actions of an unwholesome type. This explains the preoccupation with the notion of *attā* in explaining wrong-view. Belief in the self leads away from wholesome action (action not based upon craving and attachment), and by definition away from knowledge. This also suggests why familiar groups of views such as the *avyākata* are classified as wrong-views.

As I suggested in the Introduction, wrong-views, expressed by the ideas of *uccheda* and *sassata-diṭṭhi*, were considered in the early texts, to be particularly destructive. These classifications have already been met in the discussion of *sakkāya-diṭṭhi*. One explanation of these two views is the following from the *Sammohavinodanī*:

> To state that, 'I have a self' (*atthi me attā vā*) is the view of eternalism (*sassata-diṭṭhi*) which assumes the existence of a self at all times. However, to state 'I have no self' (*n' atthi me attā*) is the view of annihilationism (*uccheda-diṭṭhi*) because it assumes the annihilation of an existing being.[136]

This suggests that the view 'there is no self' is as much a wrong-view as the view 'there is a self'. To posit or deny a self are wrong-views. To say that right-view is the understanding of *anattā* is quite different. It suggests that there should not be attachment to the idea of a self; it does not posit or deny a self. Wrong-view, as I am arguing, is primarily a form of greed and attachment to the idea of a self. I will consider the problem of how there can be a right-view that corrects the wrong-view of self in Chapter 5. For the moment I wish to stress how wrong-views are classified as attachment and craving. For example, there is a discussion in the *Vibhaṅga* (Vibh 340) of the 'inclination (of thought) of beings' (*sattānaṃ āsayo*). This is to depend on 'views of becoming' (*bhava-diṭṭhi-sannissitā*), and 'views of non-becoming' (*vibhava-diṭṭhi-sannissitā*), according to the ten *avyākata*.[137] According to the *Vibhaṅga*, there is an inclination for the mind to take a position. One of the simplest ways to understand *sammā-diṭṭhi* is to take it as expressing the middle-way. It is to see the rise and fall of *dhammas*. By the idea of *micchā-diṭṭhi* the texts perhaps intend to suggest a rigidity of thought, in which *only* rise, or *only* fall is seen. The *suttas* suggest that if only rise is seen then the mind will incline to *sassata-diṭṭhi*, and if only fall is seen then the mind will incline to *uccheda-diṭṭhi*.[138] These ideas are expressed by the ten *avyākata*:

The ten avyākata

The world is eternal;
The world is not eternal;
The world is finite;
The world is infinite;
The soul and the body are the same;
The soul is one thing, the body is another;
The Tathāgata exists after death;
The Tathāgata does not exist after death;
The Tathāgata both exists and does not exist after death;
The Tathāgata neither exists nor does not exist after death.[139]

In the *Vibhaṅga* (Vibh 366–7) there is a consideration of the unwholesome action that arises from holding to any of these views. This comes in an explanation of 'seeking supreme practice' (*brahmacariyesanā*)[140] described as holding to the ten *avyākata*.[141] It is said that unwholesome actions of body, speech and mind occur with these views (*akusalaṃ kāyakammaṃ, vacīkammaṃ, manokammaṃ*). Wrong-view gives rise to unwholesome actions of body, speech and mind. As I argued above, this invalidates certain views as correct means of knowledge.[142]

CONCLUSION

In this chapter I have attempted to classify all those views understood as wrong-views in the four primary Nikāyas. In undertaking this I have followed the classifications of the *Vibhaṇga*, the *Brahmajāla-sutta* and the *Diṭṭhi-saṃyutta*. Wrong-views can be understood according to two categories: the first of these explains a view as wrong if it states that actions do not have consequences. These views deny the law of *kamma*. The second explains a view as wrong if it posits (or denies) a self. Views of this type are wrong-views because they express attachment to the idea of a self, whether existing or not existing. It would be incorrect to understand the view that denies a self to be a right-view. To deny or posit a self is a wrong-view. Technically speaking, wrong views of self posit attachment to the *khandhas*, to what is seen, heard, thought and cognized, to *attā* and *loka*. They deny that attachments have consequences. According to the Nikāyas, all views can be explained according to the category of *sakkāya-diṭṭhi* and this can further be understood as either *uccheda* or *sassata-diṭṭhi*, the views of annihilationism and eternalism. It seems clear that many of the views could be reduced to one of these categories. This reflects a preoccupation with *attā* found in the classification of wrong-views. I have suggested that this preoccupation is based upon the strong link between knowledge and action found in the Nikāyas. Indeed, this is the link between the views that deny that actions have consequences and views about the self. They both strongly influence the way that the holder of the view acts. This reflects the relationship between greed and ignorance found in the notion of wrong-view. Certain terms appear repeatedly in the Nikāyas with reference to *micchā-diṭṭhi*. We find the terms 'engagement' (*upaya*), 'attachment' (*upādāna*), 'adherence' (*abhinivesa*), 'mental-basis' (*cetaso adhiṭṭhānam*)[143] and 'clinging' (*parāmāsa*).[144] All these terms point to an essential feature of the notion of *micchā-diṭṭhi*: that it is the grasping, attached, obstinate side of the cognitive process.[145] Buddhaghosa states that 'clinging' is a term for wrong-view because it occurs in the aspect of missing the individual essence of a given state (*dhamma*) and apprehending (*āmasana*) elsewhere (*parato*) an unreal individual essence.[146] I think all this suggests that the link between craving and ignorance is made precisely because the early tradition emphasises that action and thought are intimately bound.

2

THE CONTENT OF RIGHT-VIEW

The notion of 'right-view' (*sammā-diṭṭhi*) is most familiar to us as the first stage of the noble eightfold path. The Buddhist path, aiming for the eradication of *dukkha*, begins with right-view. What doctrines does right-view have knowledge of? We may expect that it is the central Buddhist notions of the 'three marks' (*tilakkhaṇa*). Right-view has knowledge of *anicca, dukkha* and *anattā*. When a view accords with these notions, it is a right-view. Achieving this view, one enters upon the path. Right-view entails perceiving the world according to the *dhamma*. In this chapter I will classify all those views described as 'right-view' in the Nikāyas. Is right-view any view that agrees with the *dhamma*? What is the content of right-view, what does it propose? Does right-view state what is fact or of value? It is these questions that I will aim to answer.

Of particular interest to me is how far we are to understand right-view as the opposite of the wrong-views that I considered in the previous chapter. For example, I suggested in the Introduction that right-view is not another view opposed to wrong-view, but that it implies a different order of seeing. For example, the view that 'actions do not have consequences' is not *corrected* by adopting the view that 'actions have consequences', but by practising right-view. This practice reflects the knowledge that 'actions have consequences', and leads to an insight into the way things are. Right-view is a statement of 'is' and 'ought' and cannot be properly understood without appreciating that it expresses these notions, which we may all too easily separate. When we understand that this is the nature of right-view, we may realise that right-view cannot be a simple correction of wrong-view, but an essential factor on the path to the overcoming of *dukkha*.

In the Buddhist texts it is often suggested that the aim of the Buddhist path is 'seeing things as they are' (*yathābhūtadassana*). In fact, the commentaries often gloss *sammā-diṭṭhi* as *yāthāva-diṭṭhika* 'the view of things as they are'.[1] Rupert Gethin has pointed out that *sammā-diṭṭhi* is essentially knowledge of suffering, its arising, cessation and the way to its cessation.[2] This is the apprehending of a process, the process of 'rise and fall' (*udayabbaya*). I shall return to this idea in Chapter 4. Sue Hamilton has argued that seeing things as they are relates to the adaptation of experience, the way our cognition perceives the world, and entails an insight into the very nature of cognition. It is the truth of knowing that we are no longer bound to continuity;[3] it is knowing 'how our experience operates'.[4] Seeing things as they are is a soteriological truth, best explained as insight into the nature of knowledge. Hamilton argues that this understanding of the cognitive process is epistemological, and that the primary aim of the Buddhist path is not an ontological understanding of self and world:[5]

> The problem that needs solving, according to the Buddha, is an epistemological one, and following the Buddha's teaching leads to insight into the arising and nature of knowledge, and into the status of what one knows. But the process that leads to that insight, and the solving of the epistemological problem, does not itself affect Reality.[6]

These ideas lead Hamilton to translate *sammā-diṭṭhi* as 'right understanding'.[7] As a form of understanding, *sammā-diṭṭhi* may be better understood as wholesome awareness. I suggest this for the following reason: the texts make a distinction between different levels of right-view. While I will discuss this distinction fully later in this chapter, for the moment it is important to understand that *sammā-diṭṭhi* is classified into two types. First, it is understood to comprehend a group of views primarily concerned with *kamma* and rebirth. Second, *sammā-diṭṭhi* is explained as 'wisdom' (*paññā*). The former view may have more of a propositional content than the latter, but neither entails belief in a set of propositions. When right-view is explained as wisdom it consists, to a large extent, in no longer grasping at the idea of a self (whether existing or not existing). I think the aim of both of these types of views are the same, namely, to induce non-attachment from all cognitive acts. However, they function at different stages of the path. Living according to the knowledge that our actions have consequences leads to a cognitive process that no longer grasps, that is no longer attached. The world is seen in a different way: without greed, hatred and delusion. In any discussion of *micchā-diṭṭhi* and *sammā-diṭṭhi* we are primarily concerned with the affective nature of the cognitive process. We must be aware that there is a strong emphasis in the Nikāyas on the link between action and knowledge. It is clear from the earliest tradition that 'virtue' (*sīla*) and 'wisdom' (*paññā*) are related. A passage from the *Dīgha-nikāya* states that 'wisdom is cleansed by virtue and virtue is cleansed by wisdom – where there is virtue there is wisdom and where there is wisdom there is virtue'.[8] Knowledge, or wisdom, is not knowledge for its own sake, but transforms the attitudes and actions of those who possess it.

PART ONE: VIEWS THAT AFFIRM THAT ACTIONS HAVE CONSEQUENCES

In Chapter 1 I discussed a group of views that denied that actions have consequences, that denied the law of *kamma*. I would now like to consider a group of views that are their opposite. They are the right-views that affirm that actions have consequences, they affirm the law of *kamma*.

The view of affirmation (*atthika-diṭṭhi*)

In the discussion of *micchā-diṭṭhi*, we met the formula for a type of view said to have been held by one of the 'six teachers', Ajita Kesakambalī. This view is found in the *Sāmaññaphala-sutta,* as well as a number of other *suttas*. In those, Ajita is not named as the holder of the view and the opposite to his view is often given. I would like, first, to give this opposite view along with two related views, then to discuss the contexts in which they are found:

> There is what is given and what is offered and what is sacrificed; there is fruit and result of good and bad actions; there is this world and the other world; there is mother and father; there are beings who are reborn spontaneously; there are good and virtuous recluses and brahmins in the world who have themselves realised by direct knowledge and declare this world and the other world.[9]

In the *Apaṇṇaka-sutta* (M I 400–13) at M I 404 the view is described as both a *sammā-diṭṭhi* and 'the doctrine of affirmation' (*atthika-vāda*). In the Vinaya we find the statement that there is 'a right-view founded on ten (tenets)' (*dasa-vatthukā sammā-diṭṭhi*, Vin V 138), which should be understood as the view of affirmation. This view is distinguished from 'a wrong-view founded on ten (tenets)' (*dasa-vatthukā micchā-diṭṭhi*), the view of nihilism.

The view that there is doing (*kiriya-diṭṭhi*)

The second *sammā-diṭṭhi* is the following:

> When one acts or makes others act, when one mutilates or makes others mutilate, when one tortures or makes others inflict torture, when one inflicts sorrow or makes others inflict sorrow, when one oppresses or makes others inflict oppression, when one intimidates or makes others inflict intimidation, when one kills living beings, takes what is not given, breaks into houses, plunders wealth, commits burglary, ambushes highways, seduces another's wife, utters falsehood, wrong is done by the doer. If, with a razor-rimmed wheel, one were to make the living beings on this earth into one mass of flesh, into one heap of flesh, because of this there would be wrong and the outcome of wrong. If one were to go along the South bank of the Ganges killing and slaughtering, mutilating and making others mutilate, torturing and making others torture, because of this there would be wrong and the outcome of wrong. If one were to go along the North bank of the Ganges giving gifts and making others give gifts, making offerings and making others give offerings, because

> of this there would be merit and the outcome of merit. From giving, from taming oneself, from restraint, from speaking truth, there is merit and the outcome of merit.[10]

In the *Apaṇṇaka-sutta* at M I 406 this view is called both a *sammā-diṭṭhi* and 'the doctrine that there is doing' (*kiriya-vāda*). It is the opposite to the view of non-doing (*akiriya-diṭṭhi*), to the view attributed in the *Sāmaññaphala-sutta* to Purāṇa Kassapa.

The view of causality (*hetu-diṭṭhi*)

The third *sammā-diṭṭhi* is the following:

> There is a cause and condition for the defilement of beings; beings are defiled owing to a cause and condition. There is a cause and condition for the purification of beings; beings are purified owing to a cause and condition. There is no self-power or other-power, there is no power in humans, no strength or force, no vigour or exertion. All beings, all living things, all creatures, all that lives is without control, without power or strength they experience the fixed course of pleasure and pain through the six kinds of rebirth.[11]

In the *Apaṇṇaka-sutta* at M I 409 this view is called both a *sammā-diṭṭhi* and 'the doctrine of causality' (*hetu-vāda*). This is the opposite to the view of non-causality (*ahetu-diṭṭhi*), to the view attributed in the *Sāmaññaphala-sutta* to Makkhali Gosāla.

We have three right-views. What exactly are they proposing? Essentially they are views which state that actions have consequences. I would like to consider, first, the reasons that the Nikāyas advise the adoption of such views. In the *Apaṇṇaka-sutta* (M I 400–13) all three of these right-views are found. One of the aims of the *sutta* is to explain that certain cognitive acts lead to either wholesome or unwholesome courses of action. In one sense, a view is right if it leads to the desired course of action. At this stage of the path, *sammā* does not signify non-attachment from the act of cognition, but the correctness of the course of action; and this in turn leads to the cessation of craving and attachment. The *Apaṇṇaka-sutta* emphasises this aspect of right-view.

The *sutta* states that the holders of the three wrong-views of nihilism, non-doing and non-causality (*natthika-diṭṭhi, akiriya-diṭṭhi* and *ahetu-diṭṭhi*), will avoid three wholesome states;[12] good bodily, verbal and mental conduct.[13] They will also undertake and practise three unwholesome states; bodily, verbal and mental misconduct.[14] The text gives the reasons for this with the Buddha saying:

> Because those good recluses and brahmins do not see in the unwholesome states the danger, degradation, and defilement, nor do they see in the wholesome states the blessing of renunciation, the aspect of cleansing.[15]

The holders of the right-views of affirmation, doing and causality (*atthika-diṭṭhi, kiriya-diṭṭhi* and *hetu-diṭṭhi*) realise the opposite effects from holding their views. They avoid the unwholesome states of bodily, verbal and mental misconduct (M I 403, 406, 409) and they will undertake and practise three wholesome states, those of good bodily, verbal and mental conduct (M I 403, 406, 409). The reason for this is the opposite to that given for the wrong-views:

> Because those good recluses and brahmins see in unwholesome states the danger, degradation, and defilement, and they see in wholesome states the blessing of renunciation, the aspect of cleansing (*vodāna*).[16]

It is explained that *kusala* states 'cleanse' (*vodāna*) *akusala* states. The texts often refer to the hindrances of *taṇhā* and *avijjā*. The former is overcome by calm, the latter by insight. These hindrances appear to suggest a certain dynamic found within early Buddhism. There are not two hindrances, craving and ignorance, which are overcome by calm or insight. Wisdom (*paññā*) eradicates all defilements. The texts seem fully aware of these distinctions, but do not see it as a dichotomy. In dealing with the soteriological problem, the aim is to overcome *dukkha*. This is not seen as either a wholly cognitive or affective problem and, therefore, neither calm nor insight are sufficient alone. An explanation of this is found in a passage in the *Nettippakaraṇa* (Nett 160) which states that the *suttas* dealing with 'defilement by craving' (*taṇhā-saṃkilesa*) can be demonstrated by 'craving for sensual desire, craving for being, and craving for non-being' (*kāma-taṇhāya bhava-taṇhāya vibhava-taṇhāya*) and by the net of craving (see the *Taṇhājālinī-sutta* at A II 211–13). Those dealing with 'defilement by views' (*diṭṭhi-saṃkilesa*) can be demonstrated by 'annihilationism and eternalism' (*uccheda-sassatena*), by whatever one 'adheres to by means of view, namely "only this is true, anything else is wrong"',[17] and by 'the 62 types of views, i.e. delusion's net'.[18] Cleansing (*vodāna*) from craving can be demonstrated by calm,[19] cleansing from views can be demonstrated by insight.[20] It is the same term 'cleansing' (*vodāna*) that we find in the *Apaṇṇaka-sutta*. The aim of the Buddhist path, in some respects, is to cleanse the mind of defilements. The *Nettippakaraṇa* explains elsewhere that cleansing is of three kinds; the defilement of craving is 'purified' (*visujjhati*) by calm, and this is the concentration *khandha* (*samādhi-kkhandha*); the defilement of views is purified by insight, and this is the wisdom *khandha* (*paññā-kkhandha*); the defilement of misconduct is purified by good conduct, and this is the virtue *khandha* (*sīla-kkhandha*).[21] Cleansing is extinction free from the *āsavas*.[22] Both calm and insight cleanse *taṇhā* and *diṭṭhi*. The point seems to be that 'cleansing' consists of 'purification' (*visujjhati*), by calm, insight and good conduct. These three purifications constitute the three *khandhas* of *sīla, samādhi* and *paññā*, virtue, calm and wisdom. Action and knowledge work together and this is the achievement of right-view. It produces what is wholesome. This is the first reason given for the views of *natthika, akiriya* and *ahetu-diṭṭhi* being wrong-views, and the views of *atthika, kiriya* and *hetu-diṭṭhi* being right-views. The evaluation is based upon whether the views bring about *akusala* or *kusala* states: whether views defile or cleanse.

There is another way in which these wrong and right-views are analysed in the *Apaṇṇaka-sutta*. The text picks a central theme from each wrong and right-view and subjects it to analysis:

> Since there actually is another world, [doing, causality], one who holds the view "there is no other world", ["there is no doing", "there is no causality"], has wrong-view.[23]

The *sutta* adds that since there actually is another world, doing and causality, the one who 'thinks' (*saṅkappeti*) 'there is no other world', 'there is no doing', 'there is no causality' has 'wrong-intention' (*micchā-saṅkappa*). Further, the one who 'makes the statement' (*vācaṃ bhāsati*) that 'there is no other world', 'there is no doing', 'there is no causality' has 'wrong-speech' (*micchā-vācā*). One who says 'there is no other world', 'there is no doing', 'there is no causality' is opposed to those Arahants who know the other world, who hold the doctrine that there is doing, and the doctrine that there is causality (M I 402, 405, 408).[24]

If one convinces another that 'there is no other world', 'there is no doing', 'there is no causality', one convinces that person to accept an untrue *dhamma* (*asaddhammasaññatti*). Because of this he praises himself and disparages others, and any pure virtue that he formerly had is abandoned and is replaced by corrupt conduct. There are then six things that come into being because of the original wrong-view: wrong-view, wrong-intention, wrong-speech, opposition to noble ones, convincing another to accept an untrue *dhamma*, and self-praise and disparagement of others. All these bad states have wrong-view as their condition.[25]

This passage is compared by Jayatilleke to a correspondence theory of truth.[26] He holds that the *Apaṇṇaka-sutta* contains a 'conscious avowal' of the correspondence theory of truth.[27] He states, concerning the passage cited above, that: 'Falsity is here defined as the denial of fact or as what does not accord with fact'.[28] The *Apaṇṇaka-sutta* is an example of the Buddha stating this in terms of *yathābhūtam pajānāti*, 'one knows what is in accordance with fact'.[29] Jayatilleke translates the *Apaṇṇaka-sutta* passage in the following way:

> When in fact there is a next world, *the belief* occurs to me that there is no next world, that would be a *false belief*. When in fact there is a next world, if *one thinks* there is no next world, that would be a *false conception*. When in fact there is a next world, one *asserts the statement* that there is no next world, that would be a *false statement*.[30]

The three terms translated as 'belief', 'thinks', and 'asserts' (which I have emphasised in italic) are *diṭṭhi, saṅkappo* and *vācā*, all of which become false beliefs, false conceptions and false statements (*micchā-diṭṭhi, micchā-saṅkappo, micchā-vācā*). These are corrected by true beliefs, true conceptions and true statements. We have then the following:

Jayatilleke

1. false belief (*micchā-diṭṭhi*) → true belief (*sammā-diṭṭhi*)
2. false conception (*micchā-saṅkappo*) → true conception (*sammā-saṅkappo*)
3. false statement (*micchā-vācā*) → true statement (*sammā-vācā*)[31]

In the discussion of this passage above, however, we find:

Alternative translation

1. wrong-view (*micchā-diṭṭhi*) → right-view (*sammā-diṭṭhi*)
2. wrong-intention (*micchā-saṅkappo*) → right-intention (*sammā-saṅkappo*)
3. wrong-speech (*micchā-vācā*) → right-speech (*sammā-vācā*)

Throughout this book I translate *micchā* and *sammā* as 'wrong' and 'right' respectively. I stress, however, that the conception of 'right' as primarily cognitive, as referring to a right belief, a true belief correcting a wrong belief, may be misleading. This is what, I think, Jayatilleke's translation of this passage suggests. He claims that 'right' (*sammā*) is synonymous with 'true'.[32] He reaches this conclusion by stating that if *micchā* means 'false' then *sammā* must mean correct or true.[33] In looking at this *Apaṇṇaka* passage, and the conclusions that Jayatilleke draws from it, one should be careful not to be led astray by such translations. Jayatilleke, using the translation 'false belief' for *micchā-diṭṭhi*, is clearly influenced by a cognitive understanding of the notion of *diṭṭhi* and perhaps of religion in general. In commenting upon the *Apaṇṇaka* passage, he suggests that:

> [W]hile false propositions entertained as beliefs or conceptions or expressed as statements are considered false, when they do not correspond with or deny facts, true beliefs, conceptions or statements are said to be those which reflect or correspond with fact.[34]

This same tendency to give a cognitive understanding to the *Apaṇṇaka-sutta* is displayed by Jayatilleke in his translation of other terms. For example, *apaṇṇaka-dhamma* (from which the *sutta* takes its name) is translated as 'infallible *dhamma*'. According to Jayatilleke this infallibility is 'purely logical and rational', while *natthika-vāda* is translated as 'disbeliever' and *atthika-vāda* as 'believer'.[35] Although the *Apaṇṇaka-sutta* may be read in such a way, Jayatilleke is displaying a certain prejudice in his interpretation of these terms. I think that the passage about 'cleansing' (*vodāna*), interpreted as cleansing by calm and insight, suggests a different understanding of this *sutta* to that given by Jayatilleke. This is that thought and action work together to overcome the various defilements of the Buddhist Path. It is important that neither calm nor insight is given prominence, but that they both cleanse craving and ignorance.

The *sutta* continues in the following way: since there actually is another world, doing and causality, one who holds the view 'there is another world', 'there is doing' and 'there is causality' has right-view.[36] Since there actually is another world, doing and causality, one who thinks 'there is another world' has right-intention.[37] Further, the one who makes the statement that 'there is another world' 'there is doing' and 'there is causality' has right-speech.[38] One who says 'there is another world', 'there is doing', 'there is causality', is not opposed to those Arahants who know the other world, who hold the doctrine that there is doing and the doctrine that there is causality (M I 403, 406, 409). If one convinces another that 'there is another world', 'there is doing', 'there is causality', one convinces that person to accept a true *dhamma* (*saddhammasaññatti*). Any corrupt conduct is replaced by pure virtue. Six things come into being because of this right-view: right-view, right-intention, right-speech, non-opposition to noble ones, convincing another to accept true *dhamma* and avoidance of self-praise and disparagement of others. All these states have 'right-view as their condition' (*sammā-diṭṭhi-paccayā*).[39] Later in this chapter I will consider the *Mahācattārīsaka-sutta* (M III 71–8) in which it is also of some importance that 'right-view comes first'. This passage gives some context to such statements. Right-view is the ground, the condition, from which *kusala dhammas* come into being. Right-view could be a right belief, from which other wholesome *dhammas* are produced, but it is more likely that right-view implies an act of wholesome cognition, in which the nature of reality is glimpsed, and from which wholesome acts of body, speech and mind are produced. To put this another way, seeing things as they are produces a transformation of actions of body, speech and mind. As I have already stated, right-view is both an 'is' and 'ought' statement. It combines the notions of fact and value. Things are seen as they are and this is transformative.

The *sutta* goes on to give a third and final analysis of these views. It gives the perspective of someone looking at the position taken by the holder of any of the three wrong-views and the three right-views and how he might consider the view-holder's position. This person is the 'wise man' (*viññū puriso*), employed to assess the relative merits of the views being held, beginning with a consideration of the three wrong-views:[40]

> About this, householders, a wise man considers thus: 'If there is no other world [if there is no doing, if there is no causality], then on the dissolution of the body this good person will have made himself safe enough.'[41]

The *sutta* suggests by this statement that if there is no other world, no result of action, or no cause for defilement, then the person holding one of the wrong-views need not worry about any future state.[42] The *sutta* continues, however, that if there is another world, doing or causation, 'then on the dissolution of the body, after death, he (the holder of any of the three wrong-views) will reappear in a state of deprivation, in an unhappy destination, in perdition, even in hell.'[43] In contrast, the *sutta* also gives the way in which the *viññū puriso* may consider the position of the holder of any of the three right-views:

> About this a wise man considers thus: 'If there is another world [if there is doing, if there is causality], then on the dissolution of the body, after death, this good person will reappear in a happy destination, even in a heavenly world.'[44]

This is the first consideration of the *viññū puriso*. The text then grants the possibility that there may not be another world, doing or causality, and how the *viññū puriso* would consider the holders of the wrong and right-views under such circumstances. The *viññū puriso* considers that, whether or not the words of the holder of the *natthika, akiriya* or *ahetu-diṭṭhi* are true, let us assume that there is no other world, no doing or causality: 'Still', he considers, 'this good person is here and now censured by the wise as an immoral person, one of wrong-view who holds the doctrine of nihilism, non-doing, non-causality'.[45] That person's view may be true or false but, the *viññū puriso* considers, the person does not benefit in this life from holding any of the three views. As for the holder of the right-view, even assuming that there is no other world, doing or causality, 'still this good person is here and now praised by the wise as a virtuous person, one with right-view, who holds the doctrine of affirmation, doing, or causality'.[46] The truth or falsity of the statements 'there is another world', 'there is doing' and 'there is causality' is bracketed out, so to speak, and the positive nature of the view proposed is considered a good enough reason to hold the view.

The *sutta* continues with the *viññū puriso*, having previously considered that there may be no other world, and showing that the holder of the wrong-views does not benefit in this life and the holder of the right-views does benefit in this life, suggesting that if the wrong-views are wrong, namely, they do not apply to the true state of things, and if the right-views are right, namely, they do apply to the true state of things, those who hold them will lose or win in two ways. The holder of the wrong-view, having been censured by the wise in this life and, through holding a wrong-view, will be reborn in an unhappy destination, even in hell. He loses in two ways. Whereas the holder of the right-view is praised in this life and, through holding a right-view, will be reborn in a happy destination, even in heaven (M I 404, 407, 410). The final consideration of the *viññū puriso* is the following:

> He (the holder of the wrong-view) has wrongly accepted and undertaken this incontrovertible teaching in such a way that it extends only to one side and excludes the wholesome alternative.[47]

On the other hand, the holder of right-view has correctly undertaken the incontrovertible teaching, in a way that extends to both sides and excludes the unwholesome alternative.[48]

In these passages from the *Apaṇṇaka-sutta* two themes are prominent. First, a view is classified as *micchā* if the course of action it produces is *akusala*. A view is classified as *sammā* if the course of action it produces is *kusala*. This theme is found in other parts of the canon. For example, a passage from the *Nettippakaraṇa* suggests that the role of *sammā-diṭṭhi* is to cultivate 'wholesome *dhammas*' (*kusala dhammā*). Thus, in a person of right-view, wrong-view is abolished and with it the many bad and unwholesome things that have wrong-view as condition, and the wholesome things with right-view as condition are produced, and kept in being.[49] The idea is that wholesome *dhammas* come into being and reach perfection through *sammā-diṭṭhi* sustaining and cultivating them. Second, *micchā* and *sammā-diṭṭhi* are important in affecting the future state of the holder of these views. These two themes are found in another context in which *micchā* and *sammā-diṭṭhi* appear.

The ten wholesome and unwholesome courses of action

In this book, although I am primarily concerned with Buddhist epistemology, I am explaining that epistemology in the following way: views are evaluated according to the action they engender. The point I wish to stress in the present discussion is that the Nikāyas are keen to emphasize the strong relationship between thought and action. The way we think affects our actions, and the way we act affects the way we think.

This is suggested by two groups of practices, the 'ten wholesome courses of action' (*dasa kusala-kammapathā*) and the 'ten unwholesome courses of action' (*dasa akusala-kammapathā*). These courses of action are often found under the three headings of body, speech and mind. In the *Cunda-sutta* (A V 263–8) at A V 268 'ten wholesome courses of action' are outlined: 'threefold cleansing by body' (*tividhaṃ kāyena soceyyaṃ*), the 'fourfold cleansing by speech' (*catubbidhaṃ vācāya soceyyaṃ*) and the 'threefold cleansing by mind' (*tividhaṃ manasā soceyyaṃ,* A V 266–8). They are given in distinction to 'ten unwholesome courses of action' (A V 266). These are the 'threefold defilement by body' (*tividhaṃ* [...] *kāyena asoceyyaṃ*), the 'fourfold defilement by speech' (*catubbidhaṃ vācāya asoceyyaṃ*) and the 'threefold defilement by mind' (*tividhaṃ manasā asoceyyaṃ,* A V 264–5).

In the ten wholesome courses of action, right-view is the last practice. Of course, in the eightfold path, right-view is the first practice. Is this an inconsistency? Or is this method deliberate, informing us of something specific about the nature of Buddhist thought? I think the latter. The main reason for this conclusion is clear from my previous discussion of the inseparability of thought and action. But there is more to this issue. This formulation suggests a movement from the gross to the subtle. The cleansing of actions of body and speech are relatively straightforward. The cleansing of thought and the mind involves the cleansing of far more subtle processes. To begin the process of calming the mind, actions of body and speech must first be calmed. The ten wholesome courses of action, culminating in right-view, are representative of this. More than this, I think that they are suggestive of the circularity of the Buddhist path. If we act in a certain way there will be an effect on the way we think. In fact, it will influence the way we see. It will influence our desires and motivations. In turn, if we think in a certain way, if our mind reacts calmly, there will be an effect on the way we act. As this process unfolds, there is a movement towards increasingly more subtle forms of thought and action. This process is also indicated by the 'step-by-step discourse' (*anupubbi-kathā*), which is also indicative of the arising of right-view. I will discuss this later in this chapter. For the moment, I wish to stress the relationship between certain actions and the arising of right-view, and, in turn, the influence of right-view on certain actions. It is a reciprocal process of action affecting thought, affecting action, affecting thought, to ever more subtle actions and states of mind. This is not a simple movement from ignorance to knowledge, but from attachment to non-attachment. If our actions of body, speech and mind are unwholesome, wrong-view arises (for example, that 'actions do not have consequences'), which in turn gives rise to other unwholesome courses of action, which gives rise to other wrong-views (for example, that 'there is a self'). If our actions of body, speech and mind are wholesome, this gives rise to right-view (for example, that 'actions have consequences'), which in turn gives rise to other wholesome courses of action, which give rise to other right-views (for example, 'all that is subject to arising is subject to cessation').

The dasa kusala-kammapathā

*Threefold cleansing by body (*tividhaṃ kāyena soceyyaṃ*)*

Here, someone, abandoning the killing of living beings, abstains from killing living beings; with rod and weapon laid aside, gentle and kindly, he abides compassionate to all living beings.[50]

Abandoning the taking of what is not given, he abstains from taking what is not given; he does not take by way of theft the wealth and property of others in village or forest.[51]

Abandoning misconduct in sensual pleasures, he abstains from misconduct in sensual pleasures; he does not have intercourse with women protected by mother, father, mother and father, brother, sister or relatives, who have a husband, who are protected by law, or who are garlanded in token of betrothal.[52]

*Fourfold cleansing by speech (*catubbidhaṃ vācāya soceyyaṃ*)*

Here someone, abandoning false speech, abstains from false speech; when summoned to a court, or to a meeting, or to his relatives' presence, or to his guild, or to the royal family's presence, and questioned as a witness thus: 'So, good man, tell what you know,' not knowing he says, 'I do not know,' or knowing he says, 'I know'; not seeing, he says, 'I do not see,' or seeing, he says, 'I see'; he does not in full awareness speak falsehood for his own ends, or for another's ends, or for the sake of some trifling gain.[53]

> **Abandoning malicious speech, he abstains from malicious speech;** he does not repeat elsewhere what he has heard here in order to divide [those people] from these, nor does he repeat to these people what he has heard elsewhere in order to divide [these people] from those; thus he is one who reunites those who are divided, a promoter of friendships, who enjoys concord, rejoices in concord, delights in concord, a speaker of words that promote concord.[54]
>
> **Abandoning harsh speech, he abstains from harsh speech;** he speaks such words as are gentle, pleasing to the ear, and loveable, as go to the heart, are courteous, desired by many, and agreeable to many.[55]
>
> **Abandoning gossip, he abstains from gossip;** he speaks at the right time, speaks what is fact, speaks what is beneficial, speaks on the *dhamma* and the discipline; at the right time he speaks such words as are worth recording, reasonable, moderate and advantageous.[56]
>
> *Threefold cleansing by mind (*tividhaṃ manasā soceyyaṃ*)*
>
> **Here someone is not covetous;** he does not covet the wealth and property of others thus: 'Oh may what belongs to another be mine!'[57]
>
> **His mind is without ill will and he has intentions free from hate** thus: 'May these beings be free from enmity, affliction and anxiety! May they live happily!'[58]
>
> **He has right-view, undistorted vision,** thus: 'There is what is given and what is offered and what is sacrificed; there is fruit and result of good and bad actions; there is this world and the other world; there is mother and father; there are beings who are reborn spontaneously; there are good and virtuous recluses and brahmins in the world who have themselves realised by direct knowledge and declare this world and the other world.'[59]

The opposite to these are the ten unwholesome courses of action (*dasa akusala-kammapathā*).[60] There are a large number of occurrences in the Nikāyas of the ten wholesome and ten unwholesome courses of action, and to cite them all would require considerable repetition. I have summarised them in Appendix 3. As I have said, I think that these courses of action are, in part, suggestive of a movement from the gross to the subtle. This is signified by a commentarial analysis of the ten, which analyses them (in this case, the wholesome courses of action) according to five categories. These categories are: 'mental state' (*dhamma*); 'category' (*koṭṭhāsa*); 'object' (*ārammaṇa*); 'feeling' (*vedanā*) and 'root' (*mūla*, Ps I 204). Under mental state, the ten are further analysed in the following way: the first seven of the *dasa kusala-kammapathā* are 'abstinences' (*virati*) and 'volitions' (*cetanā*), and the final three are volitions only. According to 'category' the first seven are 'courses of action' (*kamma-pathā*), the final three are both courses of action and 'roots' (*mūla*). Thus non-covetousness is the wholesome root of non-greed, non-ill will, of non-hate, and right-view is the wholesome root of non-delusion (*sammā-diṭṭhi amoho kusala-mūla*, Ps I 205). Analysed according to 'object', each of the ten courses of action is said to have either 'volitional formations' (*saṃkhārā*) or 'beings' (*sattā*) as object. In the case of right-view, it is said that it has 'volitional formations' as object, according to the states of the three planes (of existence).[61] As to 'feeling', all ten have either pleasant or neutral feelings. The analysis as to 'root' is done according to an Abhidhamma analysis. According to the commentary, right-view always has two roots, 'non-greed' (*alobha*) and 'non-hate' (*adosa*, Ps I 205), and wrong-view has 'greed' (*lobha*) and 'delusion' (*moha*) as roots (Ps I 203).[62] All this suggests that actions of body and speech belong to the same sphere of activity, while the actions of the mind are treated separately. This is a quite natural distinction. Perhaps slightly more interesting is the prominent role which is given to actions of the mind as roots and volitions of other actions. The fact that view has such an influence on action is perhaps the reason that it has such a forceful role in the process of rebirth, and it is this role that I would now like to consider.

Action and thought as the cause of good and bad rebirths

The commentarial term 'wrong-views with fixed consequences' (*niyatamicchā-diṭṭhi*)[63] implies that certain views produce a fixed destiny for the holder; in this case the term applies only to wrong-views. Certain passages in the Nikāyas also suggest that the type of view held strongly influences one's future state. The *dasa kusala-kammapathā* and the *dasa akusala-kammapathā* are often used to show how a person achieves a good or bad rebirth. A passage at A I 31 states that there is not one thing so likely to cause the 'arising of unwholesome states [...] as wrong-view',[64] or if arisen, they will increase due to *micchā-diṭṭhi*. The opposite is then stated for *sammā-diṭṭhi*: there is not one thing more likely to cause the 'arising of wholesome states [...] as right-view',[65] and if arisen they will increase due to *sammā-diṭṭhi* (A I 31). The text continues that there is not one thing so likely to cause an unhappy rebirth as wrong-view.[66] Through being 'possessed of wrong-view' (*micchā-diṭṭhiyā* [...] *samannāgatā*) one is reborn in hell. The text then gives the opposite for right-view. There is not one thing so likely to cause a rebirth in a happy destination as right-view.[67] Through being 'possessed of right-view' (*sammā-diṭṭhiyā* [...] *samannāgatā*) one is reborn in heaven. We may be slightly surprised that the text proposes such a powerful role for wrong and right-views. What are the reasons for the important role of one's view in shaping one's future state? This *sutta*, in its concluding remarks, suggests, by way of a simile, that wrong-view is 'a seed of destructive nature' (*bījaṃ* [...] *pāpakaṃ*, A I 32) that produces suffering. Whereas right-view is a 'seed of happy nature' (*bījaṃ* [...] *bhaddakaṃ*, A I 32) which produces happiness. Hence, in one of wrong-view, all 'actions of body' (*kāya-kamma*), 'actions of speech' (*vacī-kamma*), and all 'actions of mind' (*mano-kamma*), all 'intentions' (*cetanā*), 'aspirations' (*patthanā*), 'resolves' (*paṇidhi*), and all 'volitional formations' (*saṃkhārā*), performed according to that view (*yathā-diṭṭhi*), lead to what is 'unpleasant, distasteful, repulsive, unprofitable and to suffering'.[68] This is due to the 'destructive view' (*diṭṭhi* [...] *pāpikā*, A I 32). In one of right-view, all actions of body, speech and mind, all intentions, aspirations, resolves and all activities, performed according to that view, lead to what is 'pleasant, dear, delightful, profitable and to happiness'.[69] This is due to that 'happy (constructive) view' (*diṭṭhi* [...] *bhaddikā*, A I 32).[70] The text appears to be suggesting that if one has wrong-view then all actions done according to that view will be 'unwholesome' (*akusala*); if one has right-view then all actions done according to that view will be 'wholesome' (*kusala*). This is what is expressed in other *suttas* focusing upon the *dasa kusala-kammapathā* and the *dasa akusala-kammapathā*.

Chapter 21 of the *Aṅguttara-nikāya* is called 'The Body Born of Deeds' (*Karajakāya-vagga*, A V 283). The *Saṃsappaniya-pariyāya-sutta* (A V 288–91) of this *vagga* states a familiar Buddhist theme:

> Monks, beings are responsible for their actions, heirs to their actions, they have actions as their womb, actions as their kinsmen, actions as their refuge. Whatever action they do, be it lovely or ugly, of that thing they are the heirs.[71]

In order to illustrate unwholesome courses of action, the *sutta*, first, gives the *dasa akusala-kammapathā*, beginning with the taking of life (A V 289). There is a short passage after the first and last items adding that 'he is contorted in body, speech and mind'.[72] Further, his 'actions of body, speech and mind are distorted',[73] and his rebirth is also 'distorted'.[74] The view of nihilism (*natthika-diṭṭhi*) is given in full as an explanation of wrong-view.

Practising the *dasa kusala-kammapathā*, he is not contorted in body, speech and mind.[75] Further, his actions of body, speech and mind are straight,[76] and his rebirth is straight (*uju gati ujūpapatti*). This results in rebirth either in the 'blissful heavens' (*sukhā saggā,* A V 290), or with khattiyas or brahmins. The view of affirmation (*atthika-diṭṭhi*) is given in full as an explanation of right-view (A V 290).[77]

Carol Anderson has discussed some of these passages containing the *dasa akusala-kammapathā* and *dasa kusala-kammapathā*.[78] She gives the following summary of what she thinks these two groups tell us about the nature of *sammā-diṭṭhi*:

> These passages that define right-view in terms of conduct and behaviour reveal the efficacy of right-view [...] [T]his material indicates that views lead to actions that determine one's rebirth. At points, the canon seems to define the holding of any view as a type of behaviour or action in itself. Views are thus cast as central factors in the maintenance and destruction of one's continued existence in *saṃsāra* [...] The act of holding either right or wrong-views is a type of action that can release one from or further link one to the unending cycle of existence.[79]

Anderson argues that *sammā-diṭṭhi*, understood as liberating insight, 'is related to the broader conception of the efficacy of *any* view at all'.[80] View has to do with action. At certain stages of the path *sammā-diṭṭhi* shapes physical action and at other stages it is concerned with acts of cognition.

I have argued that certain right-views are primarily concerned with the notion that actions have consequences, that action and causality are important in the ethical sphere. What we do matters, and what we think matters. Three views express this idea: the view of affirmation (*atthika-diṭṭhi*), the view that there is doing (*kiriya-diṭṭhi*), and the view of causality (*hetu-diṭṭhi*). I have attempted to show that, in the *Apaṇṇaka-sutta*, right-view is not a form of belief requiring intellectual assent. In an understanding of that type (which is proposed by Jayatilleke), *sammā* is synonymous with 'true'. This conclusion is reached, possibly, by conflating the notions of right-view and doctrine. Right-view is not correct doctrine, it is correct knowledge of doctrine. The simile of the raft shows the correct attitude to have towards the teaching and, to a large extent, *sammā-diṭṭhi* does the same. It is right-view because it goes beyond doubt and confusion. It is, in a certain way, a confidence in the way one acts, both physically and mentally. Right-view is what comes first by initiating a course of wholesome action and being the product of a course of wholesome action. There is a dual role between the hindrances of craving and ignorance. A similar point has been made by Sue Hamilton:

> The reason ignorance is of primary concern is that it is the conditioning factor of all consequential actions. In particular, it is because of ignorance as to the nature of Reality that one persists in having desires and cravings, not realising that they are the fuel of continuity in the cycle of rebirth.[81]

How do the ten wholesome and unwholesome courses of action fit into my overall argument? Right-view should be understood as an 'is' and 'ought' statement. It is not only a statement of fact, nor is its value based upon its utility. As I have said, right-view sees things as they are and this is transformative. However, we cannot learn Buddhist doctrines and then assume that we have achieved right-view. In order to achieve right-view we must practise it. To merely hold to the proposition 'actions have consequences' is not to have achieved right-view. In relation to the ten wholesome courses of action, right-view *understands* that 'actions have consequences', and this knowledge transforms the conduct of the person who has achieved right-view. Indeed, in order to achieve this right-view, one's behaviour must be adapted in accordance with this insight, which the *dasa kusala-kammapathā* in turn embody and lead to.

The distinction between different levels of right-view

At this point I wish to comment upon an important distinction occasionally made in the Nikāyas between different levels of right-view. There are three occurrences of this distinction. The first is found in the *Mahācattārīsaka-sutta* (M III 71–8).

At M III 72 it is said that right-view is twofold (*sammā-diṭṭhi dvayaṃ*). First, there is the right-view affected by corruptions (*sammā-diṭṭhi sāsavā*),[82] partaking of merit (*puññabhāgiyā*), and ripening in attachment (*upadhivepakkā*). Second, there is the right-view which is noble (*sammā-diṭṭhi ariyā*), corruptionless (*anāsavā*), supramundane (*lokuttarā*), and a factor of the path (*maggaṅgā*). The former right-view is the view of affirmation (*atthika-diṭṭhi*). The latter view is described in terms of 'wisdom' (*paññā*), and this will be discussed below. The second occurrence of this distinction is found in the *Bhaddalī-sutta* (M I 437–47). At M I 446 it is said that, possessed of ten qualities, a *bhikkhu* is an 'unsurpassed field of merit for the world' (*anuttaraṃ puññakkhettaṃ lokassa*). The ten are the usual eightfold path plus right-knowledge and right-release. The first of these qualities is to possess 'the right-view of one beyond training' (*asekha sammā-diṭṭhi*). In a similar fashion the *Samaṇamaṇṭikā-sutta* (M II 22–9) at M II 29, has the same ten, beginning with the *asekha sammā-diṭṭhi*.

The *Papañcasūdanī*, commenting on the *Sammādiṭṭhi-sutta*, makes a similar distinction to that made in the *Mahācattārīsaka-sutta* between the different levels of right-view, though the commentary is more detailed. It first explains two characteristics of the right-view that it is about to consider: this right-view is both 'beautiful' (*sobhana*) and 'praiseworthy' (*passattha*). This beautiful and praiseworthy view, according to the text, can be either 'mundane' (*lokiya*) or 'supramundane' (*lokuttara*). Mundane right-view can mean either the 'knowledge that *kamma* is one's own' (*kammassakatā-ñāṇa*), this knowledge being in conformity with the (four) truths (*saccānulomika-ñāṇa*), or it is 'wisdom accompanied by the corruptions' (*sāsavā paññā*).[83] The term 'accompanied by corruptions' (*sāsavā*) I take to imply anything with the potential to become an attachment. All *kusala*, *akusala* and *avyākata dhammas* are *sāsavā* in the Abhidhamma. Something can be wholesome, a *kusala dhamma*, but still be an object of attachment. It is an important notion that I will consider in more detail in Chapter 5. The second type of right-view, that which is *lokuttara*, is explained as 'wisdom' (*paññā*), connected with the noble paths and their fruits (*ariya-magga-phala-sampayuttā*).[84] The commentary, immediately after its description of *lokiya* and *lokuttara sammā-diṭṭhi*, emphasises the point that different right-views are held by people at different stages of the path. Consequently, the *puthujjana* can be one within and outside the 'dispensation' (*sāsana*). One outside the dispensation holds to the 'view of self' (*attā-diṭṭhi*); thus, that person's view does not accord with the truths. However, if the person holds to the doctrine of *kamma* (*kamma-vāda*) because he holds the view that *kamma* is one's own (*kammassakatā-diṭṭhi*), then he is of right-view in this respect. The *puthujjana* within the dispensation holds views in accordance with both principles (he does not hold a view of self, and holds the view that *kamma* is one's own).[85] The *sekha*, the one in higher training, the person on one of the four paths, holds 'fixed right-view' (*niyatā sammā-diṭṭhi*); fixed because it leads to the goal of *nibbāna*. For the one beyond training (*asekha*), the text does not explain clearly what view has been achieved, simply stating that this person has *asekho asekhāya* 'the (view) beyond training' (all references to Ps I 196).[86]

After making these distinctions the commentary explains that the *Sammādiṭṭhi-sutta* is concerned with a 'supramundane wholesome right-view, which is fixed in destiny and emancipating'.[87] This is the view of one who has confidence in the 'ninefold supramundane *dhamma*'.[88] The view functions, with *nibbāna* as its object (*nirodhārammaṇa*, Ps I 197), by understanding, in the case of the first right-view in the *Sammādiṭṭhi-sutta*, i.e. the right-view that understands what is wholesome and unwholesome (see below), that the ten unwholesome courses of action (*dasa akusala-kammapathā*) are suffering, and that their roots (greed, hatred and delusion) are the cause of suffering (Ps I 197). In summary, right-view is a contemplation of suffering and its cessation. At the same time, if this does not amount to the same thing, it is a practice aimed at the cessation of the unwholesome and the cultivation of the wholesome.

One final discussion is found in the *Vibhaṅga* in which there is an explanation of knowledge that *kamma* is one's own (*kammassakatā-ñāṇa*). This is to know that there is what is given, what is offered and what is sacrificed, etc. through the right-view of affirmation, the knowledge that 'actions have consequences'. This is then described as wisdom, giving the standard Abhidhamma explanation of wisdom (abbreviated in the text as *paññā pajānanā–pe–amoho dhammavicayo sammā-diṭṭhi*). The text states that, except knowledge in conformity with the truths, all knowledge that is with the *āsavas*, all wisdom that is wholesome, is knowledge that action is one's own.[89] The text also explains 'knowledge in conformity with the truths' (*saccānulomika-ñāna*). This is the knowledge that each of the *khandhas* is impermanent (*rūpaṃ aniccanti vā vedanā–pe–saññā–pe–saṃkhārā –pe–viññāṇaṃ aniccanti vā*).[90] In the *Visuddhimagga*, *saccānulomika-ñāna* is the last of nine knowledges described in Chapter 21 (Vism XXI 128–33). It is the knowledge that precedes 'change of lineage knowledge' (which has *nibbāna* as its object, Vism XXII 1).

I would suggest that in these two types of knowledge, knowledge that action is one's own (*kammassakatā-ñāṇa*) and knowledge in conformity with the truths (*saccānulomika-ñānaṃ*), we have a type of transitional knowledge, from action to thought, from the gross to the subtle. Indeed, this is very much the transitional knowledge between earlier and later stages of the path. Previous to the path of stream-attainment, the Nikāyas have already made the distinction between action and states of mind which, although wholesome, still have a tendency to attachment. Even a wholesome right-view is involved in the accumulation of good states, with rebirth and merit. At a certain stage of the path the view that 'actions have consequences' gives way to the right-view of the path, which the Theravādins explain as a type of wisdom.

Right-view as *paññā*

The *Mahācattārīsaka-sutta*, after making the distinction between right-view with corruptions and right-view without corruptions, explains the latter right-view in terms of *paññā*. This right-view is the following:

> And what, *bhikkhus*, is right-view that is noble, corruptionless, supramundane, a factor of the path? The wisdom, the faculty of wisdom, the power of wisdom, the investigation of-states enlightenment factor, the path factor of right-view in one whose mind is noble, whose mind is corruptionless, who possesses the noble path and is developing the noble path: this is right-view which is noble, corruptionless, supramundane, a factor of the path.[91]

In the Abhidhamma, *sammā-diṭṭhi* is also explained as *paññā*:

> The wisdom which there is on that occasion is understanding, search, research, searching the truth, discernment, discrimination, differentiation, erudition, proficiency, subtlety, criticism, reflection, analysis, breadth, sagacity, leading, insight, intelligence, incitement; the faculty of wisdom, the power of wisdom, the sword of wisdom, the stronghold of wisdom, the light of wisdom, the splendour of wisdom, the torch of wisdom, the jewel of wisdom; the absence of delusion, searching the truth, right-view – this is right-view.[92]

The idea of 'purification of view' (*diṭṭhi-visuddhi*), a term which I will discuss in Chapter 4, is also explained in the same terms: 'The phrase "now purification of view" means that wisdom, understanding [...] right-view.'[93] Similarly, in the expression that the *dhamma* is 'well penetrated by view',[94] view is interpreted as being equivalent to wisdom.[95] The *Nettippakaraṇa* gives a number of terms which it holds to be synonyms (*vevacanaṃ*) of wisdom (*paññā*). This list of terms includes right-view.[96] A separate list for synonyms of *vijjā* again includes right-view.[97]

Two points should be made. First, the early tradition understood right-view to be a type of wisdom. It was understood to be a type of *paññā* that did not merely cease to be of use after the path of stream-attainment had been achieved. It appears that the Theravāda tradition certainly understood *sammā-diṭṭhi* as operating at advanced stages of the path.[98] Second, as I have argued, a course of action leads to the refinement of thought, which in turn affects action. The craving for pleasures of the senses has been calmed, but the craving for ideas has not. Right-view, having held that actions have consequences, now focuses on the attachments of the mind.

PART TWO: VIEWS OF NOT-SELF

In the second part of Chapter 1 I considered a group of views which were views of the self. These views denied the destructiveness of attachment. I would now like to consider views that are the opposite to these. As I suggested in the Introduction, I consider certain aspects of the notion of right-view problematic, because it is necessary to avoid any view that can be held with attachment. Both the views of *uccheda* and *sassata-diṭṭhi* preclude the possibility of there being the 'right-view of not-self'. However, there is right-view. In understanding what is classified as right-view, the dilemma I explained in the Introduction will be seen in a new way. This dilemma stated that there are two ways in which the notion of views can be understood, the opposition understanding and the no-views understanding. In the second half of this chapter I will state exactly what the content of the right-view that denies the self is. It should be made clear however that *any* view about the nature of the self, as either existing or not existing, is a wrong-view. Therefore, right-view is a view that transcends attachment and craving to the very idea of a self.

The *Sammādiṭṭhi-sutta*

Some have argued that early Buddhist thought posits two causes of *dukkha*, craving and ignorance, which need respectively the cultivation of calm and insight to be overcome.[99] The *Sammādiṭṭhi-sutta* suggests not so much that craving and ignorance are different hindrances, different corruptions on the Buddhist path requiring different methods (different paths) to overcome them, but that action and thought, craving and ignorance are inseparable aspects of *dukkha*. To overcome *dukkha*, calm and insight (action and thought) are needed, and the notion of right-view accomplishes this. To have knowledge of the four truths and dependent-origination produces a transformation of actions, just as the knowledge that 'actions have consequences' did: one's attitude to the world is no longer based on craving, but on the cessation of craving. Seeing the true nature of things has a transformative effect. Wrong-views are primarily based upon greed. Things are not seen as they are and this produces an unwholesome effect. On the other hand, right-view entails a knowledge of *dukkha* and its cessation and it is this that the *Sammādiṭṭhi-sutta* describes.

The *Sammādiṭṭhi-sutta* gives 16 right-views. All of them, except the first view on *kusala* and *akusala*, follow the same format. In fact, they could all be interpreted as following the first view, and this could be understood as a concise summary of Buddhism: what is unwholesome and what is its cause? What is wholesome and what is its cause? Right-view constitutes the answer to this question in the form of the four truths and dependent-origination.

The 16 right-views from the *Sammādiṭṭhi-sutta*

(1)When, friends, a noble disciple understands the unwholesome and the root of the unwholesome, the wholesome and the root of the wholesome, in that way he is one of right-view.[100]
When, friends, a noble disciple understands:
(2) nutriment, the origin of nutriment, the cessation of nutriment, and the way to the cessation of nutriment, in that way he is one of right-view,
(3) suffering, the origin of suffering, the cessation of suffering, and the way to the cessation of suffering, in that way he is one of right-view,

(4) ageing and death, the origin of ageing and death, the cessation of ageing and death, and the way to the cessation of ageing and death, in that way he is one of right-view,
(5) birth, the origin of birth, the cessation of birth, and the way to the cessation of birth, in that way he is one of right-view,
(6) being, the origin of being, the cessation of being, and the way to the cessation of being, in that way he is one of right-view,
(7) attachment, the origin of attachment, the cessation of attachment, and the way to the cessation of attachment, in that way he is one of right-view,
(8) craving, the origin of craving, the cessation of craving, and the way to the cessation of craving, in that way he is one of right-view,
(9) feeling, the origin of feeling, the cessation of feeling, and the way to the cessation of feeling, in that way he is one of right-view,
(10) contact, the origin of contact, the cessation of contact, and the way to the cessation of contact, in that way he is one of right-view,
(11) the sixfold base, the origin of the sixfold base, the cessation of the sixfold base, and the way to the cessation of the sixfold base, in that way he is one of right-view,
(12) name and form, the origin of name and form, the cessation of name and form, and the way to the cessation of name and form, in that way he is one of right-view,
(13) consciousness, the origin of consciousness, the cessation of consciousness, and the way to the cessation of consciousness, in that way he is one of right-view,
(14) volitional formations, the origin of volitional formations, the cessation of volitional formations, and the way to the cessation of volitional formations, in that way he is one of right-view,
(15) ignorance, the origin of ignorance, the cessation of ignorance, and the way to the cessation of ignorance, in that way he is one of right-view,
(16) the corruptions, the origin of the corruptions, the cessation of the corruptions, and the way to the cessation of the corruptions.

In that way he is one of right-view, whose view is straight, who has perfect confidence in the *dhamma* and who has arrived at this true *dhamma*.[101]

First, to have right-view, one understands the 'unwholesome' (*akusala*) and its 'root' (*mūla*), and the 'wholesome' (*kusala*) and its root. The first view entails understanding that the unwholesome is the ten unwholesome courses of action.[102] It entails understanding that the roots of these courses of action are greed, hatred and delusion.[103] Further, right-view entails an understanding of what is wholesome, which is the ten wholesome courses of action.[104] It entails understanding that the three roots of the wholesome are non-greed, non-hatred and non-delusion.[105] With an understanding of the unwholesome and its roots, and the wholesome and its roots, the *bhikkhu* is said to have abandoned three *anusayas,* those of 'lust', 'aversion' and the 'view and conceit "I am"'.[106] The destruction of the three *anusayas* is the outcome of the attainment of all the *sammā-diṭṭhi* in the *sutta.*

All the other views entail an understanding of things according to the four truths and dependent-origination. Each view understands the dependent nature of all things and the path to the eradication of *dukkha.* As may be expected, the understanding of *sammā-diṭṭhi* as the four truths is found elsewhere.[107] The four truths are being treated in the *Sammādiṭṭhi-sutta* together with the notion of dependent-origination in order to show how they are part of the process of cultivating what is wholesome. At an earlier stage of the path, what is wholesome is the view that 'actions have consequences' and this constitutes *sammā-diṭṭhi.* At a later stage of the path the focus is on the more subtle cravings and attachments of the mind, and the four truths, as *sammā-diṭṭhi,* are the wholesome outlook of the *bhikkhu.* The four truths appear to be part of a group of practices that aim for the purification of actions (*kamma*) of body, speech and mind. I have already considered the ten wholesome and unwholesome courses of action. I would like to consider a group of practices which appear to express a similar understanding of purifying body, speech and mind, but might perhaps aim at the eradication of more subtle hindrances.

The *Sāpūgiya-sutta* (A II 194–6) outlines 'four factors of exertion for utter purification'[108] which are said to lead to *nibbāna.* These are the 'factor for the purification of virtue',[109] the 'factor for the purification of mind',[110] the 'factor for the purification of view',[111] and the 'factor for the purification of release'.[112]

To achieve the purification of virtue the *bhikkhu* is virtuous (*sīlavā*) and practises the precepts (*pātimokkha-saṃvara-saṃvuto,* A II 195) and this is called 'purification of virtue' (*sīla-pārisuddhi*). The resolve and exertion to bring about this purification is called 'a factor of exertion for the utter purification of virtue'.[113] The 'purification of mind' (*citta-pārisuddhi*) is the practice of the four *jhānas.* The resolve and exertion to bring these about is called 'a factor of exertion for the utter purification of thought'.[114] The formula for the 'factor of exertion for the purification of views'[115] will be given in full:

> And what [...] is the factor of exertion for the utter purification of view? In this case [...] a *bhikkhu* comes to understand as it really is: 'This is suffering. This is the arising of suffering. This is the cessation of suffering. This is the way leading to the cessation of suffering.' This is called 'utter purification of view'.[116]

This is the first part of the formula showing the purification of views itself. The second half, which I have abbreviated for the first two items, is given in full now and is repeated for each of the four items, with the appropriate changing of terms. This shows the 'factor of exertion':

> (the resolve): I will bring to perfection such a purification of view [and of virtue, mind, release] if it be incomplete, and if complete I will

> supplement it here by wisdom. The desire to do, the effort, exertion, endeavour, persistence, mindfulness and attention applied thereto is called 'a factor of exertion for the utter purification of view [and of virtue, mind, release]'.[117]

The 'purification of release' (*vimutti-pārisuddhi*) is to be possessed by the very factor of exertion for the purification of virtue, mind and views.[118] The resolve and exertion to bring this about is 'a factor of exertion for the utter purification of release'.[119] It seems clear from the context of the 'purification of view' that the four truths, as *sammā-diṭṭhi*, are the cultivation of insight into the nature of things, combined with the purification of action. Such lists of items, be they the ten wholesome courses of action, or these factors of purification, suggest how right-view is realised and then functions with other factors of the path. The clearest understanding of this is found in the *Mahācattārīsaka-sutta* (M III 71–8), which I will discuss below. For the moment I wish to consider the way in which right-view is practised and, if understood as a proposition, should be understood as proposing a course of action.

I do not think that the four truths, as *sammā-diṭṭhi*, are intended to assert a proposition in purely cognitive terms. In an interesting discussion, Carol Anderson has considered a related issue. She states that, in studies of Buddhism, thought has been separated from action, and this has tended to distort our ideas of Buddhism. She argues that:

> The challenge [...] is to begin to put these categories of human experience back together; first, in order to highlight thinking and feeling with respect to the four noble truths, we should retain the categories of proposition and symbol in order to avoid conflating these two kinds of experience, and second, place both into a context of acting. This is [...] what the category of *sammādiṭṭhi* requires.[120]

Anderson claims that to understand the notion of *sammā-diṭṭhi*, the ideas of symbol and thought (in her terms, the evocative and the rational), must not be separated.[121] It is when the four noble truths are explained as *sammā-diṭṭhi* that, according to her, the Theravāda canon is suggesting this very specific aspect of the four truths. They are neither doctrinal proposition nor symbol but a transformative liberating insight.[122] In this understanding, the tendency to explain *sammā-diṭṭhi* as 'belief in' or 'holding to' a correct proposition is less pronounced. The tendency to explain *sammā-diṭṭhi* in such a way has led to some misunderstanding of what *sammā-diṭṭhi* is. A correct understanding of right-view is reflected by Buddhaghosa and his comments on how right-view functions:

> When a meditator is progressing towards the penetration of the four truths, his eye of understanding with *nibbāna* as its object eliminates the inherent

> tendency of *avijjā*, and that is *sammā-diṭṭhi*. It has right seeing as its characteristic. Its function is to reveal elements. It is manifested as the abolition of the darkness of *avijjā*.[123]

It is in this way that the right-views in the *Sammādiṭṭhi-sutta* are to be understood. They are neither correct views in opposition to other views, nor the eradication of all views, but a form of insight which transcends all views.

Dependent-origination and the *Sammādiṭṭhi-sutta*

This is the first part of the process described in the *sutta*: right-view is knowledge of the four truths. The second explanation of right-view is that it is knowledge of dependent-origination. Of the sixteen views, twelve right-views entail seeing each factor of dependent-origination: its rise and fall. Other occurrences of this are found in the Nikāyas. We have already met a *micchā-diṭṭhi* from the *Mahātaṇhāsaṅkhaya-sutta* (M I 256–71), attributed to Sāti, which stated that: 'As I understand the *dhamma* taught by the Blessed One, it is this same consciousness that runs and wanders through the round of rebirths, not another'.[124] The *sutta*, as we might expect, shows the Buddha arguing that consciousness is dependently-arisen: without a condition there is no origination of consciousness.[125] The right-view that expresses this is the following:

> *Bhikkhus*, has it been well seen by you as it actually is with proper wisdom thus: 'This has come to be?' [...] *Bhikkhus*, has it been well seen by you as it actually is with proper wisdom thus: 'Its origination occurs with this as nutriment?' [...] *Bhikkhus*, has it been well seen by you as it actually is with proper wisdom thus: 'With the cessation of that nutriment, what has come to be is subject to cessation?'[126]

The *sutta* then describes this *diṭṭhi* as 'purified and bright'.[127] It is advised that this view should not be cherished or treated as a possession for, the text explains, the *dhamma* is similar to a raft, for the purpose of crossing over, it is not for the purpose of grasping.[128] In a similar way, in the *Aggivacchagotta-sutta* (M I 483–90), Vacchagotta asks the Buddha if he holds any 'speculative view'.[129] The Buddha replies that he has put away that type of view.[130] He, the Tathāgata, has seen (*diṭṭha*) each of the *khandhas*, their origin and their cessation.[131] The correct way of seeing, *sammā-diṭṭhi*, is to see the conditioned nature of phenomena. That the Buddha is said to have seen (*diṭṭha*) is a play on words, implying that *sammā-diṭṭhi* is not a *diṭṭhi*, but a way of seeing.

In the *Kiṃdiṭṭhika-sutta* (A V 185–90) is found a right-view expressed by Anāthapiṇḍika in opposition to the ten *avyākata* (A V 186). Each of the *avyākata* are given individually as views held by a group of *paribbājakas*. The *sammā-diṭṭhi* given in opposition to them is the following:

> Whatever has become, is put together, is thought out, is dependent on something else, that is impermanent. What is impermanent, that is *dukkha*, what is *dukkha*: 'This is not mine, this I am not, this is not my self'.[132]

In the *sutta*, the view is given in the same fashion as the evaluation of each of the *avyākata* (A V 187). Just as each of those views 'has become, is put together [...] is *dukkha*', right-view is the knowledge that 'whatever has become, is put together [...] is *dukkha*' and that is not-self. This insight is right-view.[133] Right-view entails seeing the unwholesome process and, in so doing, stopping that process. It entails seeing dependent-origination and realising that attachment to what is conditioned leads to *dukkha*. By achieving right-view the process is broken for one is no longer attached to what is conditioned. Right-view has the opposite effect to wrong-view, it leads to the cessation of *dukkha*. Since dependent-origination has been seen, as it really is, with insight, i.e. right-view, one's actions are no longer founded on not seeing. Actions no longer lead to *dukkha* but to the cessation of *dukkha*.

I would now like to look at an important explanation of right-view as dependent-origination, keeping in mind the underlying focus which the *Sammādiṭṭhi-sutta* has suggested: right-view is expressive of action leading to the cessation of *dukkha*. The *Kaccāyanagotta-sutta* (S II 16–17), in the *Saṃyutta-nikāya*, has received much attention from scholars. This is due, in no small part, for having been, arguably, one of the Nikāya *suttas* cited by Nāgārjuna.[134] The *sutta* begins with Kaccāyana asking the Buddha, 'Venerable, we hear the phrase "right-view, right-view". Now how far is there right-view?'.[135] The Buddha replies by describing what *sammā-diṭṭhi* is not. It is not a view 'based on' (*nissita*) 'existence' or 'non-existence' (*atthita* or *natthita*). These two terms, which the commentary glosses as *sassata* and *uccheda* (Spk II 32), signify that right-view avoids these two extremes.[136] The phrase was noted above from the *Papañcasūdanī* that the straight view does not deviate to either extreme. In this *sutta* it is explained that it is by 'seeing' (*passati*) with 'right wisdom' (*sammapaññāya*) the uprising and passing away of the world 'as it really is' (*yathābhūta*) that the question of existence or non-existence is dispelled. Then there is a description of the way in which views are usually formed and an explanation of right-view:

> This world, Kaccāyana, is for the most part shackled by engagement, attachment and adherence (*upāyupādānābhinivesavinibandho*). But this one [with right-view] does not become engaged and attached through that engagement and attachment, mental basis, adherence, underlying tendency; he does not take his stand about 'my self'. He has no perplexity or doubt that what arises is only suffering arising, that what ceases is only suffering ceasing. His knowledge about this is independent of others. It is in this way, Kaccāyana, that there is right-view.[137]

There is a personal knowledge of suffering and its cessation, of the arising and cessation of *dhammas*. The holder of this view is said to be without 'perplexity' (*vicikicchati*) or 'doubt' (*kankhati*). The view itself is free from the 'extremes' (*anto*), of holding that 'everything exists' (*sabbam atthī ti*) or 'nothing exists' (*sabbaṃ n' atthī ti*). The Tathāgata approaches neither, and teaches the doctrine by the middle, or in the middle.[138] The Buddha's middle-way, the *dhamma*, or right-view, is to understand *paṭicca-samuppāda* in its *anuloma* and *paṭiloma* cycles, in forward and reverse. The former is *akusala*, the latter *kusala*. The significance of the *akusala* and *kusala* cycles of *paṭicca-samuppāda* and the role of *sammā-diṭṭhi* in the practice of the Buddhist path has been noted by Gethin,[139] who suggests that *paṭicca-samuppāda* appears to have been the understanding of the middle-way by the Buddhist tradition, and this includes Nāgārjuna who, as I suggested above, is likely to have been familiar with the *nidāna-saṃyutta*.[140] The middle-way, understood as knowledge of dependent-origination, describes the development of the Buddhist path. In its negative cycle *paṭicca-samuppāda* is understood as beginning with *avijjā* – 'dependent upon ignorance arise volitional formations', etc. This is the *anuloma* sequence. The positive cycle begins with the cessation of *avijjā* – 'from the utter fading away of ignorance, there is the ceasing of volitional formations' etc., 'with the ceasing of birth there is the ceasing of old age and grief, lamentation, suffering and despair'. This is the *paṭiloma* sequence. According to Gethin, there is a resemblance between the *anuloma* sequence of *paṭicca-samuppāda* and the path beginning with *micchā-diṭṭhi*, and the *paṭiloma* sequence of *paṭicca-samuppāda* and the path beginning with *sammā-diṭṭhi*.[141] The point is that apprehending this process leads to wholesome action. The significance of right-view is that it sees things without craving and attachment. This in itself is transformative.

Jayatilleke, in commenting upon the nature of the middle-way, cites a passage found at M I 15. According to this passage, the middle-way (*majjhimā paṭipadā*) is 'true' in the sense that it makes for knowledge (*ñāṇa-karaṇī*).[142] There appears to be something about seeing reality which is soteriological in nature. In the *Sammādiṭṭhi-sutta* each factor of *paṭicca-samuppāda* is seen, its nature known, its cessation understood, and the way to its cessation, the noble eightfold path, beginning with right-view itself, realised. This, to a large extent, is how the Nikāyas describe the notion of *sammā-diṭṭhi*.

The right-view of stream-attainment

I would now like to consider a concise explanation of right-view which reflects, I think, the same method as the *Sammādiṭṭhi-sutta*. If we read the texts that contain the stories of the Buddha's awakening, we find that, during the three watches of the night he perceived *paṭicca-samuppāda* in forward and reverse order.[143] It is the realisation of this same process which establishes one as a 'stream-attainer' (*sotāpanna*). The stream-attainer is the first of four 'noble-persons' (*ariya-puggala*) of the Pāli canon, along with the once-returners, never-returners and Arahants. The stream-attainer is one who is assured of awakening within a maximum of seven rebirths.[144] The texts give the following realisation as the *sammā-diṭṭhi* that establishes one on the path of stream-attainment:

> All that is subject to arising is subject to cessation.[145]

This realisation, in this case that of Upāli, is said by the text to be the arising of the 'vision of the *dhamma*' (*dhamma-cakkhu*), which may be understood as the achievement of the path of stream-attainment. This *sammā-diṭṭhi* appears as part of a standard formula and is found a number of times in the Nikāyas. This is the formulation of the 'step-by-step discourse' (*anupubbi-kathā*). I will give the passage in full, as it gives some context to what actually occurs when one attains *sammā-diṭṭhi*:

> Then the Blessed One gave the householder Upāli instruction step-by-step, that is, talk on giving, talk on virtue, talk on the heavens; he explained the danger, degradation, and defilement in sensual pleasures and the blessing of renunciation. When he knew that the householder Upāli's mind was ready, receptive, free from hindrances, elated, and confident, he expounded to him the teaching special to the Buddhas: suffering, its arising, its cessation, and the path. Just as a clean cloth with all marks removed would take dye evenly, so too, while the householder Upāli sat there, the spotless immaculate vision of the *dhamma* arose in him: 'All that is subject to arising is subject to cessation.' Then the householder Upāli saw the *dhamma*, attained the *dhamma*, understood the *dhamma*, fathomed the *dhamma*; he crossed beyond doubt, did away with perplexity, gained intrepidity, and became independent in the teacher's dispensation.[146]

I have already suggested that the Buddhist path develops from the cultivation of actions of body, speech and mind. This was reflected in the ten wholesome courses of action. In these actions there was a cultivation of physical and mental acts, culminating in the realisation of *sammā-diṭṭhi*. In a similar way, the step-by-step discourse progresses from instruction on giving and virtue to its culmination in the realisation of dependent-origination. In this instruction there is a very strong resemblance to the different types of right-view which, I am suggesting, are part of the Buddhist path. Right-view is at first the view that 'actions have consequences'. This affects the actions of the person who holds the view, and the actions in turn affect the mind of the person performing these actions. This, in turn, leads to the realisation of dependent-origination. With the achievement of this view, one no longer grasps or craves any view whatsoever. This is the right-view of the path which goes beyond attachment. It is the view which transcends all views.

The achievement of right-view

I would like to consider some related issues concerning the arising of right-view. How does one achieve or come to hold right-view? I have already partly answered this question in my discussion of the ten wholesome courses of action. The right-view that 'actions have consequences' occurs after a course of action and this is related to another understanding of the arising of right-view. As was the case with the ten wholesome courses of action, right-view occurs at a particular moment and after a specified practice: the Buddha gives a step-by-step discourse to a certain individual, then, knowing that the mind of his listener is receptive, he gives the teaching special to the Buddha: suffering, its arising, its cessation and the path. One may note two things from this. First, the mind of the listener is receptive. In a way, the Buddha's initial instruction eases the listener's mind and makes it calm. One is reminded of the state that is achieved in the fourth *jhāna*, a state described as having neither pain-nor-pleasure but 'purity of mindfulness due to equanimity' (*upekkhā-sati-pārisuddhi*, M I 347, *passim*).[147] It is from this state, of course, that the Buddha is said to have achieved *nirvāṇa*.[148] It may be worth considering, then, that the attainment of right-view is also achieved in a state of calm and mindful investigation, as suggested by the passages cited above. Jayatilleke has explained that the gaining of knowledge in early Buddhism is realised in states of mind characteristic of the fourth *jhāna*. He states that since the mind is 'clear and cleansed' (*parisuddhe pariyodāte*, D I 76) in these states 'it was possible to have a clearer insight into the nature of things by means of this knowledge than by normal perception'.[149] He has also suggested that one of the basic features of the treatment of knowledge found in the Nikāyas is that knowledge is not a static proposition but must be experienced. He suggests that something like a proposition can only be accepted as true when there is 'personal knowledge' of it (*attanā va jāneyyātha*, A II 191).[150] This knowledge is based upon a direct vision or 'seeing'.[151] Knowledge, he argues, can be equated with an informative kind of knowledge, valued in the middle to late Upaniṣads.[152] This experiential conception of knowledge points to 'knowing and seeing' (*jānāti passati*), being valued together in the Nikāyas. The Buddha is one who knows and sees (*tam ahaṃ jānāmi passāmī ti*, M I 329).[153] This leads Jayatilleke to conclude that, for the early Buddhist tradition, it was important that its doctrines be 'seen'.[154] This seeing, he argues, implies not only the cultivation of knowledge, but its cultivation in tandem with 'mental cultivation' (*bhāvanā*).[155] For Jayatilleke, there is an emphasis upon the experiential setting of knowledge, primarily the experiencing of the *jhānas*, in order to cultivate knowledge and vision. Knowledge is the product of 'right mental concentration' (*sammā-samādhi*).[156] This is the context of the gaining of *sammā-diṭṭhi*. It does much to dispel the idea that the achievement of right-view is the adoption of a correct doctrine in opposition to an incorrect doctrine. To achieve right-view one must behave in a way that reflects the truth of suffering and its cessation.

In the Nikāyas we find a short statement which suggests that right-view is gained in two ways. This first passage is from the *Mahāvedalla-sutta* (M I 292–8):

> Friend, how many conditions are there for the arising of right-view? Friend, there are two conditions for the arising of right-view: the voice of another and appropriate bringing to mind.[157]

If we examine the passage stating how right-view is achieved in the listeners' receptive minds mentioned above, we could conclude that a person needs another's help, and to be in an attentive frame of mind. This is similar to this formula, which has caused some debate in recent years (to which I shall return in a moment). The other occurrence of this passage is at A I 87, the only difference being that the same two conditions are said to also cause wrong-view.[158] In the *Paṭisambhidāmagga* 'inappropriate bringing to mind' and 'the voice of another' are explained as two of eight 'bases for view' (*diṭṭhiṭṭhānaṃ*).[159]

The only other information in the Nikāyas as to the meaning of these statements is appended to the statement in the *Mahāvedalla-sutta*. Immediately following the statement about how many conditions there are for the arising of right-view it is said that right-view is assisted by five factors when right-view has deliverance of mind for its fruit and benefit, and deliverance by wisdom for its fruit and benefit.[160] These five are the assistance of virtue (*sīlānuggahītā*), learning (*sutānuggahītā*), discussion (*sākacchānuggahītā*), serenity (*samathānuggahītā*), and insight (*vipassanānuggahītā*, M I 294). The relevance of these factors in the achievement of the right-view of the path is uncertain. I say this partly because of the commentarial explanation of the *Mahāvedalla* passage. In this commentary we find the following descriptions of right-view. In the case of the statement that there are two causes for the arising of right-view, it states that this is 'the right-view of insight' (*vipassanā-sammā-diṭṭhi*) and the 'right-view of the path' (*magga-sammā-diṭṭhi*) and for the right-view assisted by five factors states that this is the 'right-view of the path of Arahantship' (*arahatta-magga-sammā-diṭṭhi*, Ps II 346). This suggests that, according to the tradition, the passage is referring to different levels of right-view. What seems clear, however, is that as aspects of the path, the five factors (especially learning, discussion and serenity), would appear to support the former statement that right-view is gained by the voice of another and appropriate bringing to mind (*parato ghosa* and *yoniso manasikāra*). All these passages suggest that right-view is achieved in a specific state of mind: one assisted by virtue, calm and serenity.

There is also some analysis as to what is implied by *parato ghosa* and *yoniso manasikāra* in the *Peṭakopadesa* and *Nettippakaraṇa*. The *Peṭakopadesa*, in fact, begins with a discussion of this issue.[161] It explains *parato ghosa* as any teaching, advice, instruction or talk about or in conformity with the four truths.[162] For *yoniso manasikāra*[163] the *Peṭakopadesa* states that it is any 'reflection', or 'appropriate bringing to mind' of the *dhamma*, which of course can be the four truths, or presumably any one of the right-views.[164] It is clear that *parato ghosa* and *yoniso manasikāra* interact to bring about right-view.[165] This seems rather what we would expect since one would reflect on what has been taught.

The debate about these two factors that cause the arising of *sammā-diṭṭhi* has focused upon the term *parato ghosa*. In Woodward's translation of the *Aṅguttara-nikāya*,[166] at A I 87, *parato ghosa* is given as 'a voice from another (world)'. Woodward states that he takes it as meaning 'clairaudience from another (world)'. The reasons he gives are that if ordinary speech were meant, the phrase *vācā* or *vacī* would have been used, instead of the unusual form *ghosa*. In a similar way, if another person were implied, why is the term *parato* used, when in the context of a person it would be more normal to use a term such as *aññassa* or *aññatarassa*?[167] These are unusual forms, but it is an unusual formula. More recently, Peter Masefield has considered this issue. In a discussion of these passages, he has focused upon *parato ghosa* arguing that the texts maintain that the gaining of 'noble right-view' is through the mediation of the Buddha and his immediate disciples, the suggestion being that right-view is religious truth which is 'revealed' in sound.[168] The 'voice of another' (*parato ghosa*), according to Masefield, is a 'sound from the Beyond'.[169] The tradition itself does not appear to understand *parato ghosa* in this way. Indeed, as Rupert Gethin has pointed out, Masefield's conclusions are based on one commentarial passage which he translates wrongly.[170] The commentaries explain *parato ghosa* as *sappāyadhammasavana* 'hearing of beneficial *dhamma*', which does not preclude that it is, in a sense, 'from another world', but one would imagine that the commentary would state this if it understood the expression in such a way. Gethin suggests that the sound of the *dhamma* is, in a sense, 'the sound from beyond'[171] because the *dhamma* is wholly other; its sound, to borrow a familiar Buddhist phrase, is in the world but not of the world, in many respects, the voice of the other.

A consideration of this issue supports my main point, that right-view is realised after a long course of action and the cultivation of the mind. One of the conditions for the arising of right-view is 'appropriate bringing to mind'. The arising of right-view may not only require hearing 'the voice of another' but considering it appropriately after a period of contemplation. This discussion has highlighted that the early tradition held that the arising of insight into the conditioned nature of *dhammas* (the achievement of right-view) is an occurrence of profound importance which happens after the transformation of action. The nature of this insight will be considered in more detail in Chapter 4. At this point I wish to stress two things. First, that the cultivation of right-view begins with the purification of body, speech and mind and leads to the realisation of insight, an insight that cannot be separated from the transformation of action. Second, right-view is realised in a state of calm and contemplation. Whether we are considering the realisation of the view that 'actions have consequences', or the view that 'all that is subject to arising is subject to cessation', these views are based upon a specific course of action and are the product of a particular state of mind.

The *Mahācattārīsaka-sutta*: right-view comes first

We know from the eightfold path that right-view comes first (*sammā-diṭṭhi pubbaṅgamā*) and I would now like to consider the unfolding of the Buddhist path beginning with right-view. In the *Mahācattārīsaka-sutta* (M III 71–8), we find an exposition of noble right-concentration (*ariya sammā-samādhi*), together with its supports and equipment (*sa-upanisa sa parikkhāra*). The text explains that by 'supports and equipment' it means the seven path factors of right-view, intention, speech, action, livelihood, effort and mindfulness. The 'unification of mind' (*cittassa ekaggatā*) equipped with these seven factors 'is called noble right-concentration with its supports and equipment' (*ariyo sammā-samādhi sa-upaniso iti pi, sa-parikkhāro iti pi*, M III 71). The *sutta* contains a description of right-view which is of a different nature from those that have been discussed so far, for, to a greater or lesser extent, those views have been concerned with some aspect of Buddhist doctrine. However, what we find in the *Mahācattārīsaka-sutta* is right-view functioning as a precursor and evaluator of the other path factors. Right-view understands five factors of the path in the following way:

> Therein, right-view comes first. And how does right-view come first?
> – One understands wrong-view as wrong-view and right-view as right-view: this is one's right-view
> – One understands wrong-intention as wrong-intention and one understands right-intention as right-intention (M III 72)
> – One understands wrong-speech as wrong-speech and one understands right-speech as right-speech (M III 73)
> – One understands wrong-action as wrong-action and one understands right-action as right-action (M III 74)
> – One understands wrong-livelihood as wrong-livelihood and one understands right-livelihood as right-livelihood : this is one's right-view (M III 75).[172]

Following the sections detailing the various types of views, intentions, speech, action and livelihood[173] the *sutta* gives an analysis of how two other factors, right-effort and right-mindfulness, work together with right-view. With right-view having understood each factor as wrong or right, there is then an effort to abandon wrong-view (M III 72), wrong-intention (M III 73), wrong-speech (M III 74), wrong-action (M III 75) and wrong-livelihood (M III 75), and to enter upon right-view, right-intention, right-speech, right-action and right-livelihood; this is right-effort. Mindfully, wrong-view, intention, speech, action and livelihood are abandoned and right-view, intention, speech, action and livelihood are entered upon and abided in; this is right-mindfulness. 'Thus these three states run and circle around right-view [intention, speech, action and livelihood] that is right-view, right-effort and right-mindfulness.'[174]

Right-view is clearly important in these passages. There is the statement that right-view comes first. According to the *Papañcasūdanī*, the right-view that comes first is of two kinds. There is the right-view of insight (*vipassanā-sammā-diṭṭhi*) and the right-view of the path (*magga-sammā-diṭṭhi*, Ps III 131).[175] The commentary explains the function of these right-views: *vipassanā-sammā-diṭṭhi* investigates the volitional formations as impermanent, unsatisfactory, and not-self,[176] whereas *magga-sammā-diṭṭhi* effects or completes the examination of the volitional formations and uproots the defilements.[177] The commentary gives further information on these views. The right-view that comes first, as the *sutta* stated, understands wrong-view as wrong-view. By this the commentary holds that right-view, presumably *vipassanā-sammā-diṭṭhi,* understands the three characteristics of wrong-view, that it is impermanent, unsatisfactory and not-self.[178] Right-view 'clears away confusion' (*asammoha*).[179] It comes first and discriminates between what is and is not the path. The commentary suggests that *vipassanā-sammā-diṭṭhi* is the precursor of the *lokuttara-sammā-diṭṭhi*, which, together with right-effort and right-mindfulness 'run and circle around right-view' (Ps III 132), the latter right-view being the right-view without *āsavas*, namely wisdom.[180] Similar ideas are found elsewhere. For example, the phrase 'the right-view running out in front' (*sammā-diṭṭhi-purejavaṃ* S I 33), which is interpreted as the right-view of insight contemplating the volitional formations. [181]

Rupert Gethin has noted that the *Mahācattārīsaka-sutta* falls into three sections, each opening by saying that right-view comes first, then explaining how this is the case.[182] I have already considered the first case. Right-view comes first by understanding wrong-view, intention, speech, action and livelihood as wrong, and their opposites as right. The second explanation of how right-view comes first is that in one of right-view, right-intention, right-speech, right-action, right-livelihood, right-effort, right-mindfulness, right-concentration, right-knowledge and right-release come into being (M III 75–6). The *sutta* is referring to a right-view that is not merely *lokiya* but the *lokuttara-sammā-diṭṭhi*. The holder or practitioner of right-view is the one in 'higher training' (*sekho*, M III 77), who, to follow Gethin's reading, begins to bring about all ten factors of the path.[183] The final reason that right-view comes first is that, in one of right-view, wrong-view is abandoned and along with wrong-view are also abandoned the *akusala dhammas* that have wrong-view as their condition. Also, the *kusala dhammas* that have right-view as their condition are developed.[184] The rest of the path unfolds and is cultivated in a similar fashion. Hence, the ten negative factors are abandoned and along with them the unwholesome *dhammas* that they caused, while the ten positive factors beginning with right-view are adopted and the wholesome *dhammas* are cultivated.

In these three explanations of the ways in which right-view comes first it is clear that right-view has a major influence on the other factors of the path. This further supports the emphasis which the Nikāyas give to the influence of thought on action and of action on thought. The achievement of right-view is not to be realised by adopting a particular view or opinion, but by acting in a certain way. It is the behaviour of a person that demonstrates the achievement of right-view. It is for this reason that right-view comes first.

One further distinction I would like to add to this discussion is the understanding of right-view as an 'equipment' (*parikkhāra*), in the sense of the instrument for the arising of the other factors of the path. As I understand the passage from the *Peṭakopadesa* which considers right-view in this way, *sammā-diṭṭhi* is the instrument for the arising of any wisdom, with right-view as the cause of right-intention.[185] This right-view, as an equipment on the path, understands conditionality.[186]

I can now begin to make some suggestions about certain aspects of the nature of right-view. To begin with, in his discussion of the *Mahācattārīsaka-sutta*, Rupert Gethin has made the following comments:

> The *Mahācattārīsaka-sutta* is an exposition of the processes involved in the passing from wrong-view, etc. to right-view, etc. that is ordinary and skilful, and from here to right-view, etc. that is *ariya* and without *āsavas*; and from here to the full development of right-view, etc. Throughout it is emphasised that right-view leads the way. Thus right-view comes first not just as the preliminary stage in spiritual practice, not just as the preparation or basis for higher stages, rather it comes first at all stages of spiritual practice. The treatment of the factors as consecutive steps takes on the character not so much of a map showing the stages of spiritual practice, as of a working model illustrating the operation of spiritual practice at whatever stage.[187]

These comments suggest that the conception of the path as given in the *Mahācattārīsaka-sutta* has important implications for our understanding of the notion of *sammā* and *micchā-diṭṭhi* at other stages of the path, not just for the *sekho, asekho* and Arahant. Steven Collins has observed that a type of view (or wisdom) that admits of 'differences of degree' cannot be a simple knowledge that something is a certain way.[188] This is clearly true when *sammā-diṭṭhi* refers to a type of *paññā* at later stages of the path, but could also be true of *sammā-diṭṭhi* at earlier stages of the path. If the aim of right-view is to cultivate what is *kusala*, then this is the aim of right-view, whether at the beginning of the path or in its more advanced stages. As Gethin suggests, the factors of the path are 'working models' that interact at all stages of the path. As mentioned earlier, the negative sequence beginning with wrong-view, and the positive sequence beginning with right-view, resemble the negative and positive cycles of *paṭicca-samuppāda*, the *anuloma* and *paṭiloma* cycles. Gethin also cites the first *sutta* of the *magga-saṃyutta*, the *Avijjā-sutta* (S V 1–2),[189] which stresses a similar cycle to both *paṭicca-samuppāda* and to the sequence found in the *Mahācattārīsaka-sutta* where ten negative factors of the path give rise to ten *akusala dhammas* and ten positive factors of the path give rise to ten *kusala dhammas*. As the *sutta* explains, ignorance comes first and causes the acquisition of unskilful *dhammas*. Shamefulness (*ahirika*) and fearlessness of wrongdoing (*anottappa*) follow from this. From ignorance, wrong-view and the other seven wrong factors are cultivated. In the wholesome cycle the text explains that knowledge comes first (*vijjā* [...] *pubbaṅgamā*), and it is knowledge that causes the acquisition of skilful *dhammas*.

A sense of shame (*hiri*) and fear of wrongdoing (*ottappa*) follow from this. From knowledge, right-view and the other seven factors are cultivated. This is the wholesome course of action that we have met so often in this study. One further example of the unfolding of the path in this way is found in the *Dasuttara-sutta* (D III 272–92) at D III 291, where it is stated that ten things should be thoroughly learnt. These ten are the 'ten causes of wearing away' (*dasa nijjara-vatthūni*). It is stated simply that by right-view, wrong-view is worn away. This causes the many bad and unwholesome states that have wrong-view as their condition to be worn away, and the many good and wholesome states that have right-view as condition to be developed.[190] This passage, in my understanding, is suggesting that the one who has achieved right-view practises what is wholesome, and abandons what is unwholesome. Right-view is not a matter of belief or adherence to a set of doctrines. It is not something that can be learned, but must be experienced. We do not acquire right-view, but achieve it through our actions.

In a study of the notion of *avidyā*, B.K. Matilal has suggested that wrong-views give rise to wrong ways of acting, and right-views to right ways of acting. There is, Matilal notes, a connection between *avidyā* and 'volitional formations' (*saṃkhāra,* Skt. *saṃskāra*). Hence, *avidyā* is a motivating force in affecting actions and this is of primary importance in making a view wrong. Matilal, in considering the *Avijjā-sutta* (S V 1–2, the same *sutta* considered by Gethin), notes that wrong-view leads to the unwholesome unfolding of the path, in terms of wrong-actions, and right-view leads to the wholesome unfolding of the path, in terms of right-actions:

> For false beliefs and wrong convictions give rise to the propensities or forces to act wrongly, and to act under misconception is to get involved in the cycle of rebirth, into the chain of conditions, into *duḥkha* and bondage. In this context, *avidyā* can hardly mean mere lack of knowledge, ignorance. For, wrong-actions, to be sure, proceed from wrong beliefs, wrong convictions, wrong understanding of the nature of reality, not from simple lack of knowledge.[191]

Although displaying the same tendency as Jayatilleke to understand *micchā-diṭṭhi* as 'wrong beliefs', Matilal's suggestion that *avidyā* is not a simple lack of knowledge suggests that wisdom is not a simple gaining of knowledge. If *avidyā* is not propositional, then neither is *paññā*. Matilal suggests that in the Indian context *avidyā* is something which binds us to *duḥkha*.[192] By definition *paññā* is not simply knowledge, but a way of apprehending things that has soteriological significance. His point is that *avidyā* is not a negation of *vidyā*, but a type of defilement which affects actions.[193] The difference between ignorance and knowledge is not one of false and correct cognition.[194] The knowledge that rids the mind of *avidyā*, argues Matilal, is one that gives us freedom to act in a soteriologically wholesome way.[195] Donald K. Swearer has called this type of knowledge immediate or non-propositional.[196]

Seeing phenomena as impermanent

Another explanation of right-view describes it as a view which agrees with certain central tenets of Buddhist doctrine and explains this insight in a specific way. These right-views express the ideas of impermanence, suffering and not-self. The first example is taken from the *Khandavagga* of the *Saṃyutta-nikāya*. The *Paṭhamanandikkhaya-sutta* (S III 51) subjects each of the five *khandhas* to right-view:

> *Bhikkhus*, a *bhikkhu* sees form as impermanent, which is actually impermanent: that is his right-view. Seeing rightly, he experiences indifference.[197] With the destruction of delight comes the destruction of lust; with the destruction of lust comes the destruction of delight. With the destruction of delight and lust the mind is liberated and is said to be well-liberated.[198]

The other four *khandhas* are treated in the same way. Seeing any of the five as impermanent is right-view. It should be noted that seeing in a certain way, apprehending the *khandhas* as impermanent, causes a specific form of behaviour: the experience of indifference (*nibbidā*). This, in turn, causes the liberation of the mind. The role of right-view is twofold: it sees things as they are and this is transformative. A similar theme is found in the *Saḷāyatanavagga* of the *Saṃyutta-nikāya*. This time, seeing the six senses as impermanent is right-view.[199] Similarly, in the following *sutta*, seeing the six external sense bases, the objects of the senses (*rūpa, sadda, gandha, rasa, phoṭṭhabba* and *dhamma*) as impermanent is right-view.[200] In three further *suttas* from the *Saḷāyatanavagga* of the *Saṃyutta-nikāya* the same teachings are found. These are the *Micchādiṭṭhippahāna-sutta* (S IV 147), the *Sakkāyadiṭṭhippahāna-sutta* (S IV 147–8) and the *Attānudiṭṭhippahāna-sutta* (S IV 148). In the first *sutta*, it is asked how one should know and see for *micchā-diṭṭhi* to be abandoned, in the second for *sakkāya-diṭṭhi* to be abandoned and in the third for *attānudiṭṭhi* to be abandoned.[201] The answer given for *micchā-diṭṭhi* is that one should see each of the senses, their objects, contact with the objects, and the type of consciousness that they produce and any feelings (whether painful, pleasurable or neither) as impermanent. This is how wrong-view is abandoned. For *sakkāya-diṭṭhi* to be abandoned one should view the same things as unsatisfactory, and for *attānudiṭṭhi* to be abandoned one should see them as not-self. The three *suttas* do not use the term *sammā-diṭṭhi*, but the way in which the views are abandoned is reminiscent of the operation of right-view upon them, particularly the *vipasannā-sammā-diṭṭhi* of the commentaries.

Right-view as seeing: 'This is not mine, this I am not, this is not my self'

In the discussion of wrong-view, we found six wrong-views from the *Alagaddūpama-sutta* (M I 136). These were called in the text six 'bases for views' (*diṭṭhi-ṭṭhāna*). By 'bases' (*ṭṭhāna*) the text may be implying that they are the object which views take as their standpoint, their position. The *ariya-sāvaka* should regard the *khandhas* as: 'This is not mine, this I am not, this is not my self' instead of: 'This is mine, this I am, this is my self', which are wrong-views.[202] The *ariya-sāvaka* is to regard what is seen, heard, sensed, cognized, encountered, sought, mentally pondered, as: 'This is not mine, this I am not, this is not my self'. Finally, the basis for views, 'This is self, this the world; after death I shall be permanent, everlasting, eternal, not subject to change; I shall endure and last as long as eternity', this too he should regard as: 'This is not mine, this I am not, this is not my self'. The suggestion is that of a detached and therefore wholesome way of seeing the world. Right-view proposes the notions of 'not mine', 'not I', and 'not-self'. It proposes the cessation of craving and attachment.

Four non-perversions of view (*na diṭṭhi-vipallāsā*)

In the idea of the four perversions and non-perversions of view, similar notions are found. In a sense, the doctrinal content of views cannot be separated from the effect of views: again the ideas of 'is' and 'ought'. In the *Vipallāsa-sutta* (A II 52) we are told that there are four perversions of apperception (*cattāro saññā-vipallāsā*), four perversions of mind (*cattāro citta-vipallāsā*) and four perversions of view (*cattāro diṭṭhi-vipallāsā*). The *vipallāsa* is an inversion and distortion of reality. The *Vipallāsa-sutta* states that to hold that in the impermanent there is the permanent, is a perversion of apperception, mind and view,[203] to hold that in suffering there is happiness, is a perversion of apperception, mind and view,[204] to hold that in the not-self there is a self, is a perversion of apperception, mind and view,[205] and to hold that in the ugly there is the beautiful is a perversion of apperception, mind and view.[206] In the verses that follows the prose, this is described as 'going to wrong-view' (*micchā-diṭṭhi-gatā*).

To see the opposite, that which is impermanent as impermanent, that which is suffering as suffering, that which is not-self as not-self, and that which is ugly as ugly, are the non-perversions of apperception, mind and view.[207] It is these four ways of seeing which, in verse, are described as 'undertaking right-view' (*sammā-diṭṭhi-samādānā*), and by this undertaking of view all suffering is overcome (*sammā-diṭṭhi-samādānā sabbaṃ dukkhaṃ upaccagun ti*, A II 52).

In the *Visuddhimagga*, the *vipallāsas* are explained in the following terms:

> There are three perversions, namely, the perversion of apperception, of consciousness and view, which occur apprehending objects that are impermanent, suffering, not-self and ugly, as permanent, pleasant, self, and beautiful.[208]

The *Nettippakaraṇa* (Nett 83–4) states that to contemplate the body as the body abandons the perversion that there is beauty in the ugly (*asubhe subhan ti vipallāsaṃ pajahati*), and this abandons the attachment to sensual desire. To contemplate feeling as feeling abandons the perversion that there is pleasure in the painful (*dukkhe sukhan ti vipallāsaṃ pajahati*), and this abandons the attachment to existence (*bhavupādāna*, this term is unusual in this context). To contemplate the mind as mind (*citta*) abandons the perversion that there is permanence in the impermanent (*anicce niccan ti vipallāsaṃ pajahati*), and this abandons the attachment to views. To contemplate *dhammas* as *dhammas*, one abandons the perversion that there is self in the not-self (*anattaniye attā ti vipallāsaṃ pajahati*), and this abandons the attachment to the doctrine of self. There is possibly a connection between the abandoning of these perversions and the cultivation of the four foundations of mindfulness (*satipaṭṭhāna*).[209] I will return to this in Chapter 3 and my discussion of the abandoning of the *āsavas*, and in Chapter 5 and the discussion of the three gateways to liberation.

The ten imperfections of insight (*vipassanā-upakkilesa*)

The central idea in these passages is one of misapprehending and grasping. Although these views may be used to explain right-view as those views that agree with Buddhist doctrine, it is the cessation of craving and attachment that they induce which is of equal importance. I have already cited the comments of Buddhaghosa at the end of Chapter 1 explaining that 'clinging' (*parāmāsa*) is a term for *micchā-diṭṭhi*, because it misses the individual essence of *dhammas*, by apprehending (*āmasana*) elsewhere an unreal individual essence.[210] Or, that those who do not have the correct attitude to the *dhamma*, who understand what is impermanent as permanent, have adherence to views (As 49). Buddhaghosa also states that 'there comes to be the removal of *diṭṭhi* in one who sees volitional formations as not-self'.[211] It is in this way that *micchā-diṭṭhi* is abandoned. It is, in fact, not only *micchā-diṭṭhi* but all *diṭṭhi* that are abandoned in this way. Attachment is not a predicate of *sammā-diṭṭhi*. This is expressed by the idea of the 'ten imperfections of insight' (*vipassanā upakkilesa*) found in the *Visuddhimagga*. These imperfections are illumination, knowledge, rapturous happiness, tranquillity, bliss, resolution, exertion, assurance, equanimity and attachment.[212] It is due to these that the *bhikkhu* does not see impermanence, unsatisfactoriness and not-self. Attachment is explained in the following terms:

> Attachment is attachment due to insight. For when his insight is adorned with illumination, etc., attachment arises in him, which is subtle and peaceful in aspect, and it relies on (clings to) that insight; and he is not able to discern that that attachment is a defilement.[213]

Attachment is then an imperfection of insight. Knowledge of what is of most importance, the eradication of *dukkha*, must not give way to craving for that knowledge. As right-view is explained as a type of wisdom (insight), so attachment and grasping are not part of its nature. If Buddhist doctrine becomes an object of attachment it is, in an important sense, incorrect doctrine. The content of Buddhist doctrine induces a cessation of craving and attachment.

CONCLUSION

I have argued that right-view can be understood in two ways. First, there are right-views that affirm the law of *kamma.* These are epitomised by the ten wholesome courses of action (*dasa kusala-kammapathā*). The opposition between right-view and wrong-view is in the form of a wholesome course of actions being adopted and an unwholesome course of actions being abandoned. Right-view in this sense stands in opposition to the wrong-views that deny that actions have consequences, that deny the law of *kamma*. In these courses of action, thought and action influence each other in the cleansing of body, speech and mind. However, a view may affirm the law of *kamma*, but it will be classified as wrong if it becomes an object of attachment. This leads to my second description of right-views. In distinction to the wrong-views that adhered and clung to various *dhammas*, most notably the *khandhas*, which I described in the second half of Chapter 1, these views are right precisely because they are not attached to *dhammas*. The *Sammādiṭṭhi-sutta* describes 16 right-views of this type. Its description of right-view suggests that to achieve right-view one has, first, knowledge of what is wholesome and unwholesome; second, knowledge of the four truths; and third, knowledge of dependent-origination. This is the content of right-view, this is what right-view proposes. We know from other parts of the Nikāyas that knowledge of the four truths or knowledge of dependent-origination is the right-view achieved at stream-attainment. It is the knowledge that, 'all that is subject to arising is subject to cessation'.[214] In the same way that one should act in a manner reflecting the knowledge of 'what is unwholesome and what is wholesome' or the right-view that 'actions have consequences' to achieve the right-view of stream-attainment, one should not adopt a right-view, the content of which is the four truths or dependent-origination, but act in a way that reflects a knowledge of *dukkha*, its arising, cessation and the way to its cessation, namely, with an attitude free from craving. This is right-view. It signifies the cessation of craving.

3

THE WAY WRONG-VIEW FUNCTIONS

I have considered the content of both wrong-view and right-view. I would now like to discuss how wrong-view functions. In Chapter 1 I used two headings to describe the content of wrong-view. First, there are wrong-views that deny that actions have consequences. These views deny the law of *kamma*. Second, there are those views about the self. I suggested that the latter views could be understood as denying that attachments have consequences. This class of view denies that craving is the cause of *dukkha*. It is wrong-view in this sense that I would like to focus upon in this chapter. Certain discussions of the notion of *diṭṭhi* suggest that it is the fact that *micchā-diṭṭhi* is associated with greed and attachment that makes it wrong. There is some justification in arguing that the primary interest of the Nikāyas is not in metaphysics but in how one should act in order to overcome *dukkha*. There is a preoccupation with the negative consequences of attachment to objects of the senses and of the mind and it is evidence for this that I would like to consider in this chapter.

The distinction between views and ignorance

My starting point are the corruptions (*āsavas*). In the list of corruptions four are occasionally listed instead of the more usual three, both views and ignorance being given as separate corruptions.[1] Why are views and ignorance separate corruptions? Aren't they both a lack of knowledge? If we examine how the corruptions are explained we may find an answer to this question. Buddhaghosa describes the corruptions in the following terms: the corruption of sensual desire (*kāmāsavo*) is the lust for the five pleasures of the senses; the corruption of becoming (*bhavāsavo*) is the passionate desire for life in a heaven of form, and formless existence, longing for *jhāna*, and lust co-existent with an eternalistic view;[2] the corruption of views (*diṭṭhāsavo*) is explained as the 62 views;[3] and the corruption of ignorance (*avijjāsavo*) is the lack of knowledge regarding eight points,[4] understood as the four truths, knowledge of the past, future or both, and of dependent-origination.[5] This explanation implies that views and ignorance refer to different things. In the following discussion I would like to explore why there are two separate corruptions:

views and ignorance, and to delineate the differences between them. My argument is that the corruption of views is the attachment to knowledge, and that the corruption of ignorance is false knowledge itself. It will be recalled that in the Introduction, I explained views as knowledge of doctrine, not doctrine itself. This leads me to understand the corruption of views as the attachment to doctrine, not doctrine itself.

The thicket, wilderness, contortion, vacillation and fetter of views

In the *Atthasālinī* (As 248), Buddhaghosa explains *micchā-diṭṭhi* as 'not seeing things as they are' (*ayāthāva-dassanaṃ*). The phrase points to the way in which certain views are held. It is not so much the content of the doctrines that posits a wrong conception of the way things are, but the fact that, by becoming an object of attachment, wrong-view distorts the true nature of things.[6] A view can be doctrinally correct but if, through giving rise to attachment, it distorts the holder's response to the world, it is a wrong-view. The early Abhidhamma emphasizes that a view is incorrect if it becomes an object of attachment, not because it is untrue. From the Abhidhamma perspective, *diṭṭhi* is exclusively connected with a mind (*citta*) rooted in greed (*lobha-mūla*). Views occur in four types of consciousness rooted in greed.[7] Views are primarily (if not exclusively) associated with greed, not delusion, in the Abhidhamma. In the *Visuddhimagga*, Buddhaghosa explains right-view as a type of knowledge,[8] and wrong-view as a type of greed (Vism XIV 90û1). As Rupert Gethin has observed '*diṭṭhi* can only be present in the mind when greed and attachment occur'.[9] This tells us that the early Theravāda understood the nature of views in relation to greed and attachment: wrong-views occur with greed and attachment, and right-views occur without greed and attachment. This connection between view and craving will now be considered.

I would like to look at an Abhidhamma passage explaining wrong-views, and Buddhaghosa's comments upon this passage. In the *Dhammasaṅgaṇi*, *micchā-diṭṭhi* is explained in the following terms :

> Gone over to view (*diṭṭhi-gata*), the thicket of view (*diṭṭhi-gahana*), a wilderness of view (*diṭṭhi-kantāra*), the contrariness of view (*diṭṭhi-visūkāyika*), the turmoil of view (*diṭṭhi-vipphandita*), the fetter of views (*diṭṭhi-saṃyojana*), holding (*gāha*), fixity (*patiṭṭhahā*), adherence (*abhinivesa*), clinging (*parāmāsa*), a bad path (*kumagga*), a false way (*micchā-patha*), falsity (*micchatta*), the realm of (other) systems of crossing over (*titthāyatana*), the hold of the perverted views (*vipariyesa-gāha*).[10]

This formula is also added in many contexts in which wrong-views are being discussed. One example of this is found in the *Vibhaṅga*. A discussion of dependent-origination explains the phrase 'with craving as condition there is attachment' (*taṇhā-paccayā upādānaṃ*) as 'gone over to view, the thicket of view, a wilderness of view', etc.[11] Craving, and the attachment that it gives rise to, are being explained as *micchā-diṭṭhi*. Wrong view is the embodiment of craving and attachment.[12]

In the *Atthasālinī*, Buddhaghosa comments on each of the *Dhammasaṅgaṇi* terms. I will summarise these comments:

> Wrong-views are 'gone over to view' (*diṭṭhi-gata*) because they are a way of seeing that, due to its being included in the sixty-two wrong-views (*dvāsaṭṭhi diṭṭhi-antogatattā*), has gone over to views in the sense of 'not seeing things as they are' (*ayāthāva-dassana*). Views are a thicket (*diṭṭhi-gahana*) because they are difficult to get beyond, like a grass thicket, a forest thicket or a mountainous region. The term 'wilderness of view' (*diṭṭhi-kantāra*) implies that view is dangerous and fearsome, like a wilderness infested by thieves and snakes, without food and water. In the sense of overthrowing and conflicting with right-view, it is the 'contrariness of view' (*diṭṭhi-visūkāyika*). This is because when the 'wrong way of seeing' (*micchā-dassana*) occurs, it overthrows and conflicts with the 'right way of seeing' (*sammā-dassana*). The 'turmoil of view' (*diṭṭhi-vipphandita*) is the turning to the other form for one who at one time holds the eternalist-view and at one time the annihilationist-view, for one lost in views is unable to stick with one position. The 'fetter of view' (*diṭṭhi-saṃyojana*) is itself considered as a fetter in the sense of 'binding' (*bandhana*), because it takes hold of its object firmly as crocodiles, and so on, take hold of a man, it is 'holding' (*gāha*). As a result of becoming fixed, it is 'fixity' (*patiṭṭhāha*). Indeed, by reason of its forceful occurrence, having become fixed it takes hold; and, because it is convinced about permanence and so on, this is an 'adherence' (*abhinivesa*). Because it misses the nature of *dhammas* and insists on holding on by way of the idea of their permanence and so on, it is 'clinging' (*parāmāsa*). A 'bad path' (*kumagga*) is a path that is vile due to its taking one to what is unbeneficial or it is a path to the vile descents. As a way that is not in accordance with the truth it is a 'false way' (*micchā-patha*). For even though one who is confused about the way takes a road thinking 'this is certainly the way to such and such a village' it does not bring him to that village, just so, even though one who is lost in view holds a view, thinking, 'this is the way to a happy destiny' it does not bring him to a happy destiny; so a 'false way' is a way not in accordance with the truth. As something that is by nature false it is 'falsity' (*micchatta*). A 'system of crossing over' (*tittha*) is where, just because of their roaming about there, it appears the foolish cross over; and because this is the realm of things unbeneficial, it is the 'realm of other systems of crossing over' (*titthāyatana*). Alternatively, the 'realm of other systems of crossing over' is a 'realm' (*āyatana*) in the sense of the dwelling place and country of birth of those belonging to other systems of crossing over. The 'hold of

> the perverted views' (*vipariyesa-gāha*) is a holding on which constitutes a perverted view; alternatively it is holding on because of perverted view; 'perverted view' (*vipallatthagāho*) is the meaning.[13]

The content of the view, what it proposes, is not ignored in this passage. A wrong-view does propose a false proposition. However, it is the tendency of views to become an object of greed and attachment that is of primary importance.[14] This suggests that the Abhidhamma is interested in how views are held, not, essentially, what they propose. Rupert Gethin has suggested that it is the fact that a view is an object of greed and attachment that the Theravāda Abhidhamma wishes to stress. He compares the definitions given of 'delusion' (*moha*) to that given for *diṭṭhi* in the *Dhammasaṅgaṇi*.[15] The list of terms describing *diṭṭhi* in the *Dhammasaṅgaṇi* were given above with the formula beginning 'gone over to view, the thicket of view, a wilderness of view'. In contrast, the list of terms in the *Dhammasaṅgaṇi* explaining *moha* is dominated by the notions of not knowing and not seeing.[16] Ignorance and delusion obscure the true nature of things. The content of the proposition is emphasised. This is clearly different to the list of terms that characterise *micchā-diṭṭhi*, which I have just discussed. These terms emphasize grasping, fixity and holding.

Gethin secondly considers Buddhaghosa's definitions of *micchā-diṭṭhi* and *moha*. Hence, *diṭṭhi* has the characteristic of inappropriate adherence (*ayoniso abhinivesa*); its function is clinging (*parāmāsa*); its manifestation is wrong-adherence (*micchābhinivesa*); its basis is the absence of desire to meet Noble Ones and the like (*ariyānaṃ adassana-kāmatādi*), and it should be seen as the ultimate fault (*paramaṃ vajjaṃ*). In contrast, delusion has the characteristic of mental blindness (*cittassa andhabhāva*), or not knowing (*aññāṇa*); its function is not penetrating (*asampaṭivedha*), or concealing the true nature of the object (*ārammaṇa-sabhāva-cchādana*); its manifestation is the absence of right practice (*asammā-paṭipatti*), or blindness (*andhakāra*); its basis is inappropriate bringing to mind (*ayoniso manasikāra*); it should be seen as the root of all that is unskilful (*sabbākusalānaṃ*).[17]

To these examples may be added others. In the *Peṭakopadesa* (Peṭ 94), *diṭṭhi* and *avijjā* are described in the following way: 'views are characterised by adherence and clinging'[18] while 'ignorance is characterised by non-penetration (of the four truths), and unawareness of ideas'.[19] The passage further explains that the *āsava* of views is 'abandoned by contemplating mind as mind' (*so citte cittanupassissa pahīyati*), while the *āsava* of ignorance is 'abandoned by contemplating *dhammas* as *dhammas*' (*so dhammesu dhammānupassissa pahīyati*). The '*āsava* of views is thus abandoned in the mind' (*diṭṭhāsavo citte pahātabbo*), while the '*āsava* of ignorance is abandoned in *dhammas*' (*avijjāsavo dhammesu pahātabbo*).[20] This is possibly a reference to the third and fourth foundations of mindfulness (*satipaṭṭhāna*). The four, which I have already cited, are to contemplate body as body, feelings as feelings, mind as mind, and *dhammas* as *dhammas*.[21] This passage could be understood using the model I considered earlier of the cleansing of body, speech and mind. In my discussion of the 'ten wholesome courses of action' (*dasa kusala-kammapathā*), I suggested that the sequence of these actions suggested a gradual transformation of conduct. In this understanding, contemplating the mind as mind implies an understanding of the working of the mind, of the cravings of the mind, in order to understand things as they are.

Earlier in the *Peṭakopadesa* it is explained that '[the view that there is] self in the mind [is the *āsava*] of views, and that there is permanence in the concomitants of consciousness (*cetasikas*)[22] [is the *āsava* of ignorance]'.[23] The *Peṭakopadesa* is analysing these ideas on different grounds and is clearly separating the corruptions of *diṭṭhi* and *avijjā*. Another example of the difference between the corruptions of *diṭṭhi* and *avijjā* is the following classification. The 'perversion that there is self in what is not-self, attachment to view, the bond of views, the bodily tie of clinging, the corruption of views, the flood of views, the barb of views' are terms found together to explain the tendency towards views.[24] In contrast, the 'perversion that there is permanence in the impermanent, attachment to the theory of self, the bond of ignorance, the bodily tie of insistence that this is truth, the corruption of ignorance, the flood of ignorance, the barb of delusion' are a set of terms found together to explain the tendency towards ignorance.[25]

One final example of the notion of *diṭṭhi* characterised in terms of grasping and attachment is found in the *Mahāniddesa*. This canonical text is the only commentary found in the Nikāyas, being (in part) a commentary upon the *Aṭṭhakavagga*. The *Mahāniddesa* asks a number of questions about different views. The answer to each question is identical. Hence the question is asked: 'What is the selfishness of view?'[26] The answer is that it is *sakkāya-diṭṭhi* with twenty bases, the wrong-view with ten bases (i.e. *natthika-diṭṭhi*), the extreme view with ten bases (*dasavatthukā antaggāhikā diṭṭhi*, i.e. the ten *avyākata*). These are then characterised as gone over to view (*diṭṭhi-gata*), the thicket of view (*diṭṭhi-gahana*), a wilderness of view (*diṭṭhi-kantāra*) etc., using the same formula as the one from the *Dhammasaṅgaṇi* considered above.[27] The *Mahāniddesa* then uses the same format to explain other terms. These terms become increasingly difficult to translate with different English words as they are all terms relating to attachment, clinging and grasping. Hence, the question is asked, 'what is attachment to view?' (*katamo diṭṭhi-nivesanā*). The same answer is given, that is *sakkāya-diṭṭhi* with twenty bases, the wrong-view with ten bases, the extreme view with ten bases, and that this is gone over to view, the thicket of view, etc.[28] The same answer is given as an explanation of 'fashioning by view',[29] 'devotion to view',[30] 'holding onto view',[31] 'dependence on view',[32] 'the stain of view',[33] 'the taking-up of view',[34] 'fixing attention on view'[35] and the 'dart of view'.[36]

All these examples illustrate that wrong-views emphasize one aspect of not knowing, and ignorance another. Though their definitions overlap, there is a definite emphasis on either attachment or not knowing. Why exactly is this distinction being made? I would like to suggest that different doctrines are being used in different ways. Or, to put this another way, different doctrines perform different roles. One doctrine may make a claim about how we perceive the world, another about the nature of the world. For one doctrine, it may be the value which that doctrine has for the treading of the Buddhist path, and for another the emphasis may be on what the doctrine explains about the nature of existence. In fact, as I have said, views are not doctrines, but knowledge of doctrines. Wrong-views insist, take hold of, and are attached to their objects (doctrines). This type of 'wrongness' may not essentially be ignorance of the true state of things, it may be a correct description of things, but the view is wrong because it is a 'perversion' (*vipallāsa*) and because the 'perverted view adheres' (*viparīta-diṭṭhi abhinivisati*, Peṭ 106). It is 'unwholesome' (*akusala*). It is wrong knowledge of doctrines and not, essentially, a wrong doctrine (though it is likely to be this as well). Wisdom knows how things are, right-view knows how to know how things are. To paraphrase the *Sammohavinodanī*: one who is attached needs to abandon views, while one who is ignorant needs to abandon delusion.[37]

Views are then a type of craving, but how are they distinguished from craving itself? Why not simply subsume the notion of views under the notion of craving? The *Peṭakopadesa* (Peṭ 26–8) discusses a passage from the Udāna (Ud 32–3), and how this passage relates to 'defilement by craving' (*taṇhā-saṃkileso*) and 'defilement by view' (*diṭṭhi-saṃkileso*). This passage further explains the nature of the type of attachment expressed by the corruption of views. The following is said to be an example of defilement by craving:

> This world is born to anguish and subject to painful contact,
> It is sickness that it calls self;
> For however it conceives [it],
> It is ever otherwise than that.
> Maintaining its being other than that,
> The world clings to being, expectantly relishing only being,
> [But] what it relishes brings fear,
> And what it fears is pain.[38]

The following is an example of defilement by view:

> Whoever have declared escape from being [to come about] through [love of] non-being, none of them, I say, escape from being. Whoever have declared liberation from being [to come about] through [love of some kind of] being, none of them, I say, are liberated from being.[39]

While the discussion of the *Peṭakopadesa* passage also deals with other issues, I would like to concentrate on what I consider it is implying by these two distinctions, between defilement by craving and defilement by view. The first distinction is relatively straightforward: what we crave changes and is different from what we want it to be. The second distinction, however, deserves more consideration. We could assume that, as defilement by craving points to sensual attachments, so defilement by views points to cognitive attachment. The early

Theravāda tradition is, to an extent, preoccupied with craving and how this affects the conduct of the person so obsessed. It seems reasonable to assume that, in the example of defilement by view, the text has in mind *sassata* and *uccheda-diṭṭhi*. Though the text has made the distinction between defilement by craving and defilement by views, it seems likely that, by using the term *diṭṭhi* instead of terms such as delusion (*moha*) or ignorance (*avijjā*), the text is implying, as in other places where the term *diṭṭhi* is used, a certain type of cognitive clinging (*parāmāsa*).[40] Being and non-being, self and not-self, are all potential objects of attachment. I would go as far as to suggest that, at a certain level, Buddhist thought is not concerned with whether there is a self or not. The issue of a 'self' is abandoned and, to an extent, not-self is *sammā-diṭṭhi* precisely because it rejects the strongest object of attachment. My overall point is that ignorance and views apply to two different forms of corruption, and that views apply to a form of craving, but a specific type of craving. So, when the right-view of *anattā* abandons the view of self, it is not knowledge abandoning ignorance, it is knowledge of craving abandoning attachment. This is what is meant when it is said that *micchā-diṭṭhi* is abandoned and *sammā-diṭṭhi* taken up. Attachment is abandoned and one sees without attachment.

The *Diṭṭhi-vagga*

I would now like to consider some important discussions of the notion of *diṭṭhi* found in the Nikāyas. There are two discussions of the notion of *diṭṭhi* found in the *Saṃyutta-nikāya*, the *Diṭṭhi-vagga* (S III 180–9) and the *Diṭṭhi-saṃyutta* (S III 201–24).

The *Diṭṭhi-vagga* begins by explaining that based on the *khandhas*, and depending on them (*upādāya*), pleasure and pain arise internally (S III 180–1). As the *khandhas* are impermanent, suffering and subject to change (*anicca, dukkha, viparināma*), without attachment to them pleasure and pain will not arise internally (S III 181). It is next explained that it is by the existence of the *khandhas*, and depending on and adhering to them (*upādāya, abhinivissa*), that one regards things: 'This is mine, this I am, this is my self' (S III 181). It is also by depending on and adhering to the *khandhas* that the view: 'That which is the self is the world; having passed away, I shall be permanent, stable, eternal, not subject to change',[41] and one of the annihilationist-views ('and it might not be for me' *no ca me siyā*, S III 183), 'wrong-view' (the text simply states *micchā-diṭṭhi*, S III 184), *sakkāya-diṭṭhi* (S III 185), and 'the view of self' (*attānu-diṭṭhi*, S III 185), arise. All these arise through depending on and adhering to the *khandhas*.

Without dependence and adherence these views would not arise.[42] It is by seeing in this way, without attachment, that the *ariya-sāvaka* feels revulsion for the *khandhas*. Feeling revulsion, there is indifference. Through indifference his mind is liberated, and the *bhikkhu* knows it is liberated.[43] This revulsion, indifference and liberation is explained throughout the *Khandha-vagga* as the result of seeing the *khandhas* in the stated way.[44] As I explained at the end of Chapter 2, I take such statements as pointing to the 'is', 'ought' relationship in Buddhist thought. This passage is similar to the attitude that I described in my discussion of the *Paṭhamanandikkhaya-sutta* (S III 51). In that *sutta*, seeing the *khandhas* as impermanent causes indifference and the destruction of delight and lust. It also seems likely that in such passages we find the same way of thinking described by the *anuloma* and *paṭiloma* cycles of dependent-origination. If things are seen as they are, with right-view, there is a wholesome effect; if things are not seen as they are, with wrong-view, there is an unwholesome effect.

The *Diṭṭhi-saṃyutta*

A similar treatment is given to *diṭṭhi* in the *Diṭṭhi-saṃyutta*. Again, it is explained that with the existence of the *khandhas* (and depending on and adhering to them), each of the wrong-views arises.[45] The *khandhas* are impermanent, suffering and subject to change. Without depending on them wrong-views do not arise.[46] In the first part of the *Diṭṭhi-saṃyutta* this is also explained of whatever is seen, heard, sensed, cognized, attained, sought after and ranged over by the mind.[47] All these things are impermanent, suffering and subject to change. By not depending on these things, none of the views could arise.[48]

It is through abandoning doubt about the *khandhas* and what is seen and heard, sensed, cognized, attained, sought after and ranged over by the mind that wrong-view is abandoned. The *Diṭṭhi-saṃyutta* then states the following:

> When the noble disciple has abandoned doubt in these six cases,[49] and when, further, he has abandoned doubt about suffering, the origin of suffering, the cessation of suffering, and the way leading to the cessation of suffering, he is then called a noble disciple who is a stream-attainer, no longer bound to the nether world, fixed in destiny, with enlightenment as his destination.[50]

Wrong-view is abandoned with the abandoning of doubt. The *khandhas* and *dukkha* are seen as they are. Later sections of the *Diṭṭhi-saṃyutta* state that all views arise in three ways. First, they arise when there is *dukkha*, by attachment to *dukkha*, and by adhering to *dukkha*.[51] Second, views arise by depending on what is impermanent and suffering.[52] Third, views arise when the *khandhas* are grasped. It is explained that the *khandhas* should be seen with proper wisdom: 'This is not mine, this I am not, this is not my self', and this stops views from arising. In this way there is revulsion towards the *khandhas*, this causes indifference and liberation of the mind (S III 223).

The *Diṭṭhi-vagga* and *Diṭṭhi-saṃyutta* have suggested that wrong-views are based on the *khandhas*. It is by not depending upon the *khandhas* that the person is free from views. Once again this is suggestive of an understanding of views as a type of craving and attachment.

Views in the *Diṭṭhi-kathā*

I would now like to move on to another discussion of *micchā diṭṭhi*. In the *Diṭṭhi-kathā* of the *Paṭisambhidāmagga* there is an extended treatment of *diṭṭhi*. This *Paṭisambhidāmagga* discussion is, in many respects, a summary of views found in earlier parts of the Nikāyas. The *Paṭisambhidāmagga* itself is a late canonical text and can be regarded as a form of early Abhidhamma in style and content.

The *Diṭṭhi-kathā* asks six questions. I will analyse the first five. The sixth question, relating to the escape from views, will be considered in the next chapter on the function of right-view. The *Diṭṭhi-kathā* begins by asking: 'What is view?' (*kā diṭṭhi ti*, Paṭis I 135). The answer given is that 'clinging by adherence is view' (*abhinivesa parāmāso diṭṭhi*, Paṭis I 135).

These two terms, *abhinivesa* and *parāmāsa* are found in other parts of the Nikāyas. In the *Aṭṭhakavagga* it is explained that 'adherence to views is not easily overcome. (One) has been grasped from among (many) doctrines, after consideration. Therefore a man lays down or takes up a doctrine from among these adherences (to views)'.[53] There is a related group of terms, often used with reference to the *khandhas*, describing what the Buddha has overcome. The Tathāgata is said to have abandoned 'desire, lust, delight, craving, attachment, the mental bases, adherences and underlying tendencies' regarding each of the *khandhas*.[54] The *Diṭṭhi-vagga* contains two '*abhinivesa suttas*', the *Paṭhama abhinivesa-sutta* and the *Dutiya abhinivesa-sutta* (S III 186–7). The term *abhinivesa* is also known in the wider Indian context. For example, in the *Yoga-sūtra* of Patañjali *abhiniveśa* is the fifth 'defilement' (*kleśa*).[55]

The *Paṭisambhidāmagga* explains exactly how there is clinging by adherence. This entails clinging by adherence to 198 *dhammas*. These are *dhammas* taken from a list of 201 *dhammas* in the opening section of the *Paṭisambhidāmagga* (Paṭis 5–8). These are the five *khandhas*, the six senses, the six kinds of sense object, the six classes of consciousness, the six elements (*dhātu*), the 32 parts of the body, the 12 spheres (*āyatanas*), the 18 elements (*dhātus*), the 19 faculties (*indriyas*), the three realms, the nine kinds of existence, the four *jhānas*, the four kinds of *ceto-vimutti* (*mettā*, etc.) and the four formless attainments (i.e. the *arūpa jhānas*).[56] The three *dhammas* not included in the *Diṭṭhi-kathā* are the three knowledge *indriyas*: 'I shall come to know the unknown faculty' (*anaññātaññassāmītindriyaṃ*), the 'final-knowledge faculty' (*aññindriyaṃ*) and the 'final-knower faculty' (*aññātāvindriyaṃ*). This list is being used, as is often the case with the five *khandhas*, to illustrate how the world is an object of attachment.[57] As I will suggest in a discussion of the *Paṭṭhāna* in Chapter 5, even Buddhist practice is a possible object of attachment. The *jhānas* and *arūpa jhānas* can be a cause of defilement. However, the paths and the fruits of the paths do not cause craving. This is suggested in this passage by the omission from the list of the three knowledge *indriyas*. The paths and the fruits of the path do not produce craving and attachment, they do not cause wrong-views. The passage explains how the 198 *dhammas* produce and give rise to wrong-views. The text states that 'clinging by adherence to form thus: "This is mine, this I am, this is my self" is view'.[58] It then goes through the other *dhammas* beginning with the remaining four *khandhas* and finishing with the 12 links of dependent-origination.[59] I take it that the text is suggesting that the minds of those not on the Buddhist path become attached to everything. Even those on the path may become attached to practice, to calm and insight. The mind is prone to clinging, adhering and misinterpreting.

The second question that the text aims to answer is: 'How many kinds of bases for views are there?' (*kati diṭṭhiṭṭhānāni ti*). It explains that there are 'eight kinds of bases for views'. These are the *khandhas*, ignorance, contact, apperception, applied thought, inappropriate bringing to mind, a bad friend and the voice of another.[60] The text states how each of the eight bases is a basis for views. Each is a cause (*hetu*) and condition (*paccayo*), for they are the origination for the arising of views.

It is worth considering certain details of this list of bases for views. The text is describing what exactly it is that views are based upon. It has already been suggested that an explanation of the origination of views is that they are caused by clinging and adherence to the *khandhas*. This is the first 'basis for view'. Of the remaining seven bases, ignorance, applied thought and inappropriate bringing to mind are bases that most easily reflect the cognitive origination of *micchā-diṭṭhi*. The remaining bases: contact, apperception, a bad friend and the voice of another suggest that as bases they are an object of attachment. It must also be remembered that in the consideration of *sammā-diṭṭhi* we already met the Nikāya statement that there are two causes[61] for the arising of wrong-view, the voice of another and inappropriate bringing to mind.[62] The *Paṭisambhidāmagga* explains these as bases for views.

The third question that the text asks is: 'How many kinds of obsession by views are there?' (*kati diṭṭhi-pariyuṭṭhānānī ti*). This is answered by stating that there are 18:

> Gone over to view (*diṭṭhi-gataṃ*), the thicket of view (*diṭṭhi-gahanaṃ*), and the wilderness of views (*diṭṭhi-kantāraṃ*), the contrariness of view (*diṭṭhi-visukaṃ*), the turmoil of view (*diṭṭhi-vipphandita*), fetter of views (*diṭṭhi-saṃyojanaṃ*), dart of views (*diṭṭhi-sallaṃ*), constraint of views (*diṭṭhi-sambādho*), impediment of views (*diṭṭhi-palibodho*), binding of views (*diṭṭhi-bandhanaṃ*), pitfall of views (*diṭṭhi-papāto*), underlying tendency to views (*diṭṭhānusayo*), burning (torment) of views (*diṭṭhi-santāpo*), fever (anguish) of views (*diṭṭhi-pariḷāho*), knot of views (*diṭṭhi-gantho*), attachment to views (*diṭṭhūpādānaṃ*), adherence to views (*diṭṭhābhiniveso*), clinging to views (*diṭṭhi-parāmāso*), all these are an obsession with views.[63]

The first six of these terms (up to 'fetter of views', *diṭṭhi-saṃyojanaṃ*) have already been met in the *Dhammasaṅgaṇi*. The *Dhammasaṅgaṇi* also effectively cites the adherence to views (*diṭṭhābhinivesa*) and clinging to views (*diṭṭhi-parāmāsa*). The remaining terms are added, though they only serve to enhance the meaning of *diṭṭhi* as a form of attachment.

The fourth question that the text aims to answer is: 'How many kinds of views are there?' (*kati diṭṭhi yo ti*). The answer is that there are 16 kinds of view (*soḷasa diṭṭhiyo*), perhaps mirroring the 16 right-views from the *Sammādiṭṭhi-sutta*:

> The gratification-view (*assāda-diṭṭhi*); views about self (*attānudiṭṭhi*); wrong-view (*micchā-diṭṭhi*); identity-view (*sakkāya-diṭṭhi*); views of eternity based on identity (*sakkāya-vatthukā sassata-diṭṭhi*); views about annihilation based on identity (*sakkāya-vatthukā uccheda-diṭṭhi*); views assuming finiteness (*antaggāhikā diṭṭhi*); views about past finiteness (*pubbantānudiṭṭhi*); views about future finiteness (*aparantānudiṭṭhi*); views that fetter (*saṃyojanikā diṭṭhi*); views that shackle with the conceit 'I' (*ahan ti mānavinibandhā diṭṭhi*); views that shackle with the conceit 'mine' (*maman ti mānavinibandhā diṭṭhi*); views associated with self-theories (*attavāda-paṭisaṃyuttā diṭṭhi*); views associated with world-theories (*loka-vāda-paṭisaṃyuttā diṭṭhi*); views of being (*bhava-diṭṭhi*); views of non-being (*vibhava-diṭṭhi*).[64]

The fifth question is: 'How many kinds of adherence to views are there?' (*kati-diṭṭhābhinivesāti*). The text goes through the 16 views, answering this question for each view (Paṭis I 139–40). For the 'gratification-view' there is adherence in 35 aspects (*ākāra*); for the 'views about self' in 20 aspects; 'wrong-view' in ten aspects; 'identity-view' in 20 aspects; 'views of eternity based on identity' in 15 aspects; 'views about annihilation based on identity' in five aspects; 'views assuming finiteness' in 50 aspects; 'views about past finiteness' in 18 aspects; 'views about future finiteness' in 44 aspects; 'views that fetter' in 18 aspects; 'views that shackle with the conceit "I"' in 18 aspects; 'views that shackle with the conceit "mine"' in 18 aspects; 'views associated with self-theories' in 20 aspects; 'views associated with world-theories' in eight aspects; 'views of being' in one aspect; 'views of non-being' in one aspect (Paṭis I 139–40).

The main part of the *Diṭṭhi-kathā* then explains the analysis of these categories using the fifth as the starting point (how many kinds of adherence to each view there are). There are differences in the wording of certain aspects of how the adherence takes place. However, there is a pattern to how most of the views are evaluated. By way of example, I will summarise this analysis for the first three views.

The first analysis is of how there is adherence through the gratification-view (*assāda-diṭṭhi*) in 35 aspects.[65] Quoting a *Saṃyutta-nikāya* passage (S III 28), the text states that any pleasure and joy that arise dependent on form are the gratification in the case of form.[66] It is the clinging and adherence to this gratification that is the wrong-view. The text then explains that 'the view is one thing, the gratification another and together they are called the gratification-view'.[67] All 35 *assāda-diṭṭhi* are formed in this way. The remaining 34 *assāda-diṭṭhi* are then explained. They consist in adhering to the remaining four *khandhas*, the six types of internal sense-base, the six external sense-bases, the six types of consciousness, the six kinds of contact, and the six kinds of feeling (Paṭis I 141–3).

Second, adherence through views about self (*attānu-diṭṭhi*) in 20 aspects are the 20 adherences (*abhinivesa*) to the *khandhas* that form *sakkāya-diṭṭhi*. For each view there is the 'ground' (*vatthu*), which is each of the *khandhas*. It is stated that the view is one thing and the ground another and together they are the view about self.[68] Of course, the *khandhas* have been given as both the first five of the 201 *dhammas* which through clinging and adherence are taken as: 'This is mine, this I am, this is my self', and as the first of the eight 'bases for view'. It is explained repeatedly that clinging by adherence is the view.[69] This, it will be remembered, is the explanation of view. Thus clinging (*parāmāsa*) to each of the *khandhas* as self, is adhering (*abhinivesa*) to them.

The third type of view, called simply *micchā-diṭṭhi*, is the view of nihilism that I discussed in Chapter 1 (*natthika-diṭṭhi*, the view beginning: 'Nothing is given, nothing offered, nothing sacrificed'). This time the ten grounds are the ten clauses of the view. Hence, 'nothing given' is the ground (*natthi dinna anti vatthu*) and 'clinging by adhering which asserts' is the view (*evaṃvādo micchābhinivesa-parāmāso diṭṭhi*). The view is one thing, the ground another, the view and the ground together are the first wrong-view with a wrong ground.[70]

This is the general principle followed for each view. For each of the 16 views a passage occurs which states that the wrong-view is called a 'non-accomplishment of view' (*diṭṭhi-vipatti*) which is 'destructive' (*pāpikā*). The text next explains that the view is one thing and greed another, together they are called 'greed for views'. The person who has this greed and holds the view is 'inflamed by view' and any gift given to that person does not produce any effect because he has a 'view that is destructive'. The text then states the familiar Nikāya evaluation of *micchā-diṭṭhi*, that the person who holds wrong-view will be reborn in an unhappy state, and that all his actions of 'body, speech and mind' (*kāya-kamma, vacī-kamma, mano-kamma*, Paṭis I 140), done according to that view, will lead to suffering. The text is clearly using a version of a passage found at A I 32, repeating the analogy from the *Aṅguttara* passage of the bad or destructive seed and the bad or destructive view.[71]

The *Diṭṭhi-kathā* is in many respects a summary of what we have found about views in the Nikāyas as a whole. I have pointed out that views are distinguished from ignorance and that this is done to describe them as a form of craving and attachment. The *Diṭṭhi-kathā* states this by explaining views as 'clinging by adherence'. Views are produced by adhering to 198 *dhammas*, which can be taken as explaining the world. This illustrates what clinging by adherence is: attachment to the world. The *Diṭṭhi-kathā* then states that there are eight bases for views. In a sense, the 198 *dhammas* (the world) become an object of craving according to these eight categories. These, in turn, give rise to obsessions by sixteen types of view analysed according to various adherences. The point appears to be that the mind becomes attached to the details of the world, makes assumptions and craves various parts of it. Much of this analysis is not concerned with what the various views assert, but with the influence that the view has on the actions of the person who holds the view. The interest is not in metaphysics but in the consequences of views: 'how will this way of thinking affect the way I act?' This is similar to the themes that I considered in relation to the ten wholesome courses of action in Chapter 2: thought and action are reciprocal.

Views and craving in the *Nettippakaraṇa*

I have so far argued that views and ignorance refer to different corruptions, and that views are a form of craving. I would like to conclude this chapter by discussing how this craving is described in the *Nettippakaraṇa*.

The *Nettippakaraṇa* quotes the Udāna 81: 'The supported is liable to dislodgement; the unsupported is not liable to dislodgement'.[72] It uses this statement to suggest how one should respond to the world. It first explains that there are two kinds of support: there is 'support by craving, and support by view'.[73] Any choice (*cetanā*) of one who is lusting (*rattassa*), is support by craving (*taṇhā-nissayo*), and any choice by one who is 'confused' (*mūḷhassa*), is 'support by views' (*diṭṭhi-nissayo*). The text then states that the act of choice or volition (*cetanā*) leads to involvement, and this is a 'formation' (*cetanā pana saṃkhārā*). This is then used to suggest that one who lusts or holds on to view is involved in the process of dependent-origination. The text gives a version of dependent-origination based upon volitional formations, i.e. with volitional formations as condition there is consciousness, etc., sorrow, lamentation, despair and suffering.[74] This negative outcome of holding to views is familiar to us. The *Nettippakaraṇa* explains that both those who hold views and those who lust and crave are involved in the same process, that of dependently-originated *dhammas*. Involvement with these *dhammas* leads to *dukkha*.

The *Nettippakaraṇa* next describes how there is escape from this cycle. When there is no liability to dislodgement, there is tranquillity; when there is tranquillity, there is no inclination (*nati*),[75] when there is no inclination, there is no coming and going; when there is no coming and going, there is no decease and reappearance; when there is no decease and reappearance, there is no here, beyond or in between, and this is the end of suffering.[76] This is the escape from *dukkha*. The text explains that the unsupported is not liable to dislodgement because it is 'unsupported by craving by virtue of calm',[77] and 'unsupported by views by virtue of insight'.[78] It states that: 'insight is knowledge and with its arising there is the cessation of ignorance',[79] and so on through the cessation of the chain of dependent-origination.[80]

The unwholesome process begins with choice or volition (*cetanā*), for both lust and views: objects of the senses and cognition. This gives rise to volitional formations (*saṃkhārā*), and to *dukkha*. The wholesome process begins with a turning away from objects of sense and cognition, through calm (*samatha*) and insight (*vipassanā*) which abandons ignorance and the chain of dependent-origination leading to *dukkha*. The *Nettippakaraṇa* is explaining in clear terms that the holding of views is part of the very process of *dukkha*.

In Chapter 2 I considered a similar process in the form of the right-view of Anāthapiṇḍika. This view was the following:

> Whatever has become is put together, is thought out, is dependent on something else, that is impermanent. What is impermanent, that is *dukkha*, what is *dukkha*: 'This is not mine, this I am not, this is not my self'.[81]

It is the cessation of craving, essential for apprehending this process, which the texts describe as *sammā-diṭṭhi*. The *Nettippakaraṇa* makes this clear by suggesting that the very holding of a view is a *cetanā* and this is a *saṃkhāra*. View is, as it were, implicated in the whole process of dependent-origination. I would argue that it is not just *micchā-diṭṭhi* that is implicated, but *sammā-diṭṭhi* is also likely to be a *cetanā* and a *saṃkhāra*, and part of the process of *dukkha*. In the *Nettippakaraṇa* passage the text is, in one sense, making a distinction about the nature of the view that 'corrects' *micchā-diṭṭhi* which, in fact, corrects *diṭṭhi*. It corrects all views, in the sense that any view is an object of attachment. In the language of the *Nettippakaraṇa*, a view cannot be 'liable to dislodgement' (*calitaṃ natthi*). It is the view that is 'not supported by views' (*diṭṭhiyā anissito*) in virtue of insight (*vipassanā-vasena*). Right-view transcends all views.

In many respects this passage sheds some light on the opposition and no-views understandings of views. It explains how it understands the attachments and cravings of the mind and the calming and escape from them. The aim is to be uninvolved and to find tranquillity. By calming the mind there is an escape from views. Where there are no views there is 'no here, beyond or in between'. This is the wholesome course of action. Wrong-view is the opposite to this. It is involved, it gives rise to volitional formations, consciousness, name and form, feelings, craving, attachment and suffering. Wrong-view is always associated with greed. It is implicated in the process of giving rise to unwholesome actions. As such, it leads away from insight, from right-view.

I began this chapter by pointing out that there is both a corruption of views and a corruption of ignorance. This clearly suggests that wrong-view and ignorance are different. Views are a type of greed whereas ignorance is a form of delusion. Views are wrong because they crave the world, ignorance is wrong because it sees the world incorrectly. In discussing the *Diṭṭhi-vagga*, *Diṭṭhi-saṃyutta* and the *Diṭṭhi-kathā* I have offered evidence for this understanding of the function of wrong-view. The understanding of wrong-views as a form of craving is important for my overall argument. It suggests that wrong-views see the world wrongly in the sense of grasping it and that this conceals the true nature of the world. It is in this sense that wrong-views do not 'see things as they are'.

4

THE WAY RIGHT-VIEW FUNCTIONS

PART ONE: DIFFERENT LEVELS OF RIGHT-VIEW

In Chapter 2 I considered the content of *sammā-diṭṭhi*, what the view proposed. In this chapter I would like to explore in more detail the ways in which *sammā-diṭṭhi* functions. The first half of this chapter will consider the notion of right-view under three headings. First, the gaining of right-view can be understood as the 'accomplishment in view' (*diṭṭhi-sampadā*). I considered this category briefly in Chapter 1, when I contrasted it with 'non-accomplishment in view' (*diṭṭhi-vipatti*). I noted that accomplishment in view is often used to refer to the view of affirmation, while non-accomplishment in view is often used to refer to the view of nihilism (i.e. Dhs 233 §§ 1362, 1364). The second heading under which I will consider right-view is 'accomplished in view' (*diṭṭhi-sampanna*). This term is often used to refer to the right-view achieved at stream-attainment, and the content of this view is usually the seeing of dependent-origination. The term *sampanna* is the past participle of *sampadā* and denotes the process whereby, after gaining accomplishment in view, the holder of the view becomes accomplished in view. The third heading is 'purification of view' (*diṭṭhi-visuddhi*). The content of this view is the knowing of 'rise and fall' (*udayabbayaṃ*). The second half of this chapter will use these categories to consider how a right-view, which holds that actions have consequences, is developed into a knowledge of dependent-origination and, in turn, into an insight into the rise and fall of all *dhammas*. How are we to understand this process? What is the nature of *sammā-diṭṭhi* on the higher paths (the paths of once-returner, never returner and Arahant) and how are we to understand the deepening of insight on the higher paths after stream-attainment?

Accomplishment in view (*diṭṭhi-sampadā*)

The term accomplishment in view (*diṭṭhi-sampadā*) suggests the view that one should strive to attain. The one who has accomplishment in view has the view that our actions have consequences.

In the *Saṅgīti-sutta* (D III 207–71), at D III 213, the statement is made that there is 'accomplishment in virtue and accomplishment in view' (*sīla-sampadā ca diṭṭhi-sampadā ca*, see also A I 95). This is followed by the statement that there is also 'purification of virtue and purification of view' (*sīla-visuddhi ca diṭṭhi-visuddhi*). This implies that accomplishment in view is part of the process towards achieving purification of view.

The term *sampadā* also appears in set lists of accomplishments. In the *Saṅgīti-sutta* again (also found at A III 147), five kinds of *sampadā* are described; those of relatives, wealth, health, virtue and view.[1] It is stated that beings do not arise in a heavenly state because of the accomplishment in relatives, wealth or health, but such states are achieved with the accomplishment in virtue and view (D III 235). These five are contrasted to five kinds of 'loss' (*vyasanāni*), of 'relatives, wealth, health, virtue and view'.[2] One does not arise in hell due to loss of relatives, wealth or health, but due to loss in virtue and view (D III 235, A III 147).[3] A *sutta* at A I 269–70 gives three *sampadā*, adding mind (*citta*) to virtue and view. The first seven *kusala-kammapathā* are the explanation of accomplishment in virtue, the eighth and ninth for accomplishment in mind, and the view of affirmation is the explanation of accomplishment in view. It is stated that it is due to these three accomplishments that beings are reborn in heaven.[4] These are contrasted to three non-accomplishments (*vipatti*): 'non-accomplishment in virtue' (*sīla-vipatti*), 'non-accomplishment in mind' (*citta-vipatti*) and 'non-accomplishment in view' (*diṭṭhi-vipatti*). The first seven *akusala-kammapathā* are the explanation of non-accomplishment in virtue, the eighth and ninth for non-accomplishment in mind, and the view of nihilism is the explanation of non-accomplishment in view. It is owing to these three non-accomplishments that beings are reborn in hell.[5] In a *sutta* at A I 270–1, accomplishments in action, livelihood and view,[6] and non-accomplishments in action, livelihood and view are found.[7]

Accomplished in view (*diṭṭhi-sampanna*)

The term accomplished in view (*diṭṭhi-sampanna*) is used to describe the *sammā-diṭṭhi* realised at stream-attainment. In the *Aṅguttara-nikāya* it is explained that whoever has come to the goal is accomplished in view.[8] Six things are abandoned when one is accomplished in view. These are identity-view (*sakkāya-diṭṭhi*), doubt (*vicikiccha*), clinging to precepts and vows (*sīlabbata-parāmāsa*), greed (*rāga*), hatred (*dosa*) and delusion (*moha*), A III 438. In one passage already cited, the term *diṭṭhi-sampanna* is used for the one who sees the four truths which, as I have shown, is one possible knowledge gained at the stage of stream-attainment (*sotāpatti*).[9] Elsewhere it is stated that there is great demerit (*apuñña*) for those who insult the person who is accomplished in view (*diṭṭhi-sampannam puggalaṃ*, A III 372). The one who is accomplished in view is further said to be free from the 'bases of view' (*diṭṭhi-ṭṭhānappahāyinaṃ*, A III 373), he is free from the causes of view. All this indicates that the person who is accomplished in view has reached the stage of stream-attainment.

A passage that occurs a number of times in the Nikāyas gives an insight into the vision of the one who is accomplished in view. This passage gives nine things that the one who is accomplished in view cannot do. It is impossible that one accomplished in view should regard any volitional formation as permanent or pleasurable or any *dhamma* as self,[10] though it is possible that the 'ordinary person' (*puthujjana*) would.[11] It is not possible that the person accomplished in view could deprive his mother, father or an Arahant of life. It is not possible that he could, with a mind of hate, shed the blood of a Tathāgata, cause a schism in the order or acknowledge another teacher.[12] Though again, it is possible that the ordinary person would. At A III 438–9 a number of other things are added that the one accomplished in view cannot do. The one accomplished in view cannot live without respect for the Buddha, *dhamma*, *saṅgha* or training. The one accomplished in view cannot fall back on the 62 wrong-views.[13] The one accomplished in view cannot be one who will produce the 'eighth state of becoming' (*aṭṭhamaṃ bhavaṃ nibbattetuṃ*, A III 438). This is again informing us that the one accomplished in view is a stream-attainer. The reference is to the one who has a maximum of seven more rebirths and so cannot have an 'eighth state of becoming'.

The *Saṃyutta-nikāya* (S II 133–40) uses 11 analogies to illustrate the amount of *dukkha* eliminated by the one accomplished in view. For example, the Buddha is shown with a small piece of soil in his fingernail, comparing this to the Earth. Then the analogy is made between this and the amount of *dukkha* destroyed by the one accomplished in view, and the amount of *dukkha* remaining:

> So too, *bhikkhus*, a noble disciple, a person accomplished in view who has made the breakthrough, the *dukkha* that has been destroyed and eliminated is more, while that which remains is trifling.[14]

From these passages it is clear that to be accomplished in view is to see the world in a way that is both radically different from the ordinary way of seeing and that has great soteriological significance. What then does the one accomplished in view see? What is the content and function of this view? In Chapter 2, I showed that *sammā-diṭṭhi* consists primarily of two things: it is either seeing the four truths or dependent-origination. It is the latter of these that appears to constitute what the one accomplished in view sees.

The centrality of seeing the process of dependent-origination is clear from such well-known statements as: 'Whoever sees dependent-origination sees the *dhamma*; whoever sees the *dhamma* sees dependent-origination'.[15] It is the seeing of this, the knowledge of this, that constitutes what is seen by one accomplished in view. It is stated that one who has realised the fruit of stream-attainment (*sotāpatti-phala-sacchi-kiriyāya*) sees the cause and causal origination of *dhammas*.[16] This is seen by the stream-attainer who is accomplished in view.[17] The *Manorathapūranī* explains that the one accomplished in view is a stream-attainer.[18] The *Sammohavinodanī* describes one who is accomplished in view as an *ariya-sāvaka*, a stream-attainer who has attained the view of the path.[19]

At this point I would like to examine five passages that consider the vision of the one who is accomplished in view. These passages explain the function of right-view. In the *Paccaya-sutta* (S II 42–3) at S II 42, the *Bhikkhu-sutta* (S II 43–5) at S II 45, the *Ñāṇavatthu-sutta* (S II 56–9) at S II 58, the *Paṭhama ariyasāvaka-sutta* (S II 77–9) at S II 79 and the *Dutiya ariyasāvaka-sutta* (S II 79–80) at S II 80, there is a recurring theme. These passages explain certain aspects of dependent-origination, then state that the one who sees dependent-origination in this way is accomplished in view.

In the *Paccaya-sutta* the usual sequence of dependent-origination is given, and each item is explained. It is explained that, with the arising of *avijjā* there is the arising of the volitional formations, with the cessation of *avijjā* there is the cessation of the volitional formations etc. and that the way to their cessation is the *ariyo-aṭṭhaṅgiko-maggo*. It is then stated that:

> When the noble disciple understands the condition, its origin, cessation and the way to its cessation, he is then called a noble disciple who is accomplished in view, accomplished in vision, who has arrived at this true *dhamma*, who sees this true *dhamma*, who possesses a trainee's knowledge, a trainee's true knowledge, who has entered on the stream of the *dhamma*, a noble one with penetrative wisdom, one who stands squarely before the door to the deathless.[20]

The *Sāratthappakāsinī* explains that the phrase 'understands the condition' means that it is understood by way of the truth of suffering, 'its origin' by way of the truth of origination.[21] To be accomplished in view is to be accomplished in the view of the path.[22] This is clearly similar to the *Sammādiṭṭhi-sutta's* description of right-view which I considered in Chapter 2.

In the *Bhikkhu-sutta* a similar analysis of knowing each of the factors of dependent-origination, their origin, cessation and the way to their cessation is found. This analysis excludes *avijjā*. This is probably because if the *bhikkhu* saw the origin and cessation of *avijjā* he would have reached the goal.[23] When the *bhikkhu* understands each item in this way 'he is then called a noble disciple who is accomplished in view, accomplished in vision, etc.'[24] In the *Ñāṇavatthu-sutta* it is stated that there are 44 cases of knowledge. These consist in knowing each of the items of dependent-origination (again excluding *avijjā*), their arising, cessation and the way to their cessation. This is called 'knowledge of the *dhamma*' (*dhamma-ñāṇa*, S II 58). The *Sāratthappakāsinī* interprets *dhamma-ñāṇa* as 'knowledge of the four truths' (*catu-sacca-dhamma*) or 'path knowledge' (*magga-ñāṇa-dhamma*).[25] The term 'knowledge of the *dhamma*' explains *sammā-diṭṭhi* as knowledge of the arising, cessation and the way to cessation of the factors of dependent-origination.

With the cleansing and purifying of two types of knowledge, 'knowledge of the *dhamma*' and 'knowledge of succession'(*anvaye ñāṇa*), one is described as 'accomplished in view'.[26] This is described in the following way: the knowledge of the *dhamma* when applied to the past and the future, by means of knowing that those ascetics and brahmins who knew ageing and death, its origin, cessation and the way to its cessation, know ageing and death in the same way, is called 'knowledge of succession' (*anvaye ñāṇa*).[27]

The *Paṭhama-ariyasāvaka-sutta* states that the *ariya-sāvaka* knows that 'when this exists, that comes to be', when there is ignorance, the other factors of dependent-origination come to be, and this is the arising of the world (S II 78).[28] The *ariya sāvaka* also knows that with the cessation of ignorance there is the cessation of the other factors of dependent-origination and this is the cessation of the world (S II 78). The *bhikkhu* who understands, as it really is, the origin and passing away of the world is described as 'accomplished in view'.[29]

It is clear from these five *suttas* that the person who is accomplished in view understands in some detail dependent-origination. This is the view of those who enter the Buddhist path. This view is the realisation that 'all that is subject to arising is subject to cessation',[30] and it is the vision of this process that is described as the purification of view.

Purification of view (*diṭṭhi-visuddhi*)

The term 'purification' (*visuddhi*) is important in Buddhist thought in explaining certain factors of the path that should be cultivated. As noted, in the Nikāyas we find the statement that there is 'purification of virtue and purification of view'.[31] There is also 'purification of view and effort to attain it'.[32] A set of seven factors is found in the *Rathavinīta-sutta* (M I 145–51). These are 'purification of virtue' (*sīla-visuddhi*); 'purification of mind' (*citta-visuddhi*); 'purification of view' (*diṭṭhi-visuddhi*); 'purification by overcoming doubt' (*kaṅkhā-vitaraṇa-visuddhi*); 'purification by knowledge and vision of what is the path and what is not the path' (*maggāmagga-ñāṇa-dassana-visuddhi*); 'purification by knowledge and vision of the way' (*paṭipadā-ñāṇa-dassana-visuddhi*) and 'purification by knowledge and vision' (*ñāṇa-dassana-visuddhi*, M I 147). These seven factors are used to explain the means towards the goal of *nibbāna*. They are not the goal, but the goal cannot be attained without them (M I 148). These factors form the framework for the *Visuddhimagga*.

At D III 288 a set of nine factors are found. It is stated that 'nine factors are to be developed'.[33] These are the 'nine factors of the effort for perfect purification'.[34] The 'factor of effort for purification of wisdom' (*paññā-visuddhi*), and the 'factor of effort for purification of release' (*vimutti-visuddhi*) are added to the seven factors found in the *Rathavinīta-sutta*.[35] I think that these factors can be used as a summary of the unfolding of the path as it is described by the Nikāyas. By purifying the way one acts (*sīla-visuddhi*), one calms the mind (*citta-visuddhi*). With the mind calmed, a glimpse of the true nature of reality is realised (*diṭṭhi-visuddhi*), which causes the overcoming of doubt (*kaṅkhā-vitaraṇa-visuddhi*). One now knows what is and is not the path (*maggāmagga-ñāṇa-dassana-visuddhi*), has knowledge and vision of the way (*paṭipadā-ñāṇa-dassana-visuddhi*), and knowledge and vision are purified (*ñāṇa-dassana-visuddhi*). In the ninefold structure, wisdom is purified (*paññā-visuddhi*) and the context of that wisdom, the effort to achieve release, is purified (*vimutti-visuddhi*). What I find of interest in these factors is the way in which, as a whole, the seeing of the way things are, the cognitive side of the path, is taken together with the pragmatic character of the path, culminating in, on the one hand, purification of *paññā* and on the other, purification of *vimutti*. For this path structure to make sense, craving and ignorance require calm and insight to reach the goal of release from *dukkha*. Purification of view is realised in a state of calm and part of its function is to overcome doubt.

To clarify exactly what *diṭṭhi-visuddhi* sees, what the content of the view is, it is helpful to look at sources other than the *Sutta-piṭaka*. The *Paṭisambhidāmagga* explains purification of view as seeing: 'through its meaning of seeing, purification of view is to be directly known'.[36] As I have already explained in Chapter 2, the *Dhammasaṅgaṇi* holds that purification of view is the equivalent of *paññā*.[37] It also explains *diṭṭhi-visuddhi* as 'knowledge that *kamma* is one's own' (*kammassakatā-ñāṇa*),[38] 'knowledge in conformity with the truths' (*saccānulomika-ñāṇa*), 'the knowledge of one who holds the path' (*maggasamaṅgissa-ñāṇa*) and 'the knowledge of one who holds the fruit of the path' (*phalasamaṅgissa-ñāṇa*, Dhs 233 § 1366).

Buddhaghosa explains that 'seeing' (*dassana*) that is capable of reaching *nibbāna* is termed purification of view (*diṭṭhi-visuddhi*, As 54). Elsewhere he explains *diṭṭhi-visuddhi* as 'the correct seeing of name and form'.[39] It is stated that not positing a being or person onto the *khandhas*, as the assumption of 'I' or 'I am', is correct vision (*yathābhūta-dassana*, Vism XVIII 28). This is 'purification of view' (*diṭṭhi-visuddhi*). The role of *diṭṭhi-visuddhi* in the *Visuddhimagga* is to explain what name and form are, and then to become 'established on the plane of non-confusion by overcoming the apperception of being'.[40] It is then similar to two views, which we have met already, *vipassanā-sammā-diṭṭhi* and *magga-sammā-diṭṭhi*. The first investigates and examines, the second establishes that knowledge on the path. Buddhaghosa states that it is by 'seeing passing away and reappearance' (*cutūpapāta-dassana*) that 'purification of view is caused'.[41] By seeing in such a way, *diṭṭhi-visuddhi* serves to avoid the annihilationist-view (*uccheda-diṭṭhi*) and 'the view that a new being appears'.[42] The knowledge of the passing away and reappearance of beings (*sattānaṃ cutūpapātañāṇāya*) is the second knowledge gained by the Buddha. Buddhaghosa is, in fact, commenting on one such passage from the *Sāmaññaphala-sutta*.[43] In the second watch of the night on his attainment of *nibbāna* the Buddha is said to have gained knowledge of how beings pass away and reappear according to their actions (e.g. M I 22–3, 248). This entails seeing how beings fare according to their actions of body, speech and mind.

In a sense the picture that we get from examining the cultivation of views is one in which there is a gradual refinement of the processes seen by the view. The content of the view moves from a proposition to an insight. Purification of view is clearly a form of *paññā*, not a correction of wrong-view. As I have been suggesting, right-view is not the opposite of wrong-view, but a completely different order of seeing and it is passages suggestive of this that I would now like to consider.

Abandoning by substitution of opposites (*tadaṅgappahāna*)

I would like at this point to explain the function of right-view as part of the path by discussing briefly the process by which *sammā-diṭṭhi* dispels ignorance. There is a discussion in the *Visuddhimagga* of this process. It is termed 'abandoning by substitution of opposites' (*tadaṅgappahāna*),[44] and is described in the following terms:

> (1) The abandoning of the identity-view [is achieved] through the means of delimitation of name and form; (2) The abandoning of both *akiriya-diṭṭhi* and *ahetu-diṭṭhi* and of the stain of doubt through the means of discerning conditions; (3) The abandoning of apprehension of conglomeration as 'I' and 'mine' through the means of comprehension by groups; (4) The abandoning of perception of the path in what is not the path through the means of definition of what is the path and what is not the path; (5) The abandoning of *uccheda-diṭṭhi* through the means of seeing rise and fall; (6) The abandoning of the perception of non-terror in what is terror through the means of appearance as terror; (7) The abandoning of the perception of enjoyment through the means of seeing danger; (8) The abandoning of the perception of delight through the means of contemplation of dispassion; (9) The abandoning of lack of desire for deliverance through the means of desire for deliverance; (10) The abandoning of non-reflection through the means of reflection; (11) The abandoning of not looking on equably through the means of equanimity; (12) The abandoning of apprehension contrary to truth through the means of conformity.[45]

Certain views are clearly abandoned (*pahāna*) in this process, not replaced or corrected. The passage describes how certain views are abandoned: the view of self is abandoned by seeing name and form. This, as was noted, is the usual explanation of purification of view (*diṭṭhi-visuddhi*). The wrong-views of *akiriya* and *ahetu-diṭṭhi* are abandoned by 'discerning conditions'. The annihilationist-view (*uccheda-diṭṭhi*) is abandoned 'through the means of seeing rise and fall'.

The abandoning by substitution of opposites is also given with reference to the eighteen principal insights (*aṭṭhārasa mahāvipassanā*):

> (1) The abandoning of the perception of permanence [is achieved] through the means of the contemplation of impermanence; (2) of the perception of pleasure through the means of the contemplation of pain; (3) of the perception of self through the contemplation of not-self; (4)

> of delight through the contemplation of dispassion; (5) of greed through the means of contemplation of fading away; (6) of originating through the means of the contemplation of cessation; (7) of grasping through the means of the contemplation of relinquishment; (8) of perception of compactness through the means of contemplation of destruction; (9) of accumulation through the contemplation of fall; (10) of the perception of lastingness through the means of contemplation of change; (11) of sign through the contemplation of the signless; (12) of desire through the means of contemplation of the desireless; (13) of adhering through the means of the contemplation of emptiness; (14) of adhering due to grasping at a core through the means of insight into states that is higher understanding; (15) of adhering due to confusion through the means of correct knowledge and vision; (16) of adhering due to reliance [on volitional formations] through the means of the contemplation of danger; (17) of non-reflection through the means of the contemplation of reflection; (18) of adhering due to bondage through the means of contemplation of turning away.[46]

Here again certain right or wholesome insights (the content of the purification of view) that abandon wrong or unwholesome insights are found. The first of the 18 insights states straightforwardly that permanence is abandoned by seeing impermanence. We find the statement that 'the perception of self [is abandoned] through the contemplation of not-self'. I think that the proper understanding of this statement is gained if we take it along with the statement at (13) that 'adhering [is abandoned] through the means of the contemplation of emptiness'. This is clearly a reference to one of the 'three gateways to liberation' (*tīhi vimokkhamukhehī*; see Nett 123), namely the emptiness gateway to liberation (*suññatā vimokkhamukhaṃ*).[47] The view of self in whatever form is a form of grasping and adherence. So, the 'contemplation of not-self' is to have an insight into the cessation of craving. It is the realisation and understanding of craving. The achievement of right-view is to behave in a way that reflects this knowledge. Just as 'adhering' is abandoned through the 'contemplation of emptiness', so the 'perception of self' is abandoned through the 'contemplation of not-self'. This is not a case of one view being abandoned and another adopted, but is an example of the transcendence of all views. In Chapter 3 I discussed such explanations of wrong-view from the *Diṭṭhi-kathā* of the *Paṭisambhidāmagga* that described views as 'clinging by adherence' (*abhinivesa-parāmāsa*, Paṭis I 135). The term *diṭṭhi-visuddhi* means the opposite of clinging and adherence. Purification of view is non-clinging and non-adherence. As the final insight states, 'adhering due to bondage [is abandoned] through the means of the contemplation of turning away'. Buddhaghosa explains that as a drop of water falls from a lotus leaf, so the mind retreats from volitional formations (Vism XXII 121). With the achievement of right-view, the mind retreats from all views.

Right-view as knowledge of knowing rise and fall (*udayabbaya*)

The passage to which I now turn brings together and summarises many of the ideas I have examined in the first half of this book. The *Nettippakaraṇa* (Nett 85) discusses a passage found in the *Udāna* (Ud 38). The passage describes how 'one travels on in Māra's power when one has an unguarded mind that is encumbered by *micchā-diṭṭhi*, and oppressed by lethargy and drowsiness'.[48] The *Nettippakaraṇa* comments that one is called encumbered by *micchā-diṭṭhi* when one sees permanence in the impermanent and this is called a perversion.[49] This view causes perversion in the 'four grounds of self-hood' (*catusu-attabhāva-vatthūsu*), by seeing according to the 20 views of *sakkāya-diṭṭhi*.

The parallel verse at *Udāna* 38 explains simply that '*sammā-diṭṭhi* comes first through knowing rise and fall' (*udayabbaya*).[50] Elsewhere, it is said that giving right-view first place is the footing for insight,[51] and knowing rise and fall is the footing for the plane of seeing,[52] presumably the path of stream-attainment.[53] This right-view is also said to be insight, and knowing rise and fall to be the diagnosis of suffering.[54] This knowledge is explained as 'the weapon of wisdom, the sword of wisdom, the jewel of wisdom, the illumination of wisdom, the goad of wisdom, and the palace of wisdom'.[55] This is then described as:

> knowledge about suffering, its arising, cessation, and the way leading to its cessation, knowledge about the way, knowledge about the path, knowledge about a cause, knowledge about causally-arisen *dhammas*, knowledge about a condition, knowledge about conditionally arisen *dhammas*.[56]

Knowing rise and fall is then explained in the following terms: 'knowing rise is to know that with ignorance as condition, there are volitional formations, etc. by knowing fall one knows that with the cessation of ignorance there is the cessation of volitional formations.'[57] Essentially, purification of view is the seeing of the rise and fall of all *dhammas*. To know the rise and fall of *dhammas* constitutes progress upon the Buddhist path.

PART TWO: THE FUNCTION OF RIGHT-VIEW ON THE HIGHER PATHS

In the second half of this chapter I would like to consider the nature and function of this view that knows, essentially, the rise and fall of *dhammas*. I have suggested that one accomplished in view (*diṭṭhi-sampanna*) is a stream-attainer who has view of the path (*magga-diṭṭhi*) and sees dependent-origination. This insight is developed into purification of view (*diṭṭhi-visuddhi*), by affecting action and being affected by action. The *Kosambī-sutta* (S II 115–18)[58] addresses issues arising from this understanding which I will explore in greater detail along with Buddhaghosa's understanding of it. This is the function and role of right-view on the higher paths. If right-view has abandoned wrong-view, what function does right-view have after stream-attainment? If the holder of right-view has knowledge of the four truths and dependent-origination, is not the notion of right-view somewhat redundant after knowledge of these processes has been realised? The answers to these questions are important to this book. The function of right-view on the higher paths suggests important characteristics about the notion of *diṭṭhi* in general. It is not simply a knowledge gained, but an insight into the nature of the world which continues to have an effect on actions of body, speech and mind after the realisation of stream-attainment.

In this *sutta* we find Saviṭṭha asking Musīla if 'apart from faith, approval, oral tradition, reasoned cogitation, or acceptance of a view as a result of reflection, he has personal knowledge that with birth as condition, ageing and death come to be'.[59] Musīla replies that 'he knows and sees this, with birth as condition, ageing and death come to be'.[60] In a similar fashion Saviṭṭha asks Musīla if, apart from the five factors, he has personal knowledge that 'with existence as condition, birth comes to be', 'with attachment as condition, there is existence', 'with craving as condition, there is attachment', 'with feeling as condition, there is craving', 'with contact as condition, there is feeling', 'with the six senses as condition, there is contact', 'with name and form as condition, there are the six senses', 'with consciousness as condition, there is name and form', 'with volitional formations as condition, there is consciousness', and 'with ignorance as condition, there are the volitional formations'.

To all these questions Musīla answers that he knows and sees these things. Saviṭṭha then asks Musīla if he knows that 'with the cessation of birth comes the cessation of ageing and death', 'with the cessation of existence there is the cessation of birth' and so on through the cessation of the remaining factors.[61] Again Musīla replies that he knows and sees the cessation of all these factors. Saviṭṭha then asks Musīla one final question. Apart from the five factors, the five means of knowledge, does Musīla have personal knowledge that *nibbāna* is the cessation of existence?[62] Musīla replies that 'he knows and sees this, *nibbāna* is the cessation of existence'.[63] The *Sāratthappakāsinī* interprets this statement as meaning that the cessation of the five *khandhas* is *nibbāna*.[64] Saviṭṭha then declares that 'Musīla is an Arahant whose *āsavas* are destroyed'.[65] Musīla does not answer and remains silent. The *Sāratthappakāsinī* interprets Musīla's silence as signifying that he is a *khīṇāsava*, an Arahant.[66]

At this point Nārada, who is also present, asks Saviṭṭha to question him in the same way. The same questions are asked and the same replies given. This concludes with Saviṭṭha declaring, as he had done to Musīla, that 'Nārada is an Arahant whose *āsavas* are destroyed'.[67] Nārada however does not remain silent. He declares that 'though he has seen as it really is with correct wisdom that *nibbāna* is the cessation of existence, he is not an Arahant whose *āsavas* are destroyed'.[68]

In the *Kosambī-sutta* we have an example of the difference between *sammā-diṭṭhi* and its cultivation into liberating *paññā*. This reflects, in part, the difference between being 'accomplished in view' and having 'purification of view'. Both

Musīla and Nārada have knowledge of the same process, of the arising and cessation of *dukkha*, in the form of an understanding of dependent-origination. At some point the 'knowledge of the *dhamma*' (*dhamma-ñāṇa*) is transformed into liberation. Musīla is an Arahant, Nārada is not, though they have knowledge of the same thing. They both have an understanding of dependent-origination. How can the knowledge that '*nibbāna* is the cessation of existence', which encapsulates the teaching of dependent-origination, be transformed into liberating *paññā*? In the *sutta* Nārada explains his statement that he has seen with correct wisdom that '*nibbāna* is the cessation of existence' though 'he is not an Arahant whose *āsavas* are destroyed' by way of an analogy. Suppose, along a desert road, there is a well, but there is neither a rope nor bucket. A person, thirsty and tired, could look into the well, see the water, and have knowledge that 'there is water', but not be able to touch it physically.[69] In the same way Nārada has seen, as it really is, that '*nibbāna* is the cessation of existence', but he is not an Arahant with *āsavas* destroyed.

This is reminiscent of the *Khemaka-sutta* of the *Khandha-saṃyutta* (SIII 126–32). In that *sutta* Khemaka has the knowledge that 'in the *ūpādānakkhandhas*, I do not regard anything as self or belonging to self'.[70] However, Khemaka is not an Arahant because the conceit 'I am' has not vanished in relation to the *khandhas* subject to attachment,[71] even though he does not regard the *khandhas* subject to attachment as, 'this, I am'.[72] Khemaka still has 'the residual conceit "I am", a desire "I am", an underlying tendency "I am"'.[73] In order to rid the mind of these conceits, the *bhikkhu* 'dwells contemplating the rise and fall of the five *khandhas* subject to attachment'.[74] Contemplating in this way, contemplating the rise and fall of the *khandhas*, the conceit, desire and the underlying tendency 'I am' are abandoned.[75] Khemaka sees things with right-view, he sees the rise and fall of things. It may be instructive to note that, in developed Abhidhamma, conceit and view cannot occur in the same type of consciousness. This suggests that they are either completely incompatible, or that the two terms refer to the same processes. If the latter option is true, as I think it is, then we may imagine that right-view, as the contemplation of rise and fall, continues the process of cleansing body, speech and (primarily) mind, in the higher stages of the path. Wrong-view, on the higher stages of the path, is a subtle conceit of selfhood. Right-view is a contemplation which rids the mind of this conceit. I will produce some evidence from Buddhaghosa on this subject later in this chapter that suggests how the developed Theravāda tradition understood the gaining of knowledge in such a way. Both the *Kosambī-sutta* and the *Khemaka-sutta* suggest a similar role for *sammā-diṭṭhi* on the higher paths.

The *Kosambī-sutta* clearly explains that the content of *sammā-diṭṭhi* is dependent-origination, that there can be an initial knowledge of this process, and that it is possible to cultivate and enhance this knowledge. This is the operation of right-view, which first understands dependent-origination (rise and fall), and is a vision of the path, the way to the cessation of all *dukkha*.

The view that is noble and emancipating *(diṭṭhi ariyā niyyānikā)*

How does this attitude free from craving and attachment differ from that of holding no-views? How does the person who has achieved right-view act? As I said in the Introduction, the no-views understanding is thought to be most prominent in the *Aṭṭhakavagga*. But I would suggest that the *Aṭṭhakavagga* does not teach the giving up of *all* views, but the giving up of all attachment to views, and that this is the same as the description of views found in the four primary Nikāyas. The Nikāyas, I am arguing, teach that the follower of the Buddha should neither adopt right-view in opposition to wrong-view, nor abandon all views, but that the very realisation of right-view signifies the transcendence of all views. In other words, I would suggest that the attitude free from craving and attachment is right-view. I would like to consider one specific context from the Nikāyas in which such an understanding is suggested, which describes how the person who has achieved right-view acts, before returning to how these pure views are cultivated and what role they have on the higher stages of the Buddhist path.

There is a type of *sammā-diṭṭhi* found a number of times in the Nikāyas. This view is termed 'the view that is noble and emancipating' (*diṭṭhi ariyā niyyānikā*). The *Papañcasūdanī* explains this view as 'a right-view connected with the way' (*magga-sampayuttā sammā-diṭṭhi*) or 'right-view of the stage of *sotāpatti magga*' (*sotāpatti-magga-diṭṭhi*, Ps I 401).

The *suttas* describe other things as 'noble and emancipating'. In the *Mahāsīhanāda-sutta (*M I 68–83) at M I 81 a type of wisdom is described as noble and emancipating that leads one who practises it to the complete destruction of suffering.[76] In the *Mahāsuññata-sutta* (M III 109–18) at M III 114 thoughts of renunciation, non-ill will and non-cruelty[77] are described as 'noble and emancipating and lead one who practises in accordance with them to the complete destruction of suffering'.[78] At S V 82 the 'seven limbs of wisdom', if cultivated, are described in similar terms.[79] At S V 166, the 'four foundations of mindfulness', and at S V 255 the 'four bases of psychic power' are described in a similar fashion.[80] In the *Dvayatānupassanā-sutta* (Sn 724–65) of the *Sutta-nipāta*, the *dhamma* is described as wholesome, noble, emancipating and leading to full enlightenment.[81]

I would like to concentrate on the *Kosambiya-sutta* (M I 320–5),[82] which is important in describing the nature of the right-view of the path. I have already considered in some detail the content of various views. In outlining the views found in the *Sammādiṭṭhi-sutta* I explained that these views are classified elsewhere in the Nikāyas as the right-view which is noble (*sammā-diṭṭhi ariyā*), corruptionless (*anāsavā*), supramundane (*lokuttarā*), and a factor of the path (*maggaṅgā*). It is the function of such a view which I would now like to explore.

The *sutta* finds the Buddha informing a group of *bhikkhus* that there are 'six memorable qualities that create love and respect and conduce to helpfulness, to non-dispute, to concord and to unity'.[83] The first three are to maintain bodily, verbal and mental acts of loving-kindness towards one's fellow companions in the holy life.[84] The fourth is to share any gain (*labhā*) of a kind that accords with the *dhamma*, for example, the contents of one's alms bowl. The fifth is to dwell in those virtues (*silā*) in common with one's companions in the holy life (*sīla-samaññāgato*) that, among other things, are conducive to concentration (*samādhi*, M I 322). For the sixth quality it is said that:

> A *bhikkhu* dwells both in public and in private possessing in common with his companions in the holy life that view that is noble and emancipating, and leads one who practises in accordance with it to the complete destruction of suffering.[85]

The highest of the six, the *sutta* continues, is the view that is noble and emancipating (*diṭṭhi ariyā niyyānikā*, M I 322–3). The remainder of the *sutta* explains exactly how this view leads to the complete destruction of suffering. The explanation takes the form of detailing seven knowledges (*ñāṇa*) that are noble and supramundane (*ariya*, *lokuttara*, M I 323), and which the holder of the view attains.

The first of the six is the knowledge of there being no obsession (*pariyuṭṭha*, M I 323) that will so obsess the mind (*pariyuṭṭhita-citto*), that it will 'stop the view-holder from knowing or seeing things as they are'.[86] Eight things are then given that may obsess the mind and stop the *bhikkhu* from knowing and seeing things as they are: to be obsessed by sensual lust, ill-will, sloth and torpor, restlessness and remorse, doubt, speculation about this world or the other world, or quarrels and disputes. With his mind obsessed he will not know and see things as they are. With the mind calm it can be awakened to the truths.[87]

The second knowledge is the understanding that the development and cultivation of the noble-view conduces to stillness and serenity.[88] Right-view is the embodiment of serenity. The third knowledge is to understand that this view is unique to the Buddha's followers and that no other recluses or brahmins possess such a view.[89] The fourth knowledge entails confessing to a teacher or fellow *bhikkhus* any offence that may have been committed. When he realises that he would do so, and confesses any offence, he understands that he has the character of one who is 'accomplished in view'.[90] The fifth knowledge is of a similar nature, this time, however, the explanation of the one who possesses the *diṭṭhi ariyā niyyānikā* is that, though engaged in matters of the monastic community, the holder of the view is also engaged in training in 'higher virtue, higher mind, higher wisdom',[91] and he understands that he has the character of one accomplished in view. The sixth knowledge is possessing the strength of a holder of right-view. This is to engage and to listen attentively to the *dhamma* when the *Tathāgata* is teaching it. When he understands in this way he knows he has the strength of a person who is accomplished in view.[92] The seventh knowledge is to gain inspiration and gladness when the *dhamma* is being taught. When he understands in this way he again knows that he has the strength of one who is accomplished in view.[93] The *sutta* concludes by saying that, 'with the possession of these seven factors, the view-holder possesses the fruit of stream-attainment'.[94]

All this reveals something definite about right-view: that there is nothing incongruous about the achievement of this view and the, so-called, practising of no-views found in the *Aṭṭhakavagga*. As I have explained, the achievement of right-view entails an insight into the rise and fall of things, and in order to achieve this insight, action and thought are reciprocal. Right-view cannot be achieved without acting in accordance with it. Put another way, right-view is a statement of fact and value: apprehending things in a certain way is transformative. When we are aware of the nature of right-view, then a text such as the *Aṭṭhakavagga* may be understood as describing the same thing as other passages in the Nikāyas: do not be attached to any view. The *Kosambiya-sutta* explains the gaining of knowledge in the setting of calm and serenity, away from disputes, and seems to suggest that this is somehow essential for seeing things as they are.

The function of right-view on the higher paths in the *Atthasālinī*

I would now like to move on to how the developed Buddhist tradition understood the function of right-view. I have already suggested that in the Nikāyas there was some debate as to the cultivation of knowledge between the stage of stream-attainment and the realisation of the Arahant. At stream-attainment dependent-origination is seen. This does not constitute Arahantship. To be accomplished in view is, in a sense, to be free from views. The *ariya-sāvaka* has seen arising and cessation, but this 'noble view' can be cultivated into a salvific contemplation of the rise and fall of all *dhammas*.

Buddhaghosa has addressed the role and function of right-view on the three higher paths. Buddhaghosa explains that at stream-attainment, one sees the four truths and these are also seen on the three higher paths. So the three higher paths do not see anything different than has been seen by the first path.[95] For the Theravādins, in the three higher paths, one puts away the 'defilements' (*kilesa*) not yet put away, but the truths seen remain the same.[96] If, at stream-attainment, right-view, by seeing the four truths, abandons wrong-view, and if nothing new is seen on the three higher paths, is then right-view redundant after stream-attainment?

Buddhaghosa argues that *sammā-diṭṭhi* does have a function in the three higher paths. (As 240). He first argues that right-view is not merely a name without a function after stream-attainment. He explains that there is a certain 'conceit' (*māna*) to be abandoned by the three higher paths,[97] that this conceit is 'based in view'[98] and 'right-view abandons that conceit'.[99] This recalls the *Khemaka-sutta* (S III 126–32) which I cited above, and which Buddhaghosa may have in mind. Buddhaghosa argues that, just as, at the point of stream-attainment, right-view abandons wrong-view so, in the three higher paths, right-view abandons conceit. He appears to understand *micchā-diṭṭhi* itself as a type of conceit, a form of attachment. As I have said, conceit is perhaps the equivalent of view on the higher paths. Buddhaghosa's arguments are clear if we understand *micchā-diṭṭhi* as wrong primarily because it is a form of attachment. Right-view, being a different order of seeing, can still have a function if it is understood as a detached way of seeing. In this way *sammā-diṭṭhi* has a clear function on the three higher paths by abandoning other types of conceit.

It must also be remembered that supramundane right-view (*lokuttara-sammā-diṭṭhi*) is considered to be a type of wisdom. The *Sammohavinodanī* states that each path factor has three functions. For *sammā-diṭṭhi* these are described as: first, the abandoning of *micchā-diṭṭhi* and any other defilements associated with wrong-view;[100] second, right-view makes cessation its object; third, it sees associated states as 'non-delusion by destroying the delusion that conceals them' (Vibh-a 114). The *Sammohavinodanī* goes on to explain that right-view 'as to function [...] has four names beginning with "knowledge regarding suffering (*dukkhe ñāṇa*)"' and this is the taking of the four truths as a meditation subject (Vibh-a 116). Finally, it is explained that 'in the supramundane path, it is the eye of understanding in the noble one who proceeds by penetration of the four truths, that has *nibbāna* as its object and destroys the inherent tendency to *avijjā*, which is *sammā-diṭṭhi*.' (Vibh-a 121). This is how *sammā-diṭṭhi* is understood in the developed tradition.

The question of the role of *sammā-diṭṭhi* in the three higher paths has been raised in modern scholarship by Padmanabh S. Jaini. He argues that the Vaibhāṣika system breaks down cognition into inaccurate, accurate and free of judgement, i.e. beyond all views. The Theravādins, however, only understand cognition as inaccurate and accurate.[101] In other words, the highest *paññā* for the Vaibhāṣika is free from all views, but for the Theravādins it is not. Jaini argues that the degree of understanding gained does not differ between stream-attainment and Arahantship for the Theravādins, but the distinction between the two stages of the path is one of 'defilements overcome'.[102] Clearly, if Jaini's characterisation of the Theravāda is correct, then important aspects of my book would need re-assessing. However, I do not think that he does justice to the Theravāda.

Jaini suggests that '[T]he Theravādins offered a rather unconvincing explanation [...] thereby giving *samyakdṛṣṭi* "something to do" on the path from stream-attainment to arahat.'[103] Though he is clearly aware that, for the Theravādins, all (wrong-)views are destroyed by the path of stream-attainment,[104] and that *sammā-diṭṭhi* is equated with *paññā*,[105] he does not draw the conclusion that *sammā-diṭṭhi* is a type of wisdom devoid of all attachment (*anupādāna*). If this conclusion is made then we no longer need to place the term 'wrong' in brackets, i.e. when stating that all (wrong-)views are destroyed by the path of stream-attainment. By definition, all views are destroyed by stream-attainment. Buddhaghosa has explained that there is still a certain conceit to be abandoned by right-view in the three higher paths. In the developed Abhidhamma, as I have already indicated, *diṭṭhi* and *māna* are mutually exclusive. This suggests that right-view has 'something to do' and that conceit, being the equivalent of view in the higher paths, is the natural target of right-view in the higher paths. Second, *sammā-diṭṭhi* is perhaps the equivalent to the Vaibhāṣika notion of a type of *prajñā* devoid of all judgement (*santīrikaprajñā*).[106] To say that one is not attached to an act of cognition is to say, I think, that one makes no judgements concerning that act of cognition. Right-view for the Theravādins is knowledge of rise and fall (*sammā-diṭṭhi-purekkhāro ñatvāna udayabbayaṃ*, Nett 47). This is not a *diṭṭhi* at all. 'Supramundane right-view' (*lokuttara-sammā-diṭṭhi*) cannot be a view, whether wrong or right. I am, of course, explaining terms here in a certain way. I am attempting to describe these terms in order to clarify what I think the Theravāda tradition suggests about the gaining of knowledge on the higher paths. I am doing this in order to counter Jaini's tendency to explain the Theravāda tradition in terms of Vaibhāṣika categories. For example, he notes that the Theravāda Abhidhamma was primarily concerned with wrong-view.[107] Having noted this, he then states that for the Theravāda tradition '*samyakdṛṣṭi* [...] seems to be understood as the absence of *inaccurate* views but not *all* views'.[108] This, as I have suggested, is somewhat misleading. The 'view that is noble and emancipating' is one which 'conduces to stillness and serenity' (M I 323). That the Theravāda Abhidhamma was primarily concerned with wrong-views suggests that they were interested in explaining all cognitive attachments. They were interested in cultivating an awareness free from all attachment (to views). To state, as Jaini does, that the Vaibāṣikas 'have gone beyond the simple Theravādin breakdown of cognition into "inaccurate" and "accurate modes"',[109] whereas the Vaibāṣikas classified '*all* views based on decision-making, regardless of their accuracy, as *dṛṣṭi* or *kuprajñā*' [wrong insight],[110] is, again, somewhat misleading. Jaini is suggesting that any view based on decision-making is a 'false view'. Or, to be exact, he claims that the Vaibhāṣika position is that there are two types of view based on 'discriminating', these being wrong *and* right-view. He then uses these categories to understand the Theravāda Abhidhamma. But the Theravāda Abhidhamma does not understand views in this way. Jaini thinks that it proposes something similar to an opposition understanding of views, while the Vaibāṣika's propose a no-views understanding. As I have made clear, I do not agree with either understanding. I am suggesting that a view based on decision-making (Vaibāṣika) and one based on attachment (Theravāda) amounts to the same thing. To choose between acts of cognition, to have doubt about the nature of the *khandhas*, amounts to different ways of stating the same thing. To suggest that *sammā-diṭṭhi* somehow 'corrects' *micchā-diṭṭhi* is disingenuous. As I hope to have shown, in Theravāda Buddhism *sammā-diṭṭhi* is not a proposition. It is that aspect of *paññā* that realises non-attachment from all cognitive acts.

Difficulties arise if the attainment of *sammā-diṭṭhi* and the abandoning of *micchā-diṭṭhi* is understood as the replacement of an incorrect doctrine with a correct doctrine, as Jaini claims the Theravāda system does. If this is how the early Buddhist tradition understood the unfolding of the path, then *sammā-diṭṭhi* would be redundant after stream-attainment. It has seen the four truths and dependent-origination, and this is all there is to see. But if the aim of *sammā-diṭṭhi* is to overcome a type of conceit, then it can go on functioning at other stages of the path.

The abandoning of views

Another way of understanding the function of right-view is to consider how it abandons various unwholesome mental states. Buddhaghosa explains that the path of stream-attainment abandons five unwholesome types of consciousness (*akusala-cittas*): four connected with view (*diṭṭhi-sampayutta*), and one connected with doubt (*vicikicchā-sampayutta*).[111] This leaves seven unwholesome types of consciousness to be abandoned. All seven of these are rooted in delusion.[112] The abandonment of *micchā-diṭṭhi* is the abandonment of attachment to all views. This is stated in the *Dhammasaṅgaṇi* in the following terms:

> The four arisings of consciousness associated with views, the arising of consciousness accompanied by doubt, these are the *dhammas* abandoned by seeing.[113]

The analysis of the abandoning of various defilements stated in these terms goes back to the Nikāyas. The Nikāyas hold that the path of stream-attainment abandons the first three fetters (*saṃyojana*), those of 'identity-view' (*sakkāya-diṭṭhi*), 'doubt' (*vicikicchā*) and 'clinging to precepts and vows' (*sīlabbata-parāmāsa*).[114] The once-returner abandons the first three and further weakens greed, hatred and delusion. The non-returner abandons the first, or lower, five. The Arahant abandons all ten.[115] In the *Sabbāsava-sutta* it is stated that by 'appropriate bringing to mind' (*yoniso manasikāra*) of the four truths, three fetters are abandoned in him, '*sakkāya-diṭṭhi*, doubt, and clinging to precepts and vows' (M I 9).

The later tradition, working with this model, analysed the abandonment of the defilements in different ways. In the *Dhammasaṅgaṇi*, the path of stream-attainment is said to be for the sake of abandoning views (*diṭṭhigatānaṃ pahānāya*); the path of once-return for the sake of weakening sensual desire and aversion (*kāmarāga-vyāpādānaṃ patanūbhāvāya*); the path of non-return for the sake of abandoning without remainder any sensual desire and aversion (*kāmarāga-vyāpādānaṃ anavasesa-ppahānāya*); and the path of Arahantship for the sake of abandoning without remainder any desire for the form and formless spheres, conceit, restlessness and ignorance (*rūparāga-rūparāga-māna-uddhacca-avijjāya anavasesa-ppahānāya*).[116]

One final consideration of the abandonment of defilements and the cultivation of right-view is found in the *Dhammasaṅgaṇi*. In this passage the question is asked: 'what are the *dhammas* that are to be put away by seeing?' The answer given is that it is 'the three fetters of *sakkāya-diṭṭhi*, doubt and clinging to precepts and vows'.[117] It is also stated that the causes of these three fetters are to be put away by seeing.[118] Certain other *dhammas* are to be put away by mental culture, by meditation (*bhāvanā*). This is whatever 'greed, hatred and delusion remain, any defilements, and the four *khandhas*[119] associated with them, and actions of body, speech and mind that come from them'.[120] The causes of these are also to be put away by meditation (Dhs 183 § 1011). Certain hindrances are then eradicated by *dassana* and *bhāvanā*. However, the analysis of the early Abhidhamma was aimed towards an analysis of the eradication of all *akusala dhammas*. To this end a final question is asked: 'which are the *dhammas* that are to be put away by neither *dassana* or *bhāvanā*?'[121] The answer is:

> It is those *kusala* and indeterminate *dhammas*, relating to the worlds of sense, form and the formless, or to the unincluded (*apariyāpannā*), the four *khandhas*, all form, and the uncompounded element.[122]

This is, so to speak, the arena in which right-view is active. The point is that, having abandoned wrong-view, right-view functions as *paññā*, the essential nature of *paññā* being that it sees without attachment. If we look at Buddhaghosa's comments on the first *Dhammasaṅgaṇi* passage cited above we discover what he considers 'for the sake of abandoning views' to imply. He states that the 62 views are abandoned by the path of stream-attainment. He then states that 'going to view' (*diṭṭhi-gatāni*) is also abandoned. These are *dhammas* that are 'similar in course to view' (*diṭṭhi-sadisa-gamanānī*). These are *sakkāya-diṭṭhi*, doubt, and clinging to precepts and vows (*sakkāya-diṭṭhi*, *vicikicchā*, *sīlabbata-parāmāsa*) and the unwholesome *dhammas* of greed, hatred and delusion (*rāga-dosa-mohā-kusalāni*) together with associated *dhammas*. All these are things that tend towards views (*diṭṭhi-gatāni*) and it is these *dhammas* that are abandoned by *sammā-diṭṭhi*. So, when the texts explain that *sammā-diṭṭhi* abandons *micchā-diṭṭhi* it means that right-view abandons all these *dhammas*. If we take views in the purely propositional sense, it is difficult to see how right-view accomplishes this. However, when the texts state that right-view abandons wrong-view and adds that right-view abandons the 62 views we must remember that the tradition itself is clearly aware of the shorthand it is using in this statement. An accurate cognitive process does not simply replace an inaccurate cognitive process. Jaini's argument that the Theravādins only broke down the cognitive process into inaccurate and accurate (whereas the Vaibāṣikas distinguish between inaccurate, accurate and free of all judgement), does not appear to do the Theravāda tradition justice.[123] There appears to me to be a more subtle dynamic at work within the early Theravāda texts.

A final point I wish to make is that if we understand what the texts are stating when they say that right-view abandons wrong-view, we may understand how right-view is said to function and have a role after stream-attainment. I have stated a number of times that I do not consider right-view to be propositional.[124] I do not deny that it does have a cognitive function, but that to understand the notion of *sammā-diṭṭhi* we must equally bear in mind its affective function. One way of putting this is to say that *sammā-diṭṭhi* is the non-clinging, detached aspect of *paññā*. Wrong-view is always 'rooted in greed' (*lobha-mūla*) in the Abhidhamma. A significant aspect of the right-view of the path is that it is not rooted in greed and attachment. A simple way of understanding this would be to say that *sammā-diṭṭhi* is that aspect of *paññā* that is free from attachment. Understanding may be enhanced,[125] and that aspect of the path that keeps the cognitive process detached, *sammā-diṭṭhi*, has a function. Rupert Gethin has made the following related points:

> In the Theravāda understanding the tendency to fixed opinion can only exist prior to stream-attainment. In stream-attainment, since the wisdom of stream-attainment is characterised as *sammā-diṭṭhi*, a form of *paññā* that precisely turns away from the inclination to hold fixed opinions; once the four truths have been directly seen, the mind has no inclination to either eternalism or annihilationism, the mind has no tendency to misinterpret Buddhist theory in terms of either annihilationism or eternalism.[126]

This way of understanding the texts gives us a reason for there being both *avijjā* and *micchā-diṭṭhi*, and *paññā* and *sammā-diṭṭhi*. I think that to separate the cognitive and affective natures of *paññā* and *avijjā*, to make the 'is', 'ought' distinction, may do certain aspects of early Buddhist thought a disservice. The texts appear to be claiming that the attached aspect of knowing is unwholesome, and the detached nature of knowing is wholesome. More than this, to know things as they are is somehow impossible if there is any greed and attachment for that knowledge.

To reach the higher stages of the path, calm and insight must work together. We know that the early Theravāda tradition held calm and insight to be essential for the consummation of the Buddhist path. In a sense, *sammā-diṭṭhi* holds these ideas in symmetry. We know that *sammā-diṭṭhi*, in the early Theravāda texts, is explained as a type of *paññā*, and that the Buddhist tradition is conscious of the fact that even what is correct Buddhist doctrine can be held in such a way as to make it wrong-view, then we may become aware that the right-view that abandons wrong-view is not simply accomplished by one proposition replacing another. The content of the view, what it proposes, and the way the view is held, are both related to the view being classified as wrong or right.[127] The role of *sammā-diṭṭhi* puts emphasis on the freedom from mental rigidity that stream-attainment accomplishes. A certain mental attitude is achieved in which the mind's tendency to grasp is eradicated. A new mental attitude is gained towards objects of cognition. Right-view, as it functions on the path, is perhaps a different approach or behaviour towards cognitive experience, towards even 'correct' Buddhist doctrines. It is the view that shapes experience.

Is then right-view, in fact, a view at all? It is this question that I shall consider in the final two chapters of this book. I have already discussed how the *Paṭisambhidāmagga* explains wrong-view in Chapter 3. It will be remembered that it explains views by answering six questions. The first five of these relate to wrong-views and I would now like to consider the final question which describes the function of right-view. The *Paṭisambhidāmagga* asks the question: 'What is the abolition of all bases for views?' (*katamo diṭṭhi-ṭṭhāna-samugghāto ti*, Ps I 135). The answer is that the path of stream-attainment is the abolition of all bases for views. In a verse cited explaining this, it is stated that rationalists (*takki*) make the views of being and non-being (*vibhava-diṭṭhi* and *bhava-diṭṭhi*) their foundation (*nissitāse*). They have no knowledge of cessation,[128] causing the world to have wrong perception (*loko viparītasaññī*, Ps I 159). The foundations of wrong-view, being and non-being, are removed by the correct apperception of cessation. Throughout the discussion of the function of *sammā-diṭṭhi* earlier in this chapter it was this idea, the seeing of the rise and fall of phenomena, of *dhammas*, that was shown to constitute right-view. The *Paṭisambhidāmagga* then explains how the *bhikkhu* aims to overcome the hindrances of being and non-being. It is stated simply that the *bhikkhu* sees what is as what is (*bhūtaṃ bhūtato passati*), presumably dependent-origination, or simply *dukkha*. Having seen this, the *bhikkhu* will have entered on the way to dispassion, to the fading away and greed for it, to its cessation.[129] It is the seeing of this, of things as they are, and the cessation of craving for it, that constitutes the way to the overcoming of all *micchā-diṭṭhi* (Ps I 159). As I have said, in seeing things as they are, I think things really are seen in their true nature, and apprehending things in this way is transformative. The terms used by the text to describe these wrong and right perceptions of reality are the 'unaccomplished' or 'imperfect view' (*vipanna-diṭṭhi*) and the 'accomplished' or 'perfect view' (*sampanna-diṭṭhi*). The three non-accomplished or imperfect views are: 'This is mine', 'this I am', 'this is my self'. The three accomplished or perfect views are: 'This is not mine', 'this I am not', 'this is not my self' (Ps I 160). Right-view functions as a form of non-attachment.

5

THE TRANSCENDENCE OF VIEWS

In this penultimate chapter I would like to consider what I think is the proper understanding of the notion of *diṭṭhi* in the Pāli canon. Stated briefly this is the following: it is usually thought that there are two tendencies in the Nikāyas. The first proposes right-view in opposition to wrong-views, the second rejects all views, wrong or right, as all views are potential causes of craving and attachment. I do not think either of these offers the correct understanding of *diṭṭhi* in the Nikāyas and early Abhidhamma. My previous arguments have suggested that the Pāli canon is interested in how views affect actions and how actions affect views. Wrong-views, indeed all views, can cause craving and attachment, but the Pāli canon does propose a right-view. However, this view is not essentially a correction of wrong-views, but a different order of seeing, one that is free from craving and attachment. In this chapter I would like to look at various passages from the Nikāyas and Abhidhamma which suggest what this different order of seeing is.

The *Brahmajāla-sutta*: attachment to views

I would like to begin with one of the most extensive treatments of the notion of *diṭṭhi* found in the Nikāyas, the *Brahmajāla-sutta*. Far from being an anomaly in the early Buddhist understanding of views, the *Brahmajāla-sutta* sets out the proper understanding of the nature of all views.

The *Brahmajāla-sutta*'s importance for the Buddhist tradition is suggested by its place as the first *sutta* in the first collection of discourses, the *Sutta-piṭaka* of the *Dīgha-nikāya*.[1] Buddhaghosa holds that the classification of the diversity of creeds (*samayantara*) is one of four occasions when the greatness of the Buddhas' knowledge becomes manifest, their teachings deep, stamped with the three characteristics of emptiness. The four are: the promulgation of the discipline (*vinaya-paññatti*), the classification of the diversity of planes (*bhūmantara*, i.e. analysis of the *Abhidhamma*), the exposition of conditionality (*paccayākāra*, i.e. analysis of dependent-origination), and the classification of the diversity of creeds. It is said of the classification of the diversity of creeds that it is the analysis, disentangling, and unravelling of the 62 speculative views.[2]

The *Brahmajāla-sutta* has attracted much attention.[3] The reason for the attention is twofold. First, in the exposition of the 62 views, we can discover something of the religious practices and systems of philosophy contemporaneous with the early Buddhist community.[4] Second, the *Brahmajāla-sutta* is seen by some to be a reflection of the no-views understanding of some parts of the Nikāyas.[5] It is the latter which I would like to focus upon in the following discussion.

Steven Collins has suggested that the '*locus classicus*' for the tendency to explain any view as wrong if it is held with attachment is the *Brahmajāla-sutta*.[6] As he suggests, it is not the conceptual content of the 62 views which makes them inferior to the Buddha's teaching, but the fact that they are conditioned. Though Collins describes the *Brahmajāla-sutta* as part of the no-views understanding of views, an understanding that I do not agree with, I think he is making an important point in explaining *all* views as wrong-views: right-view is the transcendence of views. I have suggested that views, explained as 'volitional formations' (*saṃkhāra*), or 'feelings' (*vedanā*), are subject to craving and attachment and, as such, are part of the process of dependent-origination and lead to *dukkha*. Though it is not explicitly stated in the Nikāyas, I would suggest that the implication is that any view held with attachment is a wrong-view. I hope to show that this is the conclusion of the *Brahmajāla-sutta*.

As I have argued, the term *sammā-diṭṭhi* implies the opposite of craving and attachment. In a sense, and again this is not explicitly stated in the Nikāyas, with the realisation of right-view, the very possibility of attachment is abandoned. Although there is wrong-view and right-view, paradoxically, the very possibility of holding views has been extinguished. As I have suggested, when the Nikāyas consider *sammā-diṭṭhi* that is supramundane (*lokuttara*), they are, in a sense, not talking about a view at all. I am not saying that it does not propose anything but that, ultimately, what it proposes is the non-attachment from all views. By supramundane right-view (*lokuttara sammā-diṭṭhi*) the Nikāyas are offering a way of seeing that is completely detached, in which no-views are held. In one respect, *sammā-diṭṭhi* presents similarities with the notion of 'emptiness' (*śunyatā*) in later Buddhist thought. It is true of *sammā-diṭṭhi*, in common with emptiness, that it becomes wrong if it is held with attachment.[7] Also, the content of both notions is the same: dependent-origination. It is no coincidence that Nāgārjuna wrote a chapter on *dṛṣṭi* in his *Mūlamadhyamakakārikā*.

The *Brahmajāla-sutta* opens with a long section detailing the reasons why the ordinary person (*puthujjana*) would praise the Buddha. The ordinary person praises the Buddha for his virtuous qualities. The *sutta* refers to these as 'trifling and insignificant matters, minor details of mere moral virtue'.[8] The *sutta* goes on to state that:

> There are other things (*dhammas*), deep, difficult to see, difficult to understand, peaceful and sublime, beyond the sphere of reasoning, subtle, comprehensible only to the wise, which the Tathāgata, having realised for himself with direct knowledge, propounds to others.[9]

It is concerning these *dhammas* that 'those who rightly praise the Tathāgata would speak in accordance with the way things are'.[10] The *sutta* then expounds the 62 views. After each set of views (there are ten sets), the *sutta* states what the *dhammas* are whereby one would rightly praise the Tathāgata. I feel that this passage is extremely important for a correct understanding of the notion of views in the Nikāyas. It states that the Tathāgata understands each group of views. He understands that these 'bases for views' (*diṭṭhiṭṭhānā*),[11] grasped (*gahitā*) and clung to (*parāmaṭṭhā*), lead to a certain future rebirth.[12] The Tathāgata also understands what transcends (*uttaritaraṃ*)[13] this, yet he does not cling to even that understanding (*taṃ ca pajānanaṃ na parāmasati*), and because of not clinging (*aparāmasato*) he has 'realised within himself the state of perfect peace'.[14] The *sutta* then states that:

> Having understood as they really are the origin and passing away of feelings, their satisfaction, unsatisfactoriness, and the escape from them, the Tathāgata [...] is emancipated through non-attachment.[15]

It is these *dhammas*, or this knowledge, that is deep, difficult to see, etc., concerning which the Tathāgata would rightly be praised.[16] The Buddha is not attached to the 'highest', for this knowledge 'transcends' (*uttaritaraṃ*). It is a knowledge beyond attachment. This is the transcendence of views. It is the same as the description of what constitutes right-view. Therefore, the transcendence of views is right-view.

First, this passage is clearly explaining views as objects held with attachment. It is likely that it is the source for the later Abhidhamma association of *parāmāsa* and *diṭṭhi*. The Abhidhamma describes views as a form of clinging and attachment and this is exactly what is stated here.

Second, the statement about having understood as they really are the origin and passing away of 'feelings' (*vedanā*) is of some interest. In other contexts seeing the rise and fall of the factors of dependent-origination is called *sammā-diṭṭhi*, and it is 'having understood as they really are' (*yathābhūtaṃ viditvā*) these factors that the Buddha is emancipated and this is the reason that he should be praised. As the *sutta* states, the Buddha is not attached to this knowledge, the knowledge of *paṭicca-samuppāda*, of rise and fall, of the four truths. The *sutta* is, in effect, stating that he is not attached to knowledge, to his view, and it is this that, to a large extent, makes it correct knowledge or right-view. In Chapter 3 on the function of wrong-view, I suggested the difference between the corruption of views and that of ignorance. I argued that the corruption of views is the attachment to knowledge and that the corruption of ignorance is false knowledge itself. In a similar way, the *Brahmajāla-sutta* is not explaining right-view as correct knowledge, but as correct knowledge of doctrine, namely, knowledge that does not produce craving.

That the *Brahmajāla-sutta* is an exposition on *paṭicca-samuppāda*, on right-view, is made clear if we look at the final four sections of the *sutta*. The first section states for each of the ten groups of views that these are 'only the feeling of those who do not know and do not see [...]; only the agitation and vacillation of those immersed in craving'.[17] This statement suggests the bringing together of ignorance and craving. The developed tradition made much of the interplay of ignorance and craving, and this is suggested in this early passage. Next, it is stated for each group of views that they are 'conditioned by contact' (*phassa-paccayā*)[18] and that 'it is impossible for those [who hold these views] to experience them without contact'.[19] Third, it is stated that all view-holders experience these feelings only by repeated contacts through the six bases of contact.[20] Then part of the standard *paṭicca-samuppāda* formula is given:

> With feeling as condition, there arises in them [the view-holders] craving; with craving as condition, attachment arises; with attachment as condition, existence; with existence as condition, birth; and with birth as condition, ageing and death, sorrow, lamentation, pain, grief and despair arise.[21]

Finally, it is explained that when a *bhikkhu* understands as they really are the origin and passing away of the six bases of contact, their satisfaction, unsatisfactoriness and the escape from them, then he 'understands what transcends all these [views]' (*sabbeheva uttaritaraṃ pajānāti*).[22] This, in the *Sammādiṭṭhi-sutta*, is *sammā-diṭṭhi*, as I pointed out in Chapter 2.[23] Right-view is explained as what transcends views. It is explained as a detached form of knowledge, a type of wisdom that does not crave knowledge or truth.

The *Brahmajāla-sutta*, we may think, does not explicitly contain a sixty-third view which is the *sammā-diṭṭhi* that gives the correct proposition in opposition to the 62 views. This is true as far as it goes, but also misleading. In my understanding, the *Brahmajāla-sutta* does suggest what *sammā-diṭṭhi* is. This *sammā-diṭṭhi* is knowledge (or understanding) of rise and fall, the *anuloma* and *paṭiloma* knowledge (or understanding) of *paṭicca-samuppāda.* By definition, and by the nature of these doctrines, they must be seen without any degree of craving and attachment. This process, as has been shown, is what the Nikāyas mean by *sammā-diṭṭhi*. Until we are clear about exactly what it is that constitutes *sammā-diṭṭhi* it is difficult to understand the process by which right-view 'corrects' wrong-view. It is a major concern of this book to decide whether the Pāli canon proposes a right-view in opposition to wrong-views or whether all views are wrong if they are held with attachment.[24] It is my contention that when the nature of *sammā-diṭṭhi* is understood, the Nikāyas should be understood as teaching the transcendence of all views. This is precisely what is found in the *Brahmajāla-sutta.*

The *Brahmajāla-sutta* proposes neither a sixty-third view (the opposition understanding), nor the rejection of all views (the no-views understanding), but knowledge of the cessation of craving. This is right-view. It is a clear example of *sammā-diṭṭhi* signifying that all views have been transcended.

In the discussion of the nature of *micchā-diṭṭhi* and *sammā-diṭṭhi*, comments have been made as to those tendencies which are prominent, and those that are less prominent. As I explained in Chapter 2, the content of right-view, at a certain stage of the path, is either the four truths or dependent-origination. Seeing dependent origination, as I explained in Chapter 4, constitutes the knowledge of those who achieve stream-attainment. If we accept that dependent-origination is right-view, then the *Brahmajāla-sutta* describes *sammā-diṭṭhi*. Far from being anomalous, the *Brahmajāla-sutta* is coherent with the general Nikāya understanding of the notions of *micchā-diṭṭhi* and *sammā-diṭṭhi*. Right-view is precisely that view which transcends and goes beyond all views. If we are clear about what constitutes right-view it is, perhaps, obvious that there is no opposition in the Nikāyas between wrong-view and right-view, but between craving and the cessation of craving.

This is the way in which the tradition, I would argue, understood the texts. Right-view is the seeing of things as they are through a knowledge of the four truths and dependent-origination. Seeing the rise and fall of *dhammas* is *sammā-diṭṭhi*. As I discussed in Chapter 4, in the *Visuddhimagga* Buddhaghosa explains 'purification of view' (*diṭṭhi-visuddhi*) as the correct seeing of name and form, and the correct seeing of the *khandhas* (Vism XVIII). The Buddhist path, in aiming to see things as they are, attempts to see the world without attachment, and this is what is meant by the term *sammā-diṭṭhi*. It is a way of seeing and understanding that is detached. This process is precisely what is found in the *Brahmajāla-sutta*. This understanding is also implicit in other parts of the Nikāyas.

The 'view' that transcends *sakkāya-diṭṭhi*

I would now like to consider two contexts in which wrong-views are transcended by right-view. These are in relation to *sakkāya-diṭṭhi* and the *avyākata*. In the Introduction, I suggested that it is difficult to see how the wrong-views of eternalism and annihilationism are corrected by the right-view of dependent-origination. This is partly because wrong-views are a type of craving and attachment. How is craving and attachment 'corrected'? I have already suggested how this process takes place. The process by which *sammā-diṭṭhi* abandons *micchā-diṭṭhi* is one by which attachment is abandoned by calm and insight. In the following I would like to give examples of this process in operation.

By way of introduction I will consider briefly a passage in the *Peṭakopadesa* that speaks of the inner and outer tangle (*anto-jaṭā bahi-jaṭā*).[25] This passage suggests why the texts were eager to combine the twin hindrances of craving and lust with those of views. The passage explains the inner tangle in two ways and the outer tangle in two ways. 'Lust' (*rāga*), which has what is in oneself for its ground, is the inner tangle, while lust, which has what is external for its ground, is the outer tangle.[26] In the next sentence the term lust is replaced by *sakkāya-diṭṭhi*, and this is explained as the inner tangle,[27] while the outer tangle are the 61 views.[28] Elsewhere the *Peṭakopadesa* states that the *khandhas* are a footing for *sakkāya-diṭṭhi*, and the 61 views are a footing for lust for views.[29] In these passages views are clearly being described as a type of craving. They are what the mind craves and has greed for. When right-view abandons wrong-view craving and greed are abandoned. It is the opposite to craving, not a correct proposition. Right-view is not essentially a type of knowledge, but a way of seeing that is free from defilement. It is in this context that the idea of *sakkāya-diṭṭhi* may also be best understood. The *khandhas*, when viewed with attachment, give rise to other attachments. The *khandhas* viewed with non-attachment become an expression of *sammā-diṭṭhi*, which is a form of seeing without craving.

It is considerations such as these that have led me to question the prevailing consensus on the notion of *diṭṭhi* in the Nikāyas, namely, the opposition and no-views understandings. As I have said in the Introduction, though it is often stated that there are only a few passages in the four primary Nikāyas which are suggestive of the no-views understanding within early Buddhism, the more one looks at the texts in which the notion of *diṭṭhi* is considered, the more common *certain* features of the no-views type become apparent. However, it is my argument that the texts do not teach the abandoning of all views, but the transcendence of views, which is something different. In many places it is stated that *sakkāya-diṭṭhi* does not come to be when one does 'not regard' (*na samanupassati*) the *khandhas*.[30] When one does not see the *khandhas* with craving and attachment, one holds no more views. This is right-view. However, this is not the same process whereby right-view replaces wrong-views in the opposition understanding. As I have argued, the attainment of right-view signifies the cessation of craving. This attainment is neither the acquisition of a correct doctrine in opposition to other doctrines, nor the rejection of all views. The attainment of right-view signifies the transcendence of all views. It is through transcending all views that right-view sees things as they are. My point is that the wrong-view of *sakkāya-diṭṭhi* is not somehow corrected by a right-view, but that by right-view a different order of seeing is implied, one that sees the world in a radically different way.

In certain passages of the *Khandha-vagga* of the *Saṃyutta-nikāya*, ignorance (*avijjā*) is explained simply as not knowing the *khandhas*, their arising, their cessation and the way to their cessation.[31] Knowledge (*vijjā*), on the other hand, is explained as understanding the *khandhas*, their arising, their cessation and the way to their cessation.[32] To have knowledge of the 'arising and passing away, gratification, danger and escape in the case of the *khandhas* subject to attachment' is described as the understanding of the stream-attainer and Arahant.[33] It is this idea of seeing the origination and cessation of the *khandhas* which I feel is important for understanding the way in which *sakkāya-diṭṭhi* is not replaced by a *sammā-diṭṭhi*, but the nature of phenomena are seen in a different way. It is this way of seeing that constitutes *sammā-diṭṭhi*.

There is the sense that one should simply not grasp or have any attachment for the *khandhas*. The aim is to see them as they are and this will cause the cessation of attachment. For example, at S III 45–6 it is stated that as the *khandhas* are impermanent, suffering and not-self, they should be seen with correct wisdom: 'This is not mine, this I am not, this is not my self'. Seeing in this way, as it really is, one holds no more views concerning the past and the future and there is no more 'obstinate clinging' (*thāmasā parāmāsa*).[34] This 'obstinate clinging', the

Sāratthappakāsinī interprets as the obstinate clinging of views (*diṭṭhi-thāmaso*, Spk II 269).

Other passages suggest that to regard the *khandhas* with attachment, in other words to form views about them, is the cause of affliction and agitation. At S III 1–5 it is explained that 'to be afflicted in body and mind'[35] one regards form as self, etc. That person lives obsessed by the notions 'I am form', 'form is mine' and so on for the other *khandhas*.[36] With the changing of the *khandhas*, suffering arises. The *sutta* then explains how one is 'afflicted in body but not afflicted in mind'.[37] This time one does not regard the *khandhas* as self, etc. The person does not live obsessed by the notions that 'I am form', 'form is mine' and so on for the other *khandhas*.[38] With the changing of the *khandhas*, suffering does not arise.

At S III 16 it is asked: 'How [...] is there agitation due to attachment?'[39] The answer given is that the person 'regards form as self, or self as possessed of form, or form as in self, or self as in form'. After this it is stated that:

> That form changes and becomes otherwise. With the change and becoming otherwise of form, his consciousness is preoccupied with the change of form. Agitated mental states born of preoccupation with the change of form arise together and remain obsessing his mind. Because his mind is obsessed, he is anxious, distressed, and concerned, and due to attachment he becomes agitated.[40]

This formula is repeated for the remaining four *khandhas*. The *sutta* next asks: 'How is there non-agitation due to non-attachment?'[41] Again, it is explained that 'by not regarding form as self' etc. there is non-agitation due to non-attachment (*anupādā*). The reason for regarding the *khandhas* in this way is that they change and become otherwise and by not regarding the *khandhas* as self etc. that person's consciousness is not preoccupied with the changing of the *khandhas*. Agitated mental states do not arise and obsess the mind. When the person's mind is not obsessed, that person is not anxious, distressed or concerned. It is due to 'non-attachment' that the person does not become agitated.[42] This non-attachment is how I understand the notion of right-view.

In the *Attadīpa-sutta* (S III 42–3) it is stated that sorrow, lamentation, pain, displeasure and despair arise from regarding the *khandhas* as self, etc. When they change and alter there is suffering. However, the *sutta* states:

> When one has understood the impermanence of form, its change, fading away and cessation, when one has understood as it really is with proper wisdom that all form etc., both in the past and in the present, is impermanent, suffering and subject to change, then sorrow, lamentation, pain, displeasure and despair are abandoned. At their abandonment the *bhikkhu* does not become agitated; because he is not agitated, he dwells happily; dwelling happily the *bhikkhu* is called quenched in this respect.[43]

The *Sāratthappakāsinī* suggests that this *sutta* is referring to the quenching of the defilements through insight and that the *sutta* is a discussion of insight.[44]

One thing that is apparent in these passages is that the way of regarding (*samanupassanā*) that replaces *sakkāya-diṭṭhi* is one in which a sense of calm is engendered and affliction and agitation are avoided. There is still the regarding of something (the *khandhas*), but without craving and attachment. The *khandhas* are seen 'as they are'. Part of the problem of holding *micchā-diṭṭhi* is that it causes agitated mental states to arise. These states are unwholesome (*akusala*). As was shown in Chapter 2, a very prominent feature of *sammā-diṭṭhi* is that it causes both calm and wholesome (*kusala*) mental states. This is one explanation of *sammā-diṭṭhi* given in the *Sammādiṭṭhi-sutta* (M I 46–7). At a certain stage of the Buddhist path these ideas meet; what causes calm is also, by definition, wholesome.

In other passages holding views about the *khandhas*, which implies simply regarding them with attachment, leads to the idea of the existence of a self. At S III 43–4 it is stated that 'the way to the origination of identity'[45] is to regard form, etc. as self. The *sutta* states that 'the way to the origination of identity' has the meaning of the way of 'regarding' that leads to the origination of suffering (*dukkhasamudayagāminī samanupassanā*). According to the *Sāratthappakāsinī*, the term *samanupassanā*, in this context, is to be understood as *diṭṭhi*.[46] To regard the *khandhas* implies having a view of them, being attached to them. The 'way to the cessation of identity'[47] is to not regard form, etc. as self. The way leading to the cessation of identity means the way of regarding that leads to the ending of suffering (S III 44). The *khandhas* are seen with understanding, with wisdom.

At S III 46–7 it is stated that those ascetics and brahmins who regard anything as self all regard 'the *khandhas* subject to attachment' (*pañcupādānakkhandhe*) as self, or self as possessing the *khandhas*, etc. It is stated that: 'Thus this way of regarding things [regarding the *khandhas* according to the 20 views of *sakkāya-diṭṭhi*] and [the notion] "I am" have not vanished in him'.[48] The *Sāratthappakāsinī* again interprets this way of regarding things[49] as regarding with views (*diṭṭhi-samanupassanā*) and the notion 'I am' (*asmīti*) as the triple proliferation of craving, conceit and views.[50] The same *sutta* then adds that as 'I am' has not vanished, the five faculties (*indriyas*),[51] the eye, ear, nose, tongue and body faculties, descend. It is not clear what this statement means. It could be describing the process of rebirth. The term *avakkanti*, 'descent', implies, in other contexts, the start of a new existence, the descent of consciousness, or name and form.[52] However, Sue Hamilton suggests that the passage is explaining that 'the first five senses (that is, not including *manodhātu*) manifest [*avakkanti*] because of an erroneous belief in selfhood'. Hamilton suggests that the term *avakkanti* is used figuratively to refer to the fact, for example, that '*nāmarūpa* and *viññāṇa* arise dependently'.[53] These comments suggest the correct interpretation of this passage.[54] This short statement about the descent (the manifesting) of the five faculties may simply be shorthand for implying the negative process of dependent-origination and the dependent nature of *dhammas*.[55] If this is true it is an unusual formulation, but makes sense of the following statement, which says, immediately after the statement about the descent (or manifesting) of the five sense faculties, that 'there is the mind, there are mental phenomena, there is the element of ignorance'.[56] Hamilton translates this: '... there are [also], *bhikkhus, manas* and *dhammā* which are the basis for knowledge/ ignorance.'[57] She uses this reading to suggest how the mind is 'directly involved in the process of liberation'.[58] As the passage continues, suggesting how the mind is directly involved in ignorance also:

> When the uninstructed worldling is contacted by a feeling born of contact with ignorance,[59] [then] 'I am' occurs to him, 'I am this', 'I will be', 'I will not be', 'I will consist of form', 'I will be formless', 'I will be appercipient', 'I will be non-appercipient', 'I will be neither appercipient nor non-appercipient' occurs to him.[60]

The idea that 'contact' (*phassa*), explicitly the contact of ignorance, gives rise to views is prominent.

The *suttas* seem to understand *micchā-diṭṭhi* as a tangible mental object of attachment, which the mind touches, has contact with, and clings to, whereas *sammā-diṭṭhi* is a way of seeing that the mind cannot take hold of, become attached to, or have contact with. It is a view that the mind does not cling to. Wrong-view is, as it were, corporeal, tangible, the mundane way of seeing. Right-view is, as it were, incorporeal, intangible, the supramundane way of seeing. The *sutta* describes this process in the following way. In the first part of this *sutta* the *khandhas* are the basis for the twenty views of *sakkāya-diṭṭhi* and the conceit 'I am' has not vanished. This gives rise to renewed existence and, with ignorance as condition, with ignorance as cause, the production of various views about future existence or non-existence. As Bhikkhu Bodhi has suggested, it is possibly an 'alternative version of dependent-origination'.[61] The *sutta*, so far, has described the negative process, *micchā-diṭṭhi.* It now explains how the noble disciple sees. Although the five faculties remain (*tiṭṭhanti pañcindriyāni*), the 'instructed noble disciple abandons ignorance and arouses true knowledge towards them'.[62] With the fading of ignorance and the arising of knowledge various speculations do not occur such as 'I am', 'I am this', 'I will be', 'I will not be', 'I will consist of form', 'I will be formless', 'I will be appercipient', 'I will be non-appercipient', 'I will be neither appercipient nor non-appercipient'.[63] The knowledge that replaces *sakkāya-diṭṭhi* is a knowledge of dependent-origination, a knowledge of suffering and its cessation. This is *sammā-diṭṭhi*, but it has none of the characteristics of *diṭṭhi*. The *sutta* is clearly explaining wrong-views as involvement and attachment. Right-view is explained as seeing dependent-origination and thereby seeing the escape from both ignorance and craving.

These themes are also found in the *Pārileyyaka-sutta* (S III 94–9). This *sutta* addresses the question of how one should know and see for the immediate destruction of the corruptions (*āsavas*).[64] The *sutta* states that the *puthujjana* regards form as self, etc., and that 'regarding is a formation'.[65] It then asks about 'the source and origination of that formation, from what is it born and produced?'[66]

The answer is that when the *puthujjana* is contacted by a feeling born of contact with ignorance, craving arises, and from that the volitional formation is born.[67] The *sutta* then explains this process. The volitional formation, craving, feeling, contact and ignorance are impermanent, conditioned and dependently-arisen.[68] When one knows and sees this, the immediate destruction of the *āsavas* occurs.[69] The *sutta* explains the remaining views of *sakkāya-diṭṭhi* in the same way (S III 97–8). A *sassata-diṭṭhi*[70] and an *uccheda-diṭṭhi*[71] are also analysed as a volitional formation born of contact with ignorance from which craving arises. The volitional formation, craving, feeling, contact and ignorance are all impermanent, conditioned and dependently-arisen. To be 'perplexed, doubtful or indecisive in regard to the true *dhamma*' is explained in a similar fashion.[72] These *suttas* are clearly explaining wrong-view as a form of craving and right-view as knowledge of the cessation of craving.

These *suttas* suggest how *sammā-diṭṭhi* functions, but, if we are not aware of how the tradition understood *sammā-diṭṭhi*, we may not notice it. I would suggest that to understand why the early tradition held *sakkāya-diṭṭhi* to be such a hindrance we need to look at what these views are fundamentally doing. Each of them is forming attachment to the *khandhas*. As will become clear later in this chapter, the *khandhas* in and of themselves are not a hindrance, yet attachment to them is. This understanding is found in the Nikāyas. The *Khandha-sutta* of the *Khandha-vagga* (S III 47–8) states that there are five *khandhas* and five *khandhas* subject to attachment (*upādānakkhandhas*). The *sutta* states that whatever form (feeling, apperception, volitional formations or consciousness), there is – past, future or present, internal or external, gross or subtle, inferior or superior, far or near – this is called the *khandha* of form (feeling, apperception, volitional formations or consciousness). These are the five *khandhas*. The *sutta* then explains the five *khandhas* subject to attachment. Whatever form (feeling, apperception, volitional formations or consciousness) there is – past, future or present, internal or external, gross or subtle, inferior or superior, far or near, that is 'with corruptions' (*sāsava*), that can be an attachment – that is called the form *khandha*, etc., subject to attachment. To hold any views about the *khandhas* is to be attached to them.

My point is that views of the self, views that I considered in the second half of Chapter 1, are primarily a form of attachment. These views, together with those that deny that actions have consequences, are what constitute wrong-views. As wrong-views, views of the self are not primarily incorrect knowledge but a form of craving. As such, these views do not so much need correcting but the actions and conduct of the person holding them needs to be adapted to an attitude of calm and non-attachment. It is this which constitutes right-view.

The 'view' that transcends the *avyākata*

I am arguing that views are not essentially corrected but are transcended on the Buddhist path. I consider this very transcendence of views to be the proper understanding of right-view itself. I would like now to consider the way in which another important group of views are transcended, this time the *avyākata*. I discussed the content of the *avyākata* towards the end of Chapter 1. Any consideration of the Nikāyas would normally evaluate the *avyākata* as an example of the no-views understanding within the early Buddhist texts.[73] As I said, I disagree with this and feel that a proper understanding of views can be understood by looking at how these views are refuted. This consideration of the *avyākata*, together with my discussion of the view that transcends *sakkāya-diṭṭhi*, explains right-view as a form of seeing that does not produce any craving or attachment. As such, it is of importance to my overall argument by helping to redefine the model by which these notions are usually understood. Instead of an opposition between wrong-view and right-view, or the rejection of all views, there is a way to understand these ideas on their own terms. This uses neither model; right-view does not replace wrong-view as a correct proposition, nor are all views rejected: right-view transcends all views.

In the *Vacchagotta-saṃyutta* (S III 257–63) it is asked: 'What is the cause and reason for the various speculative views to arise?'[74] The reason is not knowing (*aññāṇa*), not seeing (*adassana*), not breaking through (*anabhisamaya*), not comprehending (*ananubodha*), not penetrating (*appaṭivedha*), not discerning (*asallakkhaṇa*), not discriminating (*anupalakkhaṇa*), not differentiating (*apaccupakkhaṇa*), not examining (*asamapekkhaṇa*), not closely examining (*appaccupekkhaṇa*), not directly cognizing (*appaccakkhakamma*) each of the *khandhas*, their arising, cessation and the way leading to their cessation. The way to avoid the arising of *diṭṭhi* is to see *dukkha*, its arising, cessation and the way to its cessation. This is *sammā-diṭṭhi*. The *Abyākata-saṃyutta* (S IV 374–404) contains eleven *suttas* on this theme. The *Khemā-sutta* concentrates on the final four *avyākata*, those concerning the after-death state of the Tathāgata. It is explained that the *khandhas* by which the Tathāgata may be described have been abandoned and are not subject to future arising. The four questions do not apply to the Tathāgata.[75] The *Upagata-sutta* (S IV 384–6) concentrates on the same four *avyākata*. The *sutta* states that to declare that the Tathāgata exists after death, etc., is 'an involvement with form' (*rūpa-gatam*), an 'involvement with feeling' (*vedanā-gatam*), an 'involvement in apperception' (*saññā-gatam*), an 'involvement in volitional formations' (*saṃkhāra-gatam*) and an 'involvement in consciousness' (*viññāṇa-gatam*). This is why these questions are not answered.[76] Clearly, wrong-views are explained as attachment to the *khandhas*. Conversely, this is the reason why, in a sense, there is no such thing as right-view, as the opposite to a wrong-view, as this would be an involvement, literally, 'going' (*gatam*) to the *khandhas*, going to views; right-view abandons all views. Wrong-views are not so much a form of ignorance that perceives a self where there is no self, but a craving that holds to the idea of a self, which causes *dukkha*.

These themes are, perhaps, best expressed in the *Āyatana-sutta* (S IV 391–5), and the *Khandha-sutta* (S IV 395–7). In the *Āyatana-sutta* it is stated that it is because the 'wanderers of other sects' (*aññatitthiyā paribbājakā*), regard the six senses as: 'This is mine, this I am, this is my self' that the ten *avyākata* are asked.[77]

The questions are asked because things are not seen in their true nature. They are asked because there is craving. However, the six senses should be regarded as: 'This is not mine, this I am not, this is not my self'.[78] The *Khandha-sutta* states that the *avyākata* are the product of regarding each of the *khandhas* as self, or self as possessing the *khandhas*, or the *khandhas* as in self, or self as in the *khandhas*.[79] This is clearly what in other places is *sakkāya-diṭṭhi*, and it is this way of regarding that gives rise to the *avyākata*. The *Paṭisambhidāmagga* explanation of *diṭṭhi* discussed in Chapter 3 is that 'clinging by adherence is view' (*abhinivesa-parāmāso diṭṭhi*, Paṭis I 135). It is this emphasis that is also given to views in relation to the *avyākata*.

Other *suttas* on the *avyākata* support this interpretation of the term right-view signifying the transcendence of all views. The *Samudaya-sutta* (S IV 386–7) answers the question as to why the final four *avyākata* are left unanswered. It states that the person who does not know the *khandhas* as they really are, their arising, cessation and the way to their cessation thinks: 'The Tathāgata exists after death', etc.[80] But the person who knows the *khandhas* as they really are, their arising, cessation and the way to their cessation does not think: 'The Tathāgata exists after death', etc. This is why the questions are left unanswered.[81] To one who sees the *khandhas* as they really are, their arising and cessation, i.e. with right-view, the questions do not occur. In the *Pema-sutta* (S IV 387–8) it is stated that one who is not devoid of lust, desire, affection, thirst, passion and craving for the *khandhas* thinks: 'The Tathāgata exists after death', etc.[82] However one devoid of lust, desire, affection, thirst, passion and craving for the *khandhas* does not think: 'The Tathāgata exists after death', etc. This is the reason that the questions are left unanswered, because the questions do not occur.[83] The *Ārāma-sutta* (S IV 388–91) gives a lengthy summary of these themes. In this *sutta* it is stated that one who takes delight in the *khandhas* (i.e. *rūpārāmassa*, etc. for the remaining *khandhas*), and rejoices in the *khandhas* (*rūpa-sammuditassa*), who does not know and see the cessation of the *khandhas* as they really are thinks: 'The Tathāgata exists after death', etc.[84] The questions arise in one who 'delights in existence' (*bhavārāmassa*), who 'rejoices in existence' (*bhava-sammuditassa*), and who does not know and see the cessation of existence as it really is.[85] The questions also arise in one who delights in attachment (*upādānārāmassa*) and rejoices in attachment (*upādānasammuditassa*) and who does not know and see the cessation of attachment as it really is.[86] The same is also stated for delighting and rejoicing in craving and not knowing the cessation of craving as it really is.[87] The opposite is said for the non-arising of the four *avyākata*. If one does not delight and rejoice in the *khandhas*, and knows and sees their cessation as it really is, one does not think 'the Tathāgata exists after death', etc.[88] If one does not delight and rejoice in existence,[89] delight and rejoice in attachment,[90] delight and rejoice in craving,[91] and knows and sees the cessation of these as they really are, that person does not think 'the Tathāgata exists after death', etc. Again, there is a clear identification of views and craving, and the cessation of craving implying the abandoning of views.

As noted in Chapter 1, at S IV 287 it is stated that the ten *avyākata* and the 62 views from the *Brahmajāla-sutta* are dependent upon *sakkāya-diṭṭhi*. When *sakkāya-diṭṭhi* comes to be, these views come to be; without *sakkāya-diṭṭhi*, these views do not come to be. I take this to mean that if things are seen as they are, i.e. the *khandhas* are not taken as self, etc., then other views do not come to be. The foregoing analysis suggests that, in the case of the arising of wrong-views, not to see things as they are implies becoming attached to certain things, primarily the *khandhas*. Different terms are used for this process such as 'depending on' (*upādāya*), 'clinging' (*parāmāsa*), and 'adherence' (*abhinivesa*). As I have said, I do not take the doctrine of *anattā* as a propositional doctrine saying 'there is no self', but as a doctrine leading to the abandonment of craving and attachment meaning 'do not become attached to the idea of self'. The view of self expressed by the notion of *sakkāya-diṭṭhi* is primarily concerned with the expression of attachment. Therefore, to abandon this attachment, there is no 'right-view' (unless right-view is explained in a specific way, as the transcendence of views). Rather, a non-attached attitude is proposed that frees the mind of the hindrance of self. To negate questions of the *avyākata* type, we do not find the 'correct' questions to be asked, or the correct answers to be given, but a completely different attitude is proposed. When right-view replaces wrong-view it is one order of seeing replacing an entirely different order of seeing, for at the stage of stream-attainment *all* views are abandoned.[92] The view of self is abandoned for '*sakkāya* is the footing for name and form',[93] for dependent-origination, and so *dukkha*, and it is knowledge of this that the Buddha claimed to have. The *avyākata* are not questions, as such, but expressions of craving. This is true of all views. It is by the cessation of this craving, expressed as the cessation of views, that the *avyākata* are overcome.[94] By stating that 'the *ariya-sāvaka* knows view, its origin, cessation and the way to its cessation'[95] the *suttas* are explaining that the follower of the Buddha knows craving, its arising, cessation and the way to its cessation. Knowing and seeing in this way, beyond views, the *ariya-sāvaka* is calm.

The *Pāṭali-sutta*

Another example of the tendency for *sammā-diṭṭhi* to go beyond or transcend *micchā-diṭṭhi* is found in the *Pāṭali-sutta* (S IV 340–58) from the *Saṃyutta-nikāya*. This *sutta* is interesting because it does not advocate views that are clearly explained as right-views in other parts of the Nikāyas. I think this again points to the correct understanding of right-view itself. Right-view is not assent to a proposition, but a way of seeing that goes beyond doubt, calms the mind and leads to wholesome action.

In the second half of this *sutta* Pāṭali informs the Buddha that he has a rest-house and that on certain occasions, ascetics and brahmins stay there. He recalls one particular occasion when 'four teachers holding different views, following different systems'[96] came to stay. Pāṭali then recounts how each teacher 'taught thus, held this view' (*evaṃ-vādi evaṃ-diṭṭhi*). The first teacher held the view of nihilism (*natthika-diṭṭhi*, S IV 348), the second teacher the view of affirmation (*atthika-diṭṭhi*, S IV 348–9), the third the view of non-doing (*akiriya-diṭṭhi*, S IV 349), and the fourth the view that there is doing (*kiriya-diṭṭhi*, S IV 349–50). On hearing these different views, Pāṭali explains to the Buddha that he has doubt (*kaṅkhā*) and uncertainty (*vicikicchā*) not knowing which recluse and brahmin was speaking truth (*sacca*) and which was speaking falsehood (*musā*, S IV 350).[97] The Buddha replies that though Pāṭali doubts and is uncertain, it is on a doubtful point that uncertainty arose.[98] Pāṭali explains to the Buddha that he has much trust (*pasanna*) in him and asks for a teaching whereby his 'doubt will be abandoned'.[99] The Buddha explains that there is a concentration of mind (*citta-samādhi*) which is attained (*paṭilabbhati*) by concentration of the *dhamma* (*dhamma-samādhi*, S IV 350). The Buddha explains what *dhamma-samādhi* is. He explains that the *ariya-sāvaka*:

> Abandoning the killing of living beings, abstaining therefrom; abandoning the taking of what is not given, abstaining therefrom; abandoning misconduct in sensual pleasure [...] abandoning false speech [...] malicious speech [...] harsh speech [...] gossip, abstaining therefrom. Abandoning covetousness, he is no more covetous. Abandoning malevolence and hatred, his heart becomes free from ill-will. Abandoning wrong-view, he becomes one of right-view.[100]

These are the abandoning of the ten unwholesome courses of action (*dasa akusala-kammapathā*), by the ten wholesome courses of action (*dasa kusala-kammapathā*). The *ariya-sāvaka* is then said to be freed from covetousness (*vigatābhijjha*), freed from malevolence (*vigatavyāpāda*), not bewildered (*asammūḷha*), but attentive (*sampajāna*) and concentrated (*patissato*), with a mind full of loving-kindness (*mettā-sahagatena cetasā*). That person then abides, suffusing the whole world with a mind possessed of loving-kindness.[101] It is in this state that the person considers each view. Firstly, he considers the view of nihilism (S IV 351), then the view of affirmation (S IV 352), then the view of non-doing (S IV 353), and then the view that there is doing (S IV 354). The views are given a final four times, firstly considering the view of nihilism with 'a mind full of compassion' and 'a mind full of sympathetic joy',[102] then the view of affirmation with 'a mind filled with equanimity',[103] then the view of non-doing (S IV 356–7) and the view that there is doing (S IV 357–8) with 'a mind filled with equanimity'. After giving each view, the noble disciple (*ariya-sāvaka*) considers that even if the view is true (*sacca*), 'for me it counts as incontrovertible',[104] that the *ariya-sāvaka* does not cause harm (*vyābādhemi*) to anything (*kiñci*) weak or strong (*tasaṃ vā thāvaraṃ vā*). Yet again the emphasis is on behaviour and action, not on correct propositions. The *ariya-sāvaka* considers that he is lucky in two ways; first, he is 'restrained in body, speech and mind';[105] second, he will achieve a happy rebirth, perhaps even in heaven.[106] The *sutta* continues that, with this thought, gladness and joy arise in him, and his body is calmed, he is happy and his mind is at peace.

It is in this 'concentration of mind' (*citta-samādhi*) that comes by 'concentration of the *dhamma*' (*dhamma-samādhī*) that the 'state of doubt is overcome'.[107] It is of some interest to note that the commentary interprets *dhamma-samādhi* as the *dasa kusala-kammapathā* and *citta-samādhi* as the four paths and insight.[108] This suggests that action is affecting thought, and this, as I have suggested in Chapter 2, is important for the realisation of right-view.

In the *Pāṭali-sutta* the practising of the *dasa-kusala-kammapathā* and suffusing the world with *mettā, karuṇā* and *muditā* causes two beneficial outcomes – the restraint of body, speech and mind, and rebirth in a happy state.[109] Of course, one of the *dasa-kusala-kammapathā* is the abandoning of wrong-view and the adoption of right-view. Unlike other descriptions of this process, the *sutta* states that wrong-view is abandoned, 'abandoning wrong-view, he becomes one of right-view'. But this statement must be taken in context. Right-view is part of a wholesome course of action, or a beneficial practice. In a sense the no-views understanding of *diṭṭhi* suggests something about the nature of right-view that may lead us to understand what it is that the texts mean by right-view. The *Pāṭali-sutta* could be read as a *sutta* that teaches 'no-views'. The *ariya-sāvaka* is not simply advised to reject wrong-view and adopt right-view, for he doubts both wrong-view and right-view. He is advised to act in a certain way, 'abandoning the taking of life, abstaining therefrom' etc., 'abandoning wrong-view, he becomes one of right-view', not by accepting that there is 'what is given, offered and sacrificed', but by acting in a certain way. It is, in a sense, placing right-view in its context as part of the Buddhist path and, importantly, as a practice and not a proposition. As I have said, right-view is practised, not adopted or believed in.

I would like at this point to move on from this discussion of the transcending of (wrong-) views by right-view to a consideration of what lies at the heart of the dichotomy of what is and is not the path: the nature of the wholesome and unwholesome.

Seeing the wholesome and unwholesome

In the study of Buddhism it has often been noted that the teachings do not point to the changing of the world, but to changing our perception of it. The problem of *dukkha* is not ultimately to do with the world, but with the fact that people tend to grasp and become attached to all sorts of things. The world is seen with greed, hatred and delusion. This aspect of Buddhist teachings is important to my argument. It suggests that Buddhist doctrines should not be used to change the world, but to change the way we view the world. They should be used to lessen greed, hatred and delusion and, in so doing, solve the problem of *dukkha*. When the teachings are understood as having this aim, then the opposition between wrong and right-views becomes somewhat irrelevant: what is needed is a way of seeing that reduces and eradicates craving. In this chapter I have, up to this point, concentrated on the Nikāyas. I would now like to turn my attention to the Abhidhamma where a similar understanding of the nature of views is found.

Throughout book 3 of the *Dhammasaṅgaṇi*, an evaluation is given of certain ways of apprehending the world. In the following discussion I would like to focus upon one aspect of what I think the text is describing. Put simply, this is that the world can be apprehended with or without craving. This aspect of Buddhist thought has been noted by Steven Collins, who has suggested that this reflects something of a dichotomising tendency within early Buddhism:

> Anything with conceptual or experiential content was to be assimilated to the impersonal, non-valued side of the dichotomy; since in this sphere everything was dominated by desire and grasping, anything with content became potentially graspable. Against this stood the empty unconditioned *nibbāna*, susceptible neither to conceptualising nor grasping.[110]

It is this dichotomising (or something similar to it) that, I have been arguing, is the correct way in which we should understand the notions of *micchā-diṭṭhi* and *sammā-diṭṭhi*. These notions are not concerned with sets of doctrines, but with different orders of seeing. I would like to look at the *Dhammasaṅgaṇi* to see how it considers this apparent dichotomy. Book 3 of the *Dhammasaṅgaṇi*, the *Nikkhepa-kaṇḍaṃ*, begins with the following question:

> Which *dhammas* are wholesome?
> The three roots of the wholesome:
> Absence of greed, hatred and delusion;
> The four *khandhas*[111] of feeling, apperception, volitional formations and consciousness when they are associated with these roots;
> Actions of body, speech and mind when they come from these three roots.
> These are wholesome *dhammas*.[112]

With reference to the *khandhas*, I take this to imply that, when they are seen in their true nature, i.e. as not-self, they are wholesome, this is *sammā-diṭṭhi*. The next question asked is:

> Which *dhammas* are unwholesome?
> The three roots of the unwholesome:
> Greed, hatred and delusion;
> The defilements (*kilesā*) united with them;
> The four *khandhas* of feeling, apperception, volitional formations and consciousness when they are associated with these roots;
> Actions of body, speech and mind when they come from these three roots.
> These are unwholesome *dhammas*.[113]

The *Dhammasaṅgaṇi* is clearly stating that the four mental *khandhas* are unwholesome when they are associated with ‘greed’, ‘hatred’ and ‘delusion’ (*lobha, dosa, moha*).[114] In this analysis it must be remembered that in the Nikāya and

Abhidhamma analysis the term *khandha* is a neutral term, but the *khandhas* can become associated with (are indeed prone to), corruption. Primarily they are prone to give rise to the corruption of *micchā-ditthi*. Rupert Gethin has commented on the nature of the *khandhas* in the Nikāyas and Abhidhamma:

> The term *upādānakkhandha* signifies the general way in which the *khandhas* are bound up with *upādāna*; the simple *khandha*, universally applicable, is used in the *nikāyas* and especially the *Abhidhamma* texts as a neutral term, allowing the specific aspects of, for example, *upādāna's* relationship to the *khandhas* to be elaborated.[115]

The *Dhammasaṅgaṇi* is using the *khandhas* in its explanation of two ways of apprehending the world, one 'wholesome' (*kusala*), and one 'unwholesome' (*akusala*). It is these descriptions of the wholesome and unwholesome which I would like to focus upon. They suggest that the text is attempting to explain two attitudes to the world that we have met before in this study, and in the dichotomy suggested by Collins. The same reality is seen, but the one based on non-attachment is wholesome, and the other, based on attachment, giving rise to corruptions, is unwholesome.

It is interesting that, a little later in the *Dhammasaṅgaṇi*, there is an explanation of the stages of the path as being free from any attachment. The text explains those *dhammas* that are 'neither the issue of attachment nor favourable to it' (*anupādinna-anupādāniyā*). These are said to be 'the paths that are the unincluded (*apariyāpannā*), and the fruits of the paths, and the uncompounded element (*asaṃkhatā ca dhātu*).[116] The text is explaining a different order of seeing, which those who have entered the path experience. The terms 'included' (*pariyāpanna*) and 'unincluded' (*apariyāpanna*) refer to these two different ways of seeing, one with attachment, one without. Wrong-view is part of the 'included'. Right-view is part of the 'unincluded'. The fact that Buddhist thought was so vehement in its condemnation of views suggests that it had no intention of the *dhamma* being taken as a view, even a right-view. By the term *sammā-diṭṭhi*, early Buddhist thought did not intend to propose an antithesis to a thesis proposed by other schools. Buddhist thought did not wish to have a thesis; it was consistently *anti*-thesis. This is right-view, the transcendence of views, not 'included' in the world – which is one of attachment and craving – but part of the 'unincluded'. The dichotomy between attachment and non-attachment is suggested by the terms included and unincluded. The terms *pariyāpannā* and *apariyāpannā* are explained in the following ways. In the *Dhammasaṅgaṇi* it is stated that all those *dhammas* with *āsavas*, wholesome, unwholesome and indeterminate, relating to the worlds of sense, form or the formless, in other words the five *khandhas*, belong to the included.[117] Thus wholesome *dhammas*, when associated with the *āsavas*, belong to the included. The *Sammohavinodanī* explains the 'included' in the following terms: 'owing to the state of being included in destinies, included in death, included in the existence of the process of the round of rebirths; they are included, not unincluded' (Vibh-a 403, see also 518). In Chapter 2 the distinction was made between right-views with and without *āsavas*. A view, or any *dhamma*, can be wholesome; a view can be right at a certain stage of the path, but still susceptible to attachment. Ultimately such *dhammas* must be left behind on the Buddhist path.

The 'unincluded' (*apariyāpannā*) is explained in the following way. It is stated that the paths, the fruits of the paths and the uncompounded element belong to the unincluded.[118] The path aims at a way of seeing beyond attachment. This is one explanation of what is *kusala* for the Theravāda Abhidhamma. What is being pointed out in these passages is those things that belong to the world of ordinary perception, and those that belong to the perception of those on the path. Importantly, one cannot be attached to the unincluded. This is essential to an understanding of the nature of *sammā-diṭṭhi*. The Abhidhamma is explaining that it is not possible to crave and grasp right-view, for, if it is grasped, it is *not* right-view.

It has already been suggested that all views are abandoned at the stage of stream-attainment, but there does appear to have been some debate on this point. There is a short passage in the *Kathāvatthu* in which it is argued that it is a disputed point as to whether wrong-view was of the unincluded (*diṭṭhi-gataṃ apariyāpannan ti*). This, it is argued, would entail wrong-views being part of the four paths or four fruits, or one of the factors of enlightenment.[119] However, this is not the position of the Theravāda, as the *Dhammasaṅgaṇi* makes clear. In the *Sammohavinodanī* it is stated quite clearly that those on the path do not view anything as permanent, satisfactory or self (Vibh-a 424). The text states that, 'the function of the fourth plane [*catuttha-bhūmata*, i.e. the four paths and fruits[120]] is not an object for view or for unprofitable things, just as an iron heated for a day is not [a target] for flies because of its excessive heat'.[121]

On the Buddhist path, views, wrong or right, can no longer be held. I would like to consider how the *Dhammasaṅgaṇi* describes and clarifies this. It explains, in terms identical to the description of the unwholesome, the *dhammas* that are defiled and defiling (*dhammā saṅkiliṭṭhasaṅkilesikā*):

> Defiled and defiling:
> The three roots of the unwholesome; greed, hatred and delusion;
> The defilements that are united with them;
> The four [mental] *khandhas* when they are associated with them;
> Whatever action of body, speech and mind that comes from them.[122]

Then it explains those *dhammas* which are not defiled, but defiling (*dhammā asaṅkiliṭṭhasaṅkilesikā*):

> Not defiled, but defiling:
> Wholesome and indeterminate *dhammas* associated with the *āsavas*, taking effect in the world of sense, form and the formless, defined as the five *khandhas*.[123]

These *dhammas* are explained later in the text as mundane (*lokiya*).[124] Finally, those *dhammas* that are neither defiled nor defiling (*dhammā asaṅkiliṭṭha-asaṅkilesikā*) are explained:

> Neither defiled nor defiling:
> The paths that are the unincluded, the fruits of the path and the uncompounded element.[125]

These *dhammas* are described later in the text as 'supramundane' (*lokuttara*).[126] It is of some interest to reflect on what is suggested in these three evaluations. Greed, hatred and delusion are defiled *dhammas* which also defile. They are unwholesome *dhammas* that lead to other unwholesome *dhammas*. The wholesome and indeterminate *dhammas* connected to the *āsavas* are not in themselves defiled but they tend to become defiled. In other words, wholesome and indeterminate *dhammas* are unwholesome if allowed to become an object of attachment. The *khandhas*, if associated with the *āsavas* (i.e. with *kāma*, *bhāva*, *diṭṭhi* and *avijjā*), are *akusala*, but in and of themselves, as noted already, are not *akusala*. As Gethin has pointed out, and this is an important distinction in understanding what is to follow, the *khandha* of *rūpa* is always in some way connected with corruptions and the only occasions on which the four mental *khandhas* are not with corruptions, when they are not subject to attachment (*upādānakkhandhas*), is when they are part of the unincluded.[127] Hence the use of the four mental *khandhas* in the descriptions above. The *Dhammasaṅgaṇi* has explained that the stages of the path are neither defiled, nor do they defile. They are wholesome *dhammas* that lead to other wholesome *dhammas*. They are inherently free of attachment. By definition, *lokuttara sammā-diṭṭhi* shares none of the characteristics of *micchā-diṭṭhi*. To summarise, I am suggesting that the early Abhidhamma does not consider anything that is part of the path, i.e. right-view, to be in any way a potential hindrance. Supramundane right-view cannot give rise to any form of attachment. Knowledge of the *dhamma*, in the form of *sammā-diṭṭhi*, is completely free from craving and attachment.

The wholesome and unwholesome in the *Dhammasaṅgaṇi*

I would like to use this discussion to focus upon an analysis of certain aspects of the Buddhist path that appear in later chapters of the *Dhammasaṅgaṇi*. Chapters 4 to 12 (excluding Chapter 11) of the *Nikkhepa-kaṇḍaṃ* of the *Dhammasaṅgaṇi* consider various hindrances on the Buddhist path, and the way in which they are overcome. This analysis follows on from the previous three chapters of the *Dhammasaṅgaṇi*, some features of which I have just outlined. The basic principle, as described above, is that there is one way of apprehending the world that is unwholesome and not the path, and another way that is wholesome and the path. Chapter 4 of the *Nikkhepa-kaṇḍaṃ* considers the *āsavas*. The chapter asks and answers 12 questions, which in the text fall into six couplets. I would like to evaluate them in an order slightly different from that of the text. I will begin with what is basically an analysis of the unwholesome path (questions 1, 3, 5, 7, 9 and 11), of what is part of the included.[128]

> Question 1: Which are the *dhammas* that are *āsavas*?[129]

There are four *āsavas*, sensual desire, becoming, views and ignorance.[130] The *āsava* of sensual desire is all sensual passion, delight and craving. The *āsava* of becoming is the passion, delight and craving for becoming. The *āsava* of views is to hold that the world is eternal, etc., and so on through the standard list of ten *avyākata*. The *āsava* of ignorance is lack of knowledge about suffering, its arising, cessation and the way to its cessation (Dhs 195 § 1097–100).

> Question 2: Which are the *dhammas* that are with *āsavas*?[131]

The answer is that it is:

> Every *dhamma*, wholesome, unwholesome and indeterminate, whether relating to the worlds of sense, form or the formless, hence, the five *khandhas*.[132]

These *dhammas* (that are with *āsavas*) are also called favourable to the fetters (*dhammā saṃyojaniyā*, Dhs 199 § 1125).[133] They are *dhammas* that tend to become tied (*dhammā ganthanīyā*, Dhs 203 § 1141).[134] They are *dhammas* favourable to the hindrances (*dhammā nīvaraṇiyā*, Dhs 206 § 1164).[135] These *dhammas* are also clinging (*dhammā parāmaṭṭhā*, Dhs 208 § 1177).[136] They are favourable to attachment (*dhammā upādāniyā*, Dhs 213 § 1219).[137] These *dhammas* are also said to be defilements (*dhammā saṅkilesikā*, Dhs 217 § 1241).[138]

> Question 3: Which are the *dhammas* that are associated with the *āsavas*?[139]

The answer given is that:

> It is the *dhammas* associated with the *āsavas*, namely, the four *khandhas*.[140]

These are also said to be associated with the fetters, associated with the ties, associated with the hindrances, associated with clinging, associated with attachment, and with the defilements.[141]

> Question 4: Which are the *dhammas* that are both *āsavas* and with *āsavas*?[142]

The answer is that:

> It is the *āsavas* themselves.[143]

> Question 5: Which are the *dhammas* that are both *āsavas* and associated with the *āsavas*?[144]

The answer to this question suggests that ignorance, as so often, lies at the root of what is corrupting. The text states that sensual desire is an *āsava* associated with ignorance, or ignorance is an *āsava* associated with sensual desire. Or becoming is an *āsava* associated with ignorance, or ignorance is an *āsava* associated with becoming. Finally, view is an *āsava* associated with ignorance, or ignorance is an *āsava* associated with view.[145]

> Question 6: Which are the *dhammas* that are disconnected from the *āsavas* but with *āsavas*?[146]

The answer is that:

> It is the *dhammas* disconnected from the *āsavas*, but which, whether wholesome, unwholesome or indeterminate, have them as concomitants, whether they belong to the world of sense, form or the formless, in other words the five *khandhas*.[147]

These same *dhammas* are disconnected from the fetters, yet favourable to them, disconnected from the ties but tending to become tied, disconnected from the hindrances but tending to become hindrances, disconnected from clinging but tending to cling, disconnected from attachment yet favourable to it, disconnected from defilements but still defiled.[148]

These are the first group of questions and answers. They suggest an evaluation of various *dhammas* which, although not essentially corrupt, tend to become corrupt through various types of attachment. It should be remembered that most wrong-views (not necessarily those denying that actions have consequences) are based upon interpreting or becoming attached to what is conditioned, the *khandhas*, which are identified with *dukkha*. The *Dhammasaṅgaṇi* is not suggesting that there is anything corrupt about the *khandhas* themselves, but that they tend to become an object of attachment. The *khandhas* are 'disconnected from corruptions' (*āsava-vipayuttā*) but 'with corruptions' (*sāsava*). Such *dhammas* can be wholesome. But the *khandhas* tend to become corrupted, the object of attachment. Right-view entails seeing the arising and cessation of *dukkha*. This implies seeing the arising and cessation of attachment to that which is impermanent, the *khandhas*. In these *Dhammasaṅgaṇi* passages the Abhidhamma is reiterating what is found in the Nikāyas, i.e. do not regard the *khandhas* as self, etc., do not see according to them, in the sense of interpreting them for what they are not, this is attachment, but see them as they are, without *taṇhā*: this is wisdom and understanding.

The *Dhammasaṅgaṇi* also goes through a further six questions and answers that suggest the way in which things should be regarded. They are the positive evaluation of the previous six questions. These are in many respects explaining what is wholesome: the path, the fruits of the path and the unincluded.

> Question 1: Which are the *dhammas* that are not *āsavas*?[149]

The answer given is that:

> It is every *dhamma*, wholesome, unwholesome and indeterminate, which is not included in the *āsavas* [etc., for subsequent passages, fetters, ties, hindrances, clingings, attachments or defilements] whether relating to the worlds of sense, form, or the formless, or to the life that is unincluded, hence, the four *khandhas*, all form, and the uncompounded element.[150]

These *dhammas* are also not fetters, nor ties, nor hindrances, nor a clinging, they do not have the attribute of attachment, nor of defilement.[151] As Bhikkhu Bodhi has noted about the *Khandha-sutta* of the *Khandha-vagga* (S III 47–8), which I discussed above, the only *khandhas* classified as without *āsavas* or attachment, as I have already considered, are the four mental *khandhas* occurring in the four *lokuttara* paths and fruits. As Bhikkhu Bodhi suggests, these passages from the *Dhammasaṅgaṇi* are describing how certain *dhammas* are capable of being with *āsavas* and attachment, though they are not in and of themselves with *āsavas* and attachment.[152] The *Dhammasaṅgaṇi* is also suggesting that the cognitive processes of the paths and the fruits are not capable of being with *āsavas* or attachment. The dichotomy between the world of attachment and non-attachment is clearly being described. This is emphasised in the second question.

> Question 2: Which are the *dhammas* that are without *āsavas*?[153]

The answer is that:

> It is the paths that are the unincluded, the fruits of the paths and the uncompounded element.[154]

These *dhammas* are also unfavourable to the fetters, tend not to become tied, are unfavourable to the hindrances, unfavourable to clinging, unfavourable to attachment and not defiled.[155] These *dhammas*, the paths and the fruits of the paths, are described as *anāsavā*, and are without all the afflictions and attachments cited.

These two descriptions explain, I think, the way of seeing the world without greed, hatred and delusion. The first explanation states that there is a world that, in and of itself, is not corrupt. The second explanation states that there is a way of perceiving the world which is without corruptions, it is wholesome and does not cause *dukkha*, even though it may perceive *dhammas* that are unwholesome. This is a description, in certain respects, of the world and the mind that perceives it. This process can also be described in the following way. The first explanation states that a *dhamma* can be 'unwholesome' (*akusala*) but need not be a corruption, fetter, etc. Whether a *dhamma* is wholesome or unwholesome is due, in part, to our reaction to it, our perception of it. The way to react to what is wholesome, unwholesome or indeterminate is given in the second explanation. It is the detached order of seeing of the Buddhist path which is not included in the world. This detached order of seeing is always wholesome. The next four questions and answers further refine certain aspects of this process.

> Question 3: Which are the *dhammas* that are disconnected from the *āsavas*?[156]

These are:

> Those *dhammas* disconnected from the *āsavas*, etc. [change for subsequent sections], namely, the four *khandhas*, all form, and the uncompounded element.[157]

These *dhammas* are also disconnected from the fetters, disconnected from the ties, disconnected from the hindrances, disconnected from clinging, disconnected from attachment, and disconnected from the defilements.[158]

> Question 4: Which are the *dhammas* that are with *āsavas* but are not *āsavas*.[159]

The answer is that it is:

> The *dhammas* that have the foregoing *dhammas* i.e. the four *āsavas*, etc. [change for subsequent sections], as their concomitants, that is all *dhammas*, wholesome, unwholesome and indeterminate, which are with *āsavas*, whether these *dhammas* relate to the worlds of sense, form, or the formless; in other words the five *khandhas*.[160]

These *dhammas* are also favourable to the fetters but are not fetters, tend to become tied but are not ties, are favourable to the hindrances but are not hindrances, cling but are not a clinging, are favourable to attachment but are not an attachment, and are defiling but not defilements.[161]

> Question 5: Which are the *dhammas* associated with the *āsavas*, but are not *āsavas*?[162]

The answer is that:

> It is the *dhammas* associated with the foregoing *dhammas* [i.e. the four *āsavas*, etc.] that is the four *khandhas*.[163]

These *dhammas* are also said to be associated with the fetters but are not fetters, they are associated with the ties but are not ties, they are associated with the hindrances, but are not hindrances.[164] These states are also associated with attachment but are not attachment, associated with defilements but are not themselves defilements.[165] Although the four *khandhas* are associated (*sampayuttā*) with these afflictions they are not in and of themselves afflictions. The *khandhas* are now described as 'associated' with the various corruptions, but not themselves corruptions. In the previous explanation all wholesome, unwholesome and indeterminate *dhammas* were with corruptions etc., but not corruptions. Now they are explained as associated with the corruptions. The point is similar to the one made in the *Khandha-sutta* of the *Khandha-vagga* (S III 47–8), which I cited above, which suggests that there are five *khandhas* and five *khandhas* subject to attachment. The *khandhas* are not themselves corrupt. However, they are liable to give rise to corruptions. If the mind is not calmed (by action) it tends to become attached to the ideas of the cognitive process. The point made in both the Nikāyas and Abhidhamma is that the world tends to attachment. To stop this, a radical adaptation of how we apprehend things, *dhammas*, is needed. This radical adaptation begins with stream-attainment. This process is made explicit in the final question, which asks:

> Question 6: Which are the *dhammas* disconnected from the *āsavas* and not with *āsavas*?[166]

The answer is that it is:

> The paths that are the unincluded, the fruits of the paths, and the uncompounded element.[167]

These *dhammas* are also said to be disconnected from the fetters and not favourable to them, disconnected from the ties and tend not to become tied, disconnected from the hindrances and unfavourable to them, disconnected from clinging and not a clinging, disconnected from attachment and not favourable to it and disconnected from the defilements and not defiling.[168] Again, the paths and the fruits are described as *anāsavā*, and also disconnected (*vippayuttā*) with all the afflictions. The Abhidhamma is clearly explaining that the *dhamma* is for the relinquishing of all bases and obsessions.

As I suggested above, these passages are reiterating certain themes found in the Nikāyas. This is that one should apprehend things as they are and this will cause non-attachment and liberation. This passage from the Abhidhamma, which I have considered at some length, is reiterating a similar theme: things should be seen without grasping them. We should apprehend the world without attachment. This is a relatively simple teaching but one which the Abhidhamma passage articulates in what at first appears an extremely complex fashion. It is a simple teaching in that, as I suggested at the outset of the present discussion, it does not point to the changing of the world but to our perception of it. This aspect of Buddhist thought suggests that the problem of *dukkha* should not be considered apart from the greed, hatred and delusion that affect our understanding of the world. This teaching suggests that there is a way of seeing the world without craving and attachment and that this is accomplished by the Buddhist path. It is also a way of apprehending the world that undermines the holding of any position or proposition.

Let me summarise my discussion of the *Dhammasaṅgaṇi*. It has suggested three things. First, the *Dhammasaṅgaṇi* explains what is wholesome and what is unwholesome. Primarily, what is unwholesome are those *dhammas* associated with greed, hatred and delusion. The wholesome are those *dhammas* not associated with greed, hatred and delusion. Part of my argument is that this is suggestive of a preoccupation with the way we perceive and act in the world, not with the world itself. Theravāda Buddhism is interested in the mind and how it works. Second, through its description of the included and unincluded, it is suggested that you cannot be attached to what is part of the path. The unincluded is not part of the world of craving and attachment. Third, the *Dhammasaṅgaṇi* explains those *dhammas* connected and disconnected from various defilements. It explains, as it were, how subtle the reactions of body, speech and mind are when they are part of the unincluded.

The *Paṭṭhāna*: turning medicine into poison and poison into medicine

I would now like to consider a passage from the *Paṭṭhāna*. It describes how wholesome and unwholesome actions and practices of body, speech and mind give rise to various wholesome and unwholesome actions.

The simile of the raft from the *Alagaddūpama-sutta* (M I 130–42), at M I 134–5, suggests that the *dhamma* is similar to a raft. As a raft should be abandoned once the river has been crossed, so the *dhamma* is for the purpose of crossing over (to *nibbāna*), it should not be grasped once its purpose has been fulfilled. Even 'good states' should be abandoned, let alone 'bad states'.[169] What the simile of the raft is stating, in my interpretation, is that even wholesome acts, if they become an object of attachment, can lead to an unwholesome outcome. Even right-views, if they are held, are unwholesome. If they are an object of attachment, they are wrong-views.

The *Papañcasūdanī* (in its commentary on the *Alagaddūpama-sutta*) illustrates the 'good states' which one should abandon, which one should not be attached to, using the examples of 'calm and insight'. As an example of attachment to calm the commentary cites the *Laṭukopama-sutta* (M I 447–56) at M I 455–6. The *Laṭukopama-sutta* states that one should successively abandon each of the *rūpa* and *arūpa-jhānas*, and not become attached to them (Ps II 109). As an example of attachment to insight the commentary cites the *Mahātaṇhāsankhaya-sutta* (M I 256–71) at M I 260. In that *sutta* it is stated that the purified and bright-view (*diṭṭhi parisuddhā pariyodātā*), which sees the conditioned nature of phenomena, should not become an object of attachment (Ps II 109).[170] In other words, right-view should not, indeed cannot, give rise to craving.

It appears that a passage from the *Paṭṭhāna* makes a similar point to the simile of the raft. The text states that '*kusala dhammas* are related to *kusala dhammas* by object condition'.[171] The term 'object condition' (*ārammaṇa-paccaya*), the second of the twenty-four conditions of the *Paṭṭhāna*, indicates an object of thought or consciousness which causes other *dhammas* to arise.[172] The conditioned *dhammas* take the former *dhammas* as their object.[173] The 'object' (*ārammaṇa*) in this context are certain aspects of the Buddhist path. The text states that 'after having offered the offering, having undertaken the precept, having fulfilled the duty of observance (one) reviews it'.[174] As I understand this passage, these various acts are being used as the object that will condition other mental states.[175] The text continues that one reviews such acts formerly well done (*pubbe suciṇṇāni*). Having emerged from *jhāna*, one reviews *jhāna* (*jhānaṃ paccavekkhati*). It is explained that learners review change of lineage[176] and purification.[177] It is next stated that learners, having emerged from the path, review the path.[178] Learners or ordinary people practise insight into the impermanence, suffering and selflessness of the wholesome,[179] which must refer to the wholesome *dhamma*, the *jhāna*. Finally, by the knowledge of penetration into others' minds they know the wholesome mind of other beings,[180] which I take to refer to the *abhiññā* of knowing others' minds.

I would like to compare this passage to one a few lines later in the text which states how 'the wholesome *dhamma* is related to the unwholesome *dhamma* by object condition'.[181] Again it is explained that the object condition (*ārammaṇa-paccaya*) is the same aspect of the Buddhist path. The text states that, after having offered the offering, having undertaken the precept, having fulfilled the duty of observance, one again reviews it (*paccavekkhati*) but this time 'enjoys and delights in it' (*taṃ assādeti abhinandati*).[182] The *Paṭṭhāna* next states that these acts are taken as object (*ārabbha*) and 'lust, wrong-views, doubt, restlessness and displeasure arise'.[183] One 'delights in these acts formerly well done'.[184] Again the text explains that taking them as object, 'lust, wrong-views, doubt, restlessness and grief arise'. Next it is stated that, 'having emerged from *jhāna*, the person enjoys and delights in them'.[185] For the third time it is stated that, taking the *jhāna* as object, there arises 'lust, wrong-views, doubt and restlessness'. Finally it is said that, when the *jhāna* has disappeared, the person regrets it and there arises grief.[186]

These are two ways of practising the *dhamma*, of using the raft. The first way, the wholesome way, reviews various practices, reviews the *jhāna*, reviews change of lineage, reviews purification and reviews the path. It practises insight into the nature of the *jhānas*. But the raft is put down. The *dhamma* is not made into an object of attachment. The second way is to make what is wholesome unwholesome. This time one enjoys and delights in the various practises and, taking them as object (*taṃ ārabbha*), there arises lust, etc. Enjoying and delighting in the *jhānas*, taking them as object, there arises lust, wrong-views, doubt and restlessness. This causes grief when the *jhānas* disappear. One carries the raft. The *dhamma* is made into an object of attachment.

The *Paṭṭhāna* is making an important point, which is that spiritual practice must be undertaken in a certain way. This Abhidhamma passage is explaining in technical terms what can be found in earlier parts of the canon. If you hold on to right practice, to what is wholesome, the result may be unwholesome. The *dhamma* should not be made an object of attachment. What is *sammā-diṭṭhi* has the possibility of becoming *micchā-diṭṭhi* if the view is held to with attachment, if one enjoys and delights in it. It is stating that the various observances and the *jhānas* are *kusala*, they are wholesome, but the way they are used can cause them to become unwholesome. The medicine is turned into poison.

As if to make these points even clearer the *Paṭṭhāna* then explains how some unwholesome *dhammas* are related to other unwholesome *dhammas*. This is quite straightforward. The text states that 'an unwholesome *dhamma* is related to an unwholesome *dhamma* by object condition'.[187] In this case, one enjoys and delights in lust. Taking lust as object causes lust, wrong-views, doubt, restlessness and displeasure to arise.[188] Alternatively, one takes wrong-view, doubt, restlessness or displeasure as object, and the same factors arise.[189]

However, of some interest is that the *Paṭṭhāna* also explains how an unwholesome *dhamma* can be related to a wholesome *dhamma*. The text states that 'an unwholesome *dhamma* is related to a wholesome *dhamma* by object condition'.[190] It is stated that 'learners review the eradicated defilements and the uneradicated defilements, and they know the defilements addicted to before'.[191] They are aware of what is unwholesome, and this awareness is wholesome. The text continues that 'learners or ordinary people practise insight into the impermanence, suffering and not-self of the unwholesome'.[192] This is the same practice carried out on the *jhānas*; this time, however, the objects of practice are unwholesome *dhammas*. The point that is being made is that even actions and practices that are usually destructive can be made constructive by correct reflection upon them. The *Paṭṭhāna* is stating how various acts can be used in different ways. Good acts can be used in a destructive way, and destructive acts can be used in a positive way. One could even suggest, using the final example, that the *Paṭṭhāna* is describing how we can learn from bad experiences. Or, to put this another way, all experiences can be used and be of benefit on the Buddhist path.[193] The poison becomes the medicine. By the same token, even wholesome acts, whether physical or mental, can be unwholesome. The medicine becomes the poison. The *Paṭṭhāna* is stating explicitly what is often only implicit in the Nikāyas. Various observances, precepts and the practising of the *jhānas* should be wholesome, but can give rise to lust, wrong-views, doubt and restlessness. On the other hand unwholesome *dhammas*, if apprehended and used in a certain way, can produce wholesome states. If there is no greed, hatred and delusion, any experience can be of benefit. A wholesome *dhamma* can produce unwholesome action, and an unwholesome *dhamma* can produce wholesome action.

The three gateways to liberation

Finally, in this chapter I would like to consider a passage from the *Nettippakaraṇa* which suggests that certain hindrances, connected with wrong-views, are overcome by one of three gateways to liberation (*tīhi vimokkhamukhehi*). This discussion aims to show how the process of achieving a state free from craving and attachment is realised. The passages that I will discuss consider in some detail exactly which hindrances are associated with various forms of craving and which practices overcome them. The three gateways are:

> The dispositionless gateway to liberation (*appaṇihitaṃ vimokkhamukhaṃ*)
> The emptiness gateway to liberation (*suññatā vimokkhamukhaṃ*)
> The signless gateway to liberation (*animittaṃ vimokkhamukhaṃ*, Nett 123).

These categories suggest how different hindrances are overcome by different practices. There appears to be some connection between these gateways and the four *satipaṭṭhānas*.[194] There is an emphasis in this analysis on emptiness overcoming corruptions based upon views. There is also an analysis of different temperaments that are defiled in different ways, requiring different practices to overcome these defilements.

Chapter 3 of the *Nettippakaraṇa* is called the 'Moulding of the Guidelines' (*Nayasamuṭṭhānaṃ*). It begins by suggesting how ignorance is a hindrance (*nīvarana*) and craving is a fetter (*saṃyojana*). The exposition is an attempt to show how those of different temperaments have different hindrances which are predominant, and so have different ways to reach their goal. Those in whom ignorance is predominant are called those of 'view-temperament' (*diṭṭhi-caritā*). Those in whom craving is predominant are called those of 'craving-temperament' (*taṇhā-caritā*, Nett 109). On one level, those of view-temperament practise self-torment, and those of craving-temperament are devoted to the pursuit of sensual pleasures (Nett 110); insight and calm overcome these. In another sense, those of view-temperament approach each of the *khandhas* as self, and those of craving-temperament approach self as possessing each of the *khandhas*, or the *khandhas* as in self, or the self as in the *khandhas* (i.e. *sakkāya-diṭṭhi*, Nett 111). The supramundane (*lokuttara*) eightfold path (encapsulating calm and insight), disconnected from worlds, is opposed to this.[195] We have again two ways of apprehending the world: the first based upon craving and attachment, the second on indifference and non-attachment. It is interesting that the distinction is made between view and craving-temperament. Though ignorance is predominant in those of view-temperament I do not take this as suggesting that ignorance is more of a hindrance in those of view-temperament than in those of craving-temperament. As I understand this, the term view-temperament applies to the craving of the mind. The *Nettippakaraṇa* is making the distinction between those who crave sensual pleasures and those who crave mental objects.

The *Nettippakaraṇa* goes on to consider these two ways of seeing in some detail. It analyses ten sets of 'defilements' (*kilesā*) and considers whether they occur in a person of 'craving-temperament' (*taṇhā-carita*), or 'view-temperament' (*diṭṭhi-carita*). It then further refines its analysis by suggesting that these defilements occur in persons of 'lusting-temperament' (*rāga-caritassa*), 'hating-temperament' (*dosa-caritassa*), 'dull-view-temperament' (*diṭṭhi-caritassa mandassa*), or 'intelligent-view-temperament' (*diṭṭhi-caritassa udatthassa*). The meaning of these two latter categories will become clear. Finally, the means of overcoming these defilements is given, whether that be by the dispositionless, emptiness, or the signless gateway to liberation.

The defilements analysed fall into ten groups of four:

'four nutriments' (*cattāro āhārā*)
'four perversions' (*cattāro vipallāsā*)
'four attachments' (*cattāri upādānāni*)
'four bonds' (*cattāro yogā*)
'four ties' (*cattāro ganthā*)
'four corruptions' (*cattāro āsavā*)
'four floods' (*cattāro oghā*)
'four barbs' (*catatāro sallā*)
'four steadying points for consciousness' (*catasso viññāṇaṭṭhitiyo*)
'four goings on bad ways' (*cattāri agatigamanāni*, Nett 114).

The first distinction made is to classify these defilement as to whether they are defilements of a person of craving-temperament or view-temperament. This is done in the following way: the first two nutriments, perversions, attachments, etc. are imperfections in a person of craving temperament:

Defilements in a person of craving-temperament (**taṇhā-caritassa puggalassa upakkilesā**, *Nett 114–15*)

'physical nutriment' (*kabaḷiṃkāro āhāro*), 'nutriment as contact' (*phasso āhāro*);
'perversion that there is beauty in the ugly' (*asubhe subhan ti vipallāso*), 'perversion that there is pleasure in the painful' (*dukkhe sukhan ti vipallāso*);
'attachment to sensual desire' (*kāmupādānaṃ*), and 'attachment to becoming' (*bhavupādānaṃ*);
'bond of sensual desire' (*kāmayogo*), 'bond of becoming' (*bhavayogo*);
'bodily tie of covetousness' (*abhijjhā-kāyagantho*), 'bodily tie of ill-will' (*byāpādo kāyagantho*);
'corruption of sensual desire' (*kāmāsavo*), 'corruption of becoming' (*bhavāsavo*);
'flood of sensual desire (*kāmogho*), 'flood of becoming' (*bhavogho*);

'barb of lust' (*rāgasallo*), 'barb of hate' (*dosasallo*);
'form as a steadying point for consciousness passing on' (*rūpūpagā viññāṇaṭṭhiti*) 'feeling as a steadying point for consciousness passing on' (*vedanūpagā viññāṇaṭṭhiti*);
'going on a bad way through will' (*chandā agatigamanaṃ*) 'going on a bad way though hate' (*dosā agatigamanaṃ*).

Defilements in a person of view-temperament (diṭṭhi-caritassa puggalassa upakkilesā, *Nett 114–15)*

'nutriment as mind-choice' (*manosañcetanāhāro*), 'nutriment as consciousness' (*viññāṇāhāro*);
'perversion that there is permanence in the impermanent' (*anicce niccan ti vipallāso*), 'perversion that there is "self in the not-self"' (*anattani attā ti vipallāso*);
'attachment to view' (*diṭṭhūpādānaṃ*), 'attachment to the doctrine of self' (*attavādūpādānaṃ*);
'bond of views' (*diṭṭhi-yogo*), 'bond of ignorance' (*avijjāyogo*);
'bodily tie of clinging [to precepts and vows]' (*parāmāsa-kāya-gantho*), 'bodily tie of adherence to truth' (*saccābhinivesa-kāya-gantho*);
'corruption of views' (*diṭṭhāsavo*), 'corruption of ignorance' (*avijjāsavo*);
'flood of views' (*diṭṭhogho*), 'flood of ignorance' (*avijjogho*);
'barb of conceit' (*mānasallo*), 'barb of delusion' (*mohasallo*);[196]
'apperception as steadying point for consciousness' (*saññūpagā viññāṇaṭṭhiti*), 'volitional formations as a steadying point for consciousness' (*saṃkhārūpagā viññāṇaṭṭiti*);
'going in a bad way through fear' (*bhayā agatigamanaṃ*) 'going in a bad way through delusion' (*mohā agatigamanaṃ*).

The text appears to be suggesting the simple distinction between what are, in the main, attachments to sense objects, and what are forms of attachment to mental objects. There are, though, as I have said, four further categories. The text introduces the categories of a person of 'lusting-temperament' (*rāga-caritassa*), a person of 'hating-temperament' (*dosa-caritassa*), a person of 'dull-view temperament' (*diṭṭhi-caritassa mandassa*), and a person of 'intelligent-view-temperament' (*diṭṭhi-caritassa udatthassa*), and analyses which defilements apply to each category. The text takes the first nutriment, perversion, attachment, bond, tie, *āsava*, flood, barb, steadying point for consciousness and going in a bad way, stating that these are all imperfections in a person of lusting-temperament (*ime rāgacaritassa puggalassa upakkilesā*, Nett 117). The same procedure is carried out for the other temperaments. Hence the second nutriment, perversion, etc. are imperfections in a person of hating-temperament.[197] The third nutriment, perversion, etc. are imperfections in a person of dull-view-temperament.[198] The fourth nutriment, perversion, etc. are imperfections in a person of intelligent-view-temperament.[199]

The text makes one final classification of these defilements, and that is the means to overcome them. This time the classification is three-fold and follows the three gateways to liberation (*tīhi vimokkhamukhehi*, Nett 119), by which they are overcome. The first two nutriments, perversions, attachments, bonds, etc. are understood as being overcome through the dispositionless gateway to liberation.[200] The third nutriment, perversion, attachment, bond, etc. are understood as being overcome through emptiness.[201] The fourth nutriment, perversion, attachment, bond, etc. are understood as being overcome through the signless.[202]

It is interesting to consider the distinctions the text is making here, particularly in the last two categories. One clue as to the reasons for these distinctions may be found a little earlier in the text. Of the one 'steady in the third perversion, that there is "permanence in the impermanent" ',[203] it is said that this person, 'assumes the view that has expectant affection for the round [of existences], and this is attachment to views'.[204] This person is 'fettered by a destructive view, through being attached to view, and this is the bond of views'.[205] On the other hand, for one 'steady in the fourth perversion, that there is "self in the not-self" ',[206] having 'supposed a self, is attached',[207] and this person is 'fettered by ignorance through attachment to the doctrine of self, and this is called the bond of ignorance'.[208] The text is explaining various degrees of attachment to acts of cognition. It has explained that all these defilements occur in a person of view-temperament, but is now making the distinction between a dull-view, or one of dull-view-temperament, and an intelligent-view, or one of intelligent-view-temperament. It is tempting to suggest that the former view is held with a greater degree of attachment than the latter. In a sense the person of dull-view-temperament craves and is ignorant. Those of intelligent-view-temperament are only ignorant. Further, we must remember that for the Theravādins, after stream-attainment there are no more wrong-views, but, as we have seen, right-view still has a function. I would suggest that the role of right-view could be its very function in destroying, or keeping in check, attachment to any form of insight (cf. the discussion of the *Paṭṭhāna*). The stream-attainer is not attached to views, but still has a degree of ignorance.

The *Nettippakaraṇa* then explains what the three gateways to liberation (*tīhi vimokkhamukhehī*) consist of. It uses another group of ten categories, each consisting of four items. This is a positive counterpart of what went before (i.e. the four nutriments, perversions etc.) but expressed as the wholesome alternative of the negative *dhammas* that 'follow the world's round' (*lokavaṭṭānūsārino dhammā*, Nett 119); these ideas 'follow the world's stopping' (*lokavivaṭṭānusārī*, Nett 113).

These 40 ideas are the:

'four ways' (*catasso paṭipadā*)[209]
'four foundations of mindfulness' (*cattāro satipaṭṭhānā*)[210]
'four meditations' (*cattāri jhānāni*)
'four abidings' (*cattāro vihārā*)[211]
'four right-endeavours' (*cattāro sammappadhānā*)[212]

'four wonderful, marvellous ideas' (*cattāro acchariyā abbhūtā dhammā*)[213]
'four expressions' (*cattārī adhiṭṭhānāni*)[214]
'four ways of keeping concentration in being' (*catasso samādhibhāvanā*)[215]
'four ideas dealing with pleasure' (*cattāro sukhabhāgiyā dhammā*)[216]
'four measureless states' (*catasso appamāṇā*).[217]

The dispositionless gateway to liberation consists of the first and second ways, foundations of mindfulness, meditations, abidings, etc.[218] The former, the first way, etc. is also called 'medicine for a person of lusting-temperament' (*rāgacaritassa puggalassa bhesajjaṃ*), and the second way, etc. 'medicine for a person of hating-temperament' (*dosacaritassa puggalassa bhesajjaṃ*, Nett 122). The emptiness gateway to liberation is the third way, foundation of mindfulness, meditation, abiding, etc.[219] These are also 'medicine for a person of dull-view-temperament' (*diṭṭhi-caritassa mandassa puggalassa bhesajjaṃ*, Nett 122). The signless gateway to liberation consists of the fourth way, foundation of mindfulness, meditation, abiding, etc.[220] These are also said to be the 'medicine for a person of intelligent-view-temperament' (*diṭṭhi-caritassa mandassa puggalassa bhesajjaṃ*, Nett 122).[221] Clearly, in this exposition, the person of view-temperament is described more precisely, and the overcoming of the defilements in a person of view-temperament can be overcome by the emptiness or the signless gateway to liberation.[222]

The *Nettippakaraṇa* is describing, I think, how different defilements are overcome by different methods. There appears to be some connection between not-self, right-view and emptiness. Buddhaghosa equates these notions by citing the *Paṭisambhidāmagga*: 'When one who has great wisdom brings [volitional formations] to mind as not-self, he acquires the emptiness liberation.'[223] As I have already said, it is tempting to understand *sammā-diṭṭhi* as a way of seeing that incorporates the notion of *śūnyatā* (emptiness) in other parts of Buddhist thought. In later Buddhist thought there is the connection between *paṭicca-samuppāda* and *śūnyatā*. Emptiness is equated with *paṭicca-samuppāda*.[224] In a well-known *Saṃyutta* passage, the Buddha refuses to assert whether there is or is not a self precisely because this would give the mind an object of attachment in the form of permanence or impermanence.[225] The *dhamma* is an empty doctrine in the sense that attachment to it is wrong-view. Knowledge of the *dhamma* must not produce craving and this is the function and significance, in fact one of the meanings of the term *sammā-diṭṭhi*. The *dhamma*, by definition, cannot be a view. In the same way, *sammā-diṭṭhi* requires, ultimately, the destruction of all views and is 'empty' of content in the sense of not producing craving and attachment. In this way it is the emptiness gateway to liberation.

I am suggesting that right-view is not intended to be a view at all. There is a danger that in the practice of breaking things down into *dhammas* the Buddhist ascetic could become attached to the *dhammas* themselves. The early texts seem aware of this problem and often stress the 'non-viewness' of right-view.

In this chapter I have suggested that right-view, understood as part of the *lokuttara* path, does not have any of the attributes that views normally have. It is not an object that you can be attached to. It does not state a position, it is intended to express the middle-way. I have attempted to show that the understanding of views as a type of attachment is found in the Nikāyas. I showed that, in a passage from the *Brahmajāla-sutta*, views are understood as bases (*diṭṭhiṭṭhānā*), which are grasped (*gahitā*) and clung to (*parāmaṭṭhā*). These views lead to a certain negative rebirth through their influence on action. The view, or understanding, that transcends this is not clung to (*taṃ ca pajānanaṃ na parāmasati*). This view also has a definite outcome. It influences action, it leads to peace (*nibbuti*). I have suggested that the *Brahmajāla-sutta* understanding of views as clinging and adherence is likely to be the source of the early Abhidhamma understanding of all views as potential objects of attachment. This Abhidhamma understanding does not somehow distort earlier teachings but makes explicit what is implicit in the Nikāyas: that views are a source of craving and attachment. Right-view must be the opposite of this. In this sense right-view is not a view, but transcends all views.

6

VIEWS AND NON-ATTACHMENT

I began this book by suggesting that there are two ways in which the notion of *diṭṭhi* is understood: the opposition and the no-views understandings. I have argued that neither of these gives a proper interpretation of the notion of views. By the term *sammā-diṭṭhi* is meant neither a correct view which stands in opposition to wrong-views, nor the rejection of all views, but a completely different order of seeing that transcends all views. In this concluding chapter I would like to consider some of the issues at stake in this understanding. To begin with, I would like to explore in more detail the issue I considered in the Introduction on whether right-view can express a teaching that advises complete non-attachment from all acts of cognition.

The Buddha's teachings and no-views

Grace Burford has posed the following question:

> Can a *dhamma* that consists of the rejection of all attachment, even to *dhammas* themselves, be presented coherently in oral or written form? Can the truth, so conceived, ever be expressed in words, as a specific teaching?[1]

Put another way: can there be a *dhamma*, a teaching, that expresses freedom from all 'conceptual contents?'[2] As Burford explains, 'the view of no-views [...] cannot explicitly deny the validity of views that deny the validity of other views without undermining its own authority.'[3] Does not the ideal of no-views become a view itself? Is there not a view needed to overcome views? There are problems with the no-views understanding of views.

My interpretation of views, the transcendence of views, points to a step-by-step, gradual path in which actions and views are reciprocal in bringing about the cessation of craving. In other words, calm and insight overcome craving and ignorance. The opposition and the no-views understandings are based upon a misunderstanding of the notion of views. If we attempt to understand the tradition on its own terms then there is coherence. The Buddha and the stream-attainer have 'put away' (*apanītam*, M I 486) all attachment to views. The transcendence of views is expressed as, 'such is form (feeling, apperceptions, volitional formations and consciousness), such is its origin, such its disappearance'.[4] This is the seeing of the rise and fall of *dhammas*.

Did the Pāli canon, originally teaching complete non-attachment, become attached to the *dhamma* and so distort much of its teaching? It is sometimes argued that the Mahāyāna emerged because the *dhamma* had become an object of attachment for those who taught non-attachment.[5] The Abhidhamma had become attached to its method of analysis. The teachings had become a mental proliferation (*papañca*), the fuel for craving and attachment. Bad *dhammas* had been abandoned, but good *dhammas* had become an object of greed and attachment. The Mahāyāna reversed this process so that the teachings could fulfil their soteriological function again. Nothing was to be reified, nothing could be an object of attachment. The raft, having served its purpose of crossing the flood of craving and attachment, could be put aside.[6] I do not agree that the early tradition succumbed to such a process. As I have said, the *Brahmajāla-sutta* is usually taken as an example of the no-views understanding in the Nikāyas because it does not propose a right-view in opposition to wrong-views.[7] I have argued that it does because it describes how the dependent nature of all views, of all *dhammas*, should be seen: they are impermanent, suffering and not-self, they rise and they fall. This is *sammā-diṭṭhi*: a radically different order of seeing which transcends all views. I am arguing that the nature of right-view is such that it should not be regarded as a view. It is the opposite of wrong-view in the sense that non-attachment is the opposite of grasping and attachment. Wrong-view is something that has become (*kiñci bhūtaṃ*), is put together (*saṃkhataṃ*), is thought out (*cetayitaṃ*), and is dependent on something else (*paṭiccasamuppannaṃ*). This, by definition, is impermanent, and what is impermanent is *dukkha*. What is *dukkha* should be regarded: 'This is not mine, this I am not, this is not my self', i.e. with right-view.[8] Right-view is something that is not become, not put together, not thought out and not dependent on something else. It is this very insight into the nature of phenomena that constitutes *sammā-diṭṭhi*.[9]

The early Buddhist tradition does then propose a right-view, but this is not a position. You can be accomplished in view (*diṭṭhi-sampanna*), and gain purification of view (*diṭṭhi-visuddhi*), but these views are right and wholesome because they are closer to the ideal of non-attachment. To achieve right-view is then to achieve a certain insight. This is the context of the realisation of right-view. To achieve right-view is to be accomplished in a different order of seeing. I would go so far as to state that the Buddhist doctrine of *anattā* is proposed because it expresses that *dhamma* which Burford argues would be difficult to express: a *dhamma* that teaches the rejection of all attachment. Any position is an expression of attachment, an apperception (*saññā*), a mental object.

The no-views understanding, as I discussed in the Introduction, is usually thought to be most pronounced in two verse collections from the *Sutta-nipāta*, the

Aṭṭhakavagga and the *Pārāyanavagga*. These texts have struck many as sounding a silent teaching beyond words.[10] However, these texts are explaining something very definite about views. For example, in the *Māgandiya-sutta* (Sn 835–47) the Buddha tells Māgandiya that purity is not got by views, learning or knowledge, or by precepts and vows, *nor* by absence of these.[11] It is by non-attachment and non-dependence that one achieves calm. Māgandiya contends that if purity is not found by means of views, learning or knowledge, or by virtuous conduct and vows, nor by absence of these then the teaching is foolish (Sn 840). The Buddha replies:

> Dependent upon view, inquiring, Māgandiya, [...] you have become infatuated in respect of what has been grasped, and hence you have not even the slightest notion (of what I am talking about). Therefore you regard (it) as foolish.[12]

The *sutta* then goes on to describe those free from attachment:

> One who has knowledge (*vedagu*) does not become proud because of view or thought, for he is not like that. He cannot be influenced by action or thought, for he is not like that. He cannot be influenced by action or learning; he is not led into clingings (to views).
>
> There are no ties for one who is devoid of apperceptions. There are no illusions for one who is released through wisdom. But those who have grasped apperception and view wander in the world, causing offence.[13]

This is similar to (if not the same as) the 'emancipation through non-attachment' (*anupādā vimutto*, D I 22) spoken of in the *Brahmajāla-sutta*. Right-view, being itself *paññā*, is the absence of grasping and attachment. One could argue that passages such as these are explaining the vision of the one who is accomplished in view (*diṭṭhi-sampanna*). It describes the vision of the stream-attainer who has no-views in the sense of having no craving for views.

In order to discuss these issues I would like to consider three related subjects in the first half of this chapter. First, I will discuss the difference in the understanding of views in the *Aṭṭhakavagga* compared to their treatment in other parts of the Pāli canon. Second, I would like to consider the *Aṭṭhakavagga's* rejection of certain means of knowledge, namely, dependence on what is seen, heard, thought and cognized. Third, I would like to discuss the arguments of Grace Burford (and others) that the Buddhism of the four primary Nikāyas and commentaries proposes a superior teaching, which contradicts the no-views understanding of the *Aṭṭhakavagga*.

The understanding of views in the *Aṭṭhakavagga* compared to other parts of the Pāli canon

In a well-known article, 'Proto-Mādhyamika in the Pāli Canon', Luis Gómez has argued that the no-views understanding is only found in the *Sutta-nipāta* and in 'isolated' Nikāya passages, and that it only found full expression in the Madhyamaka. Gómez argues that:

> With the exception of the older parts of the Suttanipāta (*Aṭṭhakavagga* and *Pārāyanavagga*) and scattered passages in the Nikāyas, the Pāli tradition has adopted a view of *avidyā* which suggests a condemnation of specific theories or views, rather than an outright rejection of the clinging to theorising and opinionating. The ineffability of the goal is not taken to imply the impossibility of theorisation (as in the Mādhyamika), and theorisation is not seen as inextricably connected to clinging (as in the Suttanipāta). Nevertheless, the Pāli tradition preserves, in the Suttanipāta and elsewhere, several important passages in which one could perhaps discover some kind of 'proto-Mādhyamika'.[14]

Gómez describes the two understandings:

> [I]t is obvious then that the Aṭṭha's intention is not to propose a different view. Nor does it propose a nonview (systematic rejection of all views). The involved rhetoric of this short text seems to be aimed at an injunction to detachment from the tendency of the mind to become fixed in cognitive and affective extremes, in immutable mind-made polarities. I do not believe we could consistently interpret the Aṭṭha as the pronouncement of a self-serving Buddhist who believes that the clash of views is counter-productive merely because there is only one correct view and that he who possesses that view (that is, the Buddhist) can afford not to enter the ring of dispute, for, after all, he knows that he is right.[15]

I do not think a 'self-serving Buddhist' believes in right-view. To believe in right-view would be to adopt a position. I have argued that the reluctance to state any position, as expressed by the middle-way, is prominent in the Nikāyas and Pāli canon in general. Gómez also equates wrong-view with a form of ignorance. As I argued in Chapter 3, to do this is to misunderstand why views are wrong. They are primarily wrong because they are a form of attachment, not essentially a form of ignorance, though these ideas are clearly related in Buddhism. The *Aṭṭhakavagga* could be taken as a description of the non-attached cognition of the stream-attainer, and as such there is nothing incongruous with this description and that found in other parts of the Pāli canon. The stream-attainer sees the dependent nature of all phenomena, which is the middle-way, grasping no extremes. However, Gómez does not acknowledge such a process in the Pāli canon as a whole and argues that such ideas were 'unfortunately neglected' by the Abhidhamma.[16] This book has suggested the contrary.

Much of his argument is based upon an apparent condemnation of certain terms denoting wisdom or insight found in the *Aṭṭhakavagga*. This in turn is used as another way of distinguishing it from other parts of the Nikāyas. It is this aspect of the no-views understanding that leads me to question it, for it appears to propose the rejection of all views and knowledge. However, the *Aṭṭhakavagga* condemns attachment to knowledge, not knowledge itself.[17] Knowledge is a valid means to overcome *dukkha* if there is no craving for knowledge. Right-view can overcome wrong-view if the content of right-view is an expression of calm and insight: if it expresses what is true and of value, 'is' and 'ought'. However, Gómez claims that there is a criticism of knowledge (*ñāṇa*) found in the *Mahāviyuha-sutta* of the *Aṭṭhakavagga*. This is in the following verse:

> The brahmin, considering, does not submit to figments. He does not follow views (and) he has no association with knowledge, and knowing commonplace opinions he is indifferent to them (saying) 'Let others take them up'.[18]

He might equally have cited the *Paṭṭhāna* as giving a criticism of knowledge. The *Paṭṭhāna* describes something very similar to the *Mahāviyuha-sutta*. This is that there should be a correct attitude to the path. It should not give rise to craving and attachment. In fact, the early Abhidhamma suggests that right-view cannot give rise to craving and attachment. To have 'no association with knowledge' is not to be bound by it (*ñāṇabandhu*).

The *Suddhaṭṭhaka-sutta* is often cited as the epitome of the anti-knowledge thesis of the *Aṭṭhakavagga*. This *sutta* states that purity does not come by knowledge. But the *sutta* is clearly explaining attachment to knowledge:

> 'I see what is purified, highest, diseaseless. Purity comes to a man by means of what is seen.' Understanding this, knowing '(It is) the highest,' (and thinking) 'I am a seer of the purified,' he believes that knowledge (leads to purity).[19]

Knowledge usually implies knowledge of something. However, knowledge is being described in a certain way in the *Aṭṭhakavagga*. The *sutta* is explaining that if knowledge is taken as asserting that it is the highest knowledge, then it is a form of attachment. This is another way of saying 'only this is true, anything else is wrong'.[20] The middle-way is the *dhamma*, and apprehending it constitutes *ñāṇa*, or right-view, the non-attached seeing of the rise and fall of all *dhammas*.

The *Aṭṭhakavagga* does not follow the no-views understanding in the sense of rejecting all knowledge and views, it proposes the same thing as the four primary Nikāyas: the transcendence of all views. It seems to me that the opposition understanding and the no-views understanding have led us away from the teachings of both the four primary Nikāyas (which do not teach the opposition understanding), and the *Aṭṭhakavagga* (which does not teach the no-views understanding). They both teach the same thing; a non-attached attitude through the cultivation of right-view.

Dependence on what is seen, heard, thought and cognized

The *Aṭṭhakavagga's* insistence that one should not depend upon apperception (*saññā*), knowledge (*ñāṇa*), views (*diṭṭhi*), on what is seen (*diṭṭha*), heard (*suta*), or thought (*muta*), or on precepts and vows (*sīlabbata*),[21] is also consistent with the four primary Nikāyas. As I described above, the *Aṭṭhakavagga* teaches that purity is not by means of views, learning, knowledge or precepts and vows, nor is it by absence of these. The *Mahāviyuha-sutta* (Sn 895–914) speaks of giving up all precepts and vows and action both blameable and blameless.[22] This suggests a *dhamma* of non-involvement, not showing preference for what is seen and heard.[23] Preference or choice (*cetanā*) is involvement in *kamma*, in *saṃsāra* (Sn 901). In the *Suribheda-sutta* (Sn 848–61), the question is asked, 'having what vision and precepts is one called "calmed" '?[24] The answer is that it is not to be dependent,[25] not to prefer (*purekkhataṃ*), not having attachment, and not going astray among *dhammas.*[26] Right-view is an insight into the nature of reality that leads to calm.[27]

As has been shown, the dependence on what is seen, heard, thought and cognized is a familiar basis for wrong-views in the Nikāyas. The *Diṭṭhi-saṃyutta* explains how views arise due to attachment to whatever is seen, heard, thought, cognized, attained, sought after, and ranged over by the mind.[28] It is also explained in the *Alagaddūpama-sutta*, as I discussed in Chapter 1, that to regard the *khandhas*[29] or what is seen, heard, sensed, cognized, attained, sought after, and ranged over by the mind as: 'This is mine, this I am, this is my self'[30] is a basis for view (*diṭṭhiṭṭhānaṃ*). Without attachment and doubt concerning these things, wrong-view does not arise.[31] This constitutes stream-attainment, when all views are abandoned.[32]

To argue, as some have, that the relinquishment of attachment to what is seen, heard, thought and cognized is an isolated teaching in the Nikāyas, is perhaps to overlook the prominence of passages condemning such attitudes.[33] The Nikāyas suggest consistently and often that attachment to the *khandhas* is the cause of wrong-views, and this, I contend, is the same as stating that one should not be attached to what is seen, heard, thought or cognized. This way of seeing, the detached way expressive of right-view, is described in the *Dhammasaṅgaṇi* as the unincluded (*apariyāpannā*) explained as 'neither the issue of attachment nor favourable to it'.[34] This attitude of non-attachment is at least comparable to that described in the *Aṭṭhakavagga* as non-attachment from what is seen, heard or thought, from any view, apperception (*saññā*),[35] contact (*phassa*), or even dependence on knowledge (*ñāṇa*, Sn 800).[36] Just as the stream-attainer, one who has achieved right-view, is described as having no dependence upon any act of cognition, so the *Aṭṭhakavagga* advises the eradication of all attachment to views, apperceptions and knowledge. The sage of the *Aṭṭhakavagga* 'does not believe in any view at all',[37] but then nor does the stream-attainer of the Nikāyas. I suggest that the Nikāyas and the *Aṭṭhakavagga* describe the same cognitive attitude toward views, wrong or right. The *Aṭṭhakavagga* verses positing non-attachment from what is seen and heard are consistent with the Nikāyas in which the *dhamma* is a raft to which one should not become attached, and with the Abhidhamma description of *sammā-diṭṭhi* as *paññā*. If we wish to find teachings similar to the *Aṭṭhakavagga* in the Nikāyas, then we must be clear about the Nikāyas understanding of what constitutes right-view. I am arguing that right-view is not depending on (*upādāya*), not being attached to, or craving, the *khandhas*. It is non-dependence on knowledge and views. The Abhidhamma explains how attachment to insight and practice can cause unwholesome *dhammas* to arise. This was described in the *Paṭṭhāna*, which I considered in Chapter 5. If the *Paṭṭhāna* is criticising the act of giving, holding the precepts, the duty of observance, and the practising of the *jhānas*, then the *Aṭṭhakavagga* is criticising knowledge and wisdom. As it is unlikely that either text is critical of practice or knowledge, then it is likely that they are stating that attachment to the path is destructive.

As I have argued, the *Aṭṭhakavagga* and the Nikāyas are not critical of knowledge and truth but hold that attachment to knowledge and truth is detrimental. The reason that attachment to knowledge and truth is detrimental can be explained by the need for both calm and insight in the process of seeing the true nature of things. I would suggest that, in the same way that action influences knowledge and knowledge influences action, so the texts are describing how calm influences insight, and insight influences calm. In other words, seeing dependent-origination involves being calm, and being truly calm involves seeing dependent-origination.

The superior teaching?

Grace Burford has argued that the tradition distorted the original no-views understanding of the *Aṭṭhakavagga*. I do not think that the *Aṭṭhakavagga* teaches a no-views understanding and that such an interpretation of it distorts its true purport, namely, 'do not be attached to any view'. In commenting upon the analysis of the *Mahāniddesa*, she suggests that *taṇhā* and *diṭṭhi* are distinguished in the *Mahāniddesa* by their object: '"*taṇhā*" applies to desire for anything, from sensations of any kind to particular material objects or possessions; "*diṭṭhi*" applies specifically to desire for wrong-views'.[38] She continues:

> We have seen that, in the *Mahāniddesa*, desire, attachment, and dependence are often defined as both '*taṇhā*' [...] and '*diṭṭhi*' [...] If the commentator were to follow the model of the *Aṭṭhakavagga*, we would expect to find in the *Mahāniddesa* an explanation of the latter form of desire (i.e. view, *diṭṭhi*) as the selfish attachment to any particular view. We find instead a very consistent interpretation of this form of desire as desire for specific wrong-views. It is important to note that, by definition,

> there is nothing wrong with allegiance to the one correct teaching of the Buddha.[39]

As I have discussed in Chapter 3, the *Mahāniddesa* is consistent in explaining views as attachment, using many different terms to stress the fact that any view is a potential object of attachment. Burford would argue that this is only attachment to wrong-views, not all views. However, the *Mahāniddesa* is consistent, I think, with the analysis of both the *Dhammasaṅgaṇi* and the *Atthasālinī* which explain views as, 'gone over to view, the thicket of view, a wilderness of view', etc., which the *Mahāniddesa* cites in its analysis. This is not only an explanation of wrong-views, as Burford claims, but of all views, if they are an object of craving and attachment.

Such an interpretation as she gives of the *Mahāniddesa* is only possible if one approaches the text with the idea that it is proposing correct and incorrect knowledge.[40] The no-views understanding misinterprets the *Aṭṭhakavagga* by assuming that it rejects all knowledge and views. This may be the reason that she, Gómez and Vetter find in the no-views understanding of the *Aṭṭhakavagga* something that is absent from other parts of the Pāli canon.

As an example of the *Mahāniddesa* positing an 'ideal' or correct teaching (contrary to the no-views understanding of the *Aṭṭhakavagga*), Burford cites its commentary on two verses from the *Sudadhaṭaṭhaka-sutta*. These verses are the following:

> If purity comes to a man through what he has seen, or if he abandons misery by means of knowledge, (then) he who has acquisitions (which lead to rebirth) is purified by something other (*aññena so sujjhati sopadhiko*).[41] For his view betrays him as he speaks thus.
>
> The Brahman does not say that purity comes from something else, (or is) in what is seen (and) heard, in virtuous conduct and vows, or in what is thought. Not clinging to merit or destruction (*puññe ca pāpe*) he abandons what has been taken up, and does not fashion (anything more) here.[42]

Burford claims that the commentary on these verses contradicts the *Aṭṭhakavagga*'s no-views understanding by proposing a view that is higher than other views:

> The commentaries ignore the *Aṭṭhakavagga*'s blanket condemnation of exclusive teachings and focus instead on determining which specific teachings are true and which are false.[43]

Gómez also considers the *Mahāniddesa's* interpretation of these verses:

> The *Mahāniddesa* fails to understand the true purport of this passage when it glosses: 'If a man were made pure … by another path [*aññena so sujjhati sopadhīko*], by a false path … other than the Noble Eightfold

> Path …' The very context of the whole poem […] shows that the view under attack is that of him who relies on knowledge (*pacceti ñāṇaṃ*) about things seen, heard or thought.[44]

The *Mahāniddesa* actually states the following:

> Purified by something other (*aññena so sujjhati sopadhīko*) means (*ti*) [a man is purified] by means of an impure path, a wrong path, a path that does not lead out [of *saṃsāra*], a path other than the foundations of mindfulness, the exertions, the bases of psychic power, the faculties, the powers, the constituents of wisdom, the noble eightfold path.[45]

The *Mahāniddesa* is stating that purity does not come by anything other than the 37 *bodhi-pakkhiyā dhammas*. A more striking example of practices to which allegiance could not be given is difficult to imagine. The *Mahāniddesa* is suggesting the reciprocity of thought and action in the achievement of right-view, which transcends all views. However, Burford argues that the *Mahāniddesa* contradicts the no-views understanding of the *Aṭṭhakavagga* by positing these practices as the ideal right-view.[46] It proclaims the *dhamma* of the Buddha as the highest. This, argues Burford, is the 'one true teaching' of the *Mahāniddesa* which contradicts the *Aṭṭhakavagga*'s condemnation of all views, truths and positions.[47] She claims that the commentary posits 'inaccurate' and 'accurate' methods of seeing which are inconsistent with the *Aṭṭhakavagga*'s condemnation of all knowledge, wrong or right.[48] However, as I have suggested, the *Aṭṭhakavagga* and the Nikāyas as a whole condemn attachment to knowledge, not knowledge itself. The *Aṭṭhakavagga* and the Nikāyas propose neither a no-views nor opposition understanding, but the cultivation of thought and action in which one behaves in accordance with the Buddha's teaching, this being an expression of right-view. As my previous argument suggested, the aim of the path is not to rely on things seen, heard and thought, etc.[49] This is precisely what the *Aṭṭhakavagga* and the *Mahāniddesa* are explaining.

Dīghanakha and the transcendence of views

As I have said, there are clearly some issues at stake in the understanding I am arguing for. I will attempt to address one of these. As I explained in the Introduction, Paul J. Griffiths has suggested that Buddhist propositions must not be susceptible to craving and attachment. According to him, Buddhists face a dilemma because the view 'all views are false' is itself a false view.[50] However, I want to argue that the Buddhist position is that 'all craving leads to *dukkha*' and that itself is a right-view, rather than 'all views are false', a no-views position. I think it is this process that the texts are describing. I will conclude by offering an example whereby the Nikāyas describe the transcendence of all views by the adoption of right-view, which, I think, sheds some light on the dilemma posed by Griffiths.

I would like to look at five views (though I am primarily interested in two) from the *Majjhima-nikāya* that I have not as yet considered. I have left them until this late point as I think that they bring certain issues into sharp focus. These views are the following:

> *micchā-diṭṭhi*: Everything is acceptable to me.
> *micchā-diṭṭhi/sammā-diṭṭhi*: Nothing is acceptable to me.
> *micchā-diṭṭhi*: Something is acceptable to me, something is not acceptable to me.[51]

These positions can be understood as saying, 'I agree with every view', 'I agree with no view' and 'I agree with some views, and disagree with other views'.[52] The second view is the closest I have found in the Pāli canon of the view 'all views are false'.[53] The *Dīghanakha-sutta* has Dīghanakha announcing his view to the Buddha. Upon hearing it, the Buddha asks Dīghanakha: 'This view of yours, Aggivessana, "Nothing is acceptable to me" – is not at least that view acceptable to you?'[54] Dīghanakha replies: 'If this view of mine were acceptable to me, Master Gotama, it too would be all the same, it too would be all the same.'[55] The Buddha is attempting to find out how this view is being held. Is Dīghanakha's view a non-position, its aim to overcome all cognitive standpoints, or is Dīghanakha holding to his view? As the *sutta* continues, there are many who would reply in the same fashion as Dīghanakha, 'yet they do not abandon that view and they still take up another view'.[56] However, there are few, adopting Dīghanakha's view, and replying as he did 'who abandon that view and do not take up some other view'.[57]

It is at this point that the other two views are introduced into the *sutta*. Then is found the following:

> The view of those recluses and brahmins who hold the doctrine and view 'Everything is acceptable to me' [the same evaluation is given to the third view] is close to lust, close to bondage, close to delighting, close to holding, close to attachment. The view of those recluses and brahmins who hold the doctrine and view 'Nothing is acceptable to me' is close to non-lust, close to non-bondage, close to non-delighting, close to non-holding, close to non-attachment.[58]

Dīghanakha is delighted and shows his delight, 'Master Gotama commends my point of view'.[59] However, Dīghanakha's view is only 'right', the *sutta* suggests, if the view is abandoned, and another not adopted. If it accomplishes a turning away from all views, it could be a *sammā-diṭṭhi*. The text continues that none of these three views should be 'obstinately adhered to'[60] with the thought 'only this is true, anything else is wrong'.[61] Holding any of the views in this way would cause 'dispute' (*viggaho*) with the holders of the other two views. This dispute would lead to 'quarrels' (*vivāda*), 'trouble' (*vighāta*) and 'vexation' (*vihesa*). All three views are condemned in the following way:

> Foreseeing for himself dispute, quarrels, trouble and vexation, he abandons that view and does not take up some other view. This is how there comes to be the abandoning of these views; this is how there comes to be the relinquishing of these views.[62]

It is in this context that Dīghanakha hears the *dhamma*, and has the knowledge that, 'all that is subject to arising is subject to cessation'.[63] This is the achievement of right-view. Dīghanakha is advised to let go of the view that 'I agree with no-views', and transcend views, through the realisation of right-view. The view, 'I agree with no-views' is a wrong-view, because this view can cause craving and attachment. To achieve the abandonment of views, there must be a transformation of thought and action which overcomes all attachment to views. It is right-view that accomplishes this. I would suggest that this is a clear example of the proper understanding of views in the Nikāyas. Wrong-views cause attachment, right-view causes the abandoning of craving and attachment.

I would like to compare the evaluation of these three views with the following two views from the *Apaṇṇaka-sutta*:

> *micchā-diṭṭhi*: There is definitely no cessation of being.
> *sammā-diṭṭhi*: There definitely is cessation of being.[64]

The *sutta* explains that the view, 'there is definitely no cessation of being' can lead to rebirth in the immaterial realms. The view, 'there definitely is cessation of being' may lead to *nibbāna*. The views are evaluated in a way which is identical to the passage from the *Dīghanakha-sutta* which I have cited. The passage runs:

> The view of those good recluses and brahmins who hold the doctrine and view 'there is definitely no cessation of being' is close to lust, close to bondage, close to delighting, close to holding, close to attachment; but the view of those good recluses and brahmins who hold the doctrine and view 'there definitely is cessation of being' is close to non-lust, close to non-bondage, close to non-delighting, close to non-holding, close to non-attachment. After practising thus, he practises the way to dispassion towards being, to the fading away and cessation of being.[65]

The only difference between this passage and the one from the *Dīghanakha-sutta* is the final sentence. However, in the *Dīghanakha-sutta*, the advice was 'to abandon that view and not take up another'.[66] In the *Apaṇṇaka-sutta*, however, the *diṭṭhi* is a means, 'after practising thus, he practises the way to dispassion towards being, to the fading away and cessation of being'.[67] One view (that of Dīghanakha), is potentially a way to the cessation of all views, the other is a means to dispassion, it is right-view. In these examples we find the transcendence of views expressed clearly by the advice to Dīghanakha, 'to abandon that view and not take up another'. In the *Apaṇṇaka-sutta* the view 'there definitely is cessation of being' is a means, a *sammā-diṭṭhi*, distinguished from a *micchā-diṭṭhi*. It accomplishes the transcendence of all views.

The transcendence of views is described in an episode at the beginning of the *Madhupiṇḍika-sutta* from the *Majjhima-nikāya*. In this, we find someone called Daṇḍapāṇi. I like to imagine him as a philosopher, round-shouldered, spending all his time disputing about ideas. His name appears to suggest this, literally meaning 'stick in hand', implying that he walks around, leaning on his stick (even though the commentary suggests he was a young man), looking somewhat arrogant. Hearing of the Buddha, he decides to find out his position, what doctrine he proclaims, and engage him in debate. The young/old philosopher approaches the Buddha and asks him, 'what is the doctrine of the recluse, what does he proclaim?' (*kiṃvādī samano kim akkhāyi*). The reply he receives from the Buddha is probably not what he had expected:

> I assert and proclaim such a doctrine that one does not quarrel with anyone in the world with its gods, its Māras, and its Brahmās, in this generation with its recluses and brahmins, its princes and its people; such a doctrine that apperceptions no more underlie that brahmin, who abides detached from sense pleasures, without perplexity, remorse cut off, free from craving for any kind of being.[68]

Daṇḍapāṇi, not a little confused, shakes his head, raises his eyebrows, grimaces three times, and walks away, leaning on his stick. It seems to me that this is the kind of response we can expect to an insight which ultimately leads to the abandoning of all positions. In a sense, Dīghanakha's view was not that different to the answer given by the Buddha to Daṇḍapāṇi. The essential difference being that *sammā-diṭṭhi* is 'right' because it cannot be grasped and it cannot be an object of attachment. This is perhaps why the *Aṭṭhakavagga* so consistently condemns all views. It is a text free from traditional formulations of the *dhamma*: in a sense it did not know of 'right-view'. However, right-view is not understood as 'right doctrine' but a way of seeing beyond craving and attachment, 'all that is subject to arising is subject to cessation'.

CONCLUSION

A different order of seeing

In conclusion, it is my argument that the Pāli canon teaches the transcendence of views. According to the opposition understanding, right-view is opposed to wrong-view. I do not think that the texts that I have been discussing understand the notion of *diṭṭhi* in this way. Right-view is not a correction of wrong-view. It is not a pro-attitude, or acquaintance with Buddhist doctrine. It is not *another* view. I also do not think that these texts teach the rejection of all views. It is not all views that should be abandoned, but all attachment to views. The no-views understanding and the understanding I am proposing would amount to something similar, if the attainment of right-view did not have a transformative effect. Right-view apprehends both what 'is' and 'ought' to be done, in other words: seeing things as they are has value, this is right-view. I am arguing that *sammā-diṭṭhi* apprehends how things are *and* is a remedy for craving.

To achieve right-view is to have an attitude free from craving and attachment. One should strive to attain right-view in the sense of striving for the cessation of attachment. It is in this way that there is an opposition between right-view and wrong-view. On the other hand, the no-views understanding suggests that all views are a hindrance, even right-view, and that one should practise no-views. However, this is precisely what right-view achieves.

The notion of *diṭṭhi* should be understood on its own terms. Views are a form of greed, and to achieve right-view and practise no-views is to have an attitude free from craving. So, in a sense, these texts teach that right-view should be adopted and wrong-views abandoned, and that one should practise no-views. These understandings amount to the same thing. Attaining right-view is to relinquish all views. I am suggesting that right-view stands in opposition to wrong-view as the absence of greed stands in opposition to greed. One practises no-views in the sense of practising the cessation of all craving for views: right-view is the practice of a course of action leading to the cessation of *dukkha*. The attitude of the holder of right-view is indicative of a course of action that leads to the abandonment of *all* views: precisely this is right-view. But to achieve right-view, it is essential to act in accordance with the insight which it describes: by abandoning greed, hatred and delusion. The attainment of right-view is an attitude free from craving any view. In other words, apprehending things without views, is right-view.

As I explained in Chapter 2, the *Sammādiṭṭhi-sutta* describes 16 right-views. This *sutta's* description of right-view suggests that to achieve right-view one has, first, knowledge of what is wholesome and unwholesome; second, knowledge of the four truths; and third, knowledge of dependent-origination. The first right-view, in understanding what is wholesome and unwholesome is reflected in other explanations of right-view found in the Nikāyas. The term *diṭṭhi-sampadā*, which I discussed in Chapter 4, describes the person who has achieved accomplishment in view. This person holds the view of affirmation (*atthika-diṭṭhi*), the view that 'actions have consequences'. As I have said, I do not think that the achievement of this view is to be realised by adopting the view that 'actions have consequences', but that to achieve this right-view one should act in a certain way. It is, I would suggest, the behaviour of a person which demonstrates the achievement of right-view. This reflects their knowledge that 'actions have consequences'. This understanding is described in the *Pāṭali-sutta* (S IV 340–58), which I discussed in Chapter 5. This *sutta* explains that one should *not* adopt right-view and abandon wrong-view, but practise the 'ten wholesome courses of action' (*dasa kusala-kammapathā*), and that, acting in such a way, one achieves right-view. This is the first view of the *Sammādiṭṭhi-sutta*, knowledge of what is wholesome and unwholesome: by achieving right-view, one gains an insight into how to act, one behaves in a way that leads towards the cessation of *dukkha*. In the *Sammādiṭṭhi-sutta*, right-view is also explained as knowledge of the four truths or dependent-origination. I explained in Chapter 4 that this is the right-view achieved at stream-attainment.[1] In the same way that one should act in a manner reflecting the knowledge of what is unwholesome and what is wholesome or the right-view that 'actions have consequences', to achieve the right-view of stream-attainment, one should not adopt a right-view, the content of which is the four truths or dependent-origination; in order to achieve right-view one should act in a way that reflects knowledge of *dukkha*, its arising, cessation and the way to its cessation, namely, with an attitude free from craving. These descriptions of right-view suggest that right-view is more than a doctrine that one should adopt in opposition to other doctrines; to simply adopt right-view is impossible: action and thought are reciprocal in its attainment. They also suggest that to reject all views, even right-view, is problematic, for it is to abandon the attitude necessary for an understanding of the Buddha's teachings.

My understanding of views, as I explained in the Introduction, is based, in part, upon the inseparability of the notions of 'is' and 'ought'. A true insight into how things are is transformative, it leads to the cessation of craving. Things are seen as they are and apprehending things in this way leads to a radical adaptation of thought and action. Right-view is the knowledge of doctrine free from craving and attachment, expressive of fact and value. Right-view entails knowledge of things as they are: *dukkha*, its arising, cessation and the way to its cessation. To have knowledge of the way things are is inseparable from acting in a way that reflects this knowledge. Knowledge and action are reciprocal. To see things as they are, action must be transformed – and the seeing of things as they are affects action. The notion of *diṭṭhi* is concerned with how we have this knowledge: whether it is known with or without craving. How we have knowledge affects what we know. To hold wrong-views is then a great hindrance. It hinders knowledge of the way things are, and hinders the transformative effect of this knowledge.

Views and ignorance are not the same thing: views grasp what is known, ignorance is false knowledge itself. To abandon wrong-views, or all views, is to abandon attachment to doctrine, not doctrine itself. The doctrine of *anattā* is not concerned with whether there is or is not a self, but with the fact that craving is the cause of *dukkha*. Knowledge of this is right-view. Knowledge consists in knowing the cessation of craving and this is knowledge of things 'as they really are'.

I have argued that we should understand the achievement of right-view in a specific way. When the texts teach that one should strive to attain right-view, they are arguing for the attainment of a very specific attitude: a way of apprehending things without any form of attachment. I have suggested that right-view sees a particular process, it apprehends the coming to be and passing away of things. An expression of this is in the explanation of right-view as 'knowing rise and fall' (*udayabbaya*). It is this which I consider to be the content of right-view on the higher paths. Essentially, right-view is the seeing of the rise and fall of all *dhammas*, the rise and fall of *dukkha*. To achieve right-view is to have the knowledge that 'all that is subject to arising is subject to cessation'.[2] As I have said, to attain knowledge of the four truths and dependent-origination is to act in a way which reflects an insight into the cessation of craving. The realisation of right-view is inseparable from the attitude that achieves it. In a sense, these texts teach both that one should strive to attain right-view and practise no-views. However, right-view is not simply another view opposed to wrong-view, nor is it the rejection of all views. The opposite of wrong-view is of a different nature, not a mere correction, but a different order of seeing.

APPENDIX

1 The views of the endless equivocators

There are four views found in the *Brahmajāla-sutta* (D I 1–46) called the views of the 'four endless equivocators' (*cattāro amarāvikkhepikā*). These are the views of those who avoided answering questions:

The first three views begin with:
Herein, *bhikkhus*, some recluse or brahmin does not understand as it really is what is wholesome and what is unwholesome. He thinks: 'I do not understand as it really is what is wholesome and what is unwholesome. If, without understanding, I were to declare something to be wholesome or unwholesome:

View 1: my declaration might be false. If my declaration should be false, that would distress me, and that distress would be an obstacle for me. Therefore, out of fear and loathing of making a false statement, he does not declare anything to be wholesome or unwholesome.

View 2: desire and lust or hatred and aversion might arise in me. Should desire and lust or hatred and aversion arise in me, that should be attachment on my part. Such attachment would distress me, and that distress would be an obstacle for me'. Therefore, out of fear and loathing of attachment, he does not declare anything to be wholesome or unwholesome.

The third view takes a slightly different form:
View 3: Now there are recluses and brahmins who are wise, clever, experienced in controversy, who wander about demolishing the views of others with their wisdom. 'If, without understanding, I were to declare something to be wholesome or unwholesome, they might cross-examine me about my views, press me for reasons, and refute my statements. If they should do so, I might not be able to reply. If I could not reply, that would distress me, and that distress would be an obstacle for me.' Therefore, out of fear and loathing of being cross-examined, he does not declare anything to be wholesome or unwholesome.

All views (including the fourth view) conclude with:
But when questioned about this or that point, he resorts to evasive statements and to endless equivocation: 'I do not take it thus, nor do I take it in that way, nor do I take it in some other way. I do not say that it is not, nor do I say that it is neither this nor that.' [1]

The fourth view takes a slightly different form:
View 4: Herein, *bhikkhus*, some recluse or brahmin is dull and stupid. Due to his dullness and stupidity, when he is questioned about this or that point, he resorts to evasive statements and endless equivocation: 'If you ask me whether there is a world beyond – if I thought there is another world, I would declare that there is. But I do not take it thus, nor do I take it in that way, nor do I take it in some other way. I do not say that it is not, nor do I say that it is neither this nor that.'

Similarly, when asked any of the following questions, he resorts to the same evasive statements and to endless equivocation:

'Is there no world beyond?' 'Is it that there both is and is not a world beyond?' 'Is it that there neither is nor is not a world beyond?'

'Are there beings spontaneously reborn?' 'Are there no beings spontaneously reborn?' 'Is it that there both are and are not beings spontaneously reborn?' 'Is it that there neither are nor are not beings spontaneously reborn?'

'Is there fruit and result of good and bad actions?' 'Is there no fruit and result of good and bad actions?' 'Is it that there both is and is not fruit and result of good and bad actions?' 'Is it that there neither is nor is not fruit and result of good and bad actions?'

'Does the Tathāgata exist after death?' 'Does the Tathāgata not exist after death?' 'Does the Tathāgata both exist and not exist after death?' 'Does the Tathāgata neither exist nor not exist after death?' D I 24–8. [2]

These views are the views of the endless equivocators. The first view claims knowledge is a 'moral danger' and a 'source of remorse'.[3] The second view sees 'attachment' (*upadāna*) as the danger, which will lead to 'mental disquietude' (*vighāta*).[4] The third view states that fear of debating, which may lead to argument or interrogation (*anuyogabhayā*), is the danger.[5] Hence, falsehood, involvement and debate are the things to be avoided by these three positions.[6] The final view is somewhat different. It is identical to that attributed in the *Sāmaññaphala-sutta* to Sañjaya Bellaṭṭhiputta. A central theme of all four views is the expression: 'I do not take it thus, nor do I take it in that way, nor do I take it in some other way. I do not say that it is not, nor do I say that it is neither this nor that'.[7] Watanabe points out that the Buddhist tradition has explained this clause as containing both four and five answers.[8] This expression is found alone in the following:

> Again [...] a certain teacher is dull and confused. Because he is dull and confused, when he is asked such and such a question, he engages in evasive statements and to endless equivocation: 'I do not take it thus, nor do I take it in that way, nor do I take it in some other way. I do not say that it is not, nor do I say that it is neither this nor that.'[9]

This passage from the *Sandaka-sutta* is described as one of four kinds of 'holy life without consolation' (*anassāsikaṃ brahmacariyam akkhātaṃ* M I 520).[10]

2 Wrong-views

Seven annihilationist theories (satta uccheda-vādā)

In the list of wrong-views from the *Vibhaṇga* (see Chapter 1) were cited 'seven wrong-views' (*satta diṭṭhi*), which are the same as the seven *uccheda-diṭṭhi* from the *Brahmajāla-sutta* These are the following:

> View 1: The self [...] has form; it is composed of the four primary elements and originates from father and mother.
>
> **Six remaining views state:**
> There is [...] such a self as you assert. That I do not deny. But it is not at this point that the self is completely annihilated.
>
> View 2: For there is [...] another self – divine, having form, pertaining to the sense sphere, feeding on edible nutriment. That you neither know nor see, but I know it and see it.
>
> View 3: For there is [...] another self, divine, having form, mind-made, complete in all its limbs and organs, not destitute of any faculties. That you neither know nor see, but I know it and see it.
>
> View 4: For there is [...] another self belonging to the base of infinite space (reached by) the complete surmounting of apperceptions of form, by the disappearance of apperceptions of resistance, by non-attention to apperceptions of diversity (by contemplating): 'Space is infinite.' That you neither know nor see, but I know it and see it.
>
> View 5: For there is [...] another self belonging to the base of infinite consciousness (reached by) completely surmounting the base of infinite space (by contemplating): 'Consciousness is infinite.' That you neither know nor see, but I know it and see it.
>
> View 6: For there is [...] another self belonging to the base of nothingness (reached by) completely surmounting the base of infinite consciousness (by contemplating): 'There is nothing.' That you neither know nor see, but I know it and see it.
>
> View 7: For there is [...] another self belonging to the base of neither apperception nor non-apperception (reached by) completely surmounting

the base of nothingness (by contemplating): 'This is peaceful, this is sublime.' That you neither know nor see, but I know it and see it.

All views end with:
Since this self [...] is annihilated and destroyed with the break-up of the body, and does not exist after death, at this point the self is completely annihilated.[11]

These are found in the *Brahmajāla-sutta* at D I 34–6. Each *micchā-diṭṭhi* is followed by the phrase 'In this way some proclaim the annihilation, destruction and extermination of an existent being'.[12] This may be regarded as the main thesis of the seven *uccheda-diṭṭhi*.[13]

Eight theories on having non-apperception (aṭṭha asaññī-vādā)

A further eight views found in the *Brahmajāla-sutta* are the *assaññī-vāda*:

They proclaim the self is immutable after death, non-appercipient and:
View 1: material
View 2: immaterial
View 3: both material and immaterial
View 4: neither material nor immaterial
View 5: finite
View 6: infinite
View 7: both finite and infinite
View 8: neither finite nor infinite.[14]

Eight theories of neither apperception nor-non-apperception (aṭṭha nevasaññī-nā-saññī-vādā)

They proclaim the self is immutable after death, neither appercipient nor non-appercipient and:
View 1: material
View 2: immaterial
View 3: both material and immaterial
View 4: neither material nor immaterial
View 5: finite
View 6: infinite
View 7: both finite and infinite
View 8: neither finite nor infinite. [15]

These are from the *Brahmajāla-sutta* and are there called 'theories of neither apperception nor non-apperception' (*nevasaññī-nā-saññī-vāda*). The *micchā-diṭṭhi* of this type are dealing with the *jhānic* experience, and speculations based upon the *jhānas* may be suggested by the usage of the language.

Five theories on nibbāna in the present existence (pañca diṭṭha-dhamma-nibbāna-vādā)

The following five views are speculations upon the point at which the *attā* realises *nibbāna*. They are the five 'theories on *nibbāna* in the present existence' (*diṭṭha-dhamma-nibbāna-vāda*) from the *Brahmajāla-sutta*:

> View 1: When this self [...] furnished and supplied with five kinds of sense pleasures, revels in them – at this point the self attains supreme *nibbāna* here and now.
>
> **All views state that:**
> There is [...] such a self as you assert. That I do not deny. But it is not at that point that the self attains supreme *nibbāna* here and now. What is the reason?
>
> View 2: Because, good sir, sense pleasures are impermanent, suffering, subject to change, and through their change and transformation, sorrow, lamentation, pain, grief and despair arise. But when the self, quite secluded from sense pleasures, secluded from unwholesome states enters and abides in the first *jhāna*, which is accompanied by initial and sustained thought and contains the rapture and happiness born of seclusion – at this point [...] the self attains supreme *nibbāna* here and now.
>
> View 3: Because that *jhāna* contains initial and sustained thought; therefore it is declared to be gross. But when, with the subsiding of initial and sustained thought, the self enters and abides in the second *jhāna*, which is accompanied by internal confidence and unification of mind, is free from initial and sustained thought, and contains the rapture and happiness born of concentration – at this point [...] the self attains supreme *nibbāna* here and now.
>
> View 4: Because that *jhāna* contains rapture and exhilaration; therefore it is declared to be gross. But when, with the fading away of rapture, one abides in equanimity, mindful and clearly comprehending, and still experiencing happiness with the body, enters and abides in the third *jhāna*, so that the ariyans announce: 'He abides happily, in equanimity and mindfulness' – at this point [...] the self attains supreme *nibbāna* here and now.
>
> View 5: Because that *jhāna* contains a mental concern over happiness; therefore it is declared to be gross. But when, with the abandoning of pleasure and pain, with the disappearance of previous joy and grief, one enters and abides in the fourth *jhāna*, which is without pleasure and pain

> and contains purification of mindfulness through equanimity – at this point [...] the self attains supreme *nibbāna* here and now.[16]

The first *diṭṭha-dhamma-nibbāna-vāda* has been compared to a *Lokāyata* view.[17] It is clear that the remaining four are based upon *jhānic* experience. It may be assumed that these *micchā-diṭṭhi* are wrong because they mistake the goal for something which it is not.

*Two theories (of occurrences) arising without a cause (*dve adhicca samuppannikā-vāda*)*

These two views from the *Brahmajāla-sutta* are called 'theories (of occurrences) arising without a cause' (*adhicca-samuppana-vāda*).

> View 1: The self and the world originate fortuitously. What is the reason? Because previously I did not exist, but now I am living. Not having been, I sprang into existence.[18]
> View 2: The self and the world originate fortuitously.[19]

To identify a school of thought to which these views could be ascribed is problematic. Dutt[20] holds that the second view, with the way it is arrived at taken into account, could conceivably be part of Ajita Kesakambalī's (Lokāyata) view, what I have termed the view of nihilism. They are types of *anu-diṭṭhi*, 'theories regarding the remote past',[21] as are all of the first eighteen *micchā-diṭṭhi* in the *Brahmajāla-sutta*, those of *sassata-vāda, ekacca-sassata-vāda, antānanta-vāda, amarāvikkhepa-vāda.*

These two *micchā-diṭṭhi* are clearly identical. The reason that they are given in this form is to highlight a difficulty concerning the *Brahmajāla-sutta*. Although it is well known that this *sutta* is traditionally held to contain 62 philosophical viewpoints, to actually list these views is a difficult matter. Often the difference is in the reasons why they are held, not in the position which they express.

In the case of the two *adhicca-samuppana-vāda*, and this is often true for many of the other 62 views, types of *micchā-diṭṭhi* are introduced with the following: 'he speaks thus:' (*so evam āha*) or, 'he declares his view, hammered out by reason, deducted from his investigations, following his own flight of thought.'[22] The type of view expressed in the former case is more often than not preceded by a narrative, frequently set in a previous birth, where the reason for the type of view expressed can be found. For example, an experience in a previous life as a certain type of deity, which, while real enough, was often shaped by the hidden law of *kamma*. Subsequently, in a future rebirth, having gone forth into the ascetic life, and by means of meditative experience, that former birth is remembered, and the view, the *micchā-diṭṭhi*, is based upon this experience. The first *adhicca-samuppana-vāda* is based roughly on this structure. The second *adhicca-samuppana-vāda* is based upon *takka*, reason or speculation, without any meditative or experiential justification. The point is that the views themselves are the same.

Four partial eternalistic theories **(cattāro ekaccasassatikā-vāda)**

The following four views emphasise that various *micchā-diṭṭhi* are based upon mistaken ideas based upon meditative experience and *takki*. These views are the four 'partial eternalist-views' (*ekaccasassata-vāda*):

> View 1: We were created by him, by Brahmā, the great Brahmā, the vanquisher, the unvanquished, the universal seer, the wielder of power, the Lord, the master and creator, the Supreme Being, the ordainer, the Almighty, the father of all that are and are to be. He is permanent, stable, not subject to change, and he will remain the same just like eternity itself. But we who have been created by him and have come to this world – we are impermanent, unstable, short-lived, doomed to perish.[23]
>
> View 2: Those honourable gods who are not corrupted by play do not spend an excessive time indulging in the delights of laughter and play. As a consequence they do not become forgetful, they do not pass away from that place. Those gods that are permanent, stable, eternal, not subject to change, and they will remain the same just like eternity itself. But we were gods corrupted by play. We spent an excessive time indulging in the delights of laughter and play, and as a consequence we became forgetful. When we became forgetful we passed away from that plane. Coming to this world, now, we are impermanent, unstable, short-lived, doomed to perish.[24]
>
> View 3: Those honourable gods who are not corrupted by mind do not contemplate each other with excessive envy. As a result, their minds do not become corrupted by anger towards one another, their bodies and minds do not become exhausted, and they do not pass from that plane. Those gods are permanent, stable, not subject to change, and they will remain the same just like eternity itself. But we gods are corrupted by mind. We contemplated each other with excessive envy, and as a result our minds became corrupted with anger towards one another. When our minds were corrupted by anger, our bodies and minds became exhausted, and consequently we passed away from that plane. Coming to this world, now, we are impermanent, unstable, short-lived, doomed to perish.[25]
>
> View 4: That which is called the eye, the ear, the nose, the tongue, and the body – that self is impermanent, unstable, non-eternal, subject to change. But that which is called mind, or mentality, or consciousness – that self is permanent, stable, eternal, not subject to change, and it will remain the same just like eternity itself.[26]

The views posit one or a limited number of gods or 'volitional formations' (*saṃkhāra*, which could be *citta*, *mano*, *viññāṇa*, *attā*) existing eternally, while other gods, or the nose, tongue, etc. are impermanent.

3 The *dasa akusala-kammapathā* and the *dasa kusala-kammapathā*

In this appendix I will give the context of the *dasa akusala-kammapathā* and the *dasa kusala-kammapathā*. Both sets of ten, in the context of the *Cunda-sutta*, are given to show how various purifying rites of the brahmins are futile if other actions of body, speech and mind are not pure themselves.[27] The *dasa kusala-kammapathā* are described as being pure, and to lead to deva-hood or any other happy destination.[28] The *dasa akusala-kammapathā* are described as impure and to lead to an unhappy destination. In the *Sāleyyaka-sutta* (M I 285–90) the *dasa kusala-kammapathā* and the *dasa akusala-kammapathā* are discussed in some detail. The context is a group of householders from the Kosalan village of Sālā asking the Buddha about the causes and conditions for some beings to be reborn in an unhappy destination, and for some in a happy destination.[29] The Buddha replies that it is due to conduct not in accordance with the *dhamma* that some are reborn in an unhappy destination, even the *niraya* hell, and due to conduct in accordance with *dhamma* that others are reborn in a happy destination, even the *sagga* heaven.[30] The Buddha is asked to explain this in more detail. He explains that 'there are three kinds of bodily conduct not in accordance with the *dhamma*, unrighteous conduct',[31] 'there are four kinds of verbal conduct not in accordance with the *dhamma*, unrighteous conduct',[32] 'there are three kinds of mental conduct not in accordance with the *dhamma*, unrighteous conduct'.[33] These ten are the *dasa akusala-kammapathā* and it is these that lead to a negative rebirth (M I 286–7). The Buddha then explains the wholesome courses of action due to which beings achieve a positive rebirth (M I 287–8). These are the *dasa kusala-kammapathā.*

The *Mahādhammasamādāna-sutta* (M I 309–17) states that there are four ways of undertaking actions. The first is a way of undertaking actions that is painful now and results in the future as pain.[34] The text explains that in pain and grief this person kills living beings, takes what is not given, practises misconduct in sensual pleasures, speaks falsehood, speaks maliciously, speaks harshly, is a gossip, covetous, has a mind of ill-will, and holds wrong-view (M I 313). The person acting in such a way will experience the pain and grief that have these actions as their condition, and after death will appear in a bad destination, even in the *niraya* hell. The second way of undertaking things is pleasant now and results in future pain.[35] In pleasure and joy this person kills living beings, etc.; in pleasure and joy the person holds wrong-view and pleasure and joy is experienced with wrong-view as condition.[36] Though there is pleasure in acting in such a way, the actions still result in future pain, and the person is reborn in a bad destination, even in the *niraya* hell. The third way of undertaking actions is painful now but in the future results in pleasure.[37] This person in pain and grief abstains from killing living beings, taking what is not given, from misconduct in sensuous pleasures, speaking falsehood, speaking maliciously, harshly, or gossiping. In pain and grief he is not covetous, does not have a mind of ill-will, and holds right-view (M I 314–15). He experiences pain and grief from acting in this way. In pain and grief he holds right-view, and experiences pain and grief that has right-view as condition.[38] However, after death he will be reborn in a happy destination, even in the *sagga* heaven. The fourth way of undertaking things is pleasant now and results in future pleasure.[39] In pleasure and joy the person abstains from killing living beings, etc. In pleasure and joy they hold right-view and experience the pleasure and joy that has right-view as condition.[40] Once again this will result in future pleasure and joy. This way of undertaking things dispels, with its radiance, any other doctrines of ordinary recluses and brahmins.[41] In the *Dutiya mahāpañha-sutta* (A V 54–9) at A V 57 it is said that if in ten *dhammas* a *bhikkhu* has 'rightly made good growth of mind' (*sammā subhāvita-citta*), he will be free from suffering. These are the *dasa kusala-kammapathā*. In the *Brāhmaṇapaccorohaṇī-sutta* (A V 249–51), the text gives a slightly different version of the *dasa kusala-kammapathā* and the *dasa akusala-kammapathā*. The text uses the two groups of ten to indicate in what way there is 'approaching' or 'descending' (*paccorohaṇī*), to the holy life by the disciple of the Ariyan.[42] The text may be using Brahmanic language in this passage to distinguish the Buddhist practice from those of the brahmins. The term *paccorohaṇī* appears to suggest descending to the sacrificial fire (PED, s.v. *paccorohaṇī*). This appears to imply that the approaching or coming to what is holy for the brahmin and the Ariyan are two different things. The *sutta* has the *ariya-sāvaka* pondering 'of the taking of life, the ripening is destructive in this same visible state and in the state to come. Thus pondering, he abandons the taking of life; he descends (*paccorohaṇī*) from taking life'.[43] A similar explanation is given for the remainder of the *dasa akusala-kammapathā*. Thus, the *ariya-sāvaka*, realising the negative consequences (of taking what is not given, wrong conduct in things sensuous, falsehood, spiteful speech, bitter speech, gossip, coveting and harmfulness), abandons them. The *ariya-sāvaka* finally ponders, 'of wrong-view the ripening is destructive, both in this visible state and the state to come. Thus pondering, he abandons wrong-view, he descends from wrong-view'.[44]

In the *Cakkavatti-sīhanāda-sutta* (D III 58–79) the *dasa akusala-kammapathā* are used to suggest how, with the practising of each successive unwholesome action, people's life-spans gradually decreased from eighty thousand years (D III 68) to ten years (D III 71). At this point the *dasa kusala-kammapathā* will disappear and will be replaced by the *dasa akusala-kammapathā* (D III 71, the text uses these terms) and people will not even have a word for 'wholesome' (*manussesu kusalantipi na bhavissati*). Gradually, with the taking up of the *dasa kusala-kammapathā*, one by one, people's life-span increases until it returns to eighty thousand years (D III 73–5), and it is to these people that Metteyya will arise in the world.

In the *Saṅgārava-sutta* (A V 252–3), the text suggests that the *dasa akusala-kammapathā* are the near shore, while the *dasa kusala-kammapathā* are the further shore (i.e. *micchā-diṭṭhi orimaṃ tīraṃ, sammā-diṭṭhi pārimaṃ tīraṃ*, A V 251, see I. B. Horner, *The Early Buddhist Theory of Man Perfected*, p. 304). In the *Paṭhama adhamma-sutta* (A V 254), the *dasa akusala-kammapathā* are explained as 'not *dhamma* and not aim' and the *dasa kusala-kammapathā* explained as '*dhamma* and aim'. This is expanded upon in the *Dutiya adhamma-sutta* (A V 255–9) to the effect that unwholesome *dhammas* are caused by what is not *dhamma*, whereas wholesome *dhammas* have what is *dhamma* as their cause. Hence, wrong-view is not *dhamma*, right-view is *dhamma*. Destructive, unwholesome *dhammas* come into being because of wrong-view, whereas constructive and wholesome *dhammas* come into being due to right-view. In the *Kammanidāna-sutta* (A V 261–2), the *dasa akusala-kammapathā* are held to be due to three things, greed, hatred and delusion. By the destruction of these three, the 'chain of causal action' (*kamma-nidānasambhavo*, A V 262) is broken. In the *Saparikkamana-sutta* (A V 262), the *dhamma* is said to be approachable all round, not unapproachable (*saparikkamano ayaṃ bhikkhave dhammo, nāyaṃ dhammo aparikkamano*, these terms are very rare). Practising the *dasa kusala-kammapathā* is the way of all-round approach, i.e. 'for the one who has wrong-view [...] right-view is the way of all-round approach' (*micchā-diṭṭhikassa* [...] *sammā-diṭṭhi parikkamanaṃ hoti*, A V 262). In the *Sādhu-sutta* (A V 273–4), the text holds that the *dasa akusala-kammapathā* are the 'non-virtuous' (*asādhu*), and that the *dasa kusala-kammapathā* are 'the virtuous' (*sādhu*); 'wrong-view [...] is called the non-virtuous [...] right-view [...] is called the virtuous' (*micchā-diṭṭhi* [...] *vuccati bhikkhave asādhu* [...]*sammā-diṭṭhi* [...] *vuccati bhikkhave sādhū ti*, A V 274). Ten further suttas follow a similar form. The *Ariyadhamma-sutta* (A V 274) teaches that the *dasa akusala-kammapathā* are non-ariyan *dhamma* (i.e. *micchā-diṭṭhi* [...] *anariyo dhammo*), while the *dasa kusala-kammapathā* are ariyan *dhamma* (i.e. *sammā-diṭṭhi* [...] *ariyo dhammo*). The *Kusala-sutta* (A V 274–5) describes the *dasa akusala-kammapathā* as 'unwholesome' and the *dasa kusala-kammapathā* as 'wholesome' (i.e. *micchā-diṭṭhi* [...] *akusalaṃ* (A V 274), *sammā-diṭṭhī* [...] *kusalan ti*, A V 275). The *Attha-sutta* (A V 275) explains the *dasa akusala-kammapathā* as not being the aim and the *dasa kusala-kammapathā* as being the aim (*micchā-diṭṭhi* [...] *anattho, sammā-diṭṭhīti attho*). The *Dhamma-sutta* (A V 275) explains the *dasa akusala-kammapathā* as being *adhamma* and the *dasa kusala-kammapathā* as *dhamma* (*micchā-diṭṭhi* [...] *adhammo, sammā-diṭṭhī* [...] *dhammo*). The *Sāsavadhamma-sutta* (A V 272) explains the *dasa akusala-kammapatha* as being the *dhamma* with *āsavas*, and the *dasa kusala-kammapathā* as the *dhamma* without *āsavas* (*micchā-diṭṭhi* [...] *sāsavo dhammo, sammā-diṭṭhī anāsavo dhammo*). The *Sāvajja-sutta* (A V 276) explains the *dasa akusala-kammapathā* as blameworthy *dhamma*, and the *dasa kusala-kammapathā* as blameless *dhamma* (*micchā-diṭṭhi* [...] *sāvajjo dhammo, sammā-diṭṭhī anavajjo dhammo*). The *Tapanīya-sutta* (A V 276) explains the *dasa akusala-kammapathā* as a *dhamma* with remorse and the *dasa kusala-kammapathā* as a *dhamma* without remorse (*micchā-diṭṭhi tapanīyo dhammo, sammā-diṭṭhī* [...] *atapanīyo dhammo*). The *Ācayagāmī-sutta* (A V 276) explains the *dasa akusala-kammapathā* as the heaping up of *dhamma* and *dasa kusala-kammapathā* as the diminishing *dhamma* (*micchā-diṭṭhi* [...] *ācayagāmī dhammo, sammā-diṭṭhī apacayagāmī dhammo*). The *Dukkhudraya-sutta* (A V 277) explains the *dasa akusala-kammapathā* as the *dhamma* yielding pain, and the *dasa kusala-kammapathā* as the *dhamma* yielding pleasure (*micchā-diṭṭhi* [...] *dukkhudrayo dhammo, sammā-diṭṭhī sukhudrayo dhammo*). Finally, the *Dukkhavipāka-sutta* (A V 277) explains the *dasa akusala-kammapathā* as the *dhamma* producing the fruit of pain, and the *dasa kusala-kammapathā* as the *dhamma* producing the fruit of pleasure (*micchā-diṭṭhi dukkhavipāko dhammo, sammā-diṭṭhī sukhavipāko dhammo*). A further 12 *suttas* follow the same form as the previous 11. The titles of these will be given without any detail: *Ariyamagga-sutta, Kaṇhamagga-sutta, Saddhamma-sutta* (all A V 278), *Sappurisadhamma-sutta, Uppādetabbadhamma-sutta, Āsevitabbadhamma-sutta* (all A V 279), *Bhāvetabbadhamma-sutta, Bahulīkātabbadhamma-sutta, Anussaritabbadhamma-sutta* (all A V 280), *Sacchikātabbadhamma-sutta, Sevitabbādi-dvādasa-sutta, Paṇṇāsātireka-sutta* (A V 281–2) These final two take a slightly different form (see A V 247–9 for the *suttas* they follow in their description). These 23 *suttas* (from the *Sādhu-sutta*) are following a group earlier in the collection which stated the same thing, substituting a tenfold form of the path (right-view to right-release for the *dasa kusalakammapathā*), and the opposites (wrong-view to wrong release for the *dasa akusalakammapathā*).

In the *Sevitabbāsevitabba-sutta* (M III 45–61) the *dasa kusala-kammapathā* and the *dasa akusala-kammapathā* are found in a different form. The *sutta* gives a number of things that are said to be of two kinds, those to be cultivated and those that should not be cultivated. Thus, 'bodily conduct' is said to be of two kinds, to be cultivated and not to be cultivated, and it is either one or the other.[45] The same is said of 'verbal conduct', 'mental conduct', 'inclination of mind', the 'acquisition of apperception', the 'acquisition of view' and the 'acquisition of individuality'. They are all said to be 'one or the other'.[46]

These categories are evaluated by the *sutta*. The criteria for their evaluation is (to use bodily conduct as an example) the following. If bodily conduct causes unwholesome *dhammas* to increase and wholesome *dhammas* to diminish, then it should not be cultivated.[47] If bodily conduct causes unwholesome *dhammas* to diminish and wholesome *dhammas* to increase, then it should be cultivated.[48]

The first three of these categories are familiar to us. Hence, bodily, verbal and mental conduct which should not be cultivated are the first nine of the *dasa akusala-kammapathā* (M III 46–50). Bodily, verbal and mental conduct which should be cultivated are the first nine of the *dasa kusala-kammapathā* (M III 47–51). 'Inclination of mind' (*cittuppādaṃ*)[49] that is unwholesome is similar to the eighth and ninth *akusala-kammapathā*, hence 'here someone is covetous and abides with his mind imbued with covetousness'.[50] Further, 'he has ill-will and abides with his mind imbued with ill-will (*vyāpādavā hoti, vyāpādasahagatena cetasā viharati*); finally 'he is cruel and abides with his mind imbued with cruelty' (*vihesavā hoti. vihesā-sahagatena cetasā viharati*, M III 350). The opposite of these *cittuppādaṃ* cause unwholesome states to diminish and wholesome states to increase.[51] The 'acquisition of apperception' (*saññā-paṭilābhaṃ*), of both kinds, is identical to the two types of 'inclination of mind' (M III 51).[52]

The 'acquisition of view' is either that which should be 'cultivated' (followed or practised), or 'not cultivated' (*sevitabbam pi asevitabbam pi*, M III 52). As noted above for bodily conduct, if an acquisition causes unwholesome *dhammas* to increase and wholesome *dhammas* to diminish, it should not be cultivated. If a view causes unwholesome *dhammas* to diminish, and wholesome *dhammas* to increase it should be cultivated.[53] The view that should not be cultivated is the *natthika-diṭṭhi*, the view that should be cultivated is the *atthika-diṭṭhi* (M III 52). The term *diṭṭhi-paṭilābha* is not common as it appears to be the only occurrence of the term. The implication of the *sutta* passage as a whole is simply that views, if negative, lead to an unwholesome course of action, and if positive, to a wholesome course of action. This is the role I suggested that wrong-view and right-view have, as one of the ten unwholesome or wholesome courses of action.

4 The twelve unwholesome types of consciousness

The twelve unwholesome types of consciousness (dvadasa akusala-cittāni)

Consciousness rooted in greed (*lobha-mūla-cittāni*)

One consciousness, accompanied by joy, associated with wrong-view, unprompted.

One consciousness, accompanied by joy, associated with wrong-view, prompted.

One consciousness, accompanied by joy, dissociated with wrong-view, unprompted.

One consciousness, accompanied by joy, dissociated with wrong-view, prompted.

One consciousness, accompanied by equanimity, associated with wrong-view, unprompted.

One consciousness, accompanied by equanimity, associated with wrong-view, prompted.

One consciousness, accompanied by equanimity, dissociated with wrong-view, unprompted.

One consciousness, accompanied by equanimity, dissociated with wrong-view, prompted.

Consciousness rooted in hatred (*dosa-mūla-cittāni*)

One consciousness, accompanied by displeasure, associated with aversion (*paṭigha*), unprompted.

One consciousness, accompanied by displeasure, associated with aversion, prompted.

Consciousness rooted in delusion (*moha-mūla-cittāni*)

One consciousness, accompanied by equanimity, associated with doubt.
One consciousness, accompanied by equanimity, associated with restlessness.[54]

NOTES

Introduction

1 As a general rule I have usually referred to wrong-views in the plural and right-view in the singular as it is my argument that right-view is a way of seeing whereas wrong-views refer to various views such as the 62 views described in the *Brahmajāla-sutta* (D I 1–46).

2 Steven Collins, *Selfless Persons: Imagery and Thought in Theravāda Buddhism* (Cambridge, 1982), pp. 87–115; Richard Hayes, *Dignaga on the Interpretation of Signs* (Dordrecht, 1988), pp. 42, 50–2; Richard Gombrich, *How Buddhism Began: The Conditioned Genesis of the Early Teachings* (London, 1996), pp. 16–17, 28, note 1; Luis Gómez, 'Proto-Mādhyamika in the Pāli Canon', *Philosophy East and West* 26 (1976), 137–65. See also Nathan Katz, *Buddhist Images of Human Perfection: The Arahant of the Sutta Piṭaka Compared to the Bodhisattva and the Mahāsiddha* (Delhi, 1982), pp. 214–28.

3 Sn 766–1149. Collins holds that the *Aṭṭhakavagga* and the *Pārāyanavagga* 'represent the summation, in Theravāda literature, of the style of teaching which is concerned less with the content of views and theories than with the psychological state of those who hold them.' Collins, *Selfless Persons*, p. 129.

4 Gombrich, *How Buddhism Began*, p. 16.

5 Gómez, 'Proto-Mādhyamika in the Pāli Canon'.

6 Hayes, *Dignaga on the Interpretation of Signs*, p. 52. Hayes describes the Buddha's attitude in the following terms: 'In much the same way that he encouraged his followers to reduce their material needs to a bare minimum so that they could travel light, he also encouraged them to pare down their beliefs to a bare minimum.' Hayes states that this entails the negation of 'all unnecessary thinking', ibid.

7 *upayo hi dhammesu upeti vādam,*
anūpayaṃ kena kathaṃ vaddeya,
attam nirattaṃ na hi tassa atthi:
adosi so diṭṭhim idh' eva sattā ti, Sn 787.
All translations from the *Suttanipāta* are from K.R. Norman, *The Group of Discourses* II (London, 1995) with slight adaptations. All translations in this book are from PTS translations. For the sake of consistency I have often adapted these. I will consider this verse again in Chapter 6.

8 Gómez 'Proto-Mādhyamika in the Pāli Canon', p. 149.

9 Paul. J. Griffiths, *On Being Mindless: Buddhist Meditation and the Mind–Body Problem* (La Salle, 1986), p. 157, note 63.

10 For a definition of the terms apophatic and cataphatic see *A New Dictionary of Christian Theology*, A. Richardson and J. Bowden (eds) (London, 1983), s.v. apophatic.

11 Collins, *Selfless Persons*, p. 87.
12 Ibid., p. 88.
13 Ibid., pp. 89–90.
14 I follow Collins in translating the term *paññā* as 'wisdom'. However, an English term that articulates its range of meanings is difficult to find. The term could also be translated as 'understanding', 'insight' or 'knowledge'. I understand the term 'wisdom' in the sense of an ability to discern inner relationships: an insight into the nature of things. In another related sense it is an ability to judge what is true or right. For consistency I will translate *paññā* as 'wisdom', keeping in mind the wider meanings of the term.
15 Collins, *Selfless Persons*, pp. 91–2. It is clear that by these categories Collins is suggesting that there are different levels of *sammā-diṭṭhi* and, as he observes, a view which admits of degrees 'cannot be a simple knowledge *that* something is the case, but rather refers to the possession of a more or less ineffable level of "insight" or "intuition" produced by Buddhist meditation' (ibid., p. 91, Collins's emphasis). Right-view is not so much a correct opinion but a way of seeing. Indeed, one of the commentarial definitions of *sammā-diṭṭhi* is 'right-seeing' (*sammā-dassanaṃ*), found at Spk II 32 and Spk II 34; see Carol Anderson, *Pain and its Ending: The Four Noble Truths in the Theravāda Buddhist Canon* (Richmond, 1999), p. 41.
16 Collins, *Selfless Persons*, pp. 116–43.
17 Ibid., p. 117.
18 Ibid., p. 117.
19 Ñāṇananda Bhikkhu, *Concept and Reality in Early Buddhist Thought* (Ceylon, 1971), p. 17.
20 Ibid., p. 14.
21 Cited by Ñāṇananda, ibid., p. 24.
22 Ibid., p. 43.
23 Sue Hamilton, *Early Buddhism: A New Approach. The I of the Beholder* (Richmond, 2000), pp. 183–4.
24 Hamilton states this in terms of holding to any ontological position; see *Early Buddhism*, p. 186.
25 Anderson, *Pain and its Ending*, p. 40.
26 Mary Douglas, *Purity and Danger: An Analysis of Concepts of Pollution and Taboo* (London, 1966); see Anderson, *Pain and its Ending*, p. 49.
27 Anderson, *Pain and its Ending*, p. 49.
28 I have some problem with Anderson equating *diṭṭhi* with the category of doctrine. I think that a view is knowledge of a doctrine. Right-view is knowledge of the *dhamma*. I will return to this point in some detail.
29 Anderson, *Pain and its Ending*, p. 32. Scholars of doctrine may argue that religious transformation is central to the notion of doctrine. Whether right-view is a proposition that adherents give intellectual assent to has been questioned by Lance Cousins with relation to the four truths:

> When it comes to considering the four noble truths as 'propositions of doctrine', Anderson relies on three criteria for a definition of doctrine put forward by Paul Griffiths. As she recognises, this is not entirely successful – largely because the third criterion is 'Being taken by its community to be binding upon its members.' Anderson attempts to rescue this, but it is highly doubtful if any form of traditional Buddhism ever thought of belief in or assent to the four noble truths as something in any sense required. Rather they (or at least the first truth) are typically considered something to be investigated, questioned, explored, and discussed.

Pain and its Ending: The Four Noble Truths in the Theravāda Buddhist Canon, reviewed by L.S. Cousins, *Journal of Buddhist Ethics*, 8 (2001), pp. 36–41 (p. 39). Griffiths' three criteria for a definition of doctrine are:

> 1. Being taken by its community to possess to a greater or lesser degree than any of its known competitors whatever property or properties the community thinks of as making doctrine-candidates acceptable in their spheres of relevance – or, if the property controlling acceptability does not, for some community, admit of degrees (as may be the case for truth), then the doctrine-candidate must have it in the eyes of the community, and its known competitors must lack it. 2. Being taken by its community to be of significance for its religious life. 3. Being taken by its community to be binding upon its members.

Griffiths, P.J., *On Being Buddha: The Classical Doctrine of Buddhahood* (New York, 1994), p. 6.

30 This would be the view placed in Collins' category of 'pro-attitude' to ideas of *kamma* and rebirth.

31 This would be the view placed under Collins' category of right-view as 'liberating insight'.

32 See John Ross Carter, *On Understanding Buddhists: Essays on the Theravāda Tradition in Sri Lanka* (New York, 1993), pp. 83–8.

33 Collins' categories. This is part of what I have termed the opposition understanding; see Rupert Gethin, 'Wrong View (micchā-diṭṭhi) and Right View (sammā-diṭṭhi) in the Theravāda Abhidhamma', in *Recent Researches in Buddhist Studies: Essays in Honour of Professor Y. Karunadasa*, Kuala Lumpar Dhammajoti, Asanga Tilakaratne and Kapila Abhayawansa (eds) (Colombo, 1997), pp. 211–19 (p. 223).

34 Ibid., pp. 223–4.

35 Alasdair MacIntyre, *After Virtue* (South Bend, IN, 1981), pp. 54–7, 80–1; see W.D. Hudson (ed.), *The Is–Ought Question: A Collection of Papers on the Central Problem in Moral Philosophy* (London, 1969).

36 Paul Williams, *Buddhist Thought: A Complete Introduction to the Indian Tradition* (London, 2000), p. 40.

37 David Hume, *A Treatise of Human Nature: Books Two and Three*, Páll Árdal (ed.) (London, 1972), pp. 203–4.

38 Hudson, *The Is–Ought Question*, p. 16.

39 I am grateful to Paul Williams for his help in clarifying my thinking on this issue.

40 See, however, Roger R. Jackson who has discussed a passage from Vasubandhu's *Abhidharmakoṣabhāsaya*. In this passage Vasubandhu shows how the four truths 'correct' other propositions; Roger R. Jackson, *Is Enlightenment Possible? Dharmakīrti and rGyal tshab rje on Knowledge, Rebirth, No-Self and Liberation* (New York, 1993), pp. 50–51.

41 Gómez 'Emptiness and Moral Perfection', *Philosophy East and West*, 23 (1973), 361–73 (p. 371).

42 Griffiths, *On Being Mindless*, p. 157, note 63.

43 In Chapter 6 I will consider the view of Dīghanakha which suggests that it is the influence of the view on the person who holds it that is of primary importance for Buddhism. One cannot simply hold the view 'all views are false', for this will lead to attachment.

44 Gethin, 'Wrong View (micchā-diṭṭhi) and Right View (sammā-diṭṭhi) in the Theravāda Abhidhamma', pp. 217–18.

45 Ibid., p. 218. As Gethin explains:

> Since Buddhist texts furnish *micchā-diṭṭhi* with a formal content, it is all too tempting [...] to assume that *sammā-diṭṭhi* has a formal content which is

precisely the inverse of *micchā-diṭṭhi*, and that 'right-view' thus consists in a propositional attitude [...] towards that content: right-view consists in assent to the claim that things are impermanent, suffering and not-self, to the claim that the five aggregates are suffering, the cause of suffering is craving, the cessation of suffering is the cessation of craving and the way leading to the cessation of suffering is the eightfold path, and so on. Ibid., p. 223.

46 I am attempting to explain *micchā* and *sammā-diṭṭhi* in a manner in which the nature of wrong and right is not essentially propositional. The simile of the raft is not calling into question the truth or falsehood of the *dhamma*, but the correct or incorrect knowledge of it.

1 The content of wrong-view

1 There are other possible categories. For example the *Sammohavinodanī* classifies views into 'annihilationist-views' (*uccheda-diṭṭhi*), 'eternalist-views' (*sassata-diṭṭhi*), 'self-views' (*atta-diṭṭhi*), 'views of non-doing' (*akiriya-diṭṭhi*) and 'views of non-causality' (*ahetu-diṭṭhi*). Vibh-a 198–9; see Rupert Gethin, *The Foundations of Buddhism* (Oxford and New York, 1998), pp. 155–6.

2 I have calculated this number excluding repetitions of views. Including views that appear twice, I count 152.

3 The text adds for each of these views 'thus, that which is similar, wrong-view' (*yā evarūpā diṭṭhi*), 'gone over to view', etc., the text abbreviating the formula: 'Gone over to view, the thicket of view, a wilderness of view, the contrariness of view, the turmoil of view, the fetter of views, holding, fixity, adherence, clinging, a bad path, a false way, falsity, the realm of (other) systems of crossing over, the hold of the perverted views' (*diṭṭhi-gataṃ–pe–vipariyesa-gāho*, Vibh, 358). There will be an extensive discussion of this formula in chapter three.

4 The text after this view changes slightly giving: 'that which arises is wrong-view' (*yā uppajjati diṭṭhi*), instead of: 'thus, that which is similar, wrong-view' (*yā evarūpā diṭṭhi*), before giving the abbreviated 'a thicket of view, a wilderness of view', etc. (*diṭṭhi-gataṃ–pe–vipariyesa-gāho*, Vibh 359). The meaning appears clearer in the latter form implying that the view that arises is an object of attachment.

5 *sayaṃkataṃ sukhadukkhan ti saccato thetato diṭṭhi uppajjati. parakataṃ sukhadukkhan ti saccato thetato diṭṭhi uppajjati. sayaṃkatañ ca parakatañ ca sukhadukkhan ti saccato thetato diṭṭhi uppajjati. asayaṃkāraṃ aparaṃkāraṃ adhiccasamuppannaṃ sukhadukkhan ti saccato thetato diṭṭhi uppajjati*, Vibh 376–7.

The *Vibhaṅga* also discusses the 'three bases of heresy' (*tīṇi titthāyatanāni*) which appear to be related to these four views. These are described with a recluse or Brahmin holding three doctrines or views (*evaṃ vādi, evaṃ diṭṭhi*). The first is to hold that whatever pleasure, pain, or neither-pain-nor-pleasure a person experiences in the world, all this is due to past action (*yaṃ kiñcāyaṃ purisa puggalo paṭisaṃvedeti sukhaṃ vā dukkhaṃ vā adukkhamasukhaṃ vā sabban taṃ pubbekatahetū ti*). Or that all this is due to the creative activity of a supreme deity (*yaṃ kiñcāyaṃ purisapuggalo paṭisaṃvedeti sukhaṃ vā dukkhaṃ vā adukkhamasukhaṃ vā sabban taṃ issaranimmānahetū ti*). Or that they are without cause and without reason (*yaṃ kiñcāyaṃ purisapuggalo paṭisaṃvedeti sukhaṃ vā dukkhaṃ vā adukkhamasukhaṃ vā sabban taṃ ahetu-appaccayā ti*, Vibh 367–8). See Ledi Sayādaw, 'Some Points in Buddhist Doctrine', *Journal of the Pāli Text Society* (1913), pp. 115–64; see also the discussion and classification of these views in the *Sammohavinodanī*, Vibh-a 503.

6 *atthi me attāti vā assa saccato thetato diṭṭhi uppajjati, n' atthi me attāti vā assa saccato thetato diṭṭhi uppajjati. attanā va attānaṃ sañjānāmī ti vā assa saccato thetato*

diṭṭhi uppajjati. attanā va anattānaṃ sañjānāmī ti vā assa saccato thetato diṭṭhi uppajjati. anattanā va attānaṃ sañjānāmī ti vā assa saccato thetato diṭṭhi uppajjati. atha vā panassa evaṃ diṭṭhi hoti. so me ayaṃ attā vado vedeyyo. tatra tatra dīgharattaṃ kalyāṇapāpakānaṃ kammānaṃ vipākaṃ paccanubhoti na so jāto nāhosi. na so jāto na bhavissati. nicco dhuvo sassato aviparināmadhammo ti vā panassa saccato thetato diṭṭhi uppajjati, imā cha diṭṭhiyo, Vibh 382.

7 *n' atth dinnaṃ, n' atthi yiṭṭhaṃ, n' atthi hutaṃ, n' atthi sukaṭadukkaṭānaṃ kammānaṃ phalaṃ vipāko, n' atthi ayaṃ loko, n' atthi paro loko, n' atthi mātā, n' atthi pitā, n' atthi sattā opapātikā, n' atthi loke samaṇabrāhmaṇā sammaggatā sammāpaṭipannā ye imañ ca lokaṃ parañ ca lokaṃ sayaṃ abhiññā sacchikatvā pavedentī ti, ayaṃ dasavatthukā micchā-diṭṭhi*, Vibh 392.

8 *sassato loko ti vā, asassato loko ti vā antavā loko ti vā anantavā loko ti vā, taṃ jīvaṃ taṃ sarīran ti vā, aññaṃ jīvaṃ aññaṃ sarīran ti vā, hoti tathāgato param maraṇā ti vā, na hoti tathāgato param maraṇā ti vā, hoti ca na hoti ca tathāgato param maraṇā ti vā, n' eva hoti na na hoti tathāgato param maraṇā ti vā, ayaṃ dasavatthukā antaggāhikā diṭṭhi*, Vibh 392.

9 I have translated the term *saññā* as 'apperception' throughout this book; see Sue Hamilton's discussion in *Identity and Experience: The Constitution of the Human Being According to Early Buddhism* (London, 1996), pp. 53–65.

10 The six also appear in the *Kutuhalasālā-sutta* (S IV 398–400).

11 For details see Claus Vogel, *The Teachings of the Six Heretics* (Wiesbaden, 1970).

12 *n' atthi mahārāja dinnaṃ n' atthi yiṭṭham n' atthi hutaṃ, n' atthi sukaṭādukkaṭānaṃ kammānaṃ phalaṃ vipāko, n' atthi ayaṃ loko n' atthi paro loko, n' atthi mātā n' atthi pitā, n' atthi sattā opapātikā, n' atthi loke samaṇabrāhmaṇā sammaggatā sammā-paṭipannā ye imañ ca lokaṃ parañ ca lokaṃ sayaṃ abhiññā sacchikatvā pavedenti. cātum-mahābhūtiko ayaṃ puriso, yadā kālam karoti paṭhāvī paṭhavi-kāyaṃ anupeti anupagacchati, āpo āpo-kāyaṃ anupeti anupagacchati, tejo tejo-kāyaṃ anupeti anupagacchati, vāyo vāyo-kāyaṃ anupeti anupagacchati, ākāsaṃ indriyāni saṃkamanti. āsandi-pañcamā purisā mataṃ ādāya gacchanti, yāva āḷāhanā padāni paññāpenti, kāpatokāni aṭṭhīni bhavanti, bhassantâhutiyo. dattu-paññataṃ yad idaṃ dānaṃ, tesaṃ tucchaṃ musā vilāpo ye keci atthikavādaṃ vadanti. bāle ca paṇḍite ca kāyassa bhedā ucchijjanti vinassanti, na honti param maraṇā*, D I 55.

13 It is termed 'the doctrine of annihilationism' (uccheda-vāda). The formula is not specifically introduced as a *diṭṭhi*. In the *Sandaka-sutta* (M I 513–24) at M I 515 the view is not attributed to anyone. It is introduced as being the 'doctrine' (*vāda*) and 'view' (*diṭṭhi*) held by a certain ascetic. It is called one of the four ways which 'negate the living of the holy life' (*abrahmacariyavāsa*). The other three are the views of non-doing, the view of non-causality and the view of Pakudha Kaccāyana, which I will consider below. In the *Diṭṭhi-saṃyutta* (S III 201–24) at S III 205 the view is not attributed to anyone. It is called simply 'there is not' (*natthi*). In the *Pāṭali-sutta* (S IV 340–59) at S IV 347 it is described as a *vāda* and *diṭṭhi*.

14 In the *Sāleyyaka-sutta* (M I 285–90) at M I 287 (see also A V 265) it is called one of the 'three kinds of mental conduct not in accordance with the *dhamma*, unrighteous conduct' (*tividhaṃ manasā adhamma-cariyā-visamacariyā*). The other two are to covet the wealth and property of others and to have ill-will and hateful intentions. It is called both 'wrong-view' (*micchā-diṭṭhi*) and 'distorted vision' (*viparīta-dassana*, M I 189). In the *Apaṇṇaka-sutta* (M I 400–3) at M I 401 it is introduced as a *vāda* and *diṭṭhi*. It is called the 'doctrine of nihilism' (*natthika-vāda*, M I 403). In the *Cūḷapuṇṇama-sutta* (M III 20–4) at M III 22 it is introduced in the following way: 'And how, *bhikkhus*, does an untrue man hold views as an untrue man? Here, *bhikkhus*, someone holds such a view as this' (*kathañ ca bhikkhave, asappuriso asappurisadiṭṭhī hoti: idha bhikkhave, asappuriso evaṃdiṭṭhī hoti*, M III 22). The formula is then

given. In the *Sevitabbāsevitabba-sutta* (M III 45–61) at M III 52 the following introductory formula is used:

> And what kind of acquisition of view causes unwholesome states to increase and wholesome states to diminish in one who cultivates it? Here someone holds such a view as this (*kathaṃrūpaṃ bhante diṭṭhipaṭilābhaṃ sevato akusalā dhammā abhivaḍḍhanti, kusalā dhammā parihāyanti: idha bhante, ekacco evaṃdiṭṭhiko hoti*).

The formula is then given. In the *Mahācattārīsaka-sutta* (M III 71–8) at M III 71 the question is asked: 'What, *bhikkhus*, is wrong-view?' (*katamā ca bhikkhave micchā-diṭṭhi*). The formula is then given. The *Sammohavinodanī* explains the view as 'the wrong-view that has ten bases' (*dasavatthukā micchā-diṭṭhi*, Vibh-a 181).

15 *iti pi n' atthi paro loko. n' atthi sattā opapātikā. n' atthi sukaṭadukkaṭānaṃ kammānaṃ phalaṃ vipāko ti*, D II 319. This view is found in the *Pāyāsi-sutta* (D II 316–59) and is introduced as being a 'destructive view' (*pāpakaṃ diṭṭhi-gataṃ*), occurring to Prince Pāyāsi (*tena kho pana samayena Pāyāsi-rājaññassa eva-rupaṃ pāpakaṃ diṭṭhi-gataṃ uppannaṃ hoti*, D II 316).

16 I shall consider the content of this view in Chapter 2, and its function in Chapter 4.

17 Non-accomplishment in view:

> *tattha katamā diṭṭhivipatti: n' atthi dinnaṃ, n' atthi yiṭṭhaṃ, n' atthi hutaṃ, n' atthi sukaṭadukkaṭānaṃ kammānaṃ phalaṃ vipāko, n' atthi ayaṃ loko, n' atthi paro loko, n' atthi mātā, n' atthi pitā, n' atthi sattā opapātikā, n' atthi loke samaṇabrāhmaṇā sammaggatā sammāpaṭipannā ye imaṃ ca lokaṃ paraṃ ca lokaṃ sayaṃ abhiññā sacchikatvā pavedentīti yā evarūpā diṭṭhi diṭṭhi-gataṃ diṭṭhi-gahanaṃ diṭṭhi-kantāro diṭṭhi-visūkāyikaṃ diṭṭhi-vipphanditaṃ diṭṭhi-saṃyojanaṃ gāho patiggāho abhiniveso parāmāso kummaggo micchā-patho micchattaṃ titthāyatanaṃ vipariyesagāho, ayaṃ vuccati diṭṭhi-vipatti. sabbāpi micchā-diṭṭhi diṭṭhi-vipatti*, Dhs 233, § 1362.

References to the Dhs will be given by page number of the PTS edition then section number marked by §.

Accomplishment in view:

> *tattha katamā diṭṭhisampadā: atthi dinnaṃ, atthi yiṭṭhaṃ, atthi hutaṃ, atthi sukaṭadukkaṭānaṃ kammānaṃ phalaṃ vipāko. atthi ayaṃ loko, atthi paraloko, atthi mātā, atthi pitā, atthi sattā opapātikā, atthi loke samaṇabrāhmaṇā sammaggatā sammā-paṭipannā ye imaṃ ca lokaṃ parañ ca lokaṃ sayaṃ abhiññā sacchikatvā pavedentīti yā evarūpā paññā pajānanā–pe–amoho dhammavicayo sammā-diṭiṭhi, ayaṃ vuccati diṭṭhisampadā. sabbāpi sammā-diṭṭhi diṭṭhisampadā*, Dhs 233, § 1364.

See also Vibh 361, where it is stated that the view of nihilism is called a 'non-accomplishment in view' (*diṭṭhi-vipatti*), and all wrong-views are explained as non-accomplishment in view (*sabbāpi micchā-diṭṭhi diṭṭhi-vipatti*).

18 See, for example, Vibh 378 which gives five misfortunes (*pañca vyasanā*). These are misfortune through relatives; misfortune through wealth; misfortune through disease; misfortune through corrupted virtue; and misfortune through wrong-view (*ñāti-vyasanaṃ bhoga-vyasanaṃ roga-vyasanaṃ sīla-vyasanaṃ diṭṭhi-vyasanaṃ*).

19 *diṭṭhi-vipattiniddeso ca diṭṭhi-sampadā-niddesapaṭipakkhato, diṭṭhi-sampadā-niddeso ca diṭṭhūpādānaniddesapaṭipakkhato*, As 406.

20 As 385–6.

21 The attachment to the theory of self is explained using the formula for *sakkāya-diṭṭhi* which will be discussed below:

tattha katamaṃ attavādupādānaṃ: idha assutavā puthujjano ariyānaṃ adassāvī ariyadhammassa akovido ariyadhamme avinīto sappurisānaṃ adassāvī sappurisadhammassa akovido sappurisadhamme avinīto rūpaṃ attato samanupassati rūpavantaṃ vā attānaṃ attani vārūpaṃ rūpasmiṃ vā attānaṃ, vedanaṃ–pe–saññaṃ–pe–saṃkhāre–pe–viññāṇaṃ attato samanupassati. viññāṇavantaṃ vā attānaṃ attani vā viññāṇaṃ. viññāṇasmiṃ vā attānaṃ, yā evarūpā diṭṭhi diṭṭhi-gataṃ–pe–vipariyesagāho, idaṃ vuccati attavādupādānaṃ. imāni cattāri upādānāni, Vibh 375.

22 Jayatilleke, *Early Buddhist Theory of Knowledge*, p. 98. See also pp. 57–8, 74.

23 Did Ajita reject karma because it could not be known, or were there other reasons? If 'sensual pleasure' (*kāma*) were the goal, then its pursuit could not be impeded by ethical concerns. In A.K. Warder's terms, Ajita's view would 'sanction the pursuit of pleasure without fear of karma'. Warder, A.K., 'On the Relationship Between Early Buddhism and Other Contemporary Systems', *Bulletin of the School of Oriental and African Studies*, 18 (1956), pp. 43–63 (p. 55, note 3).

24 There has been a fair amount of scholarship on *Lokāyata/Cārvāka*. The standard source book on this subject, which collects together recent and not-so-recent articles on Indian Materialism is *Cārvāka/Lokāyata: An Anthology of Source Materials and Some Recent Studies*, ed. by Debiprasad Chattopadhyaya (New Delhi, 1990).

25 Tucci 'A Sketch of Indian Materialism', in Debiprasad Chattopadhyaya, *Cārvāka/ Lokāyata*, pp. 384–93 (pp. 391–2).

26 See Warder, 'On the Relationship Between Early Buddhism and Other Contemporary Systems', p. 55.

27 Tucci, 'A Sketch of Indian Materialism', p. 389. D.R. Shastri is of a similar view; Shastri, D.R., 'A Short History of Indian Materialism, Sensationalism and Hedonism', in *Cārvāka/Lokāyata*, pp. 396–431 (p. 402).

28 Tucci, 'A Sketch of Indian Materialism', p. 389. Among other parallel sources is section 108 of the *Rāmāyaṇa,* where *Lokāyata* ideas are found, none of which seem to disagree with the view of nihilism, in fact there are many parallel arguments; see J. Muir 'Verses Illustrating the Cārvāka Tenets' in *Cārvāka/Lokāyata*, pp. 351–68 (pp. 355–6); Warder, 'On the Relationship Between Early Buddhism and Other Contemporary Systems', p. 53. The phrase 'no mother no father' appears in the Jain *Praśnavyākaraṇa Sūtra* in which a description is given of the *nāstika-vādins* (P. *natthika-vādins*) using the following phrase, 'there is no mother nor father, neither is there human action', quoted by Basham, *History and Doctrines of the Ājīvikas,* p. 25; see also K.R. Norman, 'Pāli and the Language of the Heretics', in *Collected Papers*, Volume I (PTS, London, 1990), pp. 238–46). Another passage, this time in the Jain *Sūtra Kṛtaṇga*, also shows similarities to the second part of Ajita's doctrine:

> The whole soul lives; when this (body) is dead, it does not live. It lasts as long as the body lasts, it does not outlast the destruction of the body. With it (viz. the body) ends life. Other men carry it (the corpse) away to burn it. When it has been consumed by fire, only dove coloured bones remain, and the four bearers return with the hearse to the village [...]
>
> This murderer says: 'Kill, dig, slay, burn, cook, cut or break to pieces, destroy! Life ends here, there is no world beyond'. These *nāstikas* cannot inform you on the following points: whether an action is good and bad, meritorious or not well done, whether one reaches perfection or not, whether one goes to hell or not. Thus undertaking various works they engage in various pleasures and amusements for their own enjoyment.

See Jacobi, *Jaina Sutras: Part II* (Oxford, 1884), pp. 340–1. This passage is cited by Basham (*History and Doctrines of the Ājīvikas*, p. 16); see also Norman, *A Philological*

Approach to Buddhism (London, 1997), p. 73, who notes the general parallels between Buddhist and Jain sources with reference to the six teachers.

29 *karoto [...] kārayato chindato chedāpayato pacato pācayato socayato kilamayato phandato phandāpayato pāṇam atimāpayato adinnaṃ ādiyato sandhiṃ chindato nillopaṃ harato ekāgārikaṃ karoto paripanthe tiṭṭhato paradāraṃ gacchato musā bhaṇato, karoto na karīyati pāpaṃ. khura-pariyantena ce pi cakkena yo imissā paṭhaviyā pāṇe eka-maṃsa-khalaṃ eka-maṃsa-puñjaṃ kareyya, n' atthi tato-nidānaṃ pāpaṃ, n' atthi pāpassa āgamo. dakkhiṇañ ce pi Gaṅgā-tīraṃ āgaccheyya hananto ghātento chindanto chedāpento pacanto pācento, n' atthi tato-nidānaṃ pāpaṃ, n' atthi pāpassa āgamo. uttarañ ce pi Gaṅgā-tīraṃ gaccheyya dadanto dāpento yajanto yajāpento, n' atthi tato-nidānaṃ puññaṃ, n' atthi puññassa āgamo. dānena damena saṃyamena sacca-vajjena n' atthi puññaṃ, n' atthi puññassa āgamo ti*, D I 52–3.

In the *Sāmaññaphala-sutta* (D I 47–86) at D I 52–3 this view is attributed to Purāṇa Kassapa. It is called simply *akiriya*. In the *Apaṇṇaka-sutta* (M I 400–13) at M I 406 it is called *akiriya-vāda*. In the *Diṭṭhi-saṃyutta* (S III 201–24) at S III 208 it is called *karato*. In the *Sandaka-sutta* (M I 513–24) at M I 516 it is the second way which 'negates the living of the holy life' (*abrahmacariyavāsa*). In the *Pāṭali-sutta* (S IV 340–59) at S IV 347 it is described as a *vāda* and *diṭṭhi*. At S III 69 is found the first two lines of Makkhali Gosāla's view (the view of 'non-causality', see below) from the *Sāmaññaphala-sutta* (*n' atthi hetu n' atthi paccayo sattānam samkilesāya, ahetū apaccayā sattā samkilissanti n' atthi hetu, n' atthi paccayo sattānaṃ visuddhiyā, ahetū apaccayā sattā visujjhanti*) attributed to Purāṇa Kassapa. At S V 126 is found another formula attributed to Purāṇa Kassapa. This formula is part of the view (the first two lines of the Pāli) attributed in the *Sāmaññaphala-sutta* to Makkhali Gosāla (however, for 'defilement' (*samkilesa*) is found 'ignorance and lack of discernment' (*aññaṇāya adassanāya*) with other minor differences). At A III 383 is found a discussion of the 'six classes' (*abhijāti*) described in some detail. This is again attributed to Purāṇa Kassapa. Because of some of the confusion noted in these references we may surmise that Purāṇa Kassapa's view was similar to Makkhali Gosāla's; see Basham, *History and Doctrines of the Ājīvikas*, p. 84. For details of Pūraṇa Kassapa see Basham, ibid., pp. 80–90.

30 Jacobi, *Jaina Sutras*, p. 316.

31 Gómez, 'Some Aspects of the Free-Will Question in the Nikāyas', *Philosophy East and West* (1975), pp. 81–90 (p. 81).

32 *n' atthi hetu n' atthi paccayo sattānam samkilesāya, ahetu apaccayā sattā samkilissanti. n' atthi hetu, n' atthi paccayo sattānaṃ visuddhiyā, ahetu-apaccayā sattā visujjhanti. n' atthi attakāre n' atthi para-kāre, n' atthi purisa-kāre, n' atthi balaṃ n' atthi viriyaṃ, n' atthi purisa-thāmo n' atthi purisa-parakkamo. sabbe sattā sabbe pāṇā sabbe bhūtā sabbe jīvā avasā abalā aviriyā niyati-saṅgati-bhāva-pariṇatā chasvevābhijātīsu sukhadukkhaṃ paṭisaṃvedenti. cuddasa kho pan' imāni yoni-pamukha-satasahassāni saṭṭhiñca satāni cha ca satāni, pañca ca kammuno satāni pañca ca kammāni tīṇi ca kammāni kamme ca aḍḍha-kamme ca, dvaṭṭhi paṭipadā dvaṭṭh' antara-kappā, chaḷâbhijātiyo, aṭṭha purisa-bhūmiyo, ekūna-paññāsa ājīva-sate, ekūna-paññāsa paribbājaka-sate, ekūna-paññāsa nāgâvāsa-sate, vise indriya-sate, tiṃse niriya-sate, chattiṃsa rajo-dhātuyo, satta saññi-gabbhā, satta asaññi-gabbhā, satta nigaṇṭhigabbhā, satta devā, satta mānusā, satta pesācā, satta sarā, satta paṭuvā, satta paṭuvā-satāni, satta papātā, satta-papāta-satāni, satta supinā, satta supina-satāni, cullâsīti mahā-kappuno sata-sahassāni yāni bāle ca paṇḍite ca sandhāvitvā saṃsaritvā dukkhass'antaṃ karissanti. tattha n' atthi: īminâhaṃ sīlena vā vatena vā tapena vā brahamacariyena vā aparipakkaṃ vā kammaṃ paripācessāmi, paripakkaṃ vā kammaṃ phussa phussa vyanti-karissāmī ti.' h' evaṃ n' atthi doṇa-mite sukha-dukkhe pariyante-kaṭe saṃsāre, n' atthi hāyana-vaḍḍhane n' atthi*

ukkaṃsāvakaṃse. seyyathā pi nāma sutta-guḷe khitte nibbeṭhiyamānam eva phaleti, evam eva bāle paṇḍite ca sandhāvitvā saṃsaritvā dukkhass' antaṃ karissantī ti, D I 53–4.

This *diṭṭhi*, in the *Sāmaññaphala-sutta*, is the doctrine of Makkhali Gosāla. In the *Apaṇṇaka-sutta* (M I 407) it is called *ahetu-vāda*. A shorter version consisting of the first paragraph appears in the *Diṭṭhi-saṃyutta* at S III 208, and is called *hetu*. The *Sandaka-sutta* (M I 516–17), also has this shorter version. It is the third way that 'negates the living of the holy life'.

33 Pande, *Studies in the Origins of Buddhism* (Allahabad, 1957), pp. 342–3.

34 Basham considers possible reasons as to why Māgadhisms are found in the formulation of this view. They could be used in order to mock the speaker, as in Sanskrit drama, where the Māgadhi dialect was reserved to intimate lowliness (Basham, *History and Doctrines of the Ājīvikas*, p. 24). Or there is the possibility that this passage comes from a different source. Hence, by implication, they may be echoes of the original language of the teachers of these doctrines. As Norman argues: 'It seems to me that the words attributed to the six teachers probably reflect [...] the actual dialect of their teachings, at least as they were remembered at the time of the composition of the texts' (*A Philological Approach to Buddhism*, p. 73). In the first part of the formula there are few *-e* endings. They are found only in the phrase *n' atthi atta-kāre, n' atthi parakāre*. In the second part they are very prevalent. This suggests that the two parts originate from a different source (Basham, *History and Doctrines of the Ājīvikas*, pp. 24–5). If the reason for the Māgadhisms was to mock the speaker, all six teachers' views would be caricatured in a similar fashion. It seems more likely that there was an independent source for this formula. Norman has considered this issue. He agrees with Basham that in this formula we can indeed find borrowings from a non-Pāli source. In fact, due to the *-o* and *-e* endings there are probably two sources (Basham's argument), if not more (Norman, 'Pāli and the Language of the Heretics', in *Collected Papers*, Volume I (Oxford, 1990), pp. 238–46; see also Norman, 'Māgadhisms in the Kathāvatthu', in *Collected Papers*, Volume II (Oxford, 1991), pp. 59–70. In this later article, Norman notes the first scholars to recognise *-e* as Māgadhi for Pāli nominative singular *-o* were, in separate works, Kuhn and Trenckner in the 1870s).

35 *satt' ime mahārāja kāyā akaṭā akaṭā-vidhā animmitā animmātā vañjhā kūṭaṭṭhā esikaṭṭāyiṭṭhitā. te na iñjanti na vipariṇamanti na aññam-aññam vyābādhenti n' alam aññam-aññassa sukhāya vā dukkhāya vā sukha-dukkhāya vā. katame satta? paṭhavi-kāyo āpo-kāyo tejo-kāyo vāyo-kāyo sukhe dukkhe jīva-sattame. ime satta kāyā akaṭā akaṭā-vidhā animmitā animmātā vañjhā kūṭaṭṭhā esikaṭṭhāyiṭṭhitā. te na iñjanti na vipariṇamanti na aññaṃ-aññaṃ vyābādhenti nālaṃ aññaṃ-aññassa sukhāya vā dukkhāya vā sukha-dukkhāya vā. tattha n' atthi hantā vā ghātetā vā sotā vā sāvetā vā viññātā vā viññāpetā vā. yo pi tiṇhena satthena sīsaṃ chindati na koci kiñci jivitā voropeti, sattannaṃ yeva kāyānaṃ antareṇa sattha-vivaraṃ anupatati,* D I 56–7.

36 For details of Pakudha, see Basham, *History and Doctrines of the Ājīvikas*, pp. 90–3.

37 There is the following omission: *tattha n'atthi hantā vā ghātetā vā sotā vā sāvetā vā viññātā vā viññāpetā vā* of Pakudha's view in the *Sāmaññaphala-sutta* does not appear, but S III 210 does have the following: *yo pi tiṇhena satthena sīsaṃ chindati na koci kiñci jīvitā voropeti, sattannaṃ yeva kāyānaṃ antareṇa sattha-vivaraṃ anupatati* of Pakudha's view as in the *Sāmaññaphala-sutta*. The *Saṃyutta* formula then changes to the second half of Makkhali Gosāla's view as found in the *Sāmaññaphala-sutta* (see above, from *cuddassa*), with minor different readings. In a similar way the *Sandaka-sutta* (M I 513–24) at M I 517–18 has the first half of Pakudha's view with very minor variations. The second half, from *cuddassa* [...] *yoni-pamukha-satasahassāni* is Makkhali Gosāla's view as found in the *Sāmaññaphala-sutta*.

38 Bhikkhu Bodhi, *Connected Discourses of the Buddha*, Volume I (PTS, Oxford, 2000), p. 1094, note 249.

39 Basham, *History and Doctrines of the Ājīvikas,* p. 17.

40 Ibid., p. 262.

41 Jayatilleke, *Early Buddhist Theory of Knowledge*, p. 112. The view, particularly its opening section, argues Basham, echoes a static view of the universe, which may have been part of the developing ideas of Southern Ājīvikism (Basham, *History and Doctrines of the Ājīvikas,* p. 236). Basham traces these ideas as follows:

> If all future occurrences are rigidly determined and there is no room for novelty in the universe, coming events may in some sense be said to exist already. The future exists in the present, and both exist in the past. Time is thus on ultimate analysis illusory, and if so all motion and change, which take place in time, must be illusory also (ibid., p. 236).

This, argues Basham, developed into a doctrine of 'unchanging permanence' (*avikalita nityatvam*, ibid., p. 237, see also p. 262). Pande suggests that Pakudha is likely to have been a Brahmin, familiar with Upaniṣadic thought (Pande, *Origins of Buddhism*, pp. 449–50). Of some interest with this formula is that it may provide evidence of, or be an early reflection of Indian theories of indivisible entities, such as Vaiśeṣika (Basham, *History and Doctrines of the Ājīvikas,* p. 269). Again there are possible Māgadhisms found in this view. The formula mentions 'seven elementary categories' (*paṭhavi-kāyo āpo-kāyo tejo-kāyo vāyo-kāyo sukhe dukkhe jīva-sattame*; S III 210 has *jive*). The first four of these have Pāli *-o* endings, the fifth to the seventh Māgadhi *-e,* where *-aṃ* would be expected. Basham argues that the latter three were not part of standard Ājīvika theory, and were added to the earlier four (Basham, *History and Doctrines of the Ājīvikas,* p. 25 and p. 262).

42 *na vātā vāyanti na najjo sandanti na gabbhiniyo vijāyanti na candimasūriyā udenti vā apenti vā esikaṭṭhāyiṭṭhitā,* S III 200 ff. A parallel *Sūtrakṛtaṅga* passage has been noted by Jayatilleke, 'The sun does not rise or set, the moon does not wax or wane, rivers do not flow and winds do not blow; the whole world is deemed to be unreal/barren'; see Jayatilleke, *Early Buddhist Theory of Knowledge*, p. 256; see also Basham, *History and Doctrines of the Ājīvikas,* p. 262.

43 Bhikkhu Bodhi, *Connected Discourses,* Volume I, p. 1095, note 249.

44 *sassato attā ca loko ca vañjho kūṭaṭṭho esikaṭṭhāyiṭṭhito, te ca sattā sandhāvanti saṃsaranti cavanti upapajjanti, atthi tveva sassatisamaṃ,* D I 14–16. Translation from Bhikkhu Bodhi, *The Discourse on the All-Embracing Net of Views: The Brahmajāla Sutta and its Commentaries* (Kandy, 1978), p. 62. The first three views are realised through meditative experience, divided according to the number of past births which can be remembered. By *samādhi* the holder of the views attains one of the six *abhiññā*, that of realising former births (*pubbenivāsañāṇa*). Dutt observes that this is a familiar way to arrive at *micchā-diṭṭhi* in the *Brahmajāla-sutta.* Dutt, N., *Early Monastic Buddhism,* 2nd edition (Calcutta, 1971), p. 43. The final view is based upon 'reason' and 'reflection' (*takki* and *vīmaṃsi*).

45 Basham, *History and Doctrines of the Ājīvikas*, pp. 236–9.

46 Jayatilleke, *Early Buddhist Theory of Knowledge*, p. 259.

47 *idha* [...] *nigaṇṭho cātu-yāma-saṃvara-saṃvuto hoti. kathañ ca* [...] *nigaṇṭho cātu-yāma-saṃvara-saṃvuto hoti? idha* [...] *nigaṇṭho sabba-vārī-vārito ca hoti, sabba-vārī-yuto ca sabba-vārī-dhuto ca, sabba-vārī- phuṭṭho ca. evaṃ kho* [...] *nigaṇṭho cātu-yāma-saṃvara-saṃvuto hoti. yato kho* [...] *nigaṇṭho evaṃ cātu-yāma-saṃvara-saṃvuto hoti ayam vuccati* [...] *nigaṇṭho gatatto ca yatatto ca ṭhitatto cā ti,* D I 57.

The translation is from Maurice Walshe, *The Long Discourses of the Buddha: A Translation of the Dīgha Nikāya* (Boston, 1995), pp. 96–7. Basham (*History and Doctrines of the Ājīvikas*, p. 16) offers a different translation.

48 Basham, *History and Doctrines of the Ājīvikas*, p. 17.

49 Rhys Davids, T.W and Rhys Davids, C.A.F., *Dialogues of the Buddha*, Volume I (PTS, London, 1899–1921) p. 75, note 1.
50 There is a similar passage at M I 377. See the comments of Bhikkhu Bodhi, *The Middle Length Discourses of the Buddha: A New Translation of the Majjhima Nikāya* (Boston, 1995), p. 1256, note 585.
51 Walshe, *The Long Discourses of the Buddha*, p. 545, note 115.
52 *atthi paro loko ti iti ce maṃ pucchasi, atthi paro loko ti iti ce me assa, atthi paro loko ti iti te naṃ vyākareyyaṃ. evam pi me no. tathā ti pi me no. aññathā ti pi me no. no ti pi me no. no no ti pi me no. n' atthi paro loko? ti iti ce maṃ pucchasi, n' atthi paro loko ti iti ce me assa, n' atthi paro loko ti iti te naṃ vyākareyyaṃ. evanti pi me no. tathā ti pi me no. aññathā ti pi me no. no ti pi me no. no no ti pi me no. atthi ca n' atthi ca paro loko? ti iti ce maṃ pucchasi, atthi ca n' atthi ca paro loko ti iti ce me assa, atthi ca n' atthi ca paro loko ti iti te naṃ vyākareyyaṃ. evanti pi me no. tathā ti pi me no. aññathā ti pi me no. no ti pi me no. no no ti pi me no. nevatthi na n' atthi paro loko? ti iti ce maṃ pucchasi, nevatthi na n' atthi paro loko ti iti ce me assa, nevatthi na n' atthi paro loko ti iti te naṃ vyākareyyaṃ. evanti pi me no. tathā ti pi me no. aññathā ti pi me no. no ti pi me no. no no ti pi me no. atthi sattā opapātikā? ti iti ce maṃ pucchasi, atthi sattā opapātikā ti iti ce me assa, atthi sattā opapātikā'ti iti te naṃ vyākareyyaṃ. evanti pi me no. tathā ti pi me no. aññathā ti pi me no. no ti pi me no. no no ti pi me no. atthi ca n' atthi ca sattā opapātikā? ti iti ce maṃ pucchasi, atthi ca n' atthi ca sattā opapātikā ti iti ce me assa, atthi ca n' atthi ca sattā opapātikā ti iti te naṃ vyākareyyaṃ. evanti pi me no. tathā ti pi me no. aññathā'ti pi me no. no ti pi me no. no no ti pi me no. nevatthi na n' atthi sattā opapātikā? ti iti ce maṃ pucchasi, nevatthi na n' atthi sattā opapātikā ti iti ce me assa, nevatthi na n' atthi sattā opapātikā ti iti te naṃ vyākareyyaṃ. evanti pi me no. tathā ti pi me no. aññathā ti pi me no. no ti pi me no. no no ti pi me no. atthi sukaṭadukkaṭānaṃ kammānaṃ phalaṃ vipāko? ti iti ce maṃ pucchasi, atthi sukaṭadukkaṭānaṃ kammānaṃ phalaṃ vipāko ti iti ce me assa, atthi sukaṭadukkaṭānaṃ kammānaṃ phalaṃ vipāko ti iti te naṃ vyākareyyaṃ. evanti pi me no. tathā ti pi me no. aññathā ti pi me no. no ti pi me no. no no ti pi me no. n' atthi sukaṭadukkaṭānaṃ kammānaṃ phalaṃ vipāko? ti iti ce maṃ pucchasi, n' atthi sukaṭadukkaṭānaṃ kammānaṃ phalaṃ vipāko ti iti ce me assa, n' atthi sukaṭadukkaṭānaṃ kammānaṃ phalaṃ vipāko ti iti te naṃ vyākareyyaṃ. evanti pi me no. tathā ti pi me no. aññathā ti pi me no. no ti pi me no. no no ti pi me no. atthi ca n' atthi ca sukaṭadukkaṭānaṃ kammānaṃ phalaṃ vipāko? ti iti ce maṃ pucchasi, atthi ca n' atthi ca sukaṭadukkaṭānaṃ kammānaṃ phalaṃ vipāko ti iti ce me assa, atthi ca n' atthi ca sukaṭadukkaṭānaṃ kammānaṃ phalaṃ vipāko ti iti te naṃ vyākareyyaṃ. evanti'pi me no. tathā ti pi me no. aññathā ti pi me no. no ti pi me no. no no ti pi me no. nevatthi na n' atthi sukaṭadukkaṭānaṃ kammānaṃ phalaṃ vipāko? ti iti ce maṃ pucchasi, nevatthi na n' atthi sukaṭadukkaṭānaṃ kammānaṃ phalaṃ vipāko'ti iti ce me assa, nevatthi na n' atthi sukaṭadukkaṭānaṃ kammānaṃ phalaṃ vipāko ti iti te naṃ vyākareyyaṃ. evanti pi me no. tathā ti pi me no. aññathā ti pi me no. no ti pi me no. no no ti pi me no. hoti Tathāgato param maraṇā? ti iti ce maṃ pucchasi, hoti Tathāgato param maraṇā ti iti ce me assa, hoti Tathāgato param maraṇā ti iti te naṃ vyākareyyaṃ. evanti pi me no. tathā'ti pi me no. aññathā ti pi me no. no ti pi me no. no no ti pi me no. na hoti Tathāgato param maraṇā? ti iti ce maṃ pucchasi, na hoti Tathāgato param maraṇā ti iti ce me assa, na hoti Tathāgato param maraṇā ti iti te naṃ vyākareyyaṃ. evanti pi me no. tathā ti pi me no. aññathā ti pi me no. no ti pi me no. no no ti pi me no. hoti ca na hoti ca Tathāgato param maraṇā? ti iti ce maṃ pucchasi, hoti ca na hoti ca Tathāgato param maraṇā ti iti ce me assa, hoti ca na hoti ca Tathāgato param maraṇā ti iti te naṃ vyākareyyaṃ. evanti pi me no. tathā ti pi me no. aññathā ti pi me no. no ti pi me no. no no ti pi me no. neva hoti na na hoti Tathāgato param maraṇā? ti iti ce maṃ pucchasi, neva hoti na na hoti Tathāgato param maraṇā ti iti ce me assa, neva hoti na na hoti Tathāgato param*

maraṇā ti iti te naṃ vyākareyyaṃ. evanti pi me no. tathā ti'pi me no. aññathā ti pi me no. no ti pi me no. no no ti pi me no ti, D I 58–9.

53 Jayatilleke, *Early Buddhist Theory of Knowledge*, p. 474; see also Collins, *Selfless Persons*, p. 128.

54 Jayatilleke, *Early Buddhist Theory of Knowledge*, pp. 124, 128–9; Warder, *Outline of Indian Philosophy* (Delhi, 1971), pp. 45–6; Barua, B.M., *Pre-Buddhistic Indian Philosophy* (Calcutta, 1921), p. 326; Pande, *Origins of Buddhism* (Allahabad, 1957), p. 350. Pande thinks that, at the very least, this scepticism is based upon 'critical considerations'.

55 *sakkā nu kho* [...] *evaṃ diṭṭheva dhamme sandiṭṭhikaṃ sāmaññaphalaṃ paññāpetun ti*, D I 52 ff.

56 *api ca kho evam diṭṭhi hoti: no ca assaṃ, no ca me siyā,*
na bhavissāmi na me bhavissatī ti.
yā ca pana [...]
ucchedadiṭṭhi saṃkhāro so, S III 99.
See Bhikkhu Bodhi, *Connected Discourses*, Volume I, p. 1076, note 135 for this reading. A discussion of the *sutta* in which this view is found will be given in Chapter 5.

57 *tatre kho Bhagavā udānam udānesi:*
no cassa, no ca me siyā
na bhavissati na me bhavissatī ti, S III 56.
I am following the readings of both the *uccheda-diṭṭhi* and the *udāna* from Bhikkhu Bodhi, *Connected Discourses*, Volume I, p. 1076, note 135; see also pp. 1060–2, note 75.

58 See a similar practice guided by the formula at A IV 70–4 and, with a shorter version of the formula, at Ud 78; see Bhikkhu Bodhi, *Connected Discourses*, Volume I, pp. 1060–2, note 75 for a discussion of these occurrences.

59 Bhikkhu Bodhi notes that these two views are sometimes confounded in the various recensions of the text and that, from the readings of the commentaries, the uncertainty as to the meaning of the views may have existed prior to the commentaries; see Bhikkhu Bodhi, *Connected Discourses*, Volume I, p. 1061, note 75.

60 Ibid.

61 Spk III 306; see Bhikkhu Bodhi, *Connected Discourses*, Volume I, p. 1062, note 75; p. 1076, note 135.

62 Ibid.

63 Bhikkhu Bodhi, *The Middle Length Discourses*, p. 397.

64 Collins, *Selfless Persons*, pp. 93–4.

65 Gethin, *The Foundations of Buddhism*, p. 148.

66 *yā imā gahapati anekavihitā diṭṭhiyo loke uppajjanti: sassato loko ti vā, asassato loko ti vā, antavā loko ti vā, anantavā loko ti vā, taṃ jīvaṃ taṃ sarīran ti vā, aññaṃ jīvaṃ aññaṃ sarīran ti vā, hoti tathāgato param maraṇā ti vā, na hoti tathāgato param maraṇā ti vā, hoti ca na ca hoti tathāgato param maraṇā ti vā, n' eva hoti na na hoti tathāgato param maraṇā ti vā, yāni c' imāni dvāsaṭṭhi diṭṭhigatāni brahmajāle bhaṇitāni. imā kho gahapati diṭṭhiyo sakkāya-diṭṭhiyā sati honti sakkāya-diṭṭhiyā asati na hontī ti*, S IV 287.

67 *sakkāya-diṭṭhi sabbamicchā-diṭṭhiyā padaṭṭhānaṃ*, Peṭ 179.

68 *kathaṃ pana* [...] *sakkāyadiṭṭhi hotī ti. idh' āvuso assutavā puthujjano ariyānaṃ adassāvī ariyadhammassa akovido ariyadhamme avinīto, sappurisānaṃ adassāvi sappurisadhammassa akovido sappurisadhamme avinīto, rūpaṃ attato samanupassati, rūpavantaṃ vā attānaṃ, attani vā rūpaṃ, rupasmiṃ vā attāna§; vedanam attato samanupassati, vedanāvantaṃ vā attānaṃ, attani vā vedanaṃ, vedanāya vā attānaṃ; saññaṃ attato samanupassati, saññāvantam vā attānaṃ, attani vā saññaṃ, saññāya vā attānaṃ; saṃkhāre attato samanupassati, saṃkhāravantam*

vā attānaṃ, attani vā saṃkhāre, saṃkhāresu vā attānaṃ; viññāṇaṃ attato samanupassati, viññāṇavantaṃ vā attānaṃ, attani vā viññāṇaṃ, viññāṇasmiṃ vā attānaṃ, M I 300.

69 The *Sammohavinodanī* states that adherence (*abhinivesa*) to the ideas of eternalism and annihilationism is preceded by the assumption of a self (Vibh-a 182). It also explains *abhinivesa* as the conviction that the *khandhas* are self (Vibh-a 218).

70 *sakkāyavatthukāya sassataditthiyā pannarasahi ākārehi abhiniveso sabbāva tā bhavaditthiyo. sakkāyavatthukāya ucchedadiṭṭhiyā pañcahākārehi abhiniveso, sabbāva tā vibhavadiṭṭhiyo*, Ps I 157–8.

71 Nett 111.

72 Buddhaghosa interprets *pāpakāṃ diṭṭhi-gataṃ* as *lāmikā*, 'wicked', Spk I 208, Mp II 24; see Anderson, *Pain and its Ending*, p. 37. I have used the term 'destructive' throughout this book to translate *pāpaka*. It has the meaning of 'bad' or 'wicked' (see PED s.v. *pāpaka*). I use the term 'destructive' in the sense of the view destroying the Buddhist path, and in this way it is a 'bad' or 'wicked' view.

73 *tena kho pana samayena Ariṭṭhassa nāma bhikkhuno* [...] *evarūpaṃ pāpakāṃ diṭṭhi-gataṃ uppannaṃ hoti: tatra 'ha Bhagavatā dhammaṃ desitaṃ ājānāmi yathā ye 'me antarāyikā dhammā vuttā Bhagavatā te paṭisevato nâlaṃ antarāyâti*, M I 130; see also Vin II 25 and Vin IV 133–4.

74 See Gethin's comments in 'Wrong View (*micchā-diṭṭhi*) and Right View (*sammā-diṭṭhi*)', p. 228, note 20.

75 It is the 'Ariṭṭha rule' (*Ariṭṭhasikkhāpadaṃ*); see Norman, *The Pātimokkha* (PTS, London, 2001), p. 71.

76 For details of these 'acts of suspension', see Vin I 49, 53, 98, 143, 168, Vin II 27, 226, 230, 298, A I 97.

77 The Vinaya also has the idea of 'suspending an invitation' (*pavāranaṃ ṭhapetuṃ*) to various special days (the text mentioning the invitation days of the fourteenth and the fifteenth: *tadahu pavāraṇāya cātuddase vā paṇṇarase*, Vin I 170) for various types of wrong-conduct. One of the types of conduct cited which will cause such punishment is the falling away from right-view (*diṭṭhi-vipattiyā ṭhapesi*, Vin I 172). The text explains this as 'falling away from right-view [into a] wrong-view', an extreme view (*micchā-diṭṭhi antaggāhikā diṭṭhi ayaṃ diṭṭhivipatti*, Vin I 172).

78 *āpattiyā adassane ukkhittako vibbhamati.*

79 *āpattiyā appaṭikamme ukkhittako vibbhamati.*

80 *diṭṭhiyā appaṭinissagge ukkhittako vibbhamati.*

81 The passage for the giving up of wrong-view is:

> *idha pana bhikkhave, bhikkhu pāpikāya diṭṭhiyā appaṭinissagge ukkhittako vibbhamati, so puna paccāgantvā bhikkhū upasampadaṃ yācati, so evam assa vācanīyo: paṭinissajjissasi taṃ pāpikaṃ diṭṭhin ti. sacāhaṃ paṭinissajjissāmī ti, pabbājetabbo. sacāhaṃ na paṭinissajjissāmī ti, na pabbājetabbo. pabbājetvā vattabbo: paṭinissajjissasi taṃ pāpikam diṭṭhin ti. sacāhaṃ paṭinissajjissāmī ti, upasampādetabbo. sacāhaṃ na paṭinissajjissāmı ti, na upasampādetabbo. upasampādetvā vattababo: paṭinissajjissasi taṃ pāpikaṃ diṭṭhin ti. sacāhaṃ paṭinissajjissāmī ti, osāretabbo. sacāhaṃ na paṭinissajjissāmī ti na osāretabbo. osāretvā vattabbo: paṭinissajjāhi taṃ pāpikaṃ diṭṭhin ti. sace paṭinissajjati, icca etaṃ kusalaṃ no ce paṭinissajjati, labbhamānāya sāmaggiyā puna ukkhipitabbo. alabbhamānāya sāmaggiyā anāpatti sambhoge saṃvāse ti*, Vin I 98.

82 *idha pana bhikkhave, bhikkhussa na hoti āpatti daṭṭhabbā. na hoti pāpikā diṭṭhi paṭinissajjetā. tam enaṃ codeti saṅgho vā sambahulā vā ekapuggalo vā āpattiṃ tvaṃ āvuso, āpanno. passas' etaṃ āpattiṃ. pāpikā te diṭṭhi. paṭinissajj' etaṃ pāpikaṃ diṭṭhin ti. so evaṃ vadeti: n' atthi me āvuso āpatti yam ahaṃ passeyyaṃ. n' atthi me*

pāpikā diṭṭhi yam ahaṃ paṭinissajjeyyan ti. taṃ saṅgho appaṭikamme vā appaṭinissagge vā ukkhipati, adhammakammaṃ, Vin I 323.

83 *yadi saṅghassa pattakallaṃ saṅgho ariṭṭhassa bhikkhuno gaddhabādhipubbassa pāpikāya diṭṭhiyā appaṭinissagge ukkhepaniyakammaṃ kareyya, asambhogaṃ saṅghena*, Vin II 27.

84 *tena kho pana samayena Sātissa nāma bhikkhuno* [...] *evarūpaṃ pāpakāṃ diṭṭhi-gataṃ uppannaṃ hoti. tatra 'ha§ Bhagavatā dhammaṃ desitaṃ ājānāmi yathā tad ev' idaṃ viññāṇaṃ sandhāvati saṃsārati aññan ti*, M II 256.

85 Norman, *A Philological Approach to Buddhism*, p. 92.

86 Gombrich, *How Buddhism Began*, p. 78.

87 *tena kho pana* [....] *samayena Bakassa brahmuno evarūpaṃ pāpakāṃ diṭṭhi-gataṃ uppannaṃ hoti: idaṃ niccaṃ idaṃ dhuvaṃ idaṃ sassataṃ idaṃ kevalaṃ idaṃ acavanadhammaṃ, idaṃ hi na jāyati na jīyati na mīyati na cavati na upapajjati, ito ca pan' aññaṃ uttariṃ nissaraṇaṃ n' atthī ti*, M I 326.

S I 142 has a very slightly different word order. Baka is also found in the *Bakabrahmajātaka* at J III 358 ff. The *pāpakaṃ diṭṭhi-gataṃ* is slightly shorter in this *Jātaka*: 'This present existence is everlasting, permanent, eternal, unchanging; apart from it there is no *nibbāna* or release' (*idaṃ niccaṃ dhuvaṃ sassataṃ acavanadhammaṃ, ito aññaṃ loke nissaraṇaṃ nibbānaṃ nāma n' atthi*). In the *Jātaka* version this *diṭṭhi* is not preceded by the usual *pāpakāṃ ditthigataṃ uppannaṃ hoti*, but followed by *evam diṭṭhi uppajji*, 'this view arose'.

88 *tena kho pana samayena Yamakassa nāma bhikkhuno evarūpam pāpakāṃ diṭṭhi-gataṃ uppannam hoti: tathāham Bhagavatā dhammaṃ desitaṃ ājānāmi, yathā khīṇāsavo bhikkhu kāyassa bhedā ucchijjati vinassati na hoti param maraṇā ti*, S III 109.

89 *pāpakam diṭṭhi-gataṃ uppannaṃ hoti: n' atthi samaṇo vā brāhmaṇo vā yo idha āgaccheyyā ti*, S I 144.

90 *bhūtapubbaṃ* [...] *sattannaṃ brāhmaṇisīnaṃ araññāyatane paṇṇakuṭīsu sammantānaṃ evarūpaṃ pāpakaṃ diṭṭhi-gataṃ uppannaṃ hoti*: *brāhmaṇo va seṭṭho vaṇṇo, hīno añño vaṇṇo; brāhmaṇo va sukko vaṇṇo, kaṃho añño vaṇṇo; brāhmaṇā va sujjhanti no abrāhmaṇā; brāhmaṇā, va brahmuno puttā orasā mukhato jātā brahmajā brahmanimmitā brahmadāyādā ti*, M II 154–5.

91 Bhikkhu Bodhi, *The Middle Length Discourses of the Buddha*, p. 1208, note 286.

92 *ime diṭṭhi-ṭṭhāna evam-gahitā evam-parāmaṭṭhā evam-gatikā bhavanti evam-abhisamparāyā ti*, D I 16, 22, 24, 28, 30, *passim*.

93 Norman, 'A Note on *attā* in the *Alagaddūpama-sutta*', in *Collected Papers*, Volume II (PTS, Oxford, 1991), pp. 200–9 (p. 200).

94 Gombrich 'Recovering the Buddha's Message' in *The Buddhist Forum: Volume I, Seminar Papers 1987–8* (London, 1990), pp. 5–20 (p. 14).

95 *chayimāni bhikkhave diṭṭhiṭṭhānāni. katamāni cha. idha bhikkhave assutavā puthujjano ariyānaṃ adassāvī ariyadhammassa akovido ariyadhamme avinīto, sappurisānaṃ adassāvī sappurisadhammassa akovido sappurisadhamme avinīto, rūpaṃ etaṃ mama, eso 'ham asmi, eso me attā ti samanupassati. vedanaṃ etaṃ mama, eso 'ham asmi, eso me attā ti samanupassati. saññaṃ etaṃ mama, eso 'ham asmi, eso me attā ti samanupassati. saṃkhāre etaṃ mama, eso 'ham asmi, eso me attā ti samanupassati. yam pi taṃ diṭṭhaṃ sutaṃ mutaṃ viññātaṃ pattaṃ pariyesitaṃ anuvicaritaṃ manasā, tam pi etaṃ mama, eso 'ham asmi, eso me attā ti samanupassati. yam pi taṃ diṭṭhiṭṭhānaṃ so loko so attā, so pecca bhavissāmi: nicco dhuvo sassato avipariṇāmadhammo, sassatisamaṃ tatheva ṭhassāmī ti tampi etaṃ mama, esohamasmi, eso me attā ti samanupassati*, M I 135.

I have not been able to find the formula in any other place, though parts of it are familiar from other sections of the Nikāyas. Part of the formula illustrating the six views has the phrase: 'This is mine, this I am, this is my self' (*etam mama, eso 'ham asmi, eso me attā ti*). This phrase is found in the *Diṭṭhi-vagga* and *Diṭṭhi-saṃyutta* at S III 186 and S III 200 respectively. It is a wrong-view and is called, 'this is mine' (*etam mama*). The sixth view is also found in isolation to the rest of the above formula. It is repeated a little later in the *Alagaddūpama*-sutta at M I 136. The formula is: 'This is self, this the world; after death I shall be permanent, everlasting, eternal, not subject to change; I shall endure and last as long as eternity' (*so loko so attā, so pecca bhavissāmi nicco dhuvo sassato avipariṇāma-dhammo, sassatisamaṃ tath' eva ṭhassāmi*, M I 135–6). At S III 97 is found another variation: 'There may indeed be this view: "That is the self, that is the world; after death I shall be permanent, everlasting, eternal, not subject to change"' (*api ca kho evam diṭṭhi hoti, so attā so loko, so pecca bhavissāmi nicco dhuvo sassato avipariṇāmadhammo ti*, S III 97). This view is shorter than the *Majjhima* view, ending with *avipariṇāmadhammo*. The word order is slightly different, beginning with *so attā so loko* instead of *so loko so attā*. This shortened version is also found in the *Diṭṭhi-vagga* at S III 182 and the *Diṭṭhi-saṃyutta* at S III 205. In the *Diṭṭhi-vagga* it is called *eso attā* and in the *Diṭṭhi-saṃyutta, so attā*. The *sutta* describes this view as an eternalist-view (*sassata-diṭṭhi*) and as a volitional formation (*saṃkhāra*). By explaining it as such it is stating that the view is part of dependent-origination. By being part of this process it is being defined as an aspect of *dukkha* itself. A view is also found as part of six views in the *Sabbāsava-sutta* at M I 8 (to be considered in the next section of this chapter), and this also contains the second half of the formula, from *nicco*:

> It is this self of mine that speaks and feels and experiences here and there the result of good and bad actions; but this self of mine is permanent, everlasting, eternal, not subject to change, and it will endure and last forever (*yo me ayaṃ attā vado vedeyyo tatra tatra kalyāṇapāpakānaṃ kammānaṃ vipākaṃ paṭsaṃvedeti, so kho pana me ayaṃ attā nicco dhuvo sassato avipariṇāmadhammo sassatisamaṃ tath' eva ṭhassatī ti*, M I 8).

96 I will return to this below with Richard Gombrich's comments comparing this view to ideas found in the *Bṛhadāraṇyaka Upaniṣad*. I shall also discuss these ideas in Chapter 3 on the function of wrong-view and in Chapter 6 in a discussion of the *Aṭṭhakavagga*.

97 Norman, 'A Note on *attā* in the *Alagaddūpama*', pp. 200–9. Norman himself cites E.J. Thomas, *History of Buddhist Thought* (London, 1933), p. 103 (Norman, ibid., p. 201).

98 Ibid., p. 203.

99 Norman, 'A note on *attā* in the *Alagaddūpama*', p. 203.

100 Jayatilleke, *Early Buddhist Theory of Knowledge,* pp. 60–1; see also Kamaleswar Bhattacharya 'Diṭṭhaṃ, sutaṃ, mutaṃ, viññātaṃ' in *Buddhist Studies in Honour of Walpola Rahula*, S. Balasooriya, A Bareau, R. Gombrich, Siri Gunasingha, U. Mallwarachchi, and E. Perry (eds) (London, 1980), pp. 10–15.

101 Jayatilleke, *Early Buddhist Theory of Knowledge*, p. 60

102 Gombrich, 'Recovering the Buddha's Message', p. 15.

103 *Bṛhadāraṇyaka Upaniṣad* 2, 4, 5 and 4, 5, 6. Patrick Olivelle, *Upaniṣads* (Oxford, 1996).

104 As will be discussed in the next chapter, this is one of the two causes of wrong-view, together with 'the voice of another' (*parato ghosa*).

105 *tassa evaṃ ayoniso manasikarato channaṃ diṭṭhīnaṃ aññatarā diṭṭhi uppajjati: atthi me attā ti vā 'ssa saccato thetato diṭṭhi uppajjati, n' atthi me attā ti vā 'ssa saccato thetato diṭṭhi uppajjati, attanā va attānaṃ sañjānāmī ti vā 'ssa saccato thetato diṭṭhi uppajjati, attanā va anattānaṃ sañjānāmī ti vā 'ssa saccato thetato diṭṭhi uppajjati, anattanā na attānaṃ sañjānāmī ti vā 'ssa saccato thetato diṭṭhi uppajjati. atha vā pan' assa evam diṭṭhi hoti: yo me ayaṃ attā vado vedeyyo tatra tatra*

kalyāṇapāpakānaṃ kammānaṃ vipākaṃ paṭisaṃvedeti, so kho pana me ayaṃ attā nicco dhuvo sassato aviparināmadhammo sassatisamam tath' eva ṭhassatī ti, M I 8.

Translation adapted from Gethin, *The Foundations of Buddhism*, p. 149; see also Collins, *Selfless Persons*, pp. 76, 119.

106 Vibh-a 116.

107 Vibh-a 115. The four names are: suffering; its arising; cessation; and the way to its cessation.

108 Sue Hamilton uses the term 'manifoldness' as a translation for *papañca* (Hamilton, *Early Buddhism*, pp. 76–8).

109 Vibh-a 114.

110 *sassato attā ca loko ca, idam eva saccaṃ mogham aññan ti itth' eke abhivadanti. asassato attā ca loko ca* [...] *sassato ca asassato ca attā ca loko ca* [...] *neva sassato nāsassato attā ca loko ca* [...] *antavā attā ca loko ca* [...] *anantavā attā ca loko ca* [...] *antavā ca anantavā ca attā ca loko ca* [...] *nevantavā nānantavā attā ca loko ca* [...] *ekatta-saññī attā ca loko ca, idam eva saccaṃ, mogham aññan ti itth' eke abhvadanti. nānattasaññī attā ca loko ca* [...] *paritta-saññī* [...] *appamāṇasaññī* [...] *ekantasukhī* [...] *ekantadukkhī* [...] *sukhadukkhī* [...] *adukkhamasukhī attā ca loko ca, idam eva saccaṃ, mogham aññan ti itth' eke abhvadanti*, M II 233–4.

These can be compared to the 16 'theories of having apperception' (*saññī-vāda*) from the *Brahmajāla-sutta*. These are the following:

> They proclaim the self is immutable after death, appercipient and: View 1: material; View 2: immaterial; View 3: both material and immaterial; View 4: neither material nor immaterial; View 5: finite; View 6: infinite; View 7: both finite and infinite; View 8: neither finite nor infinite; View 9: of uniform apperception; View 10: of diversified apperception; View 11: of limited apperception; View 12: of boundless apperception; View 13: exclusively happy; View 14: exclusively miserable; View 15: both happy and miserable; View 16: neither happy nor miserable (*rūpī attā hoti arago param maraṇā saññī ti naṃ paññāpenti, ārūpī, rūpī ca arūpī ca attā hoti–pe–n' eva rūpī nārūpī attā hoti–pe–antavā attā hoti–pe–anantavā attā hoti–pe–anantavā ca anantavā ca attā hoti–pe–n' eva antavā nānantavā attā hoti–pe–ekatta-saññī attā hoti–pe–nānatta saññī attā hoti–pe–parittā-saññī attā hoti–pe–appamāṇā-saññī ekanta-sukhī attā hoti–pe–ekanta-dukkhī attā hoti. sukha-dukkhī attā hoti–pe–adukkham-asukhī attā hoti arago param maraṇā saññī ti naṃ paññāpenti*, D I 31).

The *Brahmajāla-sutta* calls these views speculations about the 'future' (*aparantakappika*). A group of comparable views is found in the *Saṃyutta-nikāya* (S III 218–20). Each of these *micchā-diṭṭhi* is given a name. These are the first significant word in each *micchā-diṭṭhi* which distinguishes it from the other views: *rūpī attā; arūpī attā*; *rūpī ca arūpī*; *neva rūpī nārūpī*; *ekantasukhī*; *ekantadukkhī*; *sukhadukkhī*; *adukkhamasukhī*. For example, the first two views are: 'the self has form, it is immutable/without sickness (*aroga*), after death' (*rūpī attā hoti arogo param maraṇā ti*), 'the self is formless, it is immutable/without sickness after death' (*arūpī attā hoti arogo param maraṇā ti*).

111 M II 234.

112 *paccattaṃ yeva ñāṇaṃ bhavissati parisuddhaṃ pariyodātanti*, M II 234.

113 *tatra bhikkhave, ye te samaṇabrāhmaṇā evaṃ-vādino evaṃdiṭṭhino: sassato attā ca loko ca, idam eva saccaṃ mogham aññan ti. tesaṃ vata aññatreva saddhāya aññatra ruciyā aññatra anussavā aññatra ākāraparivitakkā aññatra diṭṭhinijjhānakkhantiyā paccattaṃ yeva ñāṇaṃ bhavissati parisuddhaṃ pariyodātanti. n' etaṃ ṭhānaṃ vijjati. paccattaṃ kho pana bhikkhave ñāṇe asati parisuddhe pariyodāte, yadapi te bhonto samaṇabrāhmaṇā tattha ñāṇabhāgamattam eva pariyodapenti, tadapi tesaṃ*

bhavataṃ samaṇabrāhmaṇānaṃ upādānam akkhāyati. tayidaṃ saṃkhataṃ oḷārikaṃ, atthi kho pana saṃkhārānaṃ nirodho, atth' etan ti iti viditvā tassa nissaraṇadassāvī tathāgato tadupātivatto, M II 234.

114 Walpola Rahula, *What the Buddha Taught* (London, 1967), p. 2.

115 *samaṇabrāhmaṇā kesaputtaṃ āgacchanti, te sakaṃ yeva vādaṃ dīpenti, jotenti, paravādaṃ pana khuṃsenti, vambhenti, opapakkhiṃ karonti, paribhavanti*, A I 188.

116 In identical terms to those that we shall meet in the *Pāṭali-sutta* which I will consider in Chapter 5.

117 Again, in identical terms to the *Pāṭali-sutta*: *alaṃ hi vo kālāmā kaṅkhituṃ alaṃ vicikicchituṃ, kaṅkhanīyeva ca pana vo ṭhāne vicikicchā uppannā*, A I 189.

118 A I 189. Three of these occurred in the earlier list of five items (oral tradition, *anussavā*, reasoned cogitation, *ākāraparivitakkā*, and acceptance of a view as a result of reflection, *diṭṭhi-nijjhānakkhantiyā*); see Jayatilleke, *Early Buddhist Theory of Knowledge*, pp. 182–8, 274–6.

119 *yadā tumhe* [...] *attanā'va jāneyyātha:ime dhammā akusalā, ime dhammā sāvajjā, ime dhammā viññūgarahitā, ime dhammā samattā samādinnā ahitāya dukkhāya saṃvattantī ti: atha tumhe* [...] *pajaheyyātha*, A I 189.

120 I am arguing that when the Nikāyas state that the *dhamma* is superior they hold that it is superior because it does not give rise to craving and attachment.

121 For greed: *luddho panāyaṃ kālāmā purisapuggalo lobhena abhibhūto pariyādinnacitto pāṇampi hanti adinnam pi ādiyati, paradāram pi gacchati, musā pi bhaṇati, param pi tathattāya samādapeti, yaṃ sa hoti dīgharattaṃ ahitāya dukkhāyā ti. evaṃ bhante*, A I 189.

122 *iti kho kālāmā yaṃ taṃ avocumha. etha tumhe kālāmā mā anussavena, mā paramparāya, mā itikirāya, mā piṭakasampadānena, mā takkahetu, mā nayahetu, mā ākāraparivitakkena, mā diṭṭhinijjhānakkhantiyā, mā bhabbarūpatāya, mā samaṇo no garū ti. yadā tumhe kālāmā attanā va jāneyyātha: ime dhammā akusalā, ime dhammā sāvajjā, ime dhammā viññūgarahitā, ime dhammā samattā samādinnā ahitāya dukkhāya saṃvattantī ti. atha tumhe kālāmā pajaheyyāthā ti iti yaṃ taṃ vuttaṃ idam etaṃ paṭicca vuttaṃ*, A I 190.

123 *etha tumhe kālāmā mā anussavena, mā paramparāya, mā itikirāya, mā piṭakasampadānena, mā takkahetu, mā nayahetu, mā ākāraparivitakkena, mā diṭṭhinijjhānakkhantiyā, mā bhabbarūpatāya, mā samaṇo no garū ti. yadā tumhe kālāmā attanā va jāneyyātha, ime dhammā kusalā, ime dhammā anavajjā, ime dhammā viññuppasatthā, ime dhammā samattā samādinnā hitāya sukhāya saṃvattantī ti. atha tumhe kālāmā upasampajja vihareyyātha*, A I 190.

124 *iti kho kālāmā yaṃ taṃ avocumha: etha tumhe kālāmā mā anussavena, mā paramparāya, mā itikirāya, mā piṭakasampadānena, mā takkahetu, mā nayahetu, mā ākāraparivitakkena, mā diṭṭhinijjhānakkhantiyā, mā bhabbarūpatāya, mā samaṇo no garū ti. yadā tumhe kālāmā attanā va jāneyyātha: ime dhammā kusalā, ime dhammā anavajjā, ime dhammā viññūppasatthā, ime dhammā samattā samādinnā hitāya sukhāya saṃvattantī ti. atha tumhe kālāmā upasampajja vihareyyāthā ti iti yaṃ taṃ vuttaṃ idam etaṃ paṭicca vuttaṃ*, A I 191–2; compare to S IV 138–9.

125 In the *Devadaha-sutta* (M II 214–28) at M II 218 it is also stated that the five means of knowledge may turn out in two different ways, they may have two different outcomes. The Buddha cannot find any legitimate defence of the Jain position based upon the five.

126 *api ca bhāradvāja, susaddahitaṃ yeva hoti, tañ ca hoti rittaṃ tucchaṃ musā, no cepi susaddahitaṃ hoti, bhūtaṃ tacchaṃ anaññathā. api ca bhāradvāja, surucitaṃ yeva hoti. tañ ca hoti rittaṃ tucchaṃ musā, no cepi surucitaṃ hoti, bhūtaṃ tacchaṃ anaññathā. api ca bhāradvāja, svānussutaṃ yeva hoti. tañ ca hoti rittaṃ tucchaṃ musā, no cepi svānussutaṃ hoti, bhūtaṃ tacchaṃ anaññathā. api ca bhāradvāja suparivitakkitaṃ yeva hoti. tañ ca hoti rittaṃ tucchaṃ musā, no cepi suparivitakkitaṃ*

hoti. api ca bhāradvāja sunijjhāyitaṃ yeva hoti tañ ca hoti rittam tucchaṃ musā, no cepi sunijjhāyitaṃ hoti, bhūtaṃ taccham anaññathā, M II 170–1.

127 *evaṃ me diṭṭhi-nijjhānakkhantī ti vadaṃ saccam anurakkhati*, M II 171.

> [If] a person gains an acceptance of a view as a result of reflection, [or reaches a conclusion based upon any of the other four factors] he preserves truth when he says : "My acceptance of a view as a result of reflection is thus"; but he does not come to the definite conclusion : "only this is true, anything else is wrong" (*diṭṭhinijjhānakhanti ce pi [...] purisassa hoti, evaṃ me diṭṭhinjjhānakhantī ti iti vadaṃ saccam anurakkhati, na tveva tāva ekaṃsena niṭṭhaṃ gacchati : idam eva saccaṃ, mogham aññanti*, M II 171).

128 *ajānaṃ vā vadeyya jānāmī ti, apassaṃ vā vadeyya passāmī ti*, M II 171.

129 *paraṃ vā tadatthāya samādapeyya yaṃ paresaṃ assa dīgharattaṃ ahitāya dukkhāyā ti*, M II 172–3.

130 *dhammaṃ deseti, gambhīro so dhammo duddaso duranubodho santo paṇīto atakkāvacaro nipuṇo paṇḍitavedanīyo*, M II 172–3.

131 *na so dhammo sudesiyo luddhenā ti*, M II 172; *na so dhammo sudesiyo duṭṭhenā ti*, M II 172; *na so dhammo sudesiyo mūḷhenā ti*, M II 173.

132 Bhikkhu Bodhi, referring to the commentary, interprets this phrase as the investigation of things according to *anicca*, *dukkha* and *anattā* (*The Middle Length Discourses of the Buddha*, p. 1300, note 889).

133 *kāyena ceva paramasaccaṃ sacchikaroti. paññāya ca naṃ ativijjha passati*, M II 174.

134 Stream-attainment is realised (Bhikkhu Bodhi, *The Middle Length Discourses of the Buddha*, p. 1301, note 892).

135 *dhammānaṃ āsevanā bhāvanā bahulīkammā saccānupatti hoti*, M II 174. Arahantship realised.

136 Vibh-a 508.

137 The ideas of *bhava* and *vibhava* can be taken as synonymous with *sassata* and *uccheda*.

138 S II 17. See also Vism XIII 74. I will return to this latter passage briefly in Chapter 4 in a consideration of *diṭṭhi-visuddhi*.

139 *sassato loko ti vā, asassato loko ti vā antavā loko ti vā, anantavā loko ti vā, taṃ jīvaṃ taṃ sarīran ti vā aññaṃ jīvaṃ aññaṃ sarīran ti vā, hoti tathāgato param maraṇā ti vā, na hoti tathāgato param maraṇā ti vā, hoti ca na ca hoti tathāgato param maraṇā ti vā, neva hoti na na hoti tathāgato param maraṇā ti*, S IV 392, M I 426, S III 258, Dhs 208, § 1175, *passim*.

> In the *Pañcattaya-sutta*, as I classified above, the first four questions state that the self and world are eternal, not eternal, finite or infinite, e.g. *sassato attā ca loko ca*, M II 233. The commentaries often interpret the term 'world' as meaning 'self' (Ud-a 339). As Collins suggests, this gives the overall meaning to the first four questions (*Selfless Persons*, p. 283–4, note 1).

140 There are said to be three types of seeking: seeking sense pleasure, becoming and supreme practice (*tattha katamā tisso esāna: kāmesanā bhavesanā brahmacariyesanā*, Vibh 366).

141 *tattha katamā brahmacariyesanā: sassato loko ti vā asassato loko ti vā–pe–neva hoti. na na hoti tathāgato param maranāti vā yā evarūpā diṭṭhi diṭṭhi-gataṃ–pe–vipariyesagāho, ayaṃ vuccati brahmacariyesanā*, Vibh 366; also called the 'extremist views' (*antaggāhikā-diṭṭhi*).

142 The four *antānanta-vāda*, from the *Brahmajāla-sutta,* have many similarities with these ten *avyākata*: 'The world is finite and bounded' (*antavā ayaṃ loko parivaṭumo*, D I 22). 'The world is infinite and boundless' (*ananto ayaṃ loko apariyanto*, D I 23).

'The world is both finite and infinite' (*antavā ca ayaṃ loko ananto ca*, D I 24). 'The world is neither finite nor infinite' (*n' evâyaṃ loko antavā na panânanto*, D I 24). Bhikkhu Bodhi points out that in the sub-commentarial understanding of these views, *loko* signifies *attā* (Bhikkhu Bodhi, *The All-Embracing Net of Views*, p. 23). In many of the *micchā-diṭṭhi* being discussed we find *loko* and *attā* as the 'entity' that the *micchā-diṭṭhi* apprehends, misinterprets or adheres to. The mind inclines towards extremes and takes as its object the self and the world. There are a further group of views from the *Brahmajāla-sutta* that I have not incorporated into this chapter to avoid excessive repetition. They are found in Appendix 2. They are the following: 'seven annihilationist theories' (*satta uccheda-vādā*); 'eight theories on having non-apperception' (*aṭṭha asaññī-vādā*); 'eight theories of neither apperception nor non-apperception' (*aṭṭha nevasaññī-nāsaññī-vādā*); 'five theories on *nibbāna* in the present existence' (*pañca diṭṭha-dhamma-nibbāna-vādā*); 'two theories (of occurrences) arising without a cause' (*dve adhicca samuppannikā*).

143 S II 17, S III 181.

144 S III 181, Ps 135.

145 The early Abhidhamma gives the ten *avyākata* as an example of the clinging to views:

> *sassato loko ti vā, asassato loko ti vā, antavā loko ti vā, anantavā loko ti vā, taṃ jīvaṃ taṃ sarīran ti vā, aññaṃ jīvaṃ aññaṃ sarīran ti vā, hoti tathāgato param maraṇā ti vā, na hoti tathāgato param maraṇā ti vā, hoti ca na ca hoti tathāgato param maraṇā ti vā, neva hoti nana hoti tathāgato param maraṇā ti vā, yā evarūpā diṭṭhi diṭṭhi-gataṃ diṭṭhi-gahanaṃ diṭṭhi-kantāro diṭṭhi-visūkāyikaṃ diṭṭhi-vippanditaṃ diṭṭhi-saṃyojanaṃ gāho patiṭṭhāho abhiniveso parāmāso kummaggo micchā-patho micchattaṃ titthāyatanaṃ vipariyesaggāho, ayaṃ vuccati diṭṭhi-parāmāso, sabbāpi micchā-diṭṭhi diṭṭhi-parāmāso. ime dhammā parāmāsā*, Dhs 208, § 1180.

146 *parāmāso ti tassa tassa dhammassa sabhāvaṃ atikkammaparato abhūtaṃ sabhāvaṃ āmasanākārena pavattanato micchā-diṭṭhiyā etaṃ adhivacanaṃ*, Vism XXII 57. All references to the *Visuddhimagga* are to chapter and paragraph.

2 The content of right-view

1 Mp I 27, 355, V 66; see Peter Masefield, *Divine Revelation in Pali Buddhism*, p. 44. This idea is found in the *Mahāsaḷāyatanika-sutta* (M III 287–90). This *sutta* is concerned with seeing the 'great sixfold base' (*mahāsaḷāyatana*) as it is. The view of such a person is right-view (*yathābhūtassa diṭṭhi, sāssa hoti sammā-diṭṭhi*, M III 289) and the other path factors are 'right'.

2 Rupert Gethin, *The Buddhist Path to Awakening: A Study of the Bodhi-Pakkayā Dhammā*, p. 190.

3 Sue Hamilton *Early Buddhism*, p. 55.

4 Ibid., p. 122; see also p. 134.

5 Ibid., p. 138. As was discussed in Chapter 1, many of the *micchā-diṭṭhi* found in the Nikāyas are concerned with self and world (*attā* and *loka*).

6 Hamilton, *Early Buddhism*, p. 140.

7 Ibid., p. 67.

8 *sīlaparidhotā* [...] *paññā paññāparidhotaṃ sīlaṃ yattha sīlaṃ tattha paññā yattha paññā tattha sīlaṃ*, D I 124; see Jayatilleke, *Early Buddhist Theory of Knowledge*, p. 424.

9 *atthi dinnaṃ, atthi yiṭṭhaṃ, atthi hutaṃ, atthi sukaṭadukkaṭānaṃ kammānaṃ phalaṃ vipāko, atthi ayaṃ loko, atthi paro loko, atthi mātā, atthi pitā, atthi sattā opapātikā,*

atthi loke samaṇabrāhmaṇā sammaggatā sammā-paṭipannā ye imañ ca lokaṃ parañ ca lokaṃ sayaṃ abhiññā sacchikatvā pavedentī ti, M I 402.

10 *karoto kārayato chindato chedāpayato pacato pācapāyato socayato socāpayato kilamato kilamāpayato phandato phandāpayato pāṇam atipātayato adinnaṃ ādiyato sandhiṃ chindato nillopaṃ harato ekāgārikaṃ karoto paripanthe tiṭṭhato paradāraṃ gacchato musā bhaṇato. karoto karīyati pāpaṃ, khurapariyantena cepi cakkena yo imissā paṭhaviyā pāṇe ekamaṃsakhalaṃ ekamaṃsapuñjaṃ kareyya, atthi tato-nidānaṃ pāpaṃ, atthi pāpassa āgamo. dakkhiṇañ cepi Gaṅgāya tīraṃ gaccheyya hananto ghātento chindanto chedāpento pacanto pācento. atthi tato-nidānaṃ pāpaṃ atthi pāpassa āgamo. uttarañ cepi Gaṅgāya tīraṃ gaccheyya dadanto dāpento yajanto yājento dānena damena saṃyamena saccavajjena atthi puññaṃ, atthi puññassa āgamo ti*, M I 405.

11 *atthi hetu atthi paccayo sattānaṃ saṅkilesāya, sahetū sappaccayā sattā saṅkilissanti. atthi paccayo sattānaṃ visuddhiyā. sahetu sappaccayā sattā visujjhanti. atthi balaṃ atthi viriyaṃ atthi purisathāmo atthi purisaparakkamo, na sabbe sattā sabbe pāṇā sabbe bhūtā sabbe jīvā avasā abalā aviriyā niyatisaṅgatibhāvapariṇatā chassv evābhijātisu sukhadukkhaṃ paṭisaṃvedentī ti*, M I 407.

12 *ime tayo kusale dhamme abhinivajjetvā*, M, I 402, 405, 408.

13 *kāya-sucaritaṃ, vacī-sucaritaṃ, mano-sucaritaṃ*, M I 402, 405, 408.

14 *kāya-duccaritaṃ, vacī-duccaritaṃ, mano-duccaritaṃ*, M I 402, 405, 408.

15 *na hi te bhonto samaṇabrāhmaṇā passanti akusalānaṃ dhammānaṃ ādīnavaṃ okāraṃ saṅkilesaṃ. kusalānaṃ dhammānaṃ nekkhamme ānisaṃsaṃ vodānapakkhaṃ*, M I 402, 405, 408.

16 *passanti hi te bhonto samaṇabrāhmaṇā akusalānaṃ dhammānaṃ ādīnavaṃ okāraṃ saṅkilesaṃ kusalānaṃ dhammānaṃ nekkhamme ānisaṃsaṃ vodānapakkhaṃ*, M I 403, 406, 409.

17 *diṭṭhi-vasena abhinivisati idam eva saccaṃ mogham aññan ti*, Nett 160.

18 *dvāsaṭṭhi diṭṭhi-gatāni moha-jālaṃ*, Nett 112.

19 *taṇhā-vodāna-bhāgiyaṃ suttaṃ samathena niddisitabbaṃ*, Nett 160.

20 *diṭṭhi-vodāna-bhāgiyaṃ suttaṃ vipassanāya niddisitabbaṃ*, Nett 160.

21 *tayidaṃ vodānaṃ tividhaṃ: taṇhāsaṃkileso samathena visujjhati, so samatho samādhikkhandho. diṭṭhisaṃkileso vipassanāya visujjhati. sā vipassanā paññākkhandho. duccaritasaṃkileso sucaritena visujjhati, taṃ sucaritaṃ sīlakkhandho*, Nett 96.

22 *parinibbanti anāsāvā ti idaṃ vodānaṃ*, Nett 96; see also Nett 128.

23 *santaṃ yeva kho pana paraṃ lokaṃ n' atthi paro loko ti 'ssa diṭṭhi hoti, sāssa hoti micchā-diṭṭhi*, M I 402 [*santaṃyeva kho pana kiriyaṃ 'n' atthi kiriyā ti 'ssa diṭṭhi hoti, sāssa hoti micchā-diṭṭhi*, M I 405; *santaṃ yeva kho pana hetu n' atthi hetū ti 'ssa diṭṭhi hoti, sāssa hoti micchā-diṭṭhi*, M I 408].

24 For no other world:

> *santaṃ yeva kho pana paraṃ lokaṃ n' atthi paro loko ti 'ssa diṭṭhi hoti, sāssa hoti micchā-diṭṭhi, santaṃ yeva kho pana paraṃ lokaṃ n' atthi paro loko ti saṅkappeti, svāssa hoti micchā-saṅkappo. santaṃ yeva kho pana paraṃ lokaṃ n' atthi paro loko ti vācaṃ bhāsati, sāssa hoti micchā-vācā*, M I 402.

25 *micchā-diṭṭhi micchā-saṅkappo micchā-vācā ariyānaṃ paccanīkatā asaddhammasaññatti attukkaṃsanā paravambhanā. evaṃ ime aneke pāpakā akusalā dhammā sambhavanti micchā-diṭṭhi-paccayā*, MI 402, 406, 408.

26 Mark Siderits agrees with Jayatilleke; see Siderits, M., 'A Note on the Early Buddhist Theory of Truth', *Philosophy East and West*, 29 (1979), pp. 491–9 (p. 492).

27 Jayatilleke, *Early Buddhist Theory of Knowledge*, p. 352.

28 Ibid.

29 D I 83, 84, cited by Jayatilleke, *Early Buddhist Theory of Knowledge*, p. 352.

30 *santaṃ yeva kho pana paraṃ lokaṃ n' atthi paro loko ti 'ssa diṭṭhi hoti, sāssa hoti micchā-diṭṭhi, santaṃ yeva kho pana paraṃ lokaṃ n' atthi paro loko ti saṅkappeti, svāssa hoti micchā-saṅkappo. santaṃ yeva kho pana paraṃ lokaṃ n' atthi paro loko ti vācaṃ bhāsati, sāssa hoti micchā-vācā*, M I 402.

31 Jayatilleke, *Early Buddhist Theory of Knowledge*, pp. 352–3. For no other world:

> *santaṃ yeva kho pana paraṃ lokaṃ 'atthi paro loko tissa diṭṭhi hoti. sāssa hoti sammā-diṭṭhi. santaṃ yeva kho pana paraṃ lokaṃ atthi paro loko ti saṅkappeti, svāssa hoti sammā-saṅkappo. santaṃ yeva kho pana paraṃ lokaṃ atthi paro loko ti vācaṃ bhāsati, sāssa hoti sammā-vācā*, M I 403.

32 Jayatilleke, *Early Buddhist Theory of Knowledge*, p. 353.

33 Ibid.

34 Ibid.

35 Ibid., p. 405.

36 *santaṃ yeva kho pana paraṃ lokaṃ atthi paro loko ti 'ssa diṭṭhi hoti, sāssa hoti sammā-diṭṭhi*, M I 403, *santaṃ yeva kho pana kiriyaṃ atthi kiriyā ti 'ssa diṭṭhi hoti, sāssa hoti sammā-diṭṭhi*, M I 406, *santaṃyeva kho pana hetu atthi hetutissa diṭṭhi hoti, sāssa hoti sammā-diṭṭhi*, M I 409.

37 For another world: *santaṃ yeva kho pana paraṃ lokaṃ atthi paro loko ti saṅkappeti, svāssa hoti sammā-saṅkappo*, M I 403.

38 For another world: *santaṃ yeva kho pana paraṃ lokaṃ atthi paro loko ti vācaṃ bhāsati, sāssa hoti sammā-vācā*, M I 403.

39 *ayañ ca sammā-diṭṭhi sammā-saṅkappo sammā-vācā ariyānaṃ apaccanīkatā saddhammasaññatti. anattukkaṃsanā aparavambhanā. evam ass' ime aneke kusalā dhammā sambhavanti sammā-diṭṭhi-paccayā*, M I 404, 407, 409.

40 Jayatilleke has commented on the *viññū puriso*:

> The viññū represented for the Buddha the impartial critic at the level of intelligent common sense and the Buddha and his disciples sometimes introduce the 'viññū puriso' or the hypothetical rational critic when it seems necessary to make an impartial and intelligent assessment of the relative worth of conflicting theories (*Early Buddhist Theory of Knowledge*, p. 229).

41 *tatra gahapatayo viññū puriso iti paṭisañcikkhati: sace kho n' atthi paro loko [n' atthi kiriyā, n' atthi hetu] evam ayaṃ bhavaṃ purisapuggalo kāyassa bhedā sotthimattānaṃ karissati*, M I 403, 406, 408.

42 Bhikkhu Bodhi offers the following:

> He has made himself safe (*sotthi*) in the sense that he will not be subject to suffering in a future existence. However, he is still liable to the types of suffering to be encountered in this existence, which the Buddha is about to mention (*The Middle Length Discourses of the Buddha*, p. 1261, note 624).

43 *sace kho atthi paro loko [atthi kiriyā, atthi hetu] evam ayaṃ bhavaṃ purisapuggalo kāyassa bhedā param maraṇā apāyaṃ duggatiṃ vinīpātaṃ nirayaṃ upapajjissati*, M I 403, 406, 408.

44 *tatra gahapatayo viññū puriso iti paṭisañcikkhati: sace kho atthi paro loko [atthi kiriyā, atthi hetu] evam ayaṃ bhavaṃ purisapuggalo kāyassa bhedā param maraṇā sugatiṃ saggaṃ lokaṃ upapajjissati*, M I 404, 407, 409.

45 *atha ca panāyaṃ bhavaṃ purisapuggalo diṭṭheva dhamme viññūnaṃ gārayho: dussīlo purisapuggalo micchā-diṭṭhi natthika-vādo ti [micchā-diṭṭhi akiriya-vādo, micchā-diṭṭhi ahetu-vādo]*, M I 403, 406, 408.

46 *atha ca panāyaṃ bhavaṃ purisapuggalo diṭṭheva dhamme viññūnaṃ pāsaṃso sīlavā purisapuggalo sammā-diṭṭhī atthikavādo ti [sammā-diṭṭhi kiriyavādoti, sammā-diṭṭhi hetu-vādo]*, M I 404, 407, 409.

47 *evam assāyaṃ apaṇṇako dhammo dussamatto samādinno ekaṃsaṃ pharitvā tiṭṭhati, riñcati kusalaṃ ṭhānaṃ*, M I 403, 406, 409. On this statement Bhikkhu Bodhi glosses:

> [H]is undertaking of the incontrovertible teaching 'extends only to one side' in the sense that he makes himself safe with regard to the next life only on the presupposition that there is no afterlife, while if there is an afterlife, he loses on both counts (*The Middle Length Discourses of the Buddha*, p. 1261, note 626).

A similarity with Pascal's wager is clear.

48 *evam assāyaṃ apaṇṇako dhammo susamatto samādinno ubhayaṃsaṃ pharitvā tiṭṭhati, riñcati akusalaṃ ṭhānaṃ*, M I 404, 407, 410. One theme I have only addressed in passing is the term that gives the *sutta* its title *apaṇṇaka*. A *sutta* called the *Diṭṭhi-apaṇṇaka paṭipadā-sutta* at A II 76 states that when a *bhikkhu* is possessed of four things he has entered on the path to the 'incontrovertible' (*apaṇṇaka*) and the destruction of the *āsavās*. The four things are: dispassionate thinking, benevolent thinking, harmless thinking and right-view (*catūhi bhikkhave dhammehi samannāgato bhikkhu apaṇṇakataṃ paṭipadaṃ paṭipanno hoti, yoni cassa āraddhā hoti āsavānaṃ khayāya. katamehi catūhi? nekkhammavitakkena, avyāpādavitakkena, avihiṃsāvitakkena, sammā-diṭṭhiyā*, A II 76. This is from a section called the *Apaṇṇaka-vagga*).

49 *sammā-diṭṭhissa purisapuggalassa micchā-diṭṭhi nijjiṇṇā bhavati, ye cassa micchā-diṭṭhippaccayā uppajjeyyuṃ aneke pāpakā akusalā dhammā te cassa nijjiṇṇā honti, sammā-diṭṭhippaccayā cassa aneke kusalā dhammā sambhavanti, te cassa bhāvanā-pāripūriṃ gacchanti*, Nett 51.

50 ***idha gahapatayo ekacco pāṇātipātaṃ pahāya pāṇātipātā paṭivirato hoti***: *nihitadaṇḍo nihitasattho lajjī dayāpanno sabbapāṇabhūtahitānukampī viharati*, A V 66.

51 ***adinnādānaṃ pahāya adinnādānā paṭivirato hoti***: *yaṃ taṃ parassa paravittūpakaraṇaṃ gāmagataṃ vā araññagataṃ vā taṃ nādinnaṃ*, A V 66.

52 ***kāmesu micchā-cāraṃ pahāya kāmesu micchā-cārā paṭivirato hoti***: *yā tā māturakkhitā piturakkhitā mātāpiturakkhitā bhāturakkhitā bhaginirakkhitā ñātirakkhitā gottarakkhitā dhammarakkhitā sasāmikā saparidaṇḍā, antamaso mālāguṇaparikkhittāpi, tathārūpāsu na cārittaṃ āpajjitā hoti*, A V 266.

53 ***idha gahapatayo ekacco musāvādaṃ pahāya musāvādā paṭivirato hoti***: *sabhāggato vā parisaggato vā ñātimajjhagato vā pūgamajjhagato vā rājakulamajjhagato vā abhinīto sakkhipuṭṭho:eh' ambho purisa yaṃ jānāsi taṃ vadehī ti. so ajānaṃ vā āha na jānāmī ti, jānaṃ vā āha jānāmī ti, apassaṃ vā āha na passāmī ti, passaṃ vā āha passāmī ti. iti attahetu vā parahetu vā āmisakiñcikkhahetu vā na sampajānamusā bhāsitā hoti*, A V 67.

54 ***pisuṇaṃ vācaṃ pahāya pisuṇāya vācāya paṭivirato hoti***: *ito sutvā na amutra akkhātā imesaṃ bhedāya, amutra vā sutvā na imesaṃ akkhātā amūsaṃ bhedāya iti bhinnānaṃ vā sandhātā sahitānaṃ vā anuppadātā, samaggārāmo samaggarato samaggakaraṇiṃ vācaṃ bhāsitā hoti*, A V 67.

55 ***pharusaṃ vācaṃ pahāya pharusāya vācāya paṭivirato hoti***: *yā sā vācā nelā kaṇṇasukhā pemanīyā hadayaṅgamā porī bahujanakantā bahujanamanāpā tathārūpiṃ vācaṃ bhāsitā hoti*, A V 67.

56 ***samphappalāpaṃ pahāya samphappalāpā paṭivirato hoti***: *kālavādī bhūtavādī atthavādī dhammavādī vinayavādī, nidhānavatiṃ vācaṃ bhāsitā kālena sāpadesaṃ pariyantavatiṃ atthasaṃhitaṃ*, A V 267.

57 ***idha gahapatayo ekacco anabhijjhālu hoti***: *yaṃ taṃ parassa paravittūpakaraṇaṃ taṃ anābhijjhitā hoti. aho vata yaṃ parassa taṃ mama assā ti*, A V 67.

58 ***avyāpannacitto kho pana hoti appaduṭṭhamanasaṅkappo***: *ime sattā averā abyāpajjhā anīghā sukhī attānaṃ pariharantū ti*, A V 267.

59 ***sammā-diṭṭhiko hoti aviparītadassano:** atthi dinnaṃ, atthi yiṭṭhaṃ, atthi hutaṃ, atthi sukaṭadukkaṭānaṃ kammānaṃ phalaṃ vipāko, atthi ayaṃ loko, atthi paro loko, atthi mātā, atthi pitā, atthi sattā opapātikā, atthi loke samaṇabrāhmaṇā sammaggatā sammā-paṭipannā ye imañ ca lokaṃ parañ ca lokaṃ sayaṃ abhiññā sacchikatvā pavedentī ti*, A V 268.

The abbreviated form in which these ten are often found has been given in bold; see AS 95–104.

60 These terms are not common, but do appear in the canon. In the *Saṅgīti-sutta* (D III 207–77) at D III 269 the *dasa kusala-kammapathā* and the *dasa akusala-kammapathā* are named as such. The same are given in the *Dasuttara-sutta* (D III 272–92) at D III 290–1 where it is said that the *dasa akusala-kammapathā* lead to 'degradation' (*hānabhāgiyā*) and the *dasa kusala-kammapathā* to 'distinction' (*visesabhāgiyā*). The *Vibhaṅga* (Vibh 391) also uses the phrase *dasa akusala-kammapathā* and lists them. The *Peṭakopadesa* (Peṭ 164) uses the term *dasa kusala-kammapathā*, and the same text (Peṭ 203) cites both the *dasa kusala-kammapathā* and the *dasa akusala-kammapathā*, but in neither case elaborates on what they are. The *Nettippakaraṇa* (Nett 43) uses the term *dasa akusala-kammapathā*, defines what they are, and uses the threefold classification of bodily, verbal and mental action. At certain other places we find mention of these terms, without any clear explanation as to what they are. For example at Vin V 138 we find the statement that there are ten ways of unwholesome action and ten ways of wholesome action (*dasa akusala-kammapathā, dasa kusala-kammapathā*). Buddhaghosa states simply that the ten are called *akusala* because they are both *akusala* action (*kamma*), and they lead to 'unhappy destinies' (Vism XX II 62).

61 *sammā-diṭṭhi tebhūmakadhammavasena saṃkhārārammaṇā*. Note, this is partly from an earlier section in the commentary, explaining *micchā-diṭṭhi* according to its 'object'. In the text here it is simply stated that the analysis is the same as for the *dasa akusala-kammapathā* explained previously; see Ps I 202.

62 Buddhaghosa outlines ten bases of meritorious acts (*dasa puñña-kiriya-vatthūni*), said to give rise to the eight types of moral consciousness experienced in the realm of sense (*aṭṭha kāmāvacara-kusala-cittāni*, As 157). The last of these is rectification of view (*diṭṭhi-ujjukammaṃ*). Buddhaghosa does not give a definition of this view, only stating that to correct one's view is the basis of meritorious action of rectified view (*diṭṭhim ujuṃ karontassa diṭṭhi-ujjukammaṃ puñña-kiryavatthu*, As 159). Buddhaghosa adds that the reciters of the *Dīgha-nikāya* held that rectified view is the characteristic of assurance respecting all things, for by it there is much fruit to one doing any sort of meritorious act (*Dīghabhāṇakā panāhu: diṭṭhujjukammaṃ sabbesaṃ niyamanalakkhaṇaṃ. yaṃ kiñci puññaṃ karontassa hi diṭṭhiyā ujukabhāven' eva mahapphalaṃ hotī ti*, As 159).

63 Dhp-a III 170; see Bhikkhu Bodhi, *The All-Embracing Net of Views*, p. 4.

64 *akusalā dhammā uppajjanti* [...] *micchā-diṭṭhi*, A I 31.

65 *kusalā dhammā uppajjanti* [...] *sammā-diṭṭhi*, A I 31.

66 *nāhaṃ bhikkhave aññaṃ ekadhammam pi samanupassāmi, yen' evaṃ sattā kāyassa bhedā param maraṇā apāyaṃ duggatiṃ vinipātaṃ nirayaṃ upapajjanti, yathayidaṃ bhikkhave micchā-diṭṭhi*, A I 31.

67 *nāhaṃ bhikkhave aññaṃ ekadhammam pi samanupassāmi, yen' evaṃ sattā kāyassa bhedā param maraṇā suggatiṃ saggaṃ lokaṃ upapajjanti, yathayidaṃ bhikkhave sammā-diṭṭhi*, A I 31–2.

68 *aniṭṭhāya akantāya amanāpāya ahitāya dukkhāya*, A I 32.

69 *iṭṭhāya kantāya manāpāya hitāya sukhāya*, A I 32.

70 I am translating *pāpaka* as 'destructive' (as I explained in Chapter 1, holding these views destroys the Buddhist path), and *bhaddika* as 'happy' or 'constructive'. The root *bhadda* has the meaning of 'happy' or 'auspicious' (see PED s.v. *bhadda*). The

spellings *pāpikā* and *bhaddikā* (not *bhaddakā*) are the feminine of *pāpaka* and *bhaddaka* respectively (see PED s.v. *pāpaka*).

71 *kammassakā bhikkhave sattā kammadāyadā kammayonī kammabandhmkkū kammapaṭisaraṇā, yaṃ kammaṃ karonti kalyāṇaṃ vā pāpakaṃ vā tassa dāyadā bhavanti*, A V 288.

72 *so saṃsappati kāyena, saṃsappati vācāya, saṃsappati manasā*, A V 289. This theme is what gives the *sutta* its title, which could be translated, 'The Exposition on Creeping'. The text gives the example of being like a snake, a scorpion, a centipede, a mongoose, a cat, a mouse or an owl (A V 289), though strictly these are example of those who go 'distorted' (*jimha*); see PED s.v. *saṃsappaniyapariyāya.*

73 *jimhaṃ kāyakammaṃ hoti, jimhaṃ vacīkammaṃ, jimhaṃ manokammaṃ*, A V 289.

74 *jimhā gati jimhupapatti*, A V 289.

75 *na saṃsappati kāyena, na saṃsappati vācāya na saṃsappati manasā*, A V 289.

76 *ujuṃ-kāya kammaṃ hoti, ujuṃ vacīkammaṃ, ujuṃ mano-kammaṃ*, A V 290.

77 A further group of *suttas* preceding the *Saṃsappaniya-pariyāya-sutta* explains the effects of the *dasa kusala-kammapathā* and the *dasa akusala-kammapathā* in a similar way. In the *Paṭhamaniraya-sutta* (A V 283–5) it is stated that 'characterised by ten *dhammas* [...] one is cast into hell according to his deserts.' (*dasahi* [...] *dhammehi samannāgato yathābhataṃ nikkhitto evaṃ niraye*, A V 283. I have followed the PED translation of *yathābhataṃ* as 'according to his deserts', which could be translated as 'according to merit', PED s.v. *yathā*). The *dasa akusala-kammapathā* are given as the ten *dhammas* that produce this result. The text gives the full version of the formula including the view of nihilism (*natthika-diṭṭhi*). Following this the text states that 'characterised by ten *dhammas* one is put into the heaven according to his deserts.' (*dasahi* [...] *dhammehi samannāgato yathābhataṃ nikkhitto evaṃ sagge,* A V 284). The full version of the ten *dasa kusala-kammapathā* is given, including the full *atthika-diṭṭhi*, to show the *dhammas* that produce this wholesome outcome. The *Mātugāma-sutta* (A V 286–7), uses the *dasa kusala-kammapathā* and the *dasa akusala-kammapathā* to show the reasons for women being cast into heaven or hell. The *Upāsikā-sutta* (A V 287) uses them in a similar way, and the *Visārada-sutta* (A V 288), to show how females dwell at home with either 'hesitance' (*avisārada*) or 'confidence' (*visārada*), according to whether they practice the *dasa akusala-kammapathā* or *dasa kusala-kammapathā*. All ten are given in abbreviated form in each *sutta*. A final *sutta* on this topic is the *Paṭhamasañcetanika-sutta* (A V 292–7). The *sutta* begins by stating that one cannot negate the outcome of an intentional action, one must experience the result (*nāhaṃ* [...] *sañcetanikānaṃ kammānaṃ katānaṃ upacitānaṃ appaṭisaṃviditvā vyantībhāvaṃ vadāmi*, A V 292). This outcome can be experienced in the present life or a future life. The *sutta* then goes through the sets of the ten courses of action. As with earlier *suttas*, they are split into a group of three bodily acts, four verbal acts, and three mental acts. Hence 'threefold is the fault and guilt of bodily action done with deliberate intent, causing pain and resulting in pain', 'fourfold is the fault and guilt of action by speech done with deliberate intent, causing pain and resulting in pain', and 'threefold is the fault and guilt of mental action, done with deliberate intent, causing pain and resulting in pain.' The *dasa akusala-kammapathā* are given as an explanation of these categories, given in full in the text (A V 292–4). These are contrasted with the positive courses of action. Hence, 'threefold is the prosperity of bodily action done with deliberate good intent, causing happiness and resulting in happiness', 'fourfold is that action by speech done with deliberate good intent, causing happiness and resulting in happiness', and 'threefold is that mental action done with deliberate good intent, causing happiness and resulting in happiness'. The *dasa kusala-kammapathā* are given in full in the text as an explanation of these ten categories (A V 295). The text states that it is because of the threefold fault and guilt of bodily action, fourfold action by speech,

and the threefold action by mind that 'beings, when the body breaks up, beyond death arise again in the waste, the ill-born, the downfall'. Also, it is because of the threefold prosperity of bodily action, fourfold prosperity of action by speech and threefold action by mind that 'beings, when the body breaks up, beyond death rise up again in the happy bourne, in the heaven world'.

78 Although she does not call them *dasa akusala-kammapathā* or *dasa kusala-kammapathā* and does not appear to know their exact content; see Carol Anderson, *Pain and its Ending*, pp. 44–5.

79 Ibid., p. 47.

80 Ibid., p. 43. Anderson's emphasis.

81 Hamilton, *Early Buddhism*, p. 209.

82 I use the term 'corruption' to translate *āsava* throughout this book. I use this term in the sense of an impairment of virtue. To be affected by the *āsavas* is to have become corrupt. There is a sense of immorality, which fits well with the Pāli term *āsava*.

83 Ps I 196.

84 The *Visuddhimagga* states that *lokuttara-sammā-diṭṭhi* penetrates the four truths and has *nibbāna* as its object, and in this way it eliminates ignorance, Vism XVI 76–7.

85 Collins also notes two ways of going for refuge, the *lokiya* and *lokuttara* distinguished in the commentaries. The former uses a type of view termed *saddhāmūlikā sammā-diṭṭhi*, a 'right-view based on faith' in which the holder practises 'ten meritorious deeds' (*dasa puñña-kiriya-vatthu*, Sv I 231). The *lokuttara* way of going for refuge is that of the stream-attainer, who knows that this act is a means towards the goal of *nibbāna*; see Collins, *Selfless Persons*, p. 93.

86 See Collins' discussion of this passage, *Selfless Persons*, p. 92.

87 *niyatāya niyyānikāya lokuttara-kusala-sammā-diṭṭhiyā*, Ps I 196.

88 *navappakāra lokuttara-dhamma*, Ps I 197, i.e. the four paths, the fruits of the four paths and *nibbāna*. Though note the comments of Lance Cousins who holds that Buddhaghosa does not associate *lokuttara sammā-diṭṭhi* with the *asekha*; Cousins, Review of Anderson, *Pain and its Ending*, in *Journal of Buddhist Ethics*, 8 (2001), p. 40.

89 *ṭhapetvā saccānulomikaṃ ñāṇaṃ sabbāpi sāsavā kusalā paññā kammassakatā-ñāṇaṃ*, Vibh 328.

90 Vibh 328.

91 *katamā ca, bhikkhave, sammā-diṭṭhi ariyā anāsavā lokuttarā maggaṅgā? yā kho, bhikkhave, ariyacittassa ariyamaggassa samaṅgino ariyamaggaṃ bhāvayato paññā paññindriyaṃ paññābalaṃ dhammavicayasambojjhaṅgo sammā-diṭṭhi maggaṅgā ayaṃ, bhikkhave, sammā-diṭṭhi ariyā anāsavā lokuttarā maggaṅgā*, M III 72.

92 *katamā tasmiṃ samaye sammā-diṭṭhi hoti? yā tasmiṃ samaye paññā pajānanā vicayo pavicayo dhammavicayo sallakkhaṇā upalakkhaṇā paccupalakkhaṇā paṇḍiccaṃ kosallaṃ nepuññaṃ vebhavyā cintā upaparikkhā bhūrī medhā parināyikā vipassanā sampajaññaṃ patodo paññā paññindriyaṃ paññā-balaṃ paññā-satthaṃ paññā-pāsādo paññā-āloko paññā obhāso paññā-pajjoto paññā-ratanaṃ amoho dhammavicayo sammā-diṭṭhi—ayaṃ tasmiṃ samaye sammā-diṭṭhi hoti*, Dhs 12 § 20, 14 § 37, 63 § 297, *passim*; see also the *Vibhaṅga*: *yā paññā pajānanā–pe–amoho dhammavicayo sammā-diṭṭhi dhamma-vicaya-sambojjhaṅgo maggaṅgaṃ maggapariyāpannaṃ, ayaṃ vuccati sammā-diṭṭhi*, Vibh 237.

93 *diṭṭhivisuddhi kho panā ti: yā paññā pajānanā–pe–amoho dhammavicayo sammā-diṭṭhi*, Dhs 233 § 1366.

94 *diṭṭhiyā suppaṭividdhā*, Vin IV 51; see also Vin II 95.

95 'View means wisdom' (*diṭṭhiyā ti* [...] *paññāya*), Sp 788.

96 *paññindriyaṃ paññābalaṃ adhipaññā sikkhā paññā paññākkhandho dhammavicayasambojjhaṅgo ñāṇaṃ sammā-diṭṭhi tīraṇā vipassanā dhamme ñāṇaṃ atthe ñāṇaṃ anvaye ñāṇaṃ khaye ñāṇaṃ anuppāde ñāṇaṃ*

anaññātaññassāmītindriyaṃ aññindriyaṃ aññātāvindriyaṃ cakkhu vijjā buddhi bhūri medhā āloko, yaṃ vā pana kiñci aññam pi evaṃ jātiyaṃ paññāya etaṃ [illegible], Nett 54.

97 *tattha katamā vijjā: dukkhe ñāṇaṃ dukkhasamudaye ñāṇaṃ dukkhanirodhe ñāṇaṃ dukkhanirodhagāminiyā paṭipadāya ñāṇaṃ pubbante ñāṇaṃ aparante ñāṇaṃ pubbantāparante ñāṇaṃ idappaccayatāpaṭiccasamuppannesu dhammesu ñāṇaṃ. yā evarūpā paññā pajānanā vicayo pavicayo dhammavicaye sallakkhaṇā upalakkhaṇā paccupalakkhaṇā paṇḍiccaṃ kosallaṃ nepuññaṃ vebhavyā cintā upaparikkā bhūrī medhā pariṇāyikā vipassanā sampajaññaṃ patodo paññā paññindriyaṃ paññā-balaṃ paññā-satthaṃ paññā-pāsādo paññā-āloko paññā-obhāso paññā-pajjoto paññā-ratanaṃ amoho dhammavicayo sammā-diṭṭhi dhammavicaya sambojjhaṅgo maggaṅgaṃ maggapariyāpannaṃ*, Nett 76.

98 I will consider how the tradition and modern scholarship (particularly P.S. Jaini) have understood this process in Chapter 4.

99 Paul J. Griffiths, 'Concentration or Insight: The Problematic of Theravāda Meditation Theory', *Journal of the American Academy of Religion'*, 49 (1981), 605–24.

100 *yato kho āvuso ariyasāvako akusalañ ca pajānāti akusalamūlañ ca pajānāti, kusalañ ca pajānāti, ettāvatā pi kho āvuso ariyasāvako sammā-diṭṭhi hoti, ujugatā 'ssa diṭṭhi, dhamme aveccappasādena sammannagato, āgato imaṃ saddhammaṃ*, M I 46–7.

101 *yato kho āvuso ariyasāvako āhārañ*, M I 47–8 (*dukkhañ*, M I 48; *jarāmaraṇañ*, M I 49; *jātiñ*, M I 50; *bhavañ, upādānañ, taṇhañ*, M I 51; *vedanañ, phassañ*, M I 52; *saḷāyatanañ, nāmarupañ*, M I 53; *viññāṇaṃ, saṃkhārañ*, M I 54; *avijjañ*, M I 54; *āsavañ*, M I 55) *ca pajānāti jarāmaraṇasamudayañ ca pajānāti jarāmaraṇanirodhañ ca pajānāti jarāmaraṇanirodhagāminiṃ paṭipadañ ca ettāvatā pi kho āvuso ariyasāvako sammā-diṭṭhi hoti, ujugatā 'ssa diṭṭhi, dhamme aveccappasādena sammannagato, āgato imaṃ saddhammaṃ*, M I 49.

The introduction to the *Sammdiṭṭhi-sutta* has Sāriputta addressing the assembly of *bhikkhus*: 'One of right-view, one of right-view, is said, friends. In what way is a noble disciple one of right-view, whose view is straight, who has perfect confidence in the dhamma, and who has arrived at the true dhamma?' (*sammā-diṭṭhi sammā-diṭṭhī ti āvuso vuccati. kittāvattā nu kho āvuso ariyasāvako sammā-diṭṭhi hoti, ujugatā 'ssa diṭṭhi, dhamme aveccappasādena sammannāgato, āgato imaṃ saddhamman ti*, M I 46). First, *sammā-diṭṭhi* is described as being 'straight' (*ujugatā*). The commentary interprets this as: 'Because of its going straight without deviating to either extreme, or because of its going straight by removing all crookedness such as bodily crookedness, etc. supramundane wholesome right-view is "straight"' (*lokuttara-kusala-sammā-diṭṭhi yeva hi antadvayam anupagamma ajubhāvena gatattā, kāyavañkādīni ca sabbavañkāni samucchinditvā gatattā ujugatā hoti*, Ps I 196–7). In the *Bhikkhu-sutta* (S V 142–4) the 'view that is straight' is given along with the 'virtue that is well purified' (*sīlañ ca suvisuddhaṃ, diṭṭhi ca ujukā*) as the starting point of wholesome *dhammas* (*kusalā dhammā*) that should be purified (the same passage occurs at S V 165 and S V 166). In the *Saṃsappaniyapariyāya-sutta* (A V 288–91), which was discussed above (in relation to the ten wholesome courses of action), actions of body, speech and mind are described as being 'straight' when they are performed according to the *dasa kusala-kammapathā* (*ujuṃ kāya kammaṃ hoti, ujuṃ vacīkammaṃ, ujuṃ mano kammaṃ*, A V 290). The path itself is sometimes described as being straight: at S I 33 it is said 'the path is called straight' (*ujuko nāma so maggo*) which the *Sāratthapakāsinī* interprets as the eightfold path being straight (*aṭṭhaṅgiko magga ujuko*, Spk I 86; see Bhikkhu Bodhi, *Connected Discourses of the Buddha*, Volume I, p. 276, note 101). Sāriputta then goes on to explain what right-view is.

102 *pāṇātipāto kho āvuso akusalaṃ, adinnādānaṃ akusalaṃ, kāmesu micchācāro akusalaṃ, musāvādo akusalaṃ, pisuṇā vācā akusalaṃ, pharusā vācā akusalaṃ,*

samphappalāpo akusalaṃ, abhijjhā akusalaṃ, byāpādo akusalaṃ, micchā-diṭṭhi akusalaṃ, idaṃ vuccatāvuso akusalaṃ, M I 47.

103 *lobho akusalamūlaṃ, doso akusalamūlaṃ, moho akusalamūlaṃ*, M I 47.

104 *pāṇātipātā veramaṇī kusalaṃ, adinnādānā veramaṇī kusalaṃ, kāmesu micchācārā veramaṇī kusalaṃ, musāvādā veramaṇī kusalaṃ, pisuṇāya vācāya veramaṇī kusalaṃ, pharusāya vācāya veramaṇī kusalaṃ, samphappalāpā veramaṇī kusalaṃ, anabhijjhā kusalaṃ, abyāpādo kusalaṃ, sammā-diṭṭhi kusalaṃ*, M I 47.

105 *alobho kusalamūlaṃ, adoso kusalamūlaṃ, amoho kusalamūlaṃ*, M I 47.

106 *rāgānusayaṃ pahāya paṭighānusayaṃ paṭivinodetvā asmī ti diṭṭhi-mānānusayaṃ*, M I 47.

107 In the *Saccavibanga-sutta* (M III 248–52) at M III 251, the *Mahāsatipaṭṭhāna-sutta* (D II 290–316) at D II 311–12 and in the *Vibhaṅga-sutta* (S V 8–10) at S V 8–9, the four truths are given as a definition of the first stage of the *ariyo-aṭṭhaṅgiko-maggo*. In the *Vibhaṇga* it is stated that the four truths are right-view (Vibh 235), and that right-view is 'dependent on detachment, dependent on absence of lust, dependent on cessation, culminating in abandonment' (*idha bhikkhu sammā-diṭṭhiṃ bhāveti vivekanissitaṃ virāganissitaṃ nirodhanissitaṃ vossaggapariṇāmiṃ*, Vibh 236). The same is said for the other factors of the path, *sammā-saṅkappaṃ bhāveti–pe–sammā-vācāṃ bhāveti sammā-kammantaṃ bhāveti–pe–sammā-ājīvaṃ bhāveti–pe–sammā-vāyāmaṃ bhāveti–pe–sammā-satiṃ bhāvati–pe–sammā-samādhiṃ bhāveti vivekanissitaṃ virāganissitaṃ nirodhanissitaṃ vossaggapariṇāmiṃ*, Vibh 236. This is the analysis according to the *suttas* (*Suttanta bhājaniyaṃ*). Of course, the four truths occur in other contexts, in which right-view is not mentioned. For example, in the well-known exchange between *Bhikkhuni* Vajirā and Māra at S I 135. Insisting that Māra is immersed in wrong-views (*diṭṭhi-gataṃ*) by asking questions about 'being' (*satta*), Vajirā suggests that it is simply suffering that arises and ceases (*dukkham eva hi sambhoti dukkhaṃ tiṭṭhati veti ca, nāññatra dukkhā sambhoti nāññatra dukkhā nirujjhatī ti*, S I 135).

108 *cattārimāni byagghapajjā pārisuddhi-padhāniyaṅgāni*, A II 194.

109 *sīla-pārisuddhi-padhāniyaṅgaṃ.*

110 *citta-pārisuddhi-padhāniyaṅgaṃ.*

111 *diṭṭhi-pārisuddhi-padhāniyaṅgaṃ.*

112 *vimutti-pārisuddhi-padhāniyaṅgaṃ*, All A II 195.

113 *sīlapārisuddhipadhāniyaṅgaṃ*, A II 195.

114 *citta-pārisuddhi-padhānipadhāniyaṅgaṃ*, A II 195.

115 *diṭṭhi-pārisuddhi-padhāniyaṅgaṃ*, A II 195.

116 *katamañ ca byagghapajjā diṭṭhipārisuddhipadhāniyaṅgaṃ? idha byagghapajjā bhikkhu idaṃ dukkhan ti yathābhūtaṃ pajānāti. ayaṃ dukkhasamudayo ti yathābhūtaṃ pajānāti. ayaṃ dukkhanirodho ti yathābhūtaṃ pajānāti. ayaṃ dukkhanirodhagāminī paṭipadā ti yathābhūtaṃ pajānāti. ayaṃ vuccati byagghapajjā diṭṭhipārisuddhi*, A II 195.

117 *iti evarūpiṃ diṭṭhipārisuddhiṃ aparipūriṃ vā paripūressāmi paripūraṃ vā tattha tattha paññāya anuggahessāmī ti yo tattha chando va vāyāmo ca ussāho ca ussoḷhī ca appaṭivānī ca sati ca sampajaññañ ca idaṃ vuccati byagghapajjā diṭṭhipārisuddhipadhāniyaṅgaṃ*, A II 195–6.

118 *sa kho so byagghapajjā ariyasāvako iminā ca sīlapārisuddhipadhāniyaṅgena samannāgato iminā ca cittapārisuddhipadhāniyaṅgena samannāgato iminā ca diṭṭhipārisuddhipadhāniyaṅgena samannāgato rajanīyesu dhammesu cittaṃ virājeti, vimocanīyesu dhammesu cittaṃ vimocayati, so rajanīyesu dhammesu cittaṃ virājetvā vimocanīyesu dhammesu cittaṃ vimocetvā sammā vimuttiṃ phusati. ayaṃ vuccati byagghapajjā vimuttipārisuddhi*, A II 195–6.

119 *vimutti-pārisuddhi-padhāniyaṅgaṃ*, A II 196.

120 Anderson, *Pain and its Ending*, p. 217.

121 Ibid., p. 225.

122 Ibid., pp. 230–1.

123 *saṅkhepato hi catusaccapaṭivedhāya paṭipannassa yogino nibbāṇārammaṇaṃ avijjānusaya-samugghātakaṃ paññācakkhu sammā-diṭṭhi. sā sammā-dassanalakkhaṇā, dhātuppakāsanarasā, avijjavdhakāraviddhaṃsana-paccupaṭṭhānā*, Vism XVI 76.

124 *tathāhaṃ bhagavatā dhammaṃ desitaṃ ājānāmi yathā tadev' idaṃ viññāṇaṃ sandhāvati saṃsarati, anaññan ti*, M I 256.

125 *paṭiccasamuppannaṃ viññāṇaṃ vuttaṃ mayā, aññatra paccayā n' atthi viññāṇassa sambhavo ti*, M I 259.

126 *bhūtam idan ti bhikkhave yathābhūtaṃ sammappaññāya sudiṭṭhan ti* [...] *tadāhārasambhavan ti bhikkhave yathā bhūtaṃ sammappaññāya sudiṭṭhan ti* [...] *tadāhāranirodhā yaṃ bhūtaṃ taṃ nirodhadhamman ti bhikkhave yathābhūtaṃ sammappaññāya sudiṭṭhan ti*, M I 260.

127 *diṭṭhiṃ evaṃ parisuddhaṃ evaṃ pariyodātaṃ*, M I 260.

128 *na allīyetha na keḷāyetha na dhanāyetha na mamāyetha, api nu tumhe bhikkhave kullūpamaṃ dhammaṃ desitaṃ ājāneyyātha nittharaṇatthāya no gahaṇatthāyā ti*, M I 260–1.

129 *atthi pana bhoto gotamassa kiñci diṭṭhi-gatan ti*, M I 486.

130 *diṭṭhi-gatan ti kho vaccha apanītam etaṃ tathāgatassa*, M I 486.

131 *diṭṭhaṃ h' etaṃ vaccha tathāgatena: iti rūpaṃ, iti rūpassa samudayo, iti rūpassa atthaṅgamo, iti vedanā, iti vedanāya samudayo, iti vedanāya atthaṅgamo, iti saññā, iti saññāya samudayo, iti saññāya atthaṅgamo, iti saṃkhārā, iti saṃkhārānaṃ samudayo, iti saṃkhārānaṃ atthaṃgamo, iti viññāṇaṃ, iti viññāṇassa samudayo, iti viññāṇassa atthaṅgamoti*, M I 486.

I will consider this passage again briefly in the next chapter.

132 *yaṃ kho bhante kiñci bhūtaṃ saṃkhataṃ cetayitaṃ paṭiccasamuppannaṃ, yad aniccaṃ, tam dukkham, yaṃ dukkhaṃ, tam n' etaṃ mama n' eso 'ham asmi na me so attā ti*, A V 188.

133 This understanding of the notion of *diṭṭhi* is suggested by a passage at A V 198 which states that if a person understands going to view, the basis for view, relying on view, obsession by view, rising up from view and rooting out view (*diṭṭhi-gata, diṭṭhiṭṭhāna-adhiṭṭhāna-pariyuṭṭhāna- samuṭṭhāna-samugghāta*), then that person knows (*jānāmi*) and sees (*passāmi*).

134 Warder, 'Is Nāgārjuna a Mahāyānist?', in *The Problem of Two Truths in Buddhism and Vedānta*, Mervyn Sprung (ed.), pp. 78–88 (p. 80).

135 *sammā-diṭṭhi sammā-diṭṭhi bhante vuccati, kittāvatā nu kho bhante sammā-diṭṭhi hoti*, S II 17.

136 See Collins, *Nirvana and Other Buddhist Felicities: Utopias of the Pali Imaginaire* (Cambridge, 1998), pp. 173–4, note 94.

137 *upayupādānābhinivesavinibandho khvāyaṃ Kaccāyana loko yebhuyyena, tañ cāyaṃ upayupādānām cetaso adhiṭṭhānam abhinivesānusayaṃ na upeti na upādiyati nādhiṭṭhāti attā me ti. dukkham eva uppajjamānaṃ uppajjati, dukkhaṃ nirujjhamānaṃ nirujjhatī ti na kankhati. na vicikicchati. aparappaccayā ñāṇam evassa ettha hoti. ettāvatā kho kaccāna, sammā-diṭṭhi hoti*, S II 17.

The Pāli has been changed according to the suggested reading given by Bhikkhu Bodhi (*Connected Discourses*, Volume I, p. 736, notes 31–2).

138 *ubho ante anupagamma majjhena Tathāgato dhammam deseti*, S II 17. The following is the 'middle-way', given in the *sutta* as what constitutes right-view:

> Dependent upon ignorance arise volitional formations; dependent upon volitional formations arises consciousness; dependent upon consciousness arises name and form; dependent upon name and form arises the sixfold sense

base; dependent upon the sixfold sense base arises contact; dependent upon contact arises feeling; dependent upon feeling arises craving; dependent upon craving arises attachment; dependent upon attachment arises being; dependent upon being arises birth; dependent upon birth arises old age and grief, lamentation, suffering and despair. Thus arises this entire mass of suffering. However, from the utter fading away of ignorance, there is the ceasing of volitional formations; from the ceasing of volitional formations there is the ceasing of consciousness; with the ceasing of consciousness there is the ceasing of name and form; with the ceasing of name and form there is the ceasing of the sixfold sense base; with the ceasing of the sixfold sense base there is the ceasing of contact; with the ceasing of contact there is the ceasing of feeling; with the ceasing of feeling there is the ceasing of craving; with the ceasing of craving there is the ceasing of attachment; with the ceasing of attachment there is the ceasing of being; with the ceasing of being there is the ceasing of birth; with the ceasing of birth there is the ceasing of old age and grief, lamentation, suffering and despair. And thus there is the ceasing of this entire mass of suffering (*avijjāpaccayā saṃkhārā. saṃkhārapaccayā viññāṇaṃ. viññāṇapaccayā nāmarūpaṃ. nāmarūpapaccayā saḷāyatanaṃ. saḷāyatanapaccayā phasso. phassapaccayā vedanā. vedanāpaccayā taṇhā. taṇhāpaccayā upādānaṃ. upādānapaccayā bhavo. bhavapaccayā jāti. jātipaccayā jarāmaraṇaṃ, sokaparidevadukkhadomanassūpāyāsā sambhavanti. evam etassa kevalassa dukkhakkhandhassa samudayo hoti. avijjāya tv eva asesavirāganirodhā saṃkhāranirodho. saṃkhāranirodhā viññāṇanirodho. viññāṇanirodhā nāmarūpanirodho. nāmarūpanirodhā saḷāyatananirodho. saḷāyatananirodhā phassanirodho. phassanirodhā vedanānirodho. vedanānirodhā taṇhānirodho. taṇhānirodhā upādānanirodho. upādānanirodhā bhavanirodho. bhavanirodhā jātinirodho. jātinirodhā jarāmaraṇaṃ, sokaparidevadukkhadomanassūpāyāsā nirujjhanti. evam etassa kevalassa dukkhakkhandhassa nirodho hotī ti*, S II 17).

139 Gethin, *The Buddhist Path to Awakening*, pp. 219–20.

140 Ibid., pp. 200–1.

141 Ibid., p. 220.

142 See Jayatilleke, *Early Buddhist Theory of Knowledge*, p. 360.

143 For example, Vin I 1, though not all accounts give the awakening in these terms.

144 The 'once returner' (*sokadāgāmin*), will be reborn as a human no more than once and is assured of awakening; the 'non-returner' (*anāgāmin*) will, at death, be reborn in a 'pure abode' (*suddhāvāsa*) and gain awakening there; and the Arahant, who will never be reborn again.

145 *yaṃ kiñci samudayadhammaṃ sabbaṃtaṃ nirodhadhamman ti*, M I 380.

146 *atha kho bhagava upālissa gahapatissa ānupubbīkathaṃ kathesi. seyyathīdaṃ: dānakathaṃ, sīlakathaṃ, saggakathaṃ, kāmānaṃ ādīnavaṃ, okāraṃ saṅkilesaṃ, nekkhamme ānisaṃsaṃ pakāsesi. yadā bhagavā aññāsi upāliṃ gahapatiṃ kallacittaṃ muducittaṃ vinīvaraṇacittaṃ udaggacittaṃ pasannacittaṃ, atha yā buddhānaṃ sāmukkaṃsikā dhammadesanā, taṃ pakāsesi: dukkhaṃ samudayaṃ nirodhaṃ maggaṃ. seyyathāpi nāma suddhaṃ vatthaṃ apagatakāḷakaṃ sammadeva rajanaṃ patigaṇheyya. evam eva upālissa gahapatissa tasmiṃ yeva āsane virajaṃ vītamalaṃ dhammacakkhuṃ udapādi: yaṃ kiñci samudayadhammaṃ sabbaṃ taṃ nirodhadhamman ti. atha kho upāli gahapati diṭṭhadhammo pattadhammo viditadhammo pariyogāḷhadhammo tiṇṇavicikiccho vigatakathaṅkatho vesārajjappatto aparappaccayo satthu sāsane*, M I 379–80.

This passage is also found in the *Brahmāyu-sutta* (M II 133–46) at M II 145, where it is realised by Brahmāyu, in the *Ambaṭṭha-sutta* (D I 87–110) at D I 109–10, where it is realised by Pokkharasāti, in the *Kūṭadanta-sutta* (D I 127–49) at D I 148, where it is realised by Kūṭadanta, in the *Mahāpadāna-sutta* (D II 1–54, spoken by Buddha Vipassī) at D II 41, where it is realised by both Khaṇḍa and Tissa. The full formula is also found in the *Sīhasenāpati sutta* (A IV 179–88) at A IV 186 realised by Sīha, in the *Vesālika-ugga-sutta* (A IV 208–12) at A IV 209–10, realised by Vesāli, and at *Udāna* 49 realised by Suppabuddha. Further occurrences are found at Vin I 37, realised by twelve brahmins and householders of Magadha and King Bimbisāra. In the *Dīghanakha-sutta* (M I 497–501) at M I 501 the second half of the passage appears (from 'the spotless immaculate vision of the *dhamma* arose') and Dīghanakha realises the *dhamma-cakkhu*. In the *Sakkapañha-sutta* (D II 263–89) at D II 288–9 the *dhamma-cakkhu* arises in Sakka and 80,000 *devas*, and they utter the *sammā-diṭṭhi*. The same thing happens in the *Cūḷarāhulovāda-sutta* (M III 277–80) at M III 280 to 'many thousands of deities'. In the *Gilāna-sutta* (S IV 46–7) at S IV 47, an anonymous *bhikkhu* realises the *dhamma-cakkhu* and utters the view. Peter Masefield has looked at a longer version of this formula appearing in the canon; see Peter Masefield, *Divine Revelation in Pali Buddhism* (Colombo/London, 1986), pp. 58–71, 166. A further set of passages containing descriptions of the arising of the *dhamma-cakkhu* are found in the first book of the *Vinaya*. In these passages the Buddha's first five followers realise the *dhamma-cakkhu* and utter the view. The occurrences are Koṇḍañña at Vin I 11, Vappa and Bhaddiya at Vin I 12, and Mahānāma and Assaji at Vin I 13. At Vin I 40–2 Sāriputta and Moggallāna realise the *dhamma-cakkhu*.

147 According to the *Nettippakaraṇa*, in the fourth *jhāna*, the mind is possessed of eight factors (*catutthe hi jhāne aṭṭhaṅgasamannāgataṃ cittaṃ bhāvayati*). It is purified, bright, unblemished, rid of imperfection, malleable, wieldy, steady and attained to imperturbability (*parisuddhaṃ pariyodātaṃ anaṅgaṇaṃ vigatūpakkilesaṃ mudu kammaniyaṃ ṭhitaṃ āneñjappattaṃ*, Nett 87). It is then stated that blemish (*aṅgaṇā*) and imperfection (*upakkilesā*), belong to the side of craving (*taṇhā-pakkho*), and any perturbation (*iñjanā*), and unsteadiness (*aṭṭhiti*) of the mind belong to the side of views (*diṭṭhi-pakkho*), Nett 88.

148 See Jayatilleke, *Early Buddhist Theory of Knowledge*, p. 466.

149 Ibid., p. 437.

150 Ibid., p. 417.

151 Ibid.

152 Ibid.

153 Ibid., p. 418.

154 Ibid.

155 Ibid.

156 Ibid., p. 420.

157 *kati panāvuso paccayā sammā-diṭṭhiyā uppādāyā ti? dve kho āvuso paccayā sammā-diṭṭhiyā uppādāya: parato ca ghoso, yoniso ca manasikāro*, M I 294.

158 Of course replacing appropriate with inappropriate: *dveme bhikkhave paccayā micchā-diṭṭhiyā uppādāya. katame dve: parato ca ghoso, ayoniso ca manasikāro. ime kho bhikkhave dve paccayā micchā-diṭṭhiyā uppādāya*, A I 87.

159 *ayoniso manasikāro diṭṭhiṭṭhānaṃ* [...] *parato ghoso diṭṭhiṭṭhānaṃ*, Ps I 138. More on this in Chapter 3.

160 *anuggahītā sammā-diṭṭhi cetovimuttiphalā ca hoti cetovimuttiphalānisaṃsā ca. paññāvimuttiphalā ca hoti paññāvimuttiphalānisaṃsā ca*, M I 294.

161 *duve hetu duve paccayā sāvakassa sammā-diṭṭhiyā uppādāya: parato ca ghoso saccānusandhi, ajjhattaṃ ca yoniso manasikāro*, Peṭ 1.

162 *tattha katamo parato ghoso: yā parato desanā ovādo anusāsanī saccakathā saccānulomo. cattāri saccāni: dukkhaṃ samudayo nirodho maggo imesaṃ catunnaṃ saccānaṃ yā desanā sandassanā vivaraṇā vibhajanā uttānīkiriyā pakāsanā. ayaṃ vuccati saccānulomo ghoso ti*, Peṭ 1.

163 The text has *ajjhataṃ yoniso manasikāra*, rendered by Ñāṇamoli as 'reasoned attention in oneself', Ñāṇamoli, *Piṭaka-Disclosure*, (London, 1964), p. 1.
164 *tattha katamo ajjhattaṃ yoniso manasikāro: ajjhattaṃ yoniso manasikāro nāma: yo yathā desite dhamme bahiddhā ārammaṇaṃ anabhinīharitvā yoniso manasikāro, ayaṃ vuccati ajjhattaṃ yoniso manasikāro*, Peṭ 1.
165 See Gethin, *The Buddhist Path to Awakening*, p. 223, note 130.
166 Woodward, F.L. and Hare, M.L., *The Book of Gradual Sayings* (A Trsl.), Volume I (PTS, London 1923–6), p. 79.
167 Ibid., p. 79, note 1.
168 Masefield, *Divine Revelation in Pali Buddhism*, pp. 52–3. Gethin, *The Buddhist Path to Awakening*, p. 222.
169 Masefield, *Divine Revelation in Pali Buddhism*, p. 52.
170 Gethin, *The Buddhist Path to Awakening*, p. 222, note 123.
171 Ibid., p. 222.
172 *tatra bhikkhave, sammā-diṭṭhi pubbaṅgamā hoti. kathañ ca bhikkhave, sammā-diṭṭhi pubbaṅgamā hoti: micchā-diṭṭhiṃ micchā-diṭṭhī ti pajānāti sammā-diṭṭhiṃ sammā-diṭṭhī ti pajānāti. sāssa hoti sammā-diṭṭhi*, M III 71.
– *micchā-saṅkappaṃ micchā-saṅkappo ti pajānāti sammā-saṅkappaṃ sammā-saṅkappo ti pajānāti*, M III 72.
– *micchā-vācaṃ micchā-vācā ti pajānāti. sammā-vācaṃ sammā-vācā ti pajānāti*, M III 73.
– *micchā-kammantaṃ micchā-kammanto ti pajānāti sammā-kammantaṃ sammā-kammanto ti pajānāti*, M III 74.
– *micchā-ājīvaṃ micchā-ājīvo ti pajānāti. sammā-ājīvaṃ sammā-ājīvo ti pajānāti*, M III 75.
sāssa hoti sammā-diṭṭhi.
173 I outlined above how views are explained according to whether they are with or without corruptions, i.e. right-view with corruptions is the view of affirmation, right-view without corruptions is wisdom (M III 72). The other factors are analysed in the same way. Hence right-intention, speech, action and livelihood are each analysed as affected by corruptions, partaking of merit and on the side of attachment (*sāsavā puññabhāgiyā upadhivepakkā*). Second, they are analysed as noble, without corruptions, supramundane and a factor of the path (*ariyā anāsavā lokuttarā maggaṅgā*). See M III 73 for intention; M III 73–4 for speech; M III 74–5 for action and M III 75 for livelihood.
174 *itissime tayo dhammā sammā-diṭṭhiṃ* (right-intention, speech, action and livelihood) *anuparidhāvanti anuparivattanti. seyyathīdaṃ: sammā-diṭṭhi sammā-vāyāmo sammā-sati*, M III 72, 73, 74, 75.
175 Lance Cousins translates these terms: 'right-view that occurs during insight'; 'right-view that occurs during the path'; Cousins, Review of Anderson, *Pain and its Ending*, p. 40.
176 *vipassanā-sammā-diṭṭhi tebhūmikasaṃkhāre aniccatādivasena parivīmaṃsati*, Ps III 131.
177 *maggasammā-diṭṭhi pana parivīmaṃsanapariyosāne bhūmiladdhaṃ vaṭṭaṃ samugghāṭayamānā vūpasamayamānā sītudakaghaṭasahassaṃ matthake āsiñcamānā viya uppajjati*, Ps III 131; see Bhikkhu Bodhi, *The Middle Length Discourses of the Buddha*, p. 1322, note 1100.
178 *micchā-diṭṭhiṃ aniccaṃ dukkhaṃ anattā ti lakkhaṇapaṭivedhena ārammaṇato*, Ps III 131.
179 Ps III 131.
180 See Gethin, *Buddhist Path to Awakening*, p. 218; Bhikkhu Bodhi, *The Middle Length Discourses of the Buddha*, p. 1322, note 1104.
181 *vipassanā-sammā-diṭṭhi-purejava*, Spk I 86.

182 Gethin, *The Buddhist Path to Awakening*, p. 216. The three sections are M III 71–5, 75–6, 76–7.

183 Gethin, ibid., p. 218.

184 *sammā-diṭṭhissa bhikkhave, micchā-diṭṭhi nijjiṇṇā hoti. ye ca micchā-diṭṭhi-paccayā aneka pāpakā akusalā dhammā sambhavanti. te cassa nijjiṇṇā honti. sammā-diṭṭhipaccayā aneke kusalā dhammā bhāvanā-pāripūriṃ gacchanti*, M III 76.

185 *iti sammā-diṭṭhiyā parato ca ghoso yoniso ca manasikāro paccayo. yā paññā uppādeti. esā hetu sammā-diṭṭhiyā, sammā-saṅkappo bhavati, yā sammā-samādhi. ayaṃ parikkhāro*, Peṭ 182. Also, as is clear, this view is caused by *paratogosa* and *yoniso manisikāro.*

186 *nāmarūpassa hetu paccayo pi viññāṇaṃ hetu bījaṃ. tena avijjā ca saṃkhārā ca paccayo*, Peṭ 181.

187 Gethin, *The Buddhist Path to Awakening*, pp. 218–19.

188 Collins, *Selfless Persons*, p. 91.

189 Gethin, *The Buddhist Path to Awakening*, pp. 219–20.

190 *sammā-diṭṭhissa micchā-diṭṭhi nijjiṇṇā hoti ye ca micchā-diṭṭhi-paccayā aneke pāpakā akusalā dhammā sambhavanti. te cassa nijjiṇṇā honti. sammā-diṭṭhi-paccayā ca aneke kusalā dhammā bhāvanā pāripūriṃ gacchanti*, D III 291. The same process is described for the other nine factors of the ten-fold path.

191 B.K. Matilal, 'Ignorance or Misconception? – A Note on Avidyā in Buddhism' in *Buddhist Studies in Honour of Walpola Rahula*, S. Balasooriya *et al.* (eds) (London, 1980), pp. 154–64 (p. 157); see also Matilal's account of the *Sautrāntika* theory of *arthakriyā* as 'accordance with the function of objects', in 'Error and Truth – Classical Indian Theories', *Philosophy East and West*, 31 (1981), 215–24 (p. 223).

192 Matilal, 'Ignorance or Misconception?', pp. 160–1. Matilal notes that there must be a distinction between *avidyā* and *mithyā-dṛṣṭi* as they are distinguished in such lists of defilements as the *anuśaya*. However, I am unsure about the point that Matilal is making. I take it that he understands (using the *Abhidharmakośa* as his reference), wrong-views standing in opposition to right-views in the same way that truth does to falsehood in a correspondence theory of truth. Matilal notes that for Vasubandhu *mithyā-dṛṣṭi* is *ku-prajñā* or 'bad wisdom', whereas Matilal suggests that *avidyā* should be understood as confusion (*moha*), in opposition to some sort of soteriological insight; see Matilal 'Ignorance or Misconception?', pp. 160–1. In Chapter 3 I will explain what I think the difference is between ignorance and wrong-view.

193 Matilal, ibid., p. 162.

194 Though he does argue that this is partly the case for the Vaiśeṣika system, ibid., pp. 162–3.

195 Ibid., p. 163.

196 Donald K. Swearer, 'Two types of saving knowledge in the Pāli suttas', *Philosophy East and West*, 22 (1972), pp. 355–71.

197 I follow Sue Hamilton in translating *nibbidā* as 'indifference', instead of using translations such as 'revulsion', which are misleading. The idea is that, with the achievement of right-view, there is detachment; see Hamilton, *Identity and Experience*, p. 184.

198 *aniccaññeva bhikkhave, bhikkhu rūpaṃ aniccan ti passati. sāssa hoti sammā-diṭṭhi, sammā-passaṃ nibbindati. nandikkhayā rāgakkhayo, rāgakkhayā nandikkhayo. nandirāgakkhayā cittaṃ vimuttaṃ suvimuttan ti vuccati*, S III 51.

199 *aniccaṃ yeva bhikkhave bhikkhu cakkhuṃ* [*sotaṃ, ghānaṃ, jivham, kāyaṃ* and *manaṃ*] *aniccan ti passati. sāssa hoti sammā-diṭṭhi, sammā passaṃ nibbindati, nandikkhayā rāgakkhayo rāgakkhayā nandikkhayo nandirāgakkhayā cittaṃ suvimuttan ti vuccati*, S IV 142.

200 *anicceyeva bhikkhave bhikkhu rūpe* [*sadde, gandhe, rase, phoṭṭhabbe* and *dhamma*] *aniccāti passati. sāssa hoti sammā-diṭṭhi, sammā passaṃ nibbindati, nandikkhayā*

rāgakkhayo rāgakkhayā nandikkhayo nandirāgakkhayā cittaṃ suvimuttan ti vuccati, S IV 142.

201 *kathan nu kho bhante jānato kathaṃ passato micchā-diṭṭhi* [*sakkāya-diṭṭhi* [...] *attānudiṭṭhi*] *pahīyatī ti*, S IV 147–8.

202 As will be shown in Chapter 4, to regard things as: 'This is not mine, this I am not, this is not my self' is described as the 'perfect view' (*sampanna-diṭṭhi*) in other parts of the canon (Paṭis I 160).

203 *anicce* [...] *niccan ti saññā-vipallāso citta-vipallāso diṭṭhi-vipallāso*, A II 52.

204 *dukkhe* [...] *sukhan ti saññā-vipallāso citta-vipallāso diṭṭhi-vipallāso*, A II 52.

205 *anattani* [...] *attā ti saññā-vipallāso citta-vipallāso diṭṭhi-vipallāso*, A II 52.

206 *asubhe* [...] *bhikkhave subhan ti saññā-vipallāso citta-vipallāso diṭṭhi-vipallāso*, A II 52.

207 *anicce* [...] *aniccan ti* [...] *dukkhe* [...] *dukkhan ti* [...] *anattani* [...] *anattā ti* [...] *asubhe* [...] *asubhan ti na saññā-vipallāso na citta-vipallāso na diṭṭhi-vipallāso*, A II 52.

208 *vipallāsā ti anicca-dukkha-anatta-asubhesu yeva vatthusu niccaṃ sukhaṃ attā subhan ti evaṃ pavatto saññāvipallāso cittavipallāso diṭṭhivipallāso ti*, Vism XXII 53.

209 These are to contemplate body as body, feelings as feelings, mind as mind, and *dhammas* as *dhammas* (M I 56).

210 *parāmāso ti tassa tassa dhammassa sabhāvaṃ atikkamma parato abhūtaṃ sabhāvaṃ āmasanākārena pavattanato micchā-diṭṭhiyā etaṃ adhivacanaṃ*, Vism XXII 57.

211 *evaṃ saṃkhāre anattato passantassa diṭṭhisamugghāṭanaṃ nāma hoti*, Vism XX 87.

212 *obhāsa, ñāṇa, pīti, passaddhi, sukha, adhimokkha, paggaha, upaṭṭhāna, upekkhā, nikanti*, Vism XX 105. I am following Ñāṇamoli in translating *nikanti* as 'attachment', a term I have used in the rest of this book to translate *upādāna*; see Ñāṇamoli, *The Path of Purification* (Colombo, 1956), p. 739.

213 *nikantī ti vipassanānikanti; evaṃ obhāsādi-patimaṇḍitāya hissa vipassanāya ālayaṃ kurumānā sukhumā santākārā nikanti uppajjati, yā nikanti kileso ti pariggahetum pi na sakkā hoti*, Vism XX 122.

214 *yaṃ kiñci samudayadhammaṃ sabbaṃ taṃ nirodhadhammanti*, M I 380.

3 The way wrong-view functions

1 In the *Mahāparinibbāna-sutta* (D II 72–168) at D II 81, 91, 94 and 98 the four *āsavas* are given:

> The mind, when imbued with wisdom becomes completely free from the corruptions, that is, from the corruption of sensuality, of becoming, of wrong-views and of ignorance (*paññāparibhāvitaṃ cittaṃ sammadeva āsavehi vimuccati, seyyathīdaṃ· kāmāsavā bhavāsavā diṭṭhāsavā avijjāsavā ti*).

There is another list of terms, identical to the list of four *āsavas*, that occur in the Nikāyas. These describe sensuality, becoming, views and ignorance as the four yokes (*yoga*), sometimes found in opposition to the four unyokings (*visaṃyoga*, see D III 230, 276, S V 59). There are also the four floods (*oghas*, D III 230, S V 59), consisting of the same categories.

2 *rūpārūpabhavesu chandarāgo jhānanikanti sassatadiṭṭhisahajāto rāgo bhavavasena patthanā bhavāsavo nāma*, As 369.

3 Of the *Brahmajāla-sutta*: *dvāsaṭṭhi diṭṭhiyo diṭṭhāsavo nāma*, As 369.

4 *aṭṭhasu ṭhānesu aññāṇaṃ avijjāsavo nāma*, As 369.

5 Maung Tin, *The Expositor*, I–II (London, 1920), p. 475, note 3.

6 This certainly appears to be the understanding of wrong-views by the period of the early Abhidhamma, and, as I will suggest, seems implicit in such discussions as those found in the *Brahmajāla sutta*.

7 Dhs 79, 80–2 (this is a reference to the PTS page numbers). The formalised definition from later Abhidhamma is given in Appendix 5.

8 Buddhaghosa uses the view of affirmation to explain this view, i.e. it is a type of *paññā* (Vism XIV 84).

9 Gethin, 'Wrong View (micchā-diṭṭhi) and Right View (sammā-diṭṭhi) in the Theravāda Abhidhamma', p. 218.

10 *yā tasmiṃ samaye diṭṭhi diṭṭhi-gataṃ diṭṭhi-gahanaṃ diṭṭhi-kantāro diṭṭhi-visūkāyikaṃ diṭṭhi-vipphanditaṃ diṭṭhi-saṃyojanaṃ gāho patiṭṭhāho abhiniveso parāmāso kummaggo micchā-patho micchattaṃ titthāyatanaṃ vipariyesagāho, ayaṃ tasmiṃ samaye micchā-diṭṭhi hoti*, Dhs 78, 183, 198, 202, 208, 212, *passim* (all references to page numbers of the PTS edition).

Translation adapted from Gethin, 'Wrong View (micchā-diṭṭhi) and Right View (sammā-diṭṭhi) in the Theravāda Abhidhamma', p. 218. Most of these terms are found in the Nikāyas. In the *Sabbāsava-sutta* (M I 6–12), *diṭṭhi-gata* is described as the thicket, wilderness, contortion and vacillation of views:

> This speculative view [...] is called a thicket of views, the wilderness of views, the contortion of views, the vacillation of views, the fetter of views. Fettered by the fetter of views, the untaught ordinary person is not freed from birth, ageing, and death, from sorrow, lamentation, pain, grief, and despair; he is not freed from suffering, I say (*idaṃ vuccati* [...] *diṭṭhi-gataṃ diṭṭhi-gahanaṃ diṭṭhi-kantāro diṭṭhi-visūkaṃ diṭṭhi-vipphanditaṃ diṭṭhi-saṃyojanaṃ. diṭṭhi-saṃyojanasaṃyutto bhikkhave assutavā puthujjano na parimuccati jātiyā jarāmaraṇena sokehi paridevehi dukkhehi domanassehi upāyāsehi, na parimuccati dukkhasmā ti vadāmi*, M I 8).

In the *Aggivacchagotta-sutta* (M I 483–9), the Buddha is asked what danger he sees in the ten *avyākata*, so that he does not take up any of these views (*kim pana bhavaṃ gotamo ādīnavaṃ sampassamāno evaṃ imāni sabbaso diṭṭhi-gatāni anupagato ti*, M I 485). The Buddha replies that each of these views is a thicket, a wilderness, a contortion, a vacillation and a fetter of views (*diṭṭhi-gahanaṃ diṭṭhi-kantāraṃ diṭṭhi-visūkaṃ diṭṭhi-vipphanditaṃ diṭṭhi-saṃyojanaṃ*, M I 485). They are beset by suffering, vexation, despair and fever (*sadukkhaṃ savighātaṃ saupāyāsaṃ sapariḷāhaṃ*), and do not lead to disenchantment, dispassion, cessation, peace, direct knowledge, enlightenment or *nibbāna* (*na nibbidāya na virāgāya na nirodhāya na upasamāya na abhiññāya na sambodhāya na nibbānāya saṃvattati*, M I 485). In a sense, in this reply, as in the *Dhammasaṅgani*, the Buddha is not alluding to the content of the views but the effect upon the person that holds to them. Vacchagotta asks the Buddha if he takes up any speculative view (*atthi pana bhoto gotamassa kiñci diṭṭhi-gatan ti*). The Buddha replies that speculative view is something that he has put away (*diṭṭhi-gatan ti kho vaccha apanītam etaṃ tathāgatassa*, M I 486). What the Buddha has seen is each of the five *khandhas*, their origin and their disappearance. In the *Yoga-sutta* (A II 10–13) at A II 11, views are described as a bond (*diṭṭhi-yoga*). The bond of views is described as the lust for views, the delight in views, the affection for views, the greed for views, the thirst for views, the fever, clinging, and the craving for views (*yo diṭṭhisu diṭṭhi-rāgo diṭṭhi-nandī diṭṭhi-sineho diṭṭhi-mucchā diṭṭhi-pipāsā diṭṭhi-pariḷāho diṭṭhi-ajjhosānaṃ diṭṭhi-taṇhā*, A II 11). The term *diṭṭhi-visūkāni*, contrariness of view, occurs in the *Sutta-nipāta* where the sage is described as having gone beyond the contrariness of view (*diṭṭhivisūkāni upātivatto*), on a fixed course, wandering solitary as a rhinoceros horn, Sn 55.

11 *tattha katamaṃ taṇhāpaccayā upādānaṃ: yā diṭṭhi diṭṭhi-gataṃ diṭṭhi-gahanaṃ diṭṭhi-kantāro diṭṭhi-visukāyikaṃ diṭṭhi-vipphanditaṃ diṭṭhi-saṃyojanā gaho patiṭṭhāho abhiniveso parāmāso kummaggo micchā-patho micchattaṃ titthāyatanaṃ vipariyesagāho, idaṃ vuccati taṇhāpaccayā upādānaṃ*, Vibh, § 249, p. 145.

12 This is the analysis according to the Abhidhamma. In the analysis according to the discourses, the same connection between craving and attachment is described as the attachment of desire, wrong-view, precepts and vows, and the attachment to the theory of self (*taṇhāpaccayā upādānaṃ: kāmupādānaṃ diṭṭhupādānaṃ silabbatupādānaṃ attavādupādānaṃ, idaṃ vuccati taṇhā-paccayā upādānaṃ*, Vibh 136).

13 As 252–3. Translation adapted from Gethin, 'Wrong View (micchā-diṭṭhi) and Right View (sammā-diṭṭhi) in the Theravāda Abhidhamma', pp. 218–19.

14 A different analysis is given by Jackson. He argues that *avidyā* is 'ontological ignorance' while *mithyā-dṛṣṭi* is 'cosmological ignorance' (Jackson, R., *Is Enlightenment Possible* (New York, 1993), p. 48, note 19). Jackson holds that the four truths, as *sammā-diṭṭhi*, are a proposition which carries with it many philosophical and cosmological presuppositions (ibid. p. 43). It is in this context that he arrives at this understanding of ignorance and wrong-views.

15 Gethin, 'Wrong View (micchā-diṭṭhi) and Right View (sammā-diṭṭhi) in the Theravāda Abhidhamma', p. 220.

16 *yaṃ tasmiṃ samaye aññāṇaṃ adassanaṃ anabhisamayo ananubodho asambodho appaṭivedho asaṃgāhanā apariyogāhanā asamapekkhanā apaccavekkhanā apaccakkhakammaṃ dummejjhaṃ bālyaṃ asampajaññaṃ moho pamoho sammoho avijjā avijjogho avijjāyogo avijjānusayo avijjāpariyuṭṭhānaṃ avijjālaṅgī moho akusalamūlaṃ, ayaṃ tasmiṃ samaye moho hoti*, Dhs 78 § 390.

17 Vism XIV 163–4, As 249; see Gethin, 'Wrong View (micchā-diṭṭhi) and Right View (sammā-diṭṭhi) in the Theravāda Abhidhamma', p. 220. As Gethin explains:

> For the Theravādins what is significant about *diṭṭhi* is not simply that it is a wrong or false way of seeing, but that it is a grasping at or holding onto a particular way of seeing; it is a fixed or rigid view of things. The emphasis in the register of terms for *moha*, on the other hand, is on its not knowing, not seeing, not understanding, on its failure to penetrate (*appaṭivedha*), and get below the surface (*apariyogāhanā*) to the true nature of things. Ibid., pp. 220–1.

18 *abhiniveso ca parāmāso ca diṭṭhāsavassa lakkhaṇaṃ*, Peṭ 94.

19 *appaṭivedho ca dhammesu asampajaññā ca avijjāsavassa lakkhaṇaṃ*, Peṭ 94.

20 Note an error in the PTS edition, or a probable earlier error, which has *avijjāsavo citte pahātabbo. so citte cittānupassissa pahīyati, diṭṭhāsavo dhammesu pahātabbo, so dhammesu dhammānupassissa pahīyati*, which I have read as *diṭṭhāsavo citte pahātabbo. so citte cittānupassissa pahīyati, avijjāsavo dhammesu pahātabbo, so dhammesu dhammānupassissa pahīyati*, Peṭ 94; see Ñāṇamoli, *Piṭaka Disclosure* (London, 1964), p. 127, note 344/1.

21 *idha bhikkhave bhikkhu kāye kāyānupassī viharati ātāpī sampajāno satimā vineyya loke abhijjhādomanassaṃ. vedanāsu vedanānupassī viharati ātāpī sampajāno satimā vineyya loke abhijjhādomanassaṃ. citte cittānupassī viharati ātāpī sampajāno satimā vineyya loke abhijjhādomanassaṃ. dhammesu dhammānupassī viharati ātāpī sampajāno satimā vineyya loke abhijjhādomanassaṃ*, M I 56; see Gethin, *The Buddhist Path to Awakening*, pp. 29–68.

There is also some connection between 'the emptiness gateway to liberation' (*suññatā vimokkhamukhaṃ*), and 'the signless gateway to liberation' (*animittaṃ vimokkhamukhaṃ*, Nett 123), which I shall consider in Chapter 5.

22 Ñāṇamoli interprets the *cetasikas* as *dhammas* (Ñāṇamoli, *Piṭaka Disclosure*, p. 126, note 339/1).

23 *tattha citte attā ti diṭṭhāsavo, cetasikesu niccan ti avijjāsavo*, this is Ñāṇamoli's suggested correction or restoration of *tattha citte atthiti diṭṭhi cetasikesu niccanti* (Ñāṇamoli, *Piṭaka Disclosure* p. 136, note 333/1, Peṭ 94).

24 *anattani attā ti vipallāso, diṭṭhupādānaṃ, diṭṭhi-yogo, parāmāsa-kāya-gantho, diṭṭhāsavo, diṭṭhi-ogho, diṭṭhi-sallaṃ*, Peṭ 246.

25 *anicce niccan ti vipallāso, attavādūpādānaṃ, avijjāyogo, idaṃsaccābhiniveso kāyagantho, avijjāsavo, avijjogho, mohasallaṃ*, Peṭ 246.

26 *katamaṃ diṭṭhi-mamattaṃ*, Nidd I 51, 122, 125, 129, 276, 369, 440.

27 The *Mahāniddesa* adds 'grasping at things wrongly' (*micchā-gāho ayāthāvakasmiṃ*): *katamaṃ diṭṭhi-mamattaṃ? vīsativatthukā sakkāya-diṭṭhi, dasavatthukā micchā-diṭṭhi, dasavatthukā antaggāhikā diṭṭhi, yā evarūpā diṭṭhi diṭṭhi-gataṃ diṭṭhi-gahanaṃ diṭṭhi-kantāro diṭṭhi-visūkāyikaṃ diṭṭhi-vipphandikaṃ diṭṭhi-saṃyojanaṃ gāho paṭiggāho abhiniveso parāmāso kummaggo micchā-patho micchattaṃ titthāyatanaṃ vipariyesaggāho viparītaggāho vipallāsaggāho micchā-gāho ayāthāvakasmiṃ yāthāvakan ti gāho. yāvatā dvāsaṭṭhi diṭṭhi-gatāni, idaṃ diṭṭhi-mamattaṃ*, Nidd I 50–1.

Dhs: *yā tasmiṃ samaye diṭṭhi diṭṭhi-gataṃ diṭṭhi-gahanaṃ diṭṭhi-kantāro diṭṭhi-visūkāyikaṃ diṭṭhi-vipphanditaṃ diṭṭhi-saṃyojanaṃ gāho patiṭṭhāho abhiniveso parāmāso kummaggo micchā-patho micchattaṃ titthāyatanaṃ vipariyesagāho, ayaṃ tasmiṃ samaye micchā-diṭṭhi hoti*, Dhs 78.

28 *vīsativatthukā sakkāya-diṭṭhi, dasavatthukā micchā-diṭṭhi, dasavatthukā antaggāhikā diṭṭhi, yā evarūpā diṭṭhi diṭṭhi-gataṃ diṭṭhi-gahanaṃ diṭṭhi-kantāraṃ diṭṭhi-visūkāyikaṃ diṭṭhi-vipphanditaṃ diṭṭhi-saṃyojanaṃ gāho paṭiggāho abhiniveso parāmāso kummaggo micchā-patho micchattaṃ titthāyatanaṃ vipariyesaggāho viparītaggāho vipallāsaggāho micchā-gāho, ayāthāvakasmiṃ yāthāvakan ti gāho. yāvatā dvāsaṭṭhi diṭṭhigatāni, ayaṃ diṭṭhi-nivesanā*, Nidd I 100.

29 *diṭṭhi-kappa*, Nidd I 112–13, 251, 328, 336.

30 *diṭṭhi-purekkhāra*, Nidd I 113.

31 *diṭṭhi-pariggaha*, Nidd I 129, 275.

32 *diṭṭhi-nissaya*, Nidd I 133, 245, 431.

33 *diṭṭhi-lepa*, Nidd I 136, 332.

34 *diṭṭhi-upaya*, Nidd I 308.

35 *diṭṭhi-pakappanā*, Nidd I 316. There are two types of *pakappanā*, those of *taṇhā* and *diṭṭhi*, Nidd I 72, 186.

36 *diṭṭhi-salla*, Nidd I 414–15. There are seven darts, *rāga, dosa, moha, māna, diṭṭhi, soka* and *kathakathā*, Nidd I 59.

37 Vibh-a 300.

38 *ayaṃ loko santāpajāto*
phassapareto rogaṃ vadati attano,
yena yena hi maññati
tato taṃ hoti aññathā.
aññathābhāvī bhavasatto loko
bhavapareto bhavam evā bhinandati, yad abhinandati taṃ bhayaṃ
yassa bhāyati taṃ dukkhaṃ, Peṭ 26.

39 *ye hi keci samaṇā vā brāhmaṇā vā vibhavena bhavassa vippamokkham āhaṃsu, sabbe te avippamuttā bhavasmā ti vadāmi. ye vā pana keci samaṇā vā brāhmaṇā vā bhavena bhavassa nissaraṇam āhaṃsu, sabbe te anissaṭā bhavasmā ti vadāmi*, Peṭ 26.

40 It should be noted that the *Udāna* passage which the *Peṭakopadesa* is discussing, does use the term *avijjā*, Peṭ 27.

41 *so attā, so loko, so pecca bhavissāmi nicco dhuvo sassato avipariṇāmadhammo*, S III 182.

42 The text explains the same for the fetters, adherences, shackles and holding (*saṃyojanābhinivesa-vinibandhājjhosānāti*, S III 186–7). It is such statements from the Nikāyas, in which views are said to depend upon attachment to the *khandhas*, which has led Steven Collins to define wrong-views as 'conceptual manifestations of desire and attachment' (Collins, *Selfless Persons*, p. 119). In his discussion, he argues that this aspect of the nature of *diṭṭhi* was only one of those found in the Nikāyas. He suggests that this tendency represented part of a quietistic trend, in which all views are condemned as potential objects of cognitive attachment. No 'views' should be held. Right-view, if it becomes an object of attachment, is condemned. I agree with Collins to an extent but as I explain in the first half of this chapter I think that this is not merely a trend in the Nikāyas, but the dominant understanding of the notion of *diṭṭhi*. I cannot make sense of there being both the corruption of views and the corruption of ignorance if these terms do not apply to different things. The most logical conclusion to draw is that views apply to a type of attachment, ignorance to a type of delusion. I certainly think this is the prominent understanding of views by the time of the early Abhidhamma, and I hope to show that it is very prominent in the Nikāyas. All views rest upon attachment to *dhammas*, the most prominent being the five *khandhas*.

43 *evaṃ passaṃ bhikkhave, sutavā, ariyasāvako rūpasmim pi nibbindati. vedanāya pi nibbindati saññāya pi, nibbindati saṃkhāresu pi nibbindati. viññāṇasmim pi nibbindati. nibbindaṃ virajjati. virāgā vimuccati. vimuttasmiṃ vimuttam iti ñāṇaṃ hoti*, S III 181 and throughout the *khandha-vagga* from S III 21.

44 The non-attached attitude is also one explanation of the stage of stream-attainment. At S III 160–1 it is stated that there are five *khandhas* subject to attachment (*upādānakkhandhā*). When the *ariya-sāvaka* understands the origin and passing away of the five *khandhas* subject to attachment, he is a stream-attainer (*yato kho bhikkhave ariyasāvako imesaṃ pañcannaṃ upadānakkhandhānaṃ samudayañ ca atthagamañ ca assādañ ca ādīnavañ ca nissaraṇañ ca yathābhūtaṃ pajānanti. ayaṃ vuccati bhikkhave, ariyasāvako sotāpanno avinipātadhammo niyato sambodhiparāyaṇo ti*, S III 160–1). As I will describe in the next chapter a standard explanation of *sammā-diṭṭhi* is that it comprehends the rise and fall (*udayabbaya*) of *dhammas*. This, I think, is precisely what is being explained in the *Diṭṭhi-vagga*.

45 e.g. *rūpe kho bhikkhave sati rūpaṃ upādāya rūpaṃ abhinivissa evaṃ diṭṭhi uppajjati*, S III 202 *passim*.

46 *yaṃ panāniccaṃ dukkhaṃ vipariṇāmadhammaṃ, api nu taṃ anupādāya evaṃ diṭṭhi uppajjeyya*, S III 202.

47 *diṭṭhaṃ, sutaṃ, mutaṃ, viññātaṃ, pattaṃ, pariyesitaṃ, anuvicaritaṃ manasā*, S III 203.

48 *yaṃ panāniccaṃ dukkhaṃ vipariṇāmadhammaṃ api nu taṃ anupādāya evaṃ diṭṭhi uppajjeyya* [insert each view] *n' etaṃ bhante*, S III 203 ff.

49 The five *khandhas* plus what is seen, heard, etc. as one category.

50 *yato kho bhikkhave ariyasāvakassa imesu chasu ṭhānesu kaṅkhā pahīnā hoti, dukkhe pi 'ssa kaṅkhā pahīnā hoti, dukkhasamudaye pi 'ssa kaṅkhā pahīnā hoti, dukkhanirodhe pi 'ssa kaṅkhā pahīnā hoti, dukkha-nirodha-gāminiyā paṭipadāya pi 'ssa kaṅkhā pahīnā hoti. ayaṃ vuccati bhikkhave, ariya-sāvako sotāpanno avinipātadhammo niyato sambodhiparāyano ti*, S III 203, *passim*.

51 *dukkhe sati dukkhaṃ upādāya dukkhaṃ abhinivissa evaṃ diṭṭhi uppajjeyya*, S III 218.

52 *yad aniccaṃ taṃ dukkhaṃ tasmiṃ sati tad upādāya evaṃ diṭṭhi uppajjati*, S III 221.

53 *diṭṭhīnivesā na hi svātivattā*
dhammesu niccheyya samuggahītaṃ,
tasmā naro tesu nivesanesu,
nirassatī ādiyati-cca dhammaṃ, Sn 785.

54 *yo chando yo rāgo yā nandi yā taṇhā ye upayūpādānā cetaso adhiṭṭhānābhinivesānusayā*, S III 10, 13, 161–2. Similar terms also appeared in the *Kaccāyanagotta-sutta* which I discussed in Chapter 2:

> This world, Kaccāyana, is for the most part shackled by engagement, attachment and adherence (*upāyupādānābhinivesavinibandho*). But this one [with right-view] does not become engaged and attached through that engagement and attachment, mental basis, adherence, underlying tendency; he does not take his stand about 'my self' (*upayupādānābhinivesavinibandho khvāyaṃ Kaccāyana loko yebhuyyena, tañ cāyaṃ upayupādānām cetaso adhiṭṭhānam abhinivesānusayaṃ na upeti na upādiyati nādhiṭṭhāti attā me ti*, S II 17).

55 *The Yogadarśana of Patañjali* (*Yoga-sūtra*, 2.3), reference in Matilal, 'Ignorance or Misconception? – A Note on Avidyā in Buddhism', p. 162.
56 See Gethin, *The Buddhist Path to Awakening*, p. 123.
57 Ibid., p. 123.
58 *rūpaṃ etaṃ mama, eso 'ham asmi, eso me attā ti abhinivesa-parāmāso diṭṭhi*, Paṭis I 135.
59 i.e. for each of the *khandha*;

> *rūpaṃ etaṃ mama, eso 'ham asmi, eso me attā ti abhinivesa-parāmāso diṭṭhi, vedanaṃ etaṃ mama eso 'ham asmi, eso me attā ti abhinivesa-parāmāso diṭṭhi, saññaṃ etaṃ mama eso 'ham asmi, eso me attā ti abhinivesa-parāmāso diṭṭhi, saṃkhāre etaṃ mama eso 'ham asmi, eso me attā ti abhinivesa-parāmāso diṭṭhi, viññāṇaṃ etaṃ mama, eso 'ham asmi, eso me attā ti abhinivesa-parāmāso diṭṭhi*, Paṭis I 135.

60 *khandhā pi diṭṭhiṭṭhānaṃ, avijjā pi diṭṭhiṭṭhānaṃ, phasso pi diṭṭhiṭṭhānaṃ, saññā pi diṭṭhiṭṭhānaṃ, vitakko diṭṭhiṭṭhānaṃ, ayoniso manasikāro pi diṭṭhiṭṭhānaṃ, pāpamitto pi diṭṭhiṭṭhānaṃ, parato pi ghoso diṭṭhi-ṭṭhānaṃ*, Paṭis I 138.
61 'Condition' (*paccayo*) in the Paṭis translation.
62 *dveme bhikkhave paccayā micchā-diṭṭhiyā uppādāya. katame dve: parato ca ghoso, ayoniso ca manasikāro. ime kho bhikkhave dve paccayā micchā-diṭṭhiyā uppādāya*, A I 87.
63 Paṭis I 138. This list is also used as a definition of *micchā-diṭṭhi*, i.e. *micchā-diṭṭhi* is a *diṭṭhi-gataṃ*, a *diṭṭhi-gahanaṃ*, etc., Paṭis I 41–2.
64 Paṭis I 139. This list of views is, of course, comparable to that given in the *khuddhaka-vatthu* of the *Vibhaṅga* which I used as a framework in Chapter 1 on the content of wrong-view.
65 *assāda-diṭṭhiyā katamehi pañcatiṃsāya ākārehi abhiniveso hoti*, Paṭis I 140.
66 *yaṃ rūpaṃ paṭicca uppajjati sukhaṃ somanassaṃ, ayaṃ rūpassa assādo ti*, Paṭis I 140.
67 *diṭṭhi na assādo, assādo na diṭṭhi, aññā diṭṭhi, añño assādo. yā ca diṭṭhi, yo ca assādo, ayaṃ vuccati assāda-diṭṭhi*, Paṭis I 140.
68 e.g. for the first of the views about self with form as ground *aññā diṭṭhi, aññaṃ vatthu. yā ca diṭṭhi yañ ca vatthu, ayaṃ paṭhamā rūpavatthukā attānudiṭṭhi*, Paṭis I 144. This is different from the first view in which the view was one thing, the gratification another (*añña diṭṭhi, añño assādo*) and together they are the gratification-view.
69 *abhinivesa-parāmāso diṭṭhi*, Paṭis I 144, 145, 146, *passim*.
70 *yā ca diṭṭhi yañ ca vatthu, ayaṃ paṭhamā micchā-vatthukā micchā-diṭṭhi*, Paṭis I 149.
71 *bījaṃ pāpakaṃ* and *diṭṭhi pāpikā*, Paṭis I 141; see A I 32. The full text from the Paṭis reads:

> *assāda-diṭṭhi micchā-diṭṭhi, micchā-diṭṭhikassa purisapuggalassa dve gatiyo: nirayo vā tiracchānayoni vā. micchā-diṭṭhikassa purisapuggalassa yañ c' eva*

kāyakammaṃ yathādiṭṭīsamattaṃ samādinnaṃ, yañ ca vacīkammaṃ–pe–yañ ca manokammaṃ yathā-diṭṭhi-samattaṃ samādinnaṃ, yā ca cetanā ya ca patthanā, yo ca paṇidhi, ye ca saṃkhārā, sabbe te dhammā aniṭṭhāya akantāya amanāpāya ahitāya dukkhāya saṃvattanti. taṃ kissa hetu. diṭṭhi hissa pāpikā. seyyathāpi nimbabījaṃ vā kosatakibījaṃ vā tittakalābubījaṃ vā allāya paṭhaviyā nikkhittaṃ yañ c' eva paṭhavīrasaṃ upādiyati, yañ ca āporasaṃ upādiyati, sabbaṃ taṃ tittakatāya kaṭukatāya asāratāya saṃvattati. taṃ kissa hetu: bījaṃ hissa pāpakaṃ. evam eva micchā-diṭṭhi kassa purisapuggalassa yañ c' eva kāyakammaṃ yathā-diṭṭhi-samattaṃ samādinnaṃ, yañ ca vacīkammaṃ–pe–yañ ca manokammaṃ yathā-diṭṭhi-samattaṃ samādinnaṃ, yā ca cetanā yā ca patthanā yo ca paṇidhi ye ca saṃkhārā, sabbe te dhammā aniṭṭhāya akantāya amanāpāya ahitāya dukkhāya saṃvattanti. taṃ kisssa hetu diṭṭhi hissa pāpikā, Paṭis I 140–1.

72 *nissitassa calitaṃ anissitassa calitaṃ n' atthi,* Nett 65.

73 *nissayo nāma duvidho: taṇahānissayo diṭṭhi-nissayo ca*, Nett 65.

74 *saṃkhāra-paccayā viññāṇaṃ, viññāṇa-paccayā nāmarūpaṃ, nāmarūpa-paccayā saḷāyatanaṃ, saḷāyatana-paccayā phasso, phassa-paccayā vedanā, vedanā-paccayā taṇhā, taṇhā-paccayā upādāna, upādāna-paccayā bhavo, bhava-paccayā jāti, jāti-paccayā jarāmaraṇaṃ, sokaparidevadukkhadomanassupāyāsā sambhavanti, evam etassa kevalassa dukkhakkhandhassa samudayo hoti*, Nett 65.

75 I am translating the term *nati* as 'inclination'. To have an inclination is a subtle craving and need, the opposite to tranquillity. See a comparable passage at S II 67 which reads: *tasmiṃ patiṭṭhite viññāṇe virūḷhe nati hoti. natiyā sati āgatigati hoti. āgatigatiyā sati cutūpapāto hoti.*

76 *passaddhiyā sati nati na hoti, natiyā asati āgati-gati na hoti, āgatigatiyā asati cutūpapāto na hoti, cutūpapāte asati nev' idha na huraṃ na ubhayam antarena es' ev' anto dukkhassā*, Nett 65.

77 *samathavasena vā taṇhāya anissito*, Nett 65.

78 *vipassanāvasena vā diṭṭhiyā anissito*, Nett 65.

79 *vipassanā ayaṃ vijjā vijjuppādā avijjānirodho*, Nett 65.

80 *avijjā-nirodhā saṃkhāra-nirodho, saṃkhāra-nirodhā viññāṇa-nirodho, viññāṇa-nirodhā nāmarūpa-nirodho, nāmarūpa-nirodhā saḷāyatana-nirodho saḷāyatana-nirodhā phassa-nirodho, phassa-nirodhā vedanā-nirodho, vedanā-nirodhā taṇhā-nirodho, taṇhā-nirodhā upādāna-nirodho, upādāna-nirodhā bhava-nirodho, bhava-nirodhā jāti-nirodho, jāti-nirodhā jarāmaraṇaṃ sokaparidevadukkhadomansūpāyāsā nirujjhanti, evam etassa kevalassa dukkhakkhandhassa nirodho hoti*, Nett 65–6.

81 *yaṃ kho pana kiñci bhūtaṃ saṃkhataṃ cetayitaṃ paṭiccasamuppannaṃ, tad aniccaṃ yad aniccaṃ taṃ dukkham, yaṃ dukkham, tam n' etaṃ mama n' eso 'ham asmi na me so attā ti*, A V 188.

4 The way right-view functions

1 *ñāti-sampadā, bhoga-sampadā, ārogya-sampadā, sīla-sampadā, diṭṭhi-sampadā*, D III 235, A III 147.

2 *ñāti-vyasanāni, bhoga-vyasanāni, rogya-vyasanāni, sīla-vyasanāni, diṭṭhi-vyasanāni.* Note that the term used is not 'non-accomplishment' *vipatti*, but 'loss' (*vyasana*).

3 The importance of conduct and thought in achieving a good rebirth was discussed in Chapter 2 when considering the ten wholesome courses of action.

4 *sīla-sampadā-hetu vā bhikkhave sattā kāyassa bhedā param maraṇā sugatiṃ saggaṃ lokaṃ upapajjanti. citta-sampadā-hetu vā bhikkhave sattā kāyassa-bhedā param maraṇā sugatiṃ saggaṃ lokaṃ upapajjanti. diṭṭhi-sampadā-hetu vā bhikkhave sattā kāyassa bhedā param maraṇā sugatiṃ saggaṃ lokaṃ upapajjantī ti*, A I 270.

5 *sīla-vipatti-hetu vā bhikkhave sattā kāyassa bhedā param maraṇā apāyaṃ duggatiṃ vinipātaṃ nirayaṃ upapajjanti. citta-vipatti-hetu vā bhikkhave sattā kāyassa bhedā paraṃ maraṇā apāyaṃ duggatiṃ vinipātaṃ nirayaṃ upapajjanti. diṭṭhi-vipatti-hetu vā bhikkhave sattā kāyassa bhedā param maraṇā apāyaṃ duggatiṃ vinipātaṃ nirayaṃ upapajjanti*, A I 269. Similar themes are found in the next *sutta* at A I 270.

6 *kammanta-sampadā, ājīva-sampadā, diṭṭhi-sampadā*, A I 270.

7 *kammanta-vipatti, ājīva-vipatti, diṭṭhi-vipatti*, A I 269. The content of these are similar to those already stated. For right-livelihood, it is simply said that the person gets livelihood in a right way, with the opposite for wrong livelihood.

8 *ye keci bhikkhave mayi niṭṭhaṃ gatā, sabbe te diṭṭhi-sampannā*, A V 119.

9 *diṭṭhi-sampanno puggalo yo idaṃ dukkhan ti yathābhūtam pajānāti, la–pe–ayam dukkha-nirodha-gāminī paṭipadā ti pajānāti*, S V 442.

10 *aṭṭhānaṃ etaṃ anavakāso yaṃ diṭṭhi-sampanno puggalo kiñci saṃkhāraṃ niccato upagaccheyya* [...] *kiñci saṃkhāraṃ sukhato upagaccheyya* [...] *kiñci dhammaṃ attato sukhato upagaccheyya, n' etaṃ ṭhānaṃ vijjatī ti pajānāti*, M III 64.

11 Clearly, a variation of the 'perversions' (*vipallāsā*) are being referred to; see Chapter 2 for details of these.

12 *aṭṭhānaṃ etaṃ anavakāso yaṃ diṭṭhi-sampanno puggalo mātaraṃ jīvitā voropeyya* [...] *pitaraṃ jīvitā voropeyya* [...] *arahantaṃ jīvitā voropeyya* [...] *duṭṭhacitto tathāgatassa lohitaṃ uppādeyya* [...] *saṅghaṃ bhindeyya* [...] *aññaṃ satthāraṃ uddiseyya*, M III 64–5. These statements also occur at A I 26–7.

13 I am using the commentary to gloss the unusual phrase: *anāgamanīyaṃ vatthuṃ paccāgantuṃ*.

14 *evam eva kho bhikkhave, ariyasāvakassa diṭṭhisampannassa puggalassa abhisametāvino etad eva bahutaraṃ dukkhaṃ yadidaṃ parikkhīṇaṃ pariyādinnaṃ, appamattakaṃ avasiṭṭhaṃ*, S II 133. A further ten analogies of a similar nature are found at S V 457–65.

15 *yo paṭiccasamuppādaṃ passati, so dhammaṃ passati. yo dhammaṃ passati, so paṭiccasamuppādaṃ passati*, M I 190–1. As Sue Hamilton suggests, this passage goes on to explain dependent-origination as the *khandhas* (Hamilton, *Early Buddhism*, p. 92). The link between a correct understanding of dependent-origination and the arising of *sammā-diṭṭhi*, and adherence to and misinterpretation of the *khandhas* and the arising of *micchā-diṭṭhi* will become clear in this chapter.

16 *hetu c' assa sudiṭṭho, hetu-samuppannā ca dhammā*, A III 441.

17 All views are destroyed. A III 439 gives the following:

> The one who is accomplished in view (*diṭṭhi-sampanna*) cannot fall back on the view that pain and suffering are caused by oneself, another, both oneself and another, by chance, or both self and another (*abhabbo diṭṭhisampanno puggalo sayaṃkataṃ sukhadukkhaṃ paccāgantuṃ. abhabbo diṭṭhisampanno puggalo paraṃkataṃ sukhadukkhaṃ paccāgantuṃ. abhabbo diṭṭhisampanno puggalo sayaṃkatañ ca paraṃkatañ ca sukhadukkhaṃ paccāgantuṃ. abhabbo diṭṭhisampanno puggalo asayaṃkāraṃ adhiccasamuppannaṃ sukhadukkhaṃ paccāgantuṃ*).

18 ***diṭṭhi-sampannan*** *ti dassana-sampannaṃ, sotāpannan ti attho*, Mp III 387. When I cite from the commentaries the phrase taken from the original text will be put in bold.

19 Vibh-a 423.

20 *yato kho bhikkhave ariyasāvako evaṃ paccayaṃ pajānāti, evaṃ paccaya-samudayaṃ pajānāti, evaṃ paccayanirodhaṃ pajānāti, evaṃ paccayanirodhagāminiṃ paṭipadaṃ pajānāti, ayaṃ vuccati bhikkhave, ariyasāvako diṭṭhisampanno iti pi, dassanasampanno iti pi, āgato imaṃ saddhammaṃ iti pi, passati imaṃ saddhammaṃ iti pi, sekhena ñāṇena samannāgato iti pi, sekhayā vijjāya samannāgato iti pi,*

dhammasotaṃ samāpanno iti pi, ariyo nibbedhikapañño iti pi, amatadvāraṃ āhacca tiṭṭhati iti pī ti, S II 43.

21 ***evaṃ paccayaṃ pajānātī*** *ti, evaṃ dukkha-sacca-vasena paccayaṃ janāti,* ***paccaya-samudayādayo*** *ca samudaya-saccādīnaṃ yeva vasena veditabbā*, Spk III 59.

22 ***diṭṭhi-sampanno*** *ti, magge diṭṭhiyā sampanno*, Spk III 59.

23 However, in the *Sammādiṭṭhi-sutta* seeing *avijjā*, its arising, cessation and the way to its cessation did constitute *sammā-diṭṭhi*; see Chapter 2.

24 For example:

> *evaṃ saṃkhāre pajānāti, evaṃ saṃkhārasamudayaṃ pajānāti, evaṃ saṃkhāra-nirodhaṃ pajānāti, evaṃ saṃkhāra-nirodha-gāminiṃ paṭipadaṃ pajānāti, ayaṃ vuccati bhikkhave, bhikkhu diṭṭhi-sampanno iti pi, dassana-sampanno iti pi, āgato imaṃ saddhammaṃ iti pi, passati imaṃ saddhammaṃ iti pi, sekhena ñāṇena samannāgato iti pi, sekhāya vijjāya samannāgato iti pi, dhammasotaṃ samāpanno iti pi, ariyo nibbedhikapañño iti pi, amatadvāraṃ āhacca tiṭṭhati iti pī ti*, S II 44–5.

25 ***dhamme ñāṇan*** *ti, magga-ñāṇassa*, Spk III 69. *cattu-sacca-dhammena vā magga-ñāṇa-dhammena vā*, Spk III 69.

26 *yato kho bhikkhave ariyasāvakassa imāni dve ñāṇāni parisuddhāni honti pariyodātāni dhamme ñāṇañ ca anvaye ñāṇañ ca, ayaṃ vuccati bhikkhave ariyasāvako diṭṭhi-sampanno iti pi, dassana-sampanno iti pi, āgato imaṃ saddhammaṃ iti pi, passati imaṃ saddhammaṃ iti pi, sekhena ñāṇena samannāgato iti pi, sekhāya vijjāya samannāgato iti pi, dhammasotaṃ samāpanno iti pi, ariyo nibbedhikapañño iti pi, amatadvāraṃ āhacca tiṭṭhati iti pī ti*, S II 58–9.

27 See Jayatilleke, *Early Buddhist Theory of Knowledge*, p. 442.

28 See Hamilton's discussion on 'The World of Experience', in *Early Buddhism*, pp. 88–113.

29 *yato kho bhikkhave, ariyasāvako evaṃ lokassa samudayaṃ ca atthaṅgamaṃ ca yathābhūtaṃ pajānāti. ayaṃ vuccati bhikkhave, ariya-sāvako diṭṭhi-sampanno iti pi, dassana-sampanno iti pi, āgato imaṃ saddhammaṃ iti pi, passati imaṃ saddhammaṃ iti pi, sekhena ñāṇena samannāgato iti pi, sekhāya vijjāya samannāgato iti pi, dhammasotaṃ samāpanno iti pi, ariyo nibbedhikapañño iti pi, amatadvāraṃ āhacca tiṭṭhati iti pī ti*, S II 79.

The *Dutiya-ariyasāvaka-sutta* (SII 79–80) is the same as the preceding *sutta*, though some editions have slightly more detail; see Bhikkhu Bodhi, *Connected Discourses of the Buddha*, Volume 1, p. 586.

30 *yaṃ kiñci samudayadhammaṃ sabbaṃ taṃ nirodhadhamman ti*, M I 380.

31 *sīla-visuddhi ca diṭṭhi-visuddhi ca*, D III 214, A I 95.

32 *diṭṭhi-visuddhi kho pana yathā diṭṭhissa ca padhānaṃ*, D III 214, A I 95.

33 *nava dhammā bhāvetabbā*, D III 288.

34 *nava pārisuddhi-padhāniyaṅgāni*, D III 288.

35 *sīla-visuddhi pārisuddhipadhāniyaṅgaṃ citta-visuddhi pārisuddhipadhāniyaṅgaṃ, diṭṭhi-visuddhi pārisuddhipadhāniyaṅgaṃ, kaṅkhāvitaraṇa-visuddhi* [...] *maggāmagga ñāṇa-dassana-visuddhi* [...] *paṭipadā-ñāṇa-dassana-visuddhi* [...] *ñāṇa-dassana-visuddhi* [...] *paññā-visuddhi* [...] *vimutti-visuddhi, pārisuddhipadhāniyaṅgaṃ*, D III 288.

36 *dassanaṭṭhena diṭṭhi-visuddhi abhiññeyyā*, Paṭis I 21–2.

37 'The phrase "now purification of view" is equivalent to that wisdom, understanding [...] right-view' (*diṭṭhi-visuddhi kho panā ti: yā paññā pajānanā–pe–amoho dhammavicayo sammā-diṭṭhi*, Dhs 233, § 1366).

38 This is following the reading of Buddhaghosa found at As 406. See Dhs translation (Caroline Rhys Davids, *A Buddhist Manual of Psychological Ethics* (PTS, London, 1900), pp. 356–7, note 3). In my discussion of the *Sammādiṭṭhi-sutta* in Chapter 2 I

considered a commentarial explanation of 'mundane right-view', part of which described it as knowledge that *kamma* is one's own (*kammassakata-ñāṇa*), this knowledge being in conformity with the (four) truths (*saccānulomika-ñāṇa*, Ps I 197). This is clearly part of the explanation of *diṭṭhi-visuddhi*.

39 *tattha nāmarūpānaṃ yāthāva-dassanaṃ diṭṭhi-visuddhi nāma*, Vism XVIII 1.

40 *satta-saññaṃ abhibhavitvā asammohabhūmiyaṃ ṭhitaṃ*, Vism XVIII 28.

41 *taṃ dassanaṃ diṭṭhi-visuddhi-hetu hoti*, Vism XIII 74.

42 *nava-satta-pātubhāva-diṭṭhi*, Vism XIII 74.

43 'And so, with his mind concentrated, purified and cleansed, unblemished, free from impurities, malleable, workable, established and having gained imperturbability, he applies and directs his mind to the knowledge of the passing away and arising of beings. With the divine eye, purified and surpassing that of humans, he sees beings passing away and arising' (*so evaṃ samāhite citte parisuddhe pariyodāte anaṅgaṇe vigatūpakkilese mudubhūte kammaniye ṭhite āneñjappatte sattānaṃ cutūpapātañāṇāya cittaṃ abhinīharati abhininnāmeti. so dibbena cakkhunā visuddhena atikkantamānusakena satte passati cavamāne upapajjamāne*, D I 82).

44 'But what is called abandoning by substitution of opposites is the abandoning of any given *dhamma* that ought to be abandoned through the means of a particular factor of knowledge, which as a constituent of insight, is opposed to it, like the abandoning of darkness at night through the means of a light' (*yaṃ pana rattibhāge samujjalitena padīpena andhakārassa viya tena tena vipassanāya avayava-bhūtena ñāṇaṅgena paṭipakkhavasen' eva tassa tassa pahātabba-dhammassa pahānaṃ, idaṃ tadaṅgappahānaṃ nāma*, Vism XXII 112; see also Dhs-a 351).

45 (1) *nāmarūpa-paricchedena tāva sakkāyadiṭṭhiyā paccayapariggahena ahetuvisama-hetudiṭṭhiyā ceva kaṅkhāmalassa ca*; (2) *kalāpasammasanena ahaṃ mamā ti samūhagāhassa*; (3) *maggāmaggavavatthānena amagge maggasaññāya*; (4) *udaya-dassanena ucchedadiṭṭhiyā*; (5) *vayadassanena sassatadiṭṭhiyā*; (6) *bhayatupaṭṭhānena sabhaye abhayasaññāya*; (7) *ādīnavadassanena assādasaññāya*; (8) *nibbidānupassanena abhiratisaññāya*; (9) *muñcitukamyatāya amuñcitu-kāmabhāvassa*; (10) *paṭisaṅkhānena appaṭisaṅkhānassa*; (11) *upekkhāya anupekkhanassa*; (12) *anulomena saccapaṭilomagāhassa pahānaṃ*, Vism XXII 112.

See Ñāṇārāma who adds four more insights: knowledge of change of lineage; knowledge of the path; knowledge of the fruit and knowledge of reviewing; Mahāthera Ñāṇārāma, *The Seven Stages of Purification and The Insight Knowledges* (Kandy, 1983), p. 20.

46 (1) *aniccānupassanāya niccasaññāya*; (2) *dukkhānupassanāya sukhasaññāya*; (3) *anattānupassanāya attasaññāya*; (4) *nibbidānupassanāya nandiyā*; (5) *virāgānupassanāya rāgassa*; (6) *nirodhānupassanāya samudayassa*; (7) *paṭinissaggānupassanāya ādānassa*; (8) *hayānupassanāya ghanasaññāya*; (9) *vayānupassanāya āyūhanassa*; (10) *vipariṇāmānu-passanāya dhuvasaññāya;* (11) *animittānupassanāya nimittassa*; (12) *appaṇihitānupassanāya paṇidhiyā*; (13) *suññatānupassanāya abinivesassa*; (14) *adipaññā-dhammavipassanāya sārādānābhinivesassa*; (15) *yathābhūtañāṇadassanena sammohābhinivesassa*; (16) *ādīnavānupassanāya ālayābhinivesassa*; (17) *paṭisaṅkhānupassanāya appaṭisaṅkhāya*; (18) *vivaṭṭānupassanāya saṃyogābhinivesassa pahānaṃ*, Vism XXII 113.

47 The other two are found in (11) and (12). First, 'the signless gateway to liberation' (*animittaṃ vimokkhamukhaṃ*) is found in the statement that there is 'the abandoning of sign, through the contemplation of the signless'. Second, 'the dispositionless gateway to liberation' (*appaṇihitaṃ vimokkhamukhaṃ*) is found in the statement that there is 'the abandoning of desire through the means of contemplation of the desireless'. I will discuss these three gateways in Chapter 5.

48 *arakkhitena cittena micchā-diṭṭhi-hatena ca, thīnamiddhābhibhūtena vasaṃ mārassa gacchati*, Nett 85. The full passage, the *udāna* spoken by the Buddha is the following:

With an unguarded cognisance,
Encumbered by wrong-view, oppressed
By lethargy and drowsiness,
One travels on in Māra's power.

Ud 38. I have given the translation from Ñāṇamoli, *The Guide* (PTS, London, 1962), p. 119.

49 *miccha-diṭṭhi-hatena cā ti micchā-diṭṭhi-hataṃ nāma pavuccati yadā anicce niccan ti passati, so vipallāso*, Nett 85.

50 *sammā-diṭṭhi-purekkhāro ñatvāna udayabbayaṃ*, cited Nett 47. The full passage, following on from that given above:

So let his cognisance be guarded,
Having for pasture right-intention,
Giving right-view first place through knowing
Rise and fall; transcending drowsing
And lethargy, the *bhikkhu* may
Abandon all bad destinations.

Ud 38. Again the translation is from Ñāṇamoli, *The Guide*, p. 72.

51 *sammā-diṭṭhi-purekkhāro ti vipassanāya padaṭṭhānaṃ*, Nett 104.

52 *ñatvāna udayabbayan ti dassana-bhūmiyā padaṭṭhānaṃ*, Nett 104.

53 Ñāṇamoli, *The Guide*, p. 140.

54 *sammā-diṭṭhi-purekkhāro ti vipassani, ñatvāna udayabbaya 'nti dukkhapariññā*, Nett 105.

55 *sammā-diṭṭhi-purekkhāro ti sammā-diṭṭhi nāma paññā-satthaṃ paññā-khaggo paññā-ratataṃ paññā-pajjoto paññā-patodo paññāpāsādo*, Nett 106.

56 *sammā-diṭṭhi-purekkhāro ti ekattatā; sammā-diṭṭhi nāma yaṃ dukkhe ñāṇaṃ dukkha-samudaye ñāṇaṃ dukkha-nirodhe ñāṇaṃ dukkha-nirodha-gāminiyā paṭipadāya ñāṇaṃ magge ñāṇaṃ hetusmiṃ ñāṇaṃ hetu-samuppannesu dhammesu ñāṇaṃ paccaye ñāṇaṃ paṭicca-samuppannesu dhammesu ñāṇaṃ*, Nett 108.

57 *ñatvāna udayabbayan ti ekattatā: udayena avījjā-paccayā saṃkhārā, saṃkhāra-paccayā viññāṇaṃ; (evaṃ sabbaṃ) samudayo bhavati, vayena avijjā-nirodhā saṃkhāra-nirodho saṃkhāra-nirodhā viññāṇa-nirodho (evaṃ sabbaṃ) nirodho hoti*, Nett 108.

58 For a discussion of this *sutta* see, Gombrich, *How Buddhism Began*, pp. 127–34.

59 *aññatreva āvuso musīla, saddhāya aññatra ruciyā aññatra anussavā aññatra ākāraparivitakkā aññatra diṭṭhi-nijjhānakkhantiyā atthāyasmato mūsilassa paccattam eva ñāṇaṃ jātipaccayā jarāmaraṇan ti*, S II 115. These are the same five means of knowledge I considered in both the *Pañcattaya-sutta* and *Cankī-sutta* in Chapter 1.

60 *aham etaṃ jānāmi aham etaṃ passāmi jātipaccayā jarāmaraṇan ti*, S II 115.

61 *upādāna-nirodhā bhava-nirodho ti, taṇhā-nirodhā upādāna-nirodho ti, vedanā-nirodhā taṇhā-nirodho ti, phassā-nirodhā vedanā-nirodho ti, saḷāyatana-nirodhā phassa-nirodho ti, nāma-rūpa-nirodhā saḷāyatana-nirodho ti, viññāṇa-nirodhā nāma-rūpa-nirodho ti, saṃkhāra-nirodhā viññāṇa-nirodho ti, avijjā-nirodhā saṃkhāra-nirodho ti*, S II 116.

62 *aññatreva āvuso musīla, saddhāya aññatra ruciyā aññatra anussavā aññatra ākāraparivitakkā aññatra diṭṭhi-nijjhānakkhantiyā, atthāyasmato musīlassa paccattam eva ñāṇaṃ bhava-nirodho nibbāṇan ti*, S II 117.

63 *ahametaṃ jānāmi, ahametaṃ passāmi, bhavanirodho nibbāṇanti*, S II 117.

64 *bhavanirodho nibbānan ti pañcakkhandanirodho nibbānam*, Spk III 122.

65 *tena h' āyasmā musīlo arahaṃ khīṇāsavo ti*, S II 117.

66 Spk III 122.

67 *tena h' āyasmā nārado arahaṃ khīṇāsavo ti*, S II 117.

68 *bhava-nirodho nibbāṇan ti kho me āvuso, yathābhūtaṃ sammā-paññāya* [see Gombrich, *How Buddhism Began*, p. 128, note 23, correcting PTS *samma-paññāya*] *sudiṭṭham, na c' amhi arahaṃ khīṇāsavo*, S II 118.
69 *udakan ti kho ñāṇam assa na ca kāyena phusitvā vihareyya*, S II 118.
70 *pañcasu upādānakkhandhesu na kiñci attānaṃ vā attaniyaṃ vā samanupassāmī ti*, S III 128.
71 *pañcasu upādānakkhandhesu asmī ti adhigataṃ* (or *avigataṃ*; see Bhikkhu Bodhi, *Connected Discourses*, Volume I, pp. 1082–3, note 176).
72 *ayam aham asmī ti ca na samanupassāmī ti*, S III 128.
73 *asmi ti māno asmi ti chando asmi ti anusayo*, S III 130.
74 *pañcasu upādānakkhandhesu udayabbayānupassī viharati*, S III 131.
75 *tassa imesu pañcasu upādānakkhandhesu udayabbayānupassino viharato yo 'pi 'ssa hoti pañcasupādānakkhandhesu anusahagato asmī ti māno asmī ti chando asmi ti anusayo asamūhato, so 'pi samugghātaṃ gacchati*, S III 131; see Collins, *Selfless Persons*, pp. 94–5.
76 *paññā* [...] *ariyā niyyānikā niyyāti takkarassa sammā-dukkhakkhayāya*, M I 81.
77 *nekkhammavitakko, abyāpādavitakko, avihiṃsāvitakko*, M III 114.
78 *vitakkā ariyā niyyānikā niyyanti takkarassa sammā-dukkhakkhayāya*, M III 114.
79 *sattime* [...] *bojjhaṅgā bhāvitā bahulīkatā ariyā niyyānikā niyanti takkarassa sammā dukkhakkhayāya*, S V 82.
80 *cattāro me* [...] *satipaṭṭhānā bhāvitā bahulīkatā ariyā niyyānikā niyyanti takkarassa sammā-dukkhakkhayāya*, S V 166. *cattāro me* [...] *iddhipādā bhāvitā bahulīkatā ariyā niyyānikā niyyanti takkarassa sammā-dukkhakkhayāya*, S V 255.
81 *kusalā dhammā ariyā niyyānikā sambodha-gāmino*, Sn, p. 140. This is the page reference, as it is the introductory prose to verse 724.
82 Not to be confused with the *Kosambī-sutta*, which I considered above.
83 *chayime bhikkhave dhammā sārāṇīyā piyakaraṇā garukaraṇā saṅgahāya avivādāya sāmāggiyā ekībhāvāya saṃvattanti*, M I 322. They are described in the same terms in the *Sāmagāma-sutta* (M II 243–51) at M II 251–2. The six are also found in the *Mahāparinibbāna-sutta* (D II 72–168) at D II 80–1, called 'six things conducive to communal living' (*cha aparihāniyā* or *sārāṇīya dhammā*,). They are also found in the *Saṅgīti-sutta* (D III 207–71) at D III 245.
84 *mettaṃ kāya-kammaṃ, mettaṃ vacī-kammaṃ, mettaṃ mano-kammaṃ*, M I 322.
85 *puna ca paraṃ bhikkhave bhikkhu yā ''yaṃ diṭṭhi ariyā niyyānikā niyyāti takkarassa sammā-dukkhakkhayāya, tathārūpāya diṭṭhiyā diṭṭhi-sāmaññagato viharati sabrahmacārīhi āvī c' eva raho ca*, M I 322.
86 *yathābhūtaṃ na jāneyyaṃ na passeyyan ti*, M I 323.
87 *sace bhikkhave bhikkhu kāmarāga pariyuṭṭhito hoti, pariyuṭṭhitacitto va hoti. sace bhikkhave bhikkhu byāpādapariyuṭṭhito hoti, pariyuṭṭhitacitto va hoti. sace bhikkhave bhikkhu thīnamiddhapariyuṭṭhito hoti, pariyuṭṭhitacitto va hoti. sace bhikkhave bhikkhu uddhaccakukkuccapariyuṭṭhito hoti, pariyuṭṭhitacitto va hoti. sace bhikkhave bhikkhu vicikicchāpariyuṭṭhito hoti, pariyuṭṭhitacitto va hoti. sace bhikkhave bhikkhu idhalokacintāya pasuto hoti, pariyuṭṭhitacitto va hoti. sace bhikkhave bhikkhu paralokacintāya pasuto hoti, pariyuṭṭhitacitto va hoti. sace bhikkhave bhikkhu bhaṇḍanajāto kalahajāto vivādāpanno aññamaññaṃ mukhasattīhi vitudanto viharati, pariyuṭṭhitacitto va hoti. so evaṃ pajānāti: n' atthi kho me taṃ pariyuṭṭhānaṃ ajjhattaṃ appahīnaṃ yenāhaṃ pariyuṭṭhānena pariyuṭṭhitacitto yathābhūtaṃ na jāneyyaṃ na passeyyaṃ. suppaṇihitaṃ me mānasaṃ saccānaṃ bodhāyā ti*, M I 323.
88 *so evaṃ pajānāti:imaṃ kho ahaṃ diṭṭhiṃ āsevanto bhāvento bahulīkaronto labhāmi paccattaṃ samathaṃ, labhāmi paccattaṃ nibbutin ti*, M I 323.
89 *so evaṃ pajānāti: yathārūpāyāhaṃ diṭṭhiyā samannāgato, n' atthi ito bahiddhā añño samaṇo vā brāhmaṇo vā tathārūpāya diṭṭhiyā samannāgato ti*, M I 323–4.

90 *so evaṃ pajānāti: yathārūpāya dhammatāya diṭṭhi-sampanno puggalo samannāgato, aham pi tathārūpāya dhammatāya samannāgato ti*, M I 324. One is reminded of Ariṭṭha, discussed in Chapter 1.
91 *adhisīlasikkhāya adhicittasikkhāya adhipaññāsikkhāya*, M I 324.
92 *so evaṃ pajānāti: yathārūpāya balatāya diṭṭhi-sampanno puggalo samannāgato, aham pi tathārūpāya balatāya samannāgato ti*, M I 325.
93 *labhati dhammavedaṃ, labhati dhammūpasaṃhitaṃ pāmujjaṃ. so evaṃ pajānāti: yathārūpāya balatāya diṭṭhisampanno puggalo samannāgato, aham pi tathārūpāya balatāya samannāgato ti*, M I 325.
94 *evaṃ sattaṅgasamannāgato kho bhikkhave ariyasāvako sotāpattiphalasamannāgato hotī ti*, M I 325.
95 *imesu catūsu maggesu paṭhamamaggena cattāri saccāni diṭṭhāni uparimaggattayaṃ diṭṭhakam eva passati adiṭṭhakaṃ passatī ti diṭṭhakam eva pasatī ti*, As 241.
96 *sacca-dassanaṃ nāma apubbaṃ nattho, kilesa pana appahīne pajahati*, As 241.
97 *uparimaggattayavajjho hi eko māno atthi*, As 240, see Padmanabh S. Jaini, 'Prajñā and dṛṣṭi in the Vaibhāṣika Abhidharma', in *Prajñāpāramitā and Related Systems: Studies in Honour of Edward Conze*, Lewis Lancaster (ed.) (Berkeley, 1977), p. 409.
98 *so diṭṭhiṭṭhāne tiṭṭhati*, As 240.
99 *sā taṃ mānaṃ pajahatī ti sammā-diṭṭhi*, As 240.
100 Those defilements based upon cognitive attachment are perhaps implied, such as 'clinging to precepts and vows' (*sīlabbata-parāmāsa*).
101 Jaini, 'Prajñā and dṛṣṭi in the Vaibhāṣika Abhidharma', pp. 403–15 (p. 407); Gethin, 'Wrong View (micchā-diṭṭhi) and Right View (sammā-diṭṭhi) in the Therāvada Abhidhamma', p. 213.
102 Jaini, ibid., p. 407, Gethin, ibid., p. 213.
103 Jaini, ibid., p. 409.
104 Ibid., p. 404, 409.
105 Ibid., p. 407.
106 As Rupert Gethin suggests:

> It seems [...] that to at least some extent what the Vaibhāṣikas in their analysis of *diṭṭhi* see as a kind of 'judging' or 'determining' (*santīraṇa*) the Theravādins see as *lobha*. The difference is, however, that for the Vaibhāṣikas a subtle form of fixity of view continues after stream-attainment in the form of *samyakdṛṣṭi*, while the Theravādins apparently make no provision for its continuation since the greed-delusion that crystallises as *diṭṭhi* is abandoned by the path of stream-attainment.

Gethin, 'Wrong View (micchā-diṭṭhi) and Right View (sammā-diṭṭhi) in the Therāvada Abhidhamma', p. 221.
107 Jaini, 'Prajñā and dṛṣṭi in the Vaibhāṣika Abhidharma', p. 407.
108 Ibid., p. 407, Jaini's emphasis.
109 Ibid., p. 407.
110 Ibid., p. 407, Jaini's emphasis.
111 As I have shown in the previous chapter, it is doubt about the nature of the *khandhas* (taking them for what they are not) that is considered one of the major causes of view.
112 Four rooted in greed and delusion, which may or may not be connected with *māna*, but are not connected with *diṭṭhi*. Two are rooted in aversion and delusion, and the seventh connected with restlessness; Gethin, 'Wrong View (micchā-diṭṭhi) and Right View (sammā-diṭṭhi) in the Theravāda Abhidhamma', p. 216, As 234, 245.
113 *cattāro diṭṭhi-gata-sampayutta-cittuppādā vicikicchā-sahagato cittuppādo, ime dhammā dassanene pahātabbā*, Dhs 237 § 1404; see Gethin, *The Buddhist Path to Awakening*, p. 186–7.

114 See Gethin, *The Buddhist Path to Awakening*, p. 206.

115 i.e. M I 141–2; see Gethin, 'Wrong View (micchā-diṭṭhi) and Right View (sammā-diṭṭhi) in the Theravāda Abhidhamma', p. 227. The ten fetters are: identity-view (*sakkāyadiṭṭhi*), doubt (*vicikicchā*), clinging to precepts and vows (*sīlabbataparāmāso*), sensual desires (*kāmacchando*), aversion (*byāpāda*), desire for form (*rūparāgo*), desire for the formless (*arūparāgo*), pride (*māno*), agitation (*uddhaccaṃ*), ignorance (*avijjā*), A V 16–17, S V 61, D III 235. This is different to the list of fetters found in the *Dhammasaṅgaṇi* that I will give in Chapter 5. The explanation of the abandonment of the fetters may have undergone a transitional process. For example, a passage was cited above in which it was stated that six things are abandoned when one is accomplished in view (*diṭṭhi-sampanna*). The passage held these to be identity-view, doubt, clinging to precept and vows, greed (*rāga*), hatred (*dosa*) and delusion (*moha*), A III 438.

116 See Gethin, 'Wrong View (micchā-diṭṭhi) and Right View (sammā-diṭṭhi) in the Theravāda Abhidhamma', pp. 216–17. Gethin gives the following references to the Dhs: 60 § 277; 74–5 §§ 362, 333, 364. Buddhaghosa also considers the abandonment of the *āsavas*. The *āsava* of view is abandoned by the path of stream-attainment, the *āsava* of sensuality by the path of non-returning, and the *āsavas* of becoming and ignorance by the path of Arahantship (*sotāpatti-maggena, diṭṭhāsavo pahīyati, anāgāmi-maggena kāmāsavo, arahatta-maggena bhavāsavo, avijjāsavo cā ti*, As 372).

117 *katame dhammā dassanena pahātabbā? tīṇī saññojanāni: sakkāya-diṭṭhi vicikicchā sīlabbata-parāmāso*, Dhs 182 § 1002.

118 *katame dhammā dassanena pahātabbahetukā? tīṇi saṃyojanāni sakkāya-diṭṭhi vicikicchā sīlabbata-parāmāso*, Dhs 184 § 1009.

119 I will discuss the use of four *khandhas*, excluding *rūpa*, in Chapter 5.

120 *katame dhammā bhāvanāya pahātabbā. avaseso lobho doso moho, tad ekaṭṭhā ca kilesā, taṃ sampayutto vedanākkhandho–pe–viññāṇakkhandho, taṃ samuṭṭhānaṃ kāya-kammaṃ vacī-kammaṃ mano-kammaṃ, ime dhammā bhāvanāya pahātabbā*, Dhs 183 § 1007.

121 *katame dhammā neva dassanena na bhāvanāya pahātabbā?*

122 *kusalā vyakatā dhammā kāmāvacarā rūpāvacarā arūpāvacarā apariyāpannā, vedanākkhandho–pe–viññāṇakkhandho, sabbaṃ ca rūpaṃ, asaṅkhatā ca dhātu, ime dhammā neva dassanena na bhāvanāya pahātabbā*, Dhs 183 § 1008; The idea of *apariyāpannā* will be considered in Chapter 5.

123 Jaini, 'Prajñā and dṛṣṭi in the Vaibhāṣika Abhidharma', p. 407; Gethin, 'Wrong View (micchā-diṭṭhi) and Right View (sammā-diṭṭhi) in the Theravāda Abhidhamma', p. 213, 215.

124 I am thinking here of the right-view of the path. The propositional distinction between wrong and right-view appears to be more pronounced before stream-attainment; Gethin, 'Wrong View (micchā-diṭṭhi) and Right View (sammā-diṭṭhi) in the Theravāda Abhidhamma', pp. 212–13.

125 'Essentially the same thing may be experienced more fully and deeply'; Gethin, 'Wrong View (micchā-diṭṭhi) and Right View (sammā-diṭṭhi) in the Theravāda Abhidhamma', p. 216.

126 Ibid., p. 221.

127 Ibid., p. 222.

128 *tesaṃ nirodhamhi na h' atthi ñāṇaṃ*. The statement from the *Kosambi-sutta* (S II 115–18) should be remembered: 'to know and see *nibbāna* is the cessation of existence' (*aham etaṃ jānāmi, aham etaṃ passāmi, bhavanirodho nibbāṇan ti*). This constitutes *sammā-diṭṭhi*.

129 *nibbidāya virāgāya nirodhāya paṭipanno hoti*, Ps I 159.

5 The transcendence of views

1 Bhikkhu Bodhi, 'The Buddha's survey of views' in *Recent Researches in Buddhist Studies: Essays in Honour of Professor Y. Karunadasa*, Kuala Lumpar Dhammajoti, Asanga Tilakaratne and Kapila Abhayawansa (eds) (Colombo, 1997), pp. 51–69 (p. 51).

2 Sv I 102; see Bodhi, *The All-Embracing Net of Views*, pp. 124–6.

3 A. Syrkin, 'On the first work of the Sutta Piṭaka: The Brahmajāla-Sutta' in *Buddhist Studies Ancient and Modern*, P. Denwood and A. Piatigorsky (eds), pp. 153–66; Hayes, *Dignaga on the Interpretation of Signs*, pp. 45–8; Collins, *Selfless Persons*, pp. 128–9; Bodhi, 'The Buddha's survey of views'; Bodhi, *The All-Embracing Net of Views.*

4 Pande, *Origins of Buddhism*, p. 352.

5 Hayes, *Dignaga on the Interpretation of Signs*, pp. 45–8; Collins, *Selfless Persons*, pp. 128–9.

6 Collins, *Selfless Persons*, p. 128.

7 Cf. Nāgārjuna's famous statement that 'emptiness is a remedy for all views, but those who take emptiness to be a view are incurable' (*Mūlamadhyamakakārikā* XIII 8); see David Burton, *Emptiness Appraised* (Richmond, 1999), p. 37.

8 *appamattakaṃ kho pan' etaṃ bhikkhave oramattakaṃ sīlamattakaṃ, yena puthujjano tathāgatassa vaṇṇaṃ vadamāno vadeyya*, D I 3.

9 *atthi bhikkhave aññeva dhammā gambhīrā duddasā duranubodhā santā paṇītā atakkāvacarā nipuṇā paṇḍitavedanīyā, ye tathāgato sayaṃ abhiññā sacchikatvā pavedeti*, D I 12.

10 *yehi tathāgatassa yathābhuccaṃ vaṇṇaṃ sammā vadamānā vadeyyuṃ*, D I 12.

11 Cf. the 'eight bases' in the *Paṭisambhidhāmagga* which I discussed in Chapter 3.

12 *ime kho diṭṭhi-ṭṭhānā evaṃgahitā evaṃparāmaṭṭhā evaṃgatikā bhavissanti evaṃabhisamparāyā*, D I 16.

13 *uttaritaraṃ*, the highest, what transcends, i.e. *nibbāna*.

14 *aparāmasato c' assa paccattaññeva nibbuti viditā*, D I 16.

15 *vedanānaṃ samudayañ ca atthaṅgamañ ca assādañ ca ādīnavañ ca nissaraṇañ ca yathābhūtaṃ viditvā anupādā vimutto* [...] *tathāgato*. Whole passage: *tayidaṃ bhikkhave tathāgato pajānāti: ime diṭṭhiṭṭhānā evaṃ gahitā evaṃ parāmaṭṭhā evaṃgatikā bhavissanti evaṃ abhisamparāyā ti. tañ ca tathāgato pajānāti, tato ca uttaritaraṃ pajānāti. tañ ca pajānanaṃ na parāmasati. aparāmasato c' assa paccattaññeva nibbuti viditā. vedanānaṃ samudayañ ca atthaṅgamañ ca assādañ ca ādīnavañ ca nissaraṇañ ca yathābhūtaṃ viditvā anupādā vimutto bhikkhave tathāgato*, D I 16–17, 21–2, 24, 28, 29, 30, 31, 33, 36, 38 (x 2), 39.

This occurs 12 times in the *sutta*, once for each group of views, then for the 18 views about the past, and 44 about the future.

16 *ime kho te bhikkhave dhammā gambhīrā duddasā duranubodhā santā paṇītā atakkāvacarā nipuṇā paṇḍita vedanīyā ye tathāgato sayaṃ abhiññā sacchikatvā pavedeti yehi tathāgatassa yathābhuccaṃ vaṇṇaṃ sammā vadamānā vadeyyuṃ*, D I 17, etc.

17 *ajānataṃ apassataṃ vedayitaṃ taṇhā-gatānaṃ paritassitavipphanditam eva*, i.e. D I 39–42. Again this appears 12 times, for example: *tatra bhikkhave ye te samaṇabrāhmaṇā sassata-vādā sassataṃ attānañ ca lokañ ca paññāpenti catūhi vatthūhi, tadapi tesaṃ bhavataṃ samaṇabrāhmaṇānaṃ ajānataṃ apassataṃ vedayitaṃ taṇhā-gatānaṃ paritasitavipphanditameva*, D I 39–40.

18 i.e. *tatra bhikkhave ye te samaṇabrāhmaṇā sassata-vādā sassataṃ attānañ ca lokañ ca paññāpenti catūhi vatthūhi, tadapi phassapaccayā*, D I 41–2.

19 *te vata aññatra phassā paṭisaṃvedissantī ti n' etaṃ ṭhānaṃ vijjati*, D I 43–4.

20 *sabbe te chahi phassāyatanehi phussa phussa paṭisaṃvedenti*, D I 45.

21 *tesaṃ vedanāpaccayā taṇhā, taṇhāpaccayā upādānaṃ, upādānapaccayā bhavo, bhavapaccayā jāti, jātipaccayā jarāmaraṇaṃ sokaparidevadukkhadomanassupāyāsā sambhavanti*, D I 45.

22 *yato kho bhikkhave bhikkhu channaṃ phassāyatanānaṃ samudayañ ca atthaṅgamañ ca assādañ ca ādīnavañ ca nissaraṇañ ca yathābhūtaṃ pajānāti, ayaṃ imehi sabbeh' eva uttaritaraṃ pajānāti*, D I 45.

23 Of course applied to 'contact' and not the 'bases of contact':

> When, friends, a noble disciple understands contact, the origin of contact, the cessation of contact, and the way leading to the cessation of contact, in that way he is one of right-view, whose view is straight, who has perfect confidence in the *dhamma* and who has arrived at this true *dhamma* (*yato kho āvuso ariyasāvako phassañ ca pajānāti phassasamudayañ ca pajānāti phassanirodhañ ca pajānāti phassanirodhagāminiṃ paṭipadañ ca pajānāti, ettāvatā pi kho āvuso ariyasāvako sammā-diṭṭhi hoti, ujugatā 'ssa diṭṭhi, dhamme aveccappasādena samannāgato, āgato imaṃ saddhammaṃ*, M I 52).

24 Collins, *Selfless Persons*, p. 128.

25 Peṭ 86. A famous *sutta* about the inner and outer tangle is found at S I 13: 'A tangle inside, a tangle outside, this generation is entangled in a tangle'. The *Visuddhimagga* opens with a discussion of this verse (Vism I 1–7).

26 *ajjhattavatthuko rāgo antojaṭā, bāhiravatthuko rāgo bahi-jaṭā*, Peṭ 86.

27 *ajjhattavatthukā sakkāya-diṭṭhi, ayaṃ antojaṭā*, Peṭ 86.

28 *ekasaṭṭhi diṭṭhi-gatāni ca bāhiravatthukāni bahi-jaṭā*, Peṭ 86. The notion of '61 views' appears to be unique to the *Peṭakopadesa*.

29 *pañcakkhandhā sakkāya-diṭṭhiyā padaṭṭhānaṃ, ekasaṭṭhi diṭṭhi-gatāni diṭṭhi-rāgassa padaṭṭhānaṃ*, Peṭ 89.

30 M I 300, M III 18, S III 102.

31 e.g. *rūpaṃ na ppajānāti, rūpasamudayaṃ na ppajānāti, rūpanirodhaṃ na ppajānāti, rupanirodhagāminiṃ paṭipadaṃ na ppajānāti*, etc., S III 162, S III 176.

32 e.g. *rūpaṃ pajānāti, rūpasamudayaṃ pajānāti, rūpa-nirodhaṃ pajānāti, rupa-nirodha-gāminiṃ paṭipadaṃ pajānāti*, etc., S III 163, S III 176–7.

33 Stream-attainer: *ariyasāvako imesaṃ pañcannaṃ upādānakkhandhānaṃ samudayañ ca atthaṅgamañ ca assādañ ca ādīnavañ ca nissaraṇañ ca yathābhūtaṃ* ***pajānāti****. ayaṃ vuccati bhikkhave, ariyasāvako sotāpanno*, S III 160–1; see also S III 174. Arahant: *bhikkhu imesaṃ pañcannaṃ upādānakkhandhānaṃ samudayañ ca atthagamañaca assādañ ca ādīnavañ ca nissaraṇañ ca yathābhūtaṃ* ***viditvā*** *anupādā vimutto hoti. ayaṃ vuccati, bhikkhave, bhikkhu arahaṃ*, S III 161. The latter is described as liberated by non-attachment; see also S III 174. There is also the difference in the verb (which I have put in bold). The noble disciple understands, *pajānāti*, and the *bhikkhu* is described as having known, *viditvā*. This may suggest the degree to which the knowledge has been cultivated (though in other contexts the verb *pajānāti* is used to describe the highest knowledge attained by the Buddha). This has some connection with my discussion of Musīla and Nārada in the *Kosambī-sutta*, in Chapter 4.

34 *evam etaṃ yathābhūtaṃ sammappaññāya passato pubbantānudiṭṭhiyo na honti, pubbantānu-diṭṭhīnaṃ asati aparantānudiṭṭhiyo na honti, aparantānu-diṭṭhīnaṃ asati thāmasā parāmāso na hoti*, S III 45–6.

35 *ātura-kāyo c' eva hoti ātura-citto ca*, S III 3.

36 *ahaṃ rūpaṃ mama rūpan ti pariyuṭṭhaṭṭhāyī hoti*, S III 3.

37 *āturakāyo hi kho hoti, no ca āturacitto*, S III 4.

38 *ahaṃ rūpaṃ, mama rūpa'nti na pariyuṭṭhaṭṭhāyī hoti*, S III 4.

39 *kathaṃ ca […] upādā-paritassana hoti,* S III 16; see also M III 227.

40 *tassa taṃ rūpaṃ vipariṇamati aññathā hoti, tassa rūpavipariṇāmaññathābhāvā rūpa-vipariṇāmānuparivatti viññāṇam hoti, tassa rūpavipariṇāmānuparivattijā paritassanā dhammasamuppādā cittam pariyādāya tiṭṭhanti, cetaso pariyādānā uttāsavā ca hoti vighātavā ca apekhavā ca upādāya ca paritassati.* S III 16, M III 227.

After *vipariṇāmānuparivatti*, M III 227 has *viññānaṃ hoti, tassa rūpaṃ vipariṇāmānuparivatti viññānaṃ hoti, tassa.* It then has the same as S III 16 from *rūpavipariṇāmānuparivattajā.*

41 *kathañ cāvuso, anupādā aparitassanā hoti*, S III 16, M III 228.

42 *tassa taṃ rūpaṃ vipariṇamati. aññathā hoti. tassa rūpavipariṇāmaññathābhāvā na ca rūpavipariṇāmānuparivatti viññāṇaṃ hoti. tassa na rūpavipariṇāmānuparivattajā paritassanā dhammasamuppādā cittaṃ pariyādāya tiṭṭhanti. cetaso pariyādānā na c' eva uttāsavā hoti. na ca vighātavā na ca apekkhavā anupādāya ca na paritassati*, S III 17, M III 228.

The same themes are found in the *Majjhima-nikāya*. The *Bhaddekaratta-sutta* (M III 187–9) explains 'how one is caught in regard to presently arisen *dhammas*' (*paccuppannesu dhammesu saṃhīrati*, M III 188). The answer is that one sees according to *sakkāya-diṭṭhi*. The *sutta* then states that in order not to be caught in regard to presently arisen *dhammas* (*paccuppannesu dhammesu na saṃhīrati*, M III 189) one does not regard material form as self, etc.

43 *rūpassa tv eva, bhikkhave, aniccataṃ viditvā vipariṇāmavirāganirodhaṃ pubbe c' eva rūpaṃ etarahi ca sabbaṃ rūpaṃ aniccaṃ dukkhaṃ vipariṇāmadhamman ti evam etaṃ yathābhūtaṃ sammappaññāya passato ye sokaparidevadukkhadomanassupāyāsā te pahīyanti, tesaṃ pahānā na paritassati, aparitassaṃ sukhaṃ viharati. sukhaṃ viharaṃ bhikkhu tadaṅganibbuto ti vuccati*, S III 43.

44 ***tadaṅganibbuto*** *ti tena vipassanaṅgena kilesānaṃ nibbutattā tadaṅganibbuto. imasmiṃ sutte vipassanā va kathitā*, Spk II 268; see Bhikkhu Bodhi, *Connected Discourses*, Volume I, pp. 1055–6, note 56.

45 *sakkāya-samudaya-gāminiñ ca paṭipadaṃ*, S III 43.

46 ***dukkha-samudaya-gāminī samanupassanā*** *ti, yasmā sakkāyo dukkhaṃ tassa ca samudaya-gāminī paṭipadā nāma-rūpaṃ attato samanupassatī ti, evaṃ diṭṭhi-samanupassanā vuttā*, Spk II 269; see Bodhi, *Connected Discourses*, Volume I, p. 1056, note 57.

47 *sakkāya-nirodha-gāminiñ ca paṭipadaṃ* S III 44.

48 *iti ayañ c' eva samanupassanā asmī ti c' assa avigataṃ hoti*, S III 46.

49 *iti ayañ c' eva samanupassanā*, Spk II 269.

50 ***asmī ti c' assa avigataṃ hotī*** *ti, yassa ayaṃ samanupassanā hoti atthi tasmiṃ asmī ti taṇhā-māna-diṭṭhi-sankhātaṃ papañca-ttayaṃ avigataṃ eva hoti*, Spk II 269; see Bodhi, *Connected Discourses*, Volume I, p. 1057, note 61.

51 *asmī ti kho pana bhikkhave avigate, pañcannaṃ indriyānaṃ avakkanti hoti*, S III 46. Hamilton has: *asmī ti kho pana bhikkhave* ***adhigate atha*** *pañcannaṃ*; Hamilton, *Identity and Experience*, p. 39, note 133; see Bodhi, *Connected Discourses* Volume I, pp. 1082–3, note 176, for another occurrence of these variant readings which I referred to in Chapter 3.

52 See Bodhi, *Connected Discourses*, Volume I, p. 1057, note 62. In the *Dutiya-cetanā-sutta* at S II 66 it is stated that 'when consciousness is established there is descent of name and form' (*tasmiṃ patiṭṭhite viññāṇe virūḷhe nāmarūpassa avakkanti hoti*) and so through the series of dependent-origination, and the whole mass of suffering (S II 66). This theme is repeated in the *sutta*s preceding and succeeding the *Dutiya-cetanā-sutta* (the *Cetanā-sutta*, S II 65–6, and the *Tatiyacetanā-sutta*, S II 66–7). The three *suttas* have the theme of knowing the arising of a new existence through the establishing of consciousness, and with it the process of dependent-origination, and the removing of the basis for the maintenance of consciousness, and stopping the

arising of the process of dependent-origination and the whole mass of suffering. See Collins' discussion of *avakkanti* in *Selfless Persons*, pp. 208–13.

53 Hamilton, *Identity and Experience*, p. 85; see also Collins, *Selfless Persons*, pp. 208–13.

54 Hamilton, *Identity and Experience*, p. 27; see also p. 39, note 133.

55 See Bodhi, *Connected Discourses*, Volume I, pp. 1057–8, notes 62–3.

56 *atthi* […] *mano atthi dhammā, atthi avijjādhātu*, S III 46.

57 Hamilton, *Identity and Experience*, p. 27. Hamilton notes that only one manuscript of this passage reads *avijjādhātu*, the others *vijjādhātu*. The former makes more sense, though the latter may have some implications for an understanding of this process; see Hamilton, ibid., pp. 39–40 note 134.

58 Ibid., pp. 27–8.

59 *avijjāsamphassajena* […] *vedayitena phuṭṭhassa assutavato puthujjanassa*; see below the *Pārileyyaka-sutta*, S III 94–9, i.e. 'feeling born of contact with ignorance'.

60 *asmī ti pi 'ssa hoti, ayam aham asmī ti pi 'ssa hoti, bhavissan ti pi 'ssa hoti, na bhavissan ti pi 'ssa hoti, rūpī bhavissan ti pi 'ssa hoti, arūpī bhavissan ti pi 'ssa hoti, saññī bhavissan ti pi 'ssa hoti, asaññañī bhavissan ti pi 'ssa hoti, nevasaññīnāsañañī bhavissan ti pi 'ssa hoti*, S III 46.

61 Bodhi, *Connected Discourses*, Volume I, p. 1058, note 63.

62 *ath' ettha sutavato ariyasāvakassa avijjā pahīyati, vijjā uppajjati*, S III 46.

63 *asmī ti pi 'ssa na hoti, ayam aham asmī ti pi 'ssa na hoti, bhavissan ti pi 'ssa na hoti, na bhavissan ti pi 'ssa na hoti, rūpī bhavissan ti p' issa na hoti, arūpī bhavissan ti pi 'ssa na hoti, saññī bhavissan ti pi 'ssa na hoti, asaññī bhavissan ti pi 'ssa na hoti, nevasaññīnāsaññi bhavissan ti pi 'ssa na hotī ti*, S III 47.

64 *kathaṃ nu kho jānato kathaṃ passato anantarā āsavānaṃ khayo hotī ti*, S III 96.

65 *samanupassanā, saṃkhāro so*, S III 96.

66 *so pana saṃkhāro kinnidāno kiṃsamudayo kiñjātiko kimpabhavo ti*, S III 96.

67 *avijjāsamphassajena, bhikkhave, vedayitena phuṭṭhassa assutavato puthujjanassa uppannā taṇhā tatojo so saṃkhāro*, S III 96.

68 *so pi kho saṃkhāro anicco saṃkhato paṭiccasamuppanno, sā pi taṇhā aniccā saṃkhatā paṭicca-samuppannā, sā pi vedanā aniccā saṃkhatā paṭiccasamuppannā. so pi phasso anicco saṃkhato paṭicca-samuppanno, sā pi avijjā aniccā saṃkhatā paṭicca-samuppannā*, S III 96.

69 *jānato evaṃ passato anantarā āsavānaṃ khayo hoti*, S III 97.

70 *so attā so loko so pecca bhavissāmi nicco dhuvo sassato avipariṇāmadhammo*, S III 99.

71 *no c' assaṃ no ca me siyā na nābhavissāṃ na me bhavissatī ti*, S III 99.

72 *kaṅkhī hoti vecikicchī aniṭṭhaṅgato saddhamme*, S III 99.

73 Collins, *Selfless Persons*, pp. 131–8.

74 *ko nu kho, bho gotama, hetu ko paccayo yānimāni anekavihitāni diṭṭhigatāni loke uppajjanti*, S III 258 ff.

75 e.g. for form:

> *evam eva kho mahārāja, yena rūpena tathāgataṃ paññāpayamāno paññāpeyya, taṃ rūpaṃ tathāgatassa pahīnaṃ ucchinnamūlaṃ tālāvatthukataṃ anabhāvaṅkataṃ āyatiṃ anuppādadhammaṃ. rūpasaṅkhāya vimutto kho mahārāja tathāgato gambhīro appameyyo appariyogāho, seyyathāpi mahāsamuddo, hoti tathāgato paraṃ maraṇā ti pi na upeti, na hoti tathāgato paraṃ maraṇā ti pi na upeti. hoti ca na ca hoti tathāgato paraṃ maraṇā tipi na upeti. n' eva hoti na na hoti tathāgato paraṃ maraṇā tipi na upeti*, S IV 376.

76 *hoti tathāgato paraṃ maraṇā ti kho āvuso, rūpagatam etaṃ, na hoti tathāgato paraṃ maraṇā ti rūpagatam etaṃ, hoti ca na ca hoti tathāgato paraṃ maraṇā ti rūpagatametaṃ, n' eva hoti na na hoti tathāgato paraṃ maraṇā ti rūpagatam etaṃ. hoti tathāgato paraṃ maraṇā ti kho āvuso, vedanāgatam etaṃ, na hoti tathāgato paraṃ maraṇā ti vedanāgatam etaṃ, hoti ca na ca hoti tathāgato paraṃ maraṇā ti vedanāgatametaṃ, n' eva hoti na na hoti tathāgato paraṃ maraṇā ti vedanāgatam etaṃ. hoti tathāgato paraṃ maraṇā ti kho āvuso, saññāgatam etaṃ, na hoti tathāgato paraṃ maraṇā ti saññāgatam etaṃ, hoti ca na ca hoti tathāgato paraṃ maraṇā ti saññāgatam etaṃ, n' eva hoti na na hoti tathāgato paraṃ maraṇā ti saññāgatam etaṃ. hoti tathāgato paraṃ maraṇā ti kho āvuso, saṃkhāragatam etaṃ, na hoti tathāgato paraṃ maraṇā ti saṃkhāragatam etaṃ, hoti ca na ca hoti tathāgato paraṃ maraṇā ti saṃkhāragatam etaṃ, n' eva hoti na na hoti tathāgato paraṃ maraṇā ti saṃkhāragatam etaṃ. hoti tathāgato paraṃ maraṇā ti kho āvuso, viññāṇagatam etaṃ, na hoti tathāgato paraṃ maraṇā ti viññāṇagatam etaṃ, hoti ca na ca hoti tathāgato paraṃ maraṇā ti viññāṇagatam etaṃ, n' eva hoti na na hoti tathāgato paraṃ maraṇā ti viññāṇagatam etaṃ. ayaṃ kho āvuso, hetu ayaṃ paccayo yena taṃ avyākataṃ bhagavatā ti*, S IV 285–6.

77 *cakkhuṃ etaṃ mama, eso 'ham asmi, eso me attā ti samanupassanti. sotaṃ etaṃ mama, eso 'ham asmi, eso me attā ti samanupassanti.ghānaṃ etaṃ mama, eso 'ham asmi, eso me attā ti samanupassanti. jivhaṃ etaṃ mama, eso 'ham asmi, eso me attā ti samanupassanti. kāyaṃ etaṃ mama, eso 'ham asmi, eso me attā ti samanupassanti. manaṃ etaṃ mama, eso 'ham asmi, eso me attā ti samanupassanti. tasmā aññatitthiyānaṃ paribbājakānaṃ evaṃ puṭṭhānaṃ evaṃ vyākaraṇaṃ hoti: sassato loko ti vā, asassato loko ti vā antavā loko ti vā, anantavā loko ti vā, taṃ jīvaṃ taṃ sarīran ti vā aññaṃ jīvaṃ aññaṃ sarīran ti vā, hoti tathāgato paraṃ maraṇā ti va, na hoti tathāgato paraṃ maraṇā ti vā, hoti ca na ca hoti tathāgato paraṃ maraṇā ti vā, n' eva hoti na na hoti tathāgato paraṃ maraṇā ti vā*, S IV 393.

78 *n' etaṃ mama, n' eso 'ham asmi, na me so attā ti samanupassati*, S IV 393.

79 *aññatitthiyā kho, vaccha, paribbājakā rūpaṃ attato samanupassanti, rūpavantaṃ vā attānaṃ, attani vā rūpaṃ, rūpasmiṃ vā attānaṃ, vedanaṃ attato samanupassanti, vedanāvantaṃ vā attānaṃ, attani vā vedanaṃ, vedanasmiṃ vā attānaṃ saññaṃ attato samanupassanti, saññāvantaṃ vā attānaṃ, attani vā saññā, saññāsmiṃ vā attānaṃ, saṃkhāraṃ attato samanupassanti, saṃkhāravantaṃ vā attānaṃ, attani vā saṃkhāraṃ, saṃkhārasmiṃ vā attānaṃ, viññāṇaṃ attato samanupassanti, viññāṇavantaṃ vā attānaṃ, attani vā viññāṇaṃ, viññāṇasmiṃ vā attānaṃ*, S IV 395–6.

80 e.g. for form:

> *rūpaṃ kho āvuso, ajānato apassato yathābhūtaṃ, rūpasamudayaṃ ajānato apassato yathābhūtaṃ, rūpanirodhaṃ ajānato apassato yathābhūtaṃ, rūpanirodhagāminiṃ paṭipadaṃ ajānato apassato yathābhūtaṃ: hoti tathāgato paraṃ maraṇā ti p' issa hoti, na hoti tathāgato paraṃ maraṇā ti p' issa hoti, hoti ca na ca hoti tathāgato paraṃ maraṇā ti p' issa hoti, n' eva hoti na na hoti tathāgato paraṃ maraṇā ti p' issa hoti*, S IV 386.

81 e.g. for form:

> *rūpañ ca kho āvuso, jānato passato yathābhūtaṃ, rūpaṃ samudayaṃ jānato passato yathābhūtaṃ, rūpanirodhaṃ jānato passato yathābhūtaṃ rūpanirodhagāminiṃ paṭipadaṃ jānato passato yathābhūtaṃ hoti tathāgato paraṃ maraṇā ti p' issa na hoti, na hoti tathāgato paraṃ maraṇā ti p' issa na hoti, hoti ca na ca hoti tathāgato paraṃ maraṇā ti p' issa na hoti, n' eva hoti na na hoti tathāgato paraṃ maraṇā ti p' issa na hoti. ayaṃ kho āvuso, hetu ayaṃ paccayo yena taṃ avyākataṃ bhagavatāti*, S IV 387.

82 e.g. for form:

> *rūpe kho āvuso avigatarāgassa avigatachandassa avigatapemassa avigatapipāsassa avigatapariḷāhassa avigatataṇhassa hoti tathāgato paraṃ maraṇā ti p' issa hoti, na hoti tathāgato paraṃ maraṇā ti p' issa hoti, hoti na ca hoti tathāgato paraṃ maraṇā ti p' issa hoti. n' eva hoti na na hoti tathāgato paraṃ maraṇā ti p' issa hoti*, S IV 387.

83 e.g. for form:

> *rūpe ca kho, āvuso vigatarāgassa vigatachandassa vigatapemassa vigatapipāsassa vigatapariḷāhassa vigatataṇhassa hoti tathāgato paraṃ maraṇā ti p' issa na hoti, hoti ca na ca hoti tathāgato paraṃ maraṇā ti p' issa na hoti, n' eva hoti na na hoti tathāgato paraṃ maraṇā ti p' issa na hoti* [...] *ayaṃ kho āvuso, hetu ayaṃ paccayo yena taṃ avyākataṃ bhagavatā ti*, S IV 288.

84 e.g. for form:

> *rūpārāmassa kho āvuso, rūparatassa rūpasammuditassa rūpa-nirodhaṃ ajānato apassato yathābhūtaṃ hoti tathāgato paraṃ maraṇā ti p' issa hoti, na hoti tathāgato paraṃ maraṇā ti p' issa hoti, hoti ca na ca hoti tathāgato paraṃ maraṇā ti p' issa hoti, n' eva hoti na na hoti tathāgato paraṃ maraṇā ti p' issa hoti*, S IV 388–9.

85 e.g. for form:

> *bhavārāmassa kho āvuso, bhavaratassa bhavasammuditassa bhavanirodhaṃ ajānato apassato yathābhūtaṃ hoti tathāgato paraṃ maraṇā ti p' issa hoti, na hoti tathāgato paraṃ maraṇā ti p' issa hoti, hoti ca na ca hoti tathāgato paraṃ maraṇā ti p' issa hoti, n' eva hoti na na hoti tathāgato paraṃ maraṇā ti p' issa hoti*, S IV 389–90.

86 *upādānanirodhaṃ ajānato apassato yathābhūtaṃ*, S IV 390.

87 *taṇhārāmassa kho āvuso, taṇhāratassa taṇhāsammuditassa taṇhānirodhaṃ ajānato apassato yathābhūtaṃ hoti tathāgato paraṃ maraṇā ti p' issa hoti, na hoti tathāgato paraṃ maraṇā ti p' issa hoti, hoti ca na ca hoti tathāgato paraṃ maraṇā ti p' issa hoti, n' eva hoti na na hoti tathāgato paraṃ maraṇā ti p' issa hoti*, S IV 390–1.

88 e.g. for form:

> *na rūpārāmassa kho āvuso, na rūparatassa na rūpasammuditassa rūpa-nirodhaṃ jānato passato yathābhūtaṃ hoti tathāgato paraṃ maraṇā ti p' issa na hoti, na hoti tathāgato paraṃ maraṇā ti p' issa na hoti, hoti ca na ca hoti tathāgato paraṃ maraṇā ti p' issa na hoti, n' eva hoti na na hoti tathāgato paraṃ maraṇā ti p' issa na hoti*, S IV 389.

89 *na bhavārāmassa kho āvuso, na bhavaratassa na bhavasammuditassa bhavanirodhaṃ jānato passato yathābhūtaṃ hoti tathāgato paraṃ maraṇā ti p' issa hoti, na hoti tathāgato paraṃ maraṇā ti p' issa hoti, hoti ca na ca hoti tathāgato paraṃ maraṇā ti p' issa na hoti, n' eva hoti na na hoti tathāgato paraṃ maraṇā ti p' issa na hoti ayam pi kho āvuso pariyāyo yena taṃ avyākataṃ bhagavatā ti*, S IV 390.

90 *na upādānārāmassa kho āvuso, na upādānaratassa na upādānasammuditassa upādhānanirodhaṃ jānato passato yathābhūtaṃ hoti tathāgato paraṃ maraṇā ti p' issa hoti, na hoti tathāgato paraṃ maraṇā ti p' issa hoti, hoti ca na ca hoti tathāgato paraṃ maraṇā ti p' issa na hoti, n' eva hoti na na hoti tathāgato paraṃ maraṇā ti p' issa na hoti ayam pi kho, āvuso, pariyāyo yena taṃ avyākataṃ bhagavatā ti*, S IV 390.

91 *na taṇhārāmassa kho āvuso, na taṇhāratassa na taṇhāsammuditassa taṇhānirodhaṃ jānato passato yathābhūtaṃ hoti tathāgato paraṃ maraṇā ti p' issa na hoti, na hoti tathāgato paraṃ maraṇā ti p' issa hoti, hoti ca na ca hoti tathāgato paraṃ maraṇā ti p' issa na hoti, n' eva hoti na na hoti tathāgato paraṃ maraṇā ti p' issa na hoti ayampi kho, āvuso, pariyāyo yena taṃ avyākataṃ bhagavatā ti*, S IV 390–1.

92 This is stated in the *Peṭakopadesa*: 'He abandons [all] the types of views with the abandoning of *sakkāya-diṭṭhi*' (*sakkāya-diṭṭhippahānena vā diṭṭhi-gatāni pajahati*, Peṭ 178).

93 *sakkāyo nāma-rūpassa padaṭṭhānaṃ*, Peṭ 179, this giving rise to 'I-making' (*ahaṅkāra*, Peṭ 179).

94 It is explained that it is by the cessation of view, or the stopping of view, that doubt does not arise as to the *avyākata*: *diṭṭhi-nirodhā kho* [...] *sutavato ariyasāvakassa vicikicchā na uppajjati avyākatavatthūsu*, A IV 68.

95 *diṭṭhiṃ pajānāti, diṭṭhi-samudayaṃ, pajānāti diṭṭhi-nirodaṃ pajānāti, diṭṭhi-nirodha-gāminiṃ paṭipadaṃ pajānāti*, A IV 68.

96 *cattāro satthāro nānādiṭṭhikā nānākhantikā nānārucikā*, S IV 348.

97 Similar to the 'doubt and uncertainty' (*kaṅkhā* [...] *vicikicchā*, A I 189), of the Kālāmas; see Chapter 1.

98 *alañ hi te* [...] *kaṅkhītuṃ, alaṃ vicikicchituṃ, kaṅkhanīye ca pana te ṭhāne vicikicchā uppannā ti*, S IV 350.

99 *kaṅkhādhammaṃ pajaheyyan ti*, S IV 350.

100 *pāṇātipātam pahāya pāṇātipātā paṭivirato hoti, adinnādānam pahāya adinnādānā paṭivirato hoti, kāmesu micchācāram pahāya kāmesu micchācārā paṭivirato hoti, musāvādam pahāya musāvādā paṭivirato hoti, pisuṇaṃ vācam pahāya pisuṇāya vācāya paṭivirato hoti, pharusaṃ vācam pahāya pharusāya vācāya paṭivirato hoti, samphappalāpam pahāya samphappalāpā paṭivirato hoti, abhijjhaṃ pahāya anabhijjhālu hoti, vyāpādapadosaṃ pahāya avyāpannacitto hoti, micchā-diṭṭhiṃ pahāya sammā-diṭṭhiko hoti*, S IV 350–1.

101 *ekaṃ disaṃ pharitvā viharati, tathā dutiyaṃ, tathā tatiyaṃ, tathā catutthaṃ; iti uddhamadho tiriyaṃ sabbadhi sabbattatāya sabbāvantaṃ lokaṃ mettāsahagatena cetasā vipulena mahaggatena appamāṇena averena avyāpajjena pharitvā viharati*, S IV 351.

102 *karuṇā-sahagatena-cetasā, muditā-sahagatena cetasā*, S IV 354–5.

103 *upekkhā-sahagatena cetasā*, S IV 355–6.

104 *apaṇṇakatāya mayhaṃ*, S IV 351. Bodhi cites the Spk: 'This practice leads to what is incontrovertible for me, to absence of wrongness' (*anaparādhakatāya*); *Connected Discourses*, Volume II, p. 1453, note 364.

105 *kāyena saṃvuto vācāya saṃvuto manasā saṃvuto*, S IV 351, 352, 353, 354, 355, 356, 357, 358.

106 *kāyassa bhedā paraṃ maraṇā sugatiṃ saggaṃ lokaṃ upapajjissāmī ti*, passage occurs at S IV 351, 352, 353, 354, 355, 356, 357, 358.

107 *kaṅkhādhammaṃ pajaheyyāsi*. The full passage is: *tassa pāmojjaṃ jāyati, pamuditassa pīti jāyati, pītimanassa kāyo passambhati, passaddhakāyo sukhaṃ vedayati, sukhino cittaṃ samādhiyati. ayaṃ kho so, gāmaṇi, dhammasamādhi. tatra ce tvaṃ cittasamādhiṃ paṭilabheyyāsi, evaṃ tvaṃ imaṃ kaṅkhādhammaṃ pajaheyyāsi*, S IV 351–2, 353, 354, 355, 356, 357, 358.

108 ***dhamma-samādhī*** *ti dasa-kusala-kammapatha-dhammā*, ***citta-samādhī*** *ti, saha-vipassanā ya cattāro maggā*, Spk III 110. The Spk gives two other examples that are similar to this; see Bodhi, *Connected Discourses*, Volume II, pp. 1452–3, note 363.

109 These two outcomes of achieving right-view can be compared to the *Apaṇṇaka-sutta* discussed in Chapter 2.

110 Collins, *Selfless Persons*, p. 113.

111 I shall return to the use of four *khandhas* below.

112 *katame dhammā kusalā? tīṇi kusalamūlāni: alobho adoso amoho taṃsampayutto vedanākkhandho saññākkhandho saṃkhārakkhandho viññāṇakkhandho, taṃ samuṭṭhānaṃ kāyakammaṃ vacīkammaṃ manokammaṃ, ime dhammā kusalā*, Dhs 180 § 981.

All references to the Dhs are given by page then paragraph numbers.

113 *katame dhammā akusalā? tīṇi akusalamūlāni: lobho doso moho, tadekaṭṭhā ca kilesā taṃsampayutto vedanākkhandho saññākkhandho saṃkhārakkhandho viññāṇakkhandho, taṃsamuṭṭhānaṃ kāyakammaṃ vacīkammaṃ manokammaṃ, ime dhammā akusalā*, Dhs 180 § 982.

114 The text finally defines those *dhammas* that are indeterminate (*avyākatā*), which is not essential for the present discussion:

> *katame dhammā avyākatā kusalākusalānaṃ dhammānaṃ vipākā kāmāvacarā rūpāvacarā arūpāvacarā apariyāpannā, vedanākkhandho saññākkhandho saṃkhārakkhandho viññāṇakkhandho, ye ca dhammā kiriyā n' eva kusalā nākusalā na ca kammavipākā, sabbaṃ ca rūpaṃ, asaṃkhatā ca dhātu. ime dhammā avyākatā*, Dhs 180 § 983.

115 Gethin, 'The Five Khandhas: Their Treatment in the Nikāyas and Early Abhidhamma', *Journal of Indian Philosophy*, 14 (1986), pp. 35–53 (p. 39).

116 *katame dhammā anupādinna-anupādāniyā? apariyāpannā maggā ca maggaphalāni ca asaṃkhatā ca dhātu, ime dhammā anupādinna-anupādāniyā*, Dhs 181 § 992.

117 *katame dhammā pariyāpannā: sāsavā kusalākusalāvyākatā dhammā kāmāvacarā rūpāvacarā arūpāvacarā, rūpakkhandho–pe–viññāṇakkhandho, ime dhammā pariyāpannā*, Dhs 224 § 1286.

118 *katame dhammā apariyāpannā: maggā ca maggaphalāni ca asaṃkhatā ca dhātu, ime dhammā apariyāpannā*, Dhs 224 § 1286. In a stricter sense it may be more correct to say that the unincluded refers only to the four paths (*cattāro maggā apariyāpannā*, Dhs 184 § 1014; 224 § 1288).

119 *maggo, phalaṃ, nibbānaṃ, sotāpattimaggo, sotāpatti-phalaṃ, sakadāgāmimaggo, sakadāgāmiphalaṃ, anāgāmimaggo, anāgāmiphalaṃ, arahattamaggo, arahattaphalaṃ, satipaṭṭhānaṃ, sammappadhānaṃ iddhipādo, indriyaṃ, balaṃ, bojjhaṅgo ti*, Kv 507.

120 Ñāṇamoli, *The Dispeller of Delusion*, Part II (London, 1991), p. 216, note 41.

121 Vibh-a 424.

122 *katame dhammā saṅkiliṭṭhasaṅkilesikā? tīṇi akusalamūlāni lobho doso moho, tadekaṭṭhā ca kilesā, taṃsampayutto vedanākkhandho–pe–viññāṇakkhandho, taṃsamuṭṭhānaṃ kāya-kammaṃ vacī-kammaṃ mano-kammaṃ, ime dhammā saṅkiliṭṭhasaṅkilesikā*, Dhs 181 § 993.

123 *sāsavā kusalavyākatā dhammā kāmāvacarā rūpāvacarā arūpāvacarā, rūpakkhandho vedanākkhandho saññākkhandho saṃkhārakkhandho viññāṇakkhandho, ime dhammā asaṅkiliṭṭhasaṅkilesikā*, Dhs 181 § 994.

124 *sāsavā kusalākusalāvyākatā dhammā kāmāvacarā rūpāvacarā arūpāvacarā rūpakkhandho–pe–viññāṇakkhandho, ime dhammā lokiyā*, Dhs 193 § 1093.

125 *apariyāpannā maggā ca maggaphalāni ca asaṃkhatā ca dhātu, ime dhammā asaṅkiliṭṭha-asaṅkilesikā*, Dhs 181 § 995.

126 *apariyāpannā maggā ca maggaphalāni ca asaṃkhatā ca dhātu, ime dhammā lokuttarā*, Dhs 193 § 1094.

127 Gethin, 'The Five Khandhas: Their Treatment in the Nikāyas and Early Abhidhamma', p. 38. Gethin cites S III 3–5 as a Nikāya parallel to this understanding. This passage was discussed earlier in this Chapter in the consideration of the view that transcends *sakkāya-diṭṭhi*. I shall return to the theme of the four *khandhas* being without corruptions or attachment below.

128 Chapter 4 considers the *āsavas*, Chapter 5 the *saṃyojanā*, Chapter 6 the *ganthas*, Chapter 7 the *oghas*, Chapter 8 the *yogas*, Chapter 9 the *nīvaraṇas*, Chapter 10 *parāmasa* and Chapter 12 the *upādānas*. Chapters 7 and 8, on the *oghas* and *yogas*, will not be considered as they are the same as the *āsavas*.

129 *katame dhammā āsavā*, Dhs 195 § 1096.

130 *kāmāsavo bhavāsavo diṭṭhāsavo avijjāsavo*, Dhs 195 § 1096.

131 *katame dhammā sāsavā*, Dhs 196 § 1103.

132 *kusalākusalāvyākatā dhammā kāmāvacarā rūpāvacarā arūpāvacarā, rūpakkhandho–pe–viññāṇakkhandho, ime dhammā sāsavā*, Dhs 196 § 1103.

133 *sāsavā kusalākusalāvyākatā dhammā kāmāvacarā rūpāvacarā arūpāvacarā, rūpakkhandho–pe–viññāṇakkhandho, ime dhammā saṃyojaniyā*, Dhs 199 § 1125. Chapter 5 states that there are ten fetters (*saṃyojanā*). These are sensual desire, repulsion, conceit, views, doubt, clinging to precepts and vows, desire for becoming, envy, meanness and ignorance: *kāmarāga-saṃyojanaṃ, paṭigha-saṃyojanaṃ, māna-saṃyojanaṃ, diṭṭhi-saṃyojanaṃ, vicikicchā-saṃyojanaṃ, sīlabbata-parāmāsa-saṃyojanaṃ, bhavarāga-saṃyojanaṃ, issā-saṃyojanaṃ, macchariya-saṃyojanaṃ, avijjā-saṃyojanaṃ*, Dhs 197 § 1113. These differ from the Nikāya list of fetters that I gave in Chapter 4.

134 *sāsavā kusalākusalāvyākatā dhammā kāmāvacarā rūpāvacarā arūpāvacarā rūpakkhandho–pe–viññāṇakkhandho ime dhammā ganthanīyā*, Dhs 203 § 1141. The text gives four ties (*ganthā*), the bodily tie of covetousness (*abhijjhākāya-gantho*), the bodily tie of ill-will (*vyāpādo kāya-gantho*), the bodily tie of clinging to precepts and vows (*sīlabbata-parāmāso kāya-gantho*), the bodily tie of adherence to truth (*saccābhiniveso kāya-gantho*). For the bodily tie of covetousness a standard formula is given which is also given for 'lust' (*lobha*, i.e. at Dhs 189 § 1059). For the bodily tie of ill-will, a standard formula is given that is also given for 'hate' (*dosa*, i.e. at Dhs 190 § 1060). For the bodily tie of clinging to precepts and vows a standard formula is given for the third 'fetter' (*saṃyojana*, i.e. Dhs 183 §§ 1005, 1119). This is the theory of those outside the doctrine that purity is got by precepts of moral conduct, by vows, or both together. These are then called gone over to view (*diṭṭhi-gata*), a thicket of view (*diṭṭhi-gahana*), a wilderness of view (*diṭṭhi-kantāra*) etc., as in the standard definition of *micchā-diṭṭhi* (Dhs 202 §1138). For the bodily tie of adherence to truth the text gives the ten usual *ayākata* beginning 'the world is eternal, only this is true, anything else is wrong', adding the same formula as for the previous 'tie', i.e. gone over to view, a thicket of view, a wilderness of view, etc. The text adds that, notwithstanding the bodily tie of the clinging to precepts and vows, all wrong-views are included under the heading of the tie of adherence to truth (*ṭhapetvā sīlabbata-parāmāsaṃ kāya-ganthaṃ sabbāpi micchā-diṭṭhi idaṃsaccābhiniveso kāya-gantho*, Dhs 202 § 1139).

135 *sāsavā kusalākusalāvyākatā dhammā kāmā-vacarā rūpā-vacarā arūpā-vacarā, rūpakkhandho–pe–viññāṇakkhandho, ime dhammā nīvaraṇiyā*, Dhs 206 § 1164. The text gives six hindrances (*nīvaraṇa*), sensual desire; ill-will; tiredness and sleepiness; excitement and depression; doubt and ignorance (*kāmacchandanīvaraṇaṃ, vyāpādanīvaraṇaṃ, thīnamiddhanīvaraṇaṃ, uddhaccakukkuccanīvaraṇaṃ, vicikicchānīvaraṇaṃ, avijjānīvaraṇaṃ*, Dhs 204 § 1152).

136 *sāsavā kusalākusalāvyākatā dhammā kāmāvacarā rūpāvacarā arūpāvacarā, rūpakkhandho–pe–viññāṇakkhandho, ime dhammā parāmaṭṭhā*, Dhs 208 § 1177. The text gives one clinging, that of view (*diṭṭhi-parāmāsa*), the text gives the ten *avyākata* as an example of clinging to views: *sassato loko ti vā, asassato loko ti vā* [...] *ayaṃ vuccati diṭṭhi-parāmāso, sabbāpi micchā-diṭṭhi diṭṭhi-parāmāso. ime dhammā parāmāsā*, Dhs 208 § 1175. Buddhaghosa states that those who do not have the correct attitude to the *dhamma*, who understand what is impermanent as permanent, cling to views (As 49). The clinging and adherence to views is a term also used to describe

the adherence to the *dhamma* by, for example, Yamaka in the *Yamaka-sutta* (S III 109–16) discussed in Chapter 1: *pāpakaṃ diṭṭhi-gataṃ thāmasā parāmāsā abhinivissa voharati tathāhaṃ bhagavatā dhammaṃ desitaṃ ājānāmi yathā khīṇāsavo bhikkhu kāyassa bhedā ucchijjati vinassati na hoti paraṃ maraṇā ti*, S III 110.

137 *sāsavā kusalākusalāvyākatā dhammā kāmāvacarā rūpāvacarā arūpāvacarā, rūpakkhandho–pe–viññññāṇakkhandho, ime dhammā upādāniyā*, Dhs 213 § 1224. The text gives four states that have the attribute of attachment, these are the attachment to sensual desire, the attachment to view, the attachment to precepts and vows, and the attachment to self: *cattāri upādānāni: kāmūpādānaṃ diṭṭhūpādānaṃ sīlabbatūpādānaṃ attavādūpādānaṃ*. Most of these have already been met. The attachment to sensual desire is the same as the *āsava* (*saṃyojana* and *nīvaraṇa*) of sensual desire. The attachment to view is the view of nihilism. The attachment to precepts and vows is the same as the clinging to precepts and vows. Attachment to self is *sakkāya-diṭṭhi*.

138 *sāsavā kusalākusalāvyākatā dhammā kāmāvacarā rūpāvacarā arūpāvacarā, rūpakkhandho–pe–viññāṇakkhandho, ime dhammā saṅkilesikā*, Dhs 217 § 1214. The text gives ten defilements (*dasa kilesavatthūni*: *lobho; doso*; *moho*; *māno*; *diṭṭhi*; *vicikicchā*; *thīnaṃ*; *uddhaccaṃ*; *ahirikaṃ*; *anottappaṃ*, Dhs 214 § 1229). The text inserts two additional questions in the section on the defilements, one with an unwholesome answer, one with a wholesome answer. The first asks: 'What are the *dhammas* that are defiled?' The answer given is that it is the three roots of the unwholesome: greed, hatred and delusion, the corruptions united with them, the four *khandhas* united with them, and actions of body, speech and mind that come from these *dhammas* (*katame dhammā saṅkiliṭṭhā:tīṇi akusalamūlāni lobho doso moho, tadekaṭṭhā ca kilesā taṃ sampayutto vedanākkhandho–pe–viññāṇakkhandho taṃ samuṭṭhānaṃ kāyakammaṃ vacīkammaṃ manokammaṃ, ime dhammā saṅkiliṭṭhā*, Dhs 217 § 1243). The second question is: 'What are the *dhammas* that are not defiled?' The answer given is that it is wholesome, unwholesome and indeterminate *dhammas* relating to the worlds of sense, form or the formless, or to the life that is the unincluded, hence the four *khandhas*, all form and the uncompounded element (*katame dhammā asaṅkiliṭṭhā: kusalāvyākatā dhammā kāmāvacarā rūpāvacarā arūpāvacarā apariyāpannā, vedanākkhandho–pe–viññāṇakkhandho, sabbaṃ ca rūpaṃ asaṃkhatā ca dhātu, ime dhammā asaṅkiliṭṭhā*, Dhs 217 § 1244).

139 *katame dhammā āsava-sampayuttā*, Dhs 196 § 1105.

140 *tehi dhammehi ye dhammā sampayuttā vedanākkhandho–pe–viññāṇakkhandho, ime dhammā āsavasampayuttā*, Dhs 196 § 1105.

141 *dhammā saṃyojana-sampayuttā*, Dhs 199 § 1127; *dhammā gantha-sampayuttā*, Dhs 203 § 1143; *dhammā nīvaraṇa-sampayuttā*, Dhs 206 § 1166; *dhammā parāmāsa-sampayuttā*, Dhs 208 § 1179; *dhammā upādāna-sampayuttā*, Dhs 198–9 § 1121; *dhammā kilesa-sampayuttā*, Dhs 217 § 1244.

142 *katame dhammā āsavā c' eva sāsavā ca*, Dhs 196 § 1107.

143 *teyeva āsavā āsavā c' eva sāsavā ca*, Dhs 196 § 1107. For each subsequent chapter the text states that each of the fetters, hindrances, etc., are both fetters, etc., and favourable to them, Dhs 200 § 1129, Dhs 206 § 1168; or ties and tend to become tied, etc., Dhs 203 § 1145.

144 *katame dhammā āsavā c' eva āsavasampayuttā ca*, Dhs 196 § 1109.

145 This is an interpretation of: *kāmāsavo avijjāsavena āsavo c' eva āsava-sampayutto ca, avijjāsavo kāmāsavena āsavo c' eva āsava-sampayutto ca, bhavāsavo avijjāsavena āsavo c' eva āsava-sampayutto ca, avijjāsavo bhavāsavena āsavo c' eva āsava-sampayutto ca, diṭṭhāsavo avijjāsavena āsavo c' eva āsava-sampayutto ca, avijjāsavo diṭṭhāsavena āsavo c' eva āsava-sampayutto ca, ime dhammā āsavā c' eva āsava-sampayuttā ca*, Dhs 196–7 § 1109. Subsequent chapters have the various hindrances

in conjunction with each other. Chapter 5 uses each fetter in conjunction with ignorance, Dhs 199 § 1131; Chapter 6 has the ties in combination, Dhs 203 § 1146; Chapter 9 has the hindrances in combination with ignorance, Dhs 206–7 § 1170; Chapter 10, seeing as there is only one clinging, omits this question; Chapter 12 has the various attachments in combination, Dhs 199 § 1125; Chapter 13 has the various defilements in combination, Dhs 217–19 § 1250

146 *katame dhammā āsavavippayuttā sāsavā*, Dhs 197 § 1111.

147 *tehi dhammehi ye dhammā vippayuttā sāsavā kusalākusalāvyākatā dhammā kāmāvacarā rūpāvacarā arūpāvacarā, rūpakkhandho–pe–viññāṇakkhandho*, Dhs 197 § 1111.

148 *dhammā saṃyojanavippayuttā saṃyojaniyā*, Dhs 201 § 1133; *dhammā ganthavippayuttā ganthanīyā*, Dhs 204 § 1149; *dhammā nīvaraṇavippayuttā nīvaraṇiyā*, Dhs 207 § 1172; *dhammā parāmāsavippayuttā parāmaṭṭhā*, Dhs 209 § 1183; *dhammā upādānavippayuttā upādāniyā*, Dhs 199 § 1127; *dhammā kilesavippayuttā saṅkilesikā*, Dhs 219–20 § 1252.

149 *katame dhammā no āsavā*, Dhs 196 § 1102.

150 *te dhamme ṭhapetvā avasesā kusalākusalāvyākatā dhammā kāmāvacarā rūpāvacarā arūpāvacarā apariyāpannā vedanākkhandho–pe–viññāṇakkhandho, sabbañ ca rūpaṃ, asaṃkhatā ca dhātu, ime dhammā no āsavā*, Dhs 196 § 1102.

151 *dhammā no saṃyojanā*, Dhs 199 § 1124; *dhammā no ganthā*, Dhs 202–3 § 1140; *dhammā no nīvaraṇā*, Dhs 206 § 1163; *dhammā no parāmāsā*, Dhs 208 § 1176; *dhammā no upādānā*, Dhs 213 § 1218; *dhammā no kilesā*, Dhs 216–7 § 1240.

152 Bhikkhu Bodhi, *Connected Discourses*, Volume 1, p. 1058, note 65.

153 *katame dhammā anāsavā*, Dhs 196 § 1104.

154 *apariyāpannā maggā ca maggaphalāni ca asaṃkhatā ca dhātu, ime dhammā anāsavā*, Dhs 196 § 1104.

155 *dhammā asaṃyojaniyā*, Dhs 199 § 1126; *dhammā aganthanīyā*, Dhs 203 § 1142; *dhammā anīvaraṇiyā*, Dhs 206 § 1165; *dhammā aparāmaṭṭhā*, Dhs 208 § 1178; *dhammā anupādāniyā*, Dhs 213 § 1220; *dhammā asaṅkilesikā*, Dhs 217 § 1242.

156 *katame dhammā āsava-vippayuttā*, Dhs 196 § 1106.

157 *tehi dhammehi ye dhammā vippayuttā vedanākkhandho–pe–viññāṇakkhandho sabbañ ca rūpaṃ asaṃkhatā ca dhātu, ime dhammā āsavavippayuttā*, Dhs 196 § 1106.

158 *dhammā saṃyojanavippayuttā* Dhs 199 § 1128; *dhammā ganthavippayuttā*, Dhs 203 § 1144; *dhammā nīvaraṇavippayuttā*, Dhs 206 § 1167; *dhammā parāmāsavippayuttā*, Dhs 208 § 1180; *dhammā upādānavippayuttā*, Dhs 213 § 1222; *dhammā kilesavippayuttā*, Dhs 217 § 1245.

159 *katame dhammā sāsavā c' eva no ca āsavā*, Dhs 196 § 1108.

160 *tehi dhammehi ye dhammā sāsavā te dhamme ṭhapetvā avasesā sāsavā kusalākusalāvyākatā dhammā kāmāvacarā rūpāvacarā arūpāvacarā, rūpakkhandho–pe–viññāṇakkhandho, ime dhammā sāsavā c' eva no ca āsavā*, Dhs 196 § 1108.

161 *dhammā saṃyojaniyā c' eva no ca saṃyojanā*, Dhs 200 § 1130; *dhammā ganthanīyā c' eva no ca ganthā*, Dhs 203 § 1146, *dhammā nīvaraṇiyā c' eva no ca nīvaraṇā*, Dhs 206 § 1169; *dhammā parāmaṭṭhā c' eva no ca parāmāsā*, Dhs 208–9 § 1182; *dhammā upādāniyā c' eva no ca upādānā*, Dhs 213 § 1224; *dhammā saṅkilesikā c' eva no ca kilesā*, Dhs 217 § 1247. There is a slight variation in the text discussing the defilements at this point. The text repeats, with minor changes, question four. In the unwholesome version of the question the answer is the same, though the grammar does have a slight variation, i.e. *katame dhammā kilesā c' eva saṅkilesikā ca: teva kilesā kilesā c' eva saṅkilesikā ca*, compared to *katame dhammā kilesā c' eva saṅkiliṭṭhā ca: teva kilesā kilesā c' eva saṅkiliṭṭhā ca*. However, when the wholesome version of this question is asked, two different answers are given. The first time the standard answer is given: *katame dhammā saṅkilesikā c' eva no ca kilesā: tehi dhammehi ye dhammā*

saṅkilesikā te dhamme ṭhapetvā avasesā sāsavā kusalākusalāvyākatā dhammā kāmāvacarā rūpāvacarā arūpāvacarā, rūpakkhandho–pe–viññāṇakkhandho, ime dhammā saṅkilesikā c' eva no ca kilesā (Dhs 217 § 1247). This follows the form of the previous sections. The second time the question is asked, however, the answer to the question: 'what are the states that are defiled but not themselves defilements' is that 'it is the states that are defiled by the defilements, i.e. the four *khandhas*' (*katame dhammā saṅkiliṭṭhā c' eva no ca kilesā:tehi dhammehi ye dhammā saṅkiliṭṭhā, te dhamme ṭhapetvā vedanākkhandho–pe–viññāṇakkhandho, ime dhammā saṅkiliṭṭhā c' eva no ca kilesā*, Dhs 217 § 1249). This alteration is perhaps suggestive of the importance placed upon the defilements in the unfolding of the Buddhist path.

162 *katame dhammā āsava-sampayuttā c' eva no ca āsavā*, Dhs 197 § 1110.

163 *tehi dhammehi ye dhammā sampayuttā te dhamme ṭhapetvā vedanākkhandho–pe–viññāṇakkhandho*, Dhs 197 § 1110.

164 In Chapter 10 on 'clinging' this question and answer do not appear, as the corresponding negative evaluation did not appear.

165 *saṃyojana-sampayuttā c' eva no ca saṃyojanā* Dhs 201 § 1132; *dhammā gantha-sampayuttā c' eva no ca ganthā*, Dhs 204 § 1148; *dhammā nīvaraṇa-sampayuttā c' eva no ca nīvaraṇā*, Dhs 207 § 1171; *dhammā upādāna-sampayuttā c' eva no ca upādānā*, Dhs 214 § 1226; *katame dhammā kilesasampayuttā c' eva no ca kilesā*, Dhs 219–20 § 1252.

166 *katame dhammā āsava-vippayuttā anāsavā*, Dhs 197 § 1112.

167 *apariyāpannā maggā ca maggaphalāni ca asaṃkhatā ca dhātu, ime dhammā āsavavippayuttā anāsavā*, Dhs 197 § 1112.

168 *dhammā saṃyojana-vippayuttā asaṃyojaniyā*, Dhs 201 § 1134; *dhammā gantha-vippayuttā aganthaniyā*, Dhs 204 § 1150; *dhammā nīvaraṇa-vippayuttā anīvaraṇiyā*, Dhs 207 § 1173; *parāmāsa-vippayuttā aparāmaṭṭhā*, Dhs 209 § 1184; *dhammā upādānavippayuttā anupādāniyā*, Dhs 214 § 1228; *dhammā kilesavippayuttā asaṅkilesikā*, Dhs 220 § 1253.

169 *dhammāpi vo pahātabbā pageva adhammā*, M I 135. I follow the reading of Bodhi here (Bodhi, *The Middle Length Discourses of the Buddha*, p. 229). However, Richard Gombrich has recently argued that the phrase should be translated as, 'you will let go of my teachings, let alone things I have not taught' (Gombrich, *How Buddhism Began*, p. 24). Gombrich argues that the Buddha is stating that the teachings 'should be let go of, let alone *adhammā*, non-teachings' (ibid.), in the sense that the words and formulation of the teaching should not be clung to, but one should try to understand the spirit of the teachings. Abandoning the content of the teachings, abandoning the *dhamma*, is not being advised by the simile. The simile is not pointing to the abandonment of all 'objects [*dhammā*] of thought' (ibid., p. 25).

170 As Collins has suggested, it is not only concepts, even correct concepts, that can be harmful, but that states of mind produced by meditation are instruments towards liberation, and should not become the object of attachment; see Collins, *Selfless Persons*, p. 121–2; see also Anderson, *Pain and its Ending*, p. 38.

171 *kusalo dhammo kusalassa dhamassa ārammaṇa-paccayena paccayo*, Paṭṭh 154.

172 See Bodhi, *A Comprehensive Manual of Abhidhamma*: *The Abhidhammattha Sangaha of Ācariya Anuruddha* (Kandy, 1993), p. 315.

173 In the Abhidhamma six objects are recognised: visible form object, sound object, smell object, taste object, tangible object and mental object, these give rise to the various *cittas* and *cetasikas* of the Abhidhamma system.

174 *dānaṃ datvā, sīlaṃ samādiyitvā, uposathakammaṃ katvā, taṃ paccavekkhati*, Paṭṭh 154.

175 Cf. the ten wholesome and unwholesome courses of action conditioning right-view and wrong-view.

176 This term implies one who is no longer a *puthujjana* but an *ariya*, with *nibbāna* as their aim, this is the 'change of lineage'.
177 *sekhā gotrabhuṃ paccavekkhanti, vodānaṃ paccavekkhanti*, Paṭṭh 152.
178 *sekhā maggā vuṭṭhahitvā maggaṃ paccavekkhanti*, Paṭṭh 152.
179 *sekhā vā putthujjanā vā kusalaṃ aniccato dukkhato anattato vipassanti*, Paṭṭh 152.
180 *cetopariyañāṇena kusala-cittasamangissa cittaṃ jānanti*, Paṭṭh 152.
181 *kusalo dhammo akusalassa dhamassa ārammaṇapaccayena paccayo*, Paṭṭh 154–5.
182 The *Pañcappakaraṇa-aṭṭhakathā* interprets 'enjoys' (*assādeti*) as 'experiences and takes pleasure by means of the *cittas* associated with greed and accompanied by joy' (*somanassasahagatalobhasampayuttacittehi anubhavati c' eva rajjati ca*) and 'delights' (*abhinandati*) as 'delighting in views' (*diṭṭhābhinandanāya*), Paṭṭh-a 269.
183 *rāgo uppajjati, diṭṭhi uppajjati, vicikicchā uppajjati, uddhaccaṃ uppajjati, domanassaṃ uppajjati*, Paṭṭh 154–5.
184 *pubbe suciṇṇāni assādeti abhinandati*, Paṭṭh 155.
185 *jhānā vuṭṭhāhitvā jhānaṃ assādeti, abhinandati*, Paṭṭh 155.
186 *jhāne parihīne vippaṭisārissa domanassaṃ uppajjati*, Paṭṭh 155. The *Paṭṭhāna* is perhaps suggesting that 'lust, wrong-views, doubt and restlessness' can be experienced by those on the path. This would be somewhat different from the passage in the *Dhammasaṅgaṇi* which I considered above.
187 *akusalo dhammo akusalassa dhammassa ārammaṇa-paccayena paccayo*, Paṭṭh 155.
188 *rāgaṃ assādeti abhinandati. ārabbha rāgo uppajjati, diṭṭhiṃ uppajjati, vicikicchā uppajjati, uddhaccaṃ uppajjati, domanassaṃ uppajjati*, Paṭṭh 155.
189 *diṭṭhiṃ assādeti, abhanandati, taṃ ārabbha rāgo uppajjati, diṭṭhi uppajjati vicikicchā uppajjati, uddhaccaṃ uppajjati, domanassaṃ uppajjati, vicikicchaṃ ārabbha vicikicchā uppajjati, diṭṭhi uppajjati uddhaccaṃ uppajjati, domanassaṃ uppajjati, uddhaccaṃ ārabbha uddhaccaṃ uppajjati, diṭṭhi uppajjati, vicikicchā uppajjati. domassaṃ uppajjati, domanassaṃ ārabbha domanassaṃ uppajjati. diṭṭhi uppajjati, vicikicchā uppajjati, uddhaccaṃ uppajjati*, Paṭṭh 155.
190 *akusalo dhammo kusalassa dhammassa ārammaṇapaccayena paccayo*, Paṭṭh 155.
191 *sekkhā pahīne kilese paccave kkhanti, vikkhambhite kilese paccavekkhanti, pubbe samudāciṇṇe kilese jānanti*, Paṭṭh 155.
192 *sekkhā vā puthujjanā vā akusalaṃ aniccato dukkhato anattato vipassanti*, Paṭṭh 155.
193 I may well be describing the process that formed the basis for tantric practice: indulgence in what is unwholesome can be used in a way that is wholesome.
194 I have already cited a possible connection of the *satipaṭṭhāna* with a passage at Peṭ 94 in Chapter 3 in a discussion of the *āsavas*. I have also mentioned them in Chapter 2 in the consideration of the undertaking of right-view and the *vipallāsa*. The first two *satipaṭṭhāna* are related to the first gateway to liberation, the third *satipaṭṭhāna* to the second, and the fourth *satipaṭṭhāna* to the third; see D II 290.
195 *tassā paṭipakkho lokuttarā sammā-diṭṭhi, anvāyikā sammā-saṅkappo sammā-vācā sammā-kammanto sammā-ājīvo sammā-vāyāmo sammā-sati sammā-samādhi, ayaṃ ariyo aṭṭhaṅgiko maggo*, Nett 111.
196 Note misprint in Ñāṇamoli's translation of the *Nettippakaraṇa* (Ñāṇamoli, *The Guide* p. 155, given correctly p. 153).
197 *tattha yo ca phasso āhāro yo ca dukkhe sukhan ti vipallāso bhavūpādānaṃ bhavayogo byāpādakāyagantho bhavāsavo bhavogho dosasallo vedanūpagā viññāṇaṭṭhiti dosā agatigamanan ti imesaṃ dasannaṃ suttānaṃ eko attho byañjanam eva nānaṃ, ime dosa-caritassa puggalassa upakkilesā*, Nett 118.
198 *tattha yo ca viññāṇāhāro yo ca anicce niccan ti vipallāso diṭṭhūpādānaṃ diṭṭhayogo parāmāsakāyagantho diṭṭhāsavo diṭṭhogho mānasallo saññūpagā viññāṇaṭṭhiti bhayā agatigamanan ti imesaṃ dasannaṃ suttānaṃ eko attho vyāñnam eva nānaṃ, ime diṭṭhicaritassa mandassa upakkilesā*, Nett 118.

199 *tattha yo ca manosañcetanāhāro ye ca anattani attā ti vipallāso attavādupādānaṃ avijjāyogo idaṃsaccābhinivesakāyagantho avijjāsavo avijjogho mohasallo saṅkhārūpagā viññāṇaṭṭhiti mohā agatigamanan ti imesaṃ dasannaṃ suttānaṃ eko attho byañjanam eva nānaṃ, ime diṭṭhicaritassa udatthassa upakkilesā*, Nett 118.

200 *tattha yo ca kabaḷiṃkārāhāro yo ca phasso āhāro* [...] *yo ca asubhe subhan ti vipallāso yo ca dukkhe sukhan ti vipallāso* [...] *kāmūpādānaṃ ca bhavūpādānaṃ ca* [...] *kāma-yogo ca bhava-yogo ca appaṇihitena vimokkhamukhena pahānaṃ gacchanti*, etc., Nett 118–19.

201 *viññāṇāhāro* [...] *anicce niccan ti vipallāso* [...] *diṭṭhūpādānaṃ* [...] *diṭṭhi-yogo suññatāya* etc., Nett 18–19.

202 *manosañcetanāhāro* [...] *anattani attā ti vipallāso* [...] *attavādūpādānaṃ* [...] *avijjāyogo animittena*, etc., ibid. However, later in the text non-accomplishment in virtue, views and conduct (*sīla-vipatti, diṭṭhi-vipatti, ācāra-vipatti*), are said to be overcome by emptiness, the signless and the dispositionless (*suññataṃ animittaṃ appaṇihitan ti*) respectively, Nett 126.

203 *anicce niccan ti vipallāso*, see Nett 114.

204 *tatiye vipallāse ṭhito saṃsārābhinandiniṃ diṭṭhiṃ upādiyati, idaṃ vuccati diṭṭhūpādānaṃ*, Nett 116.

205 *diṭṭhūpādānena pāpikāya diṭṭhiyā saṃyujjati, ayaṃ vuccati diṭṭhiyogo*, Nett 116.

206 *anattani attā ti vipallāso*, Nett 115.

207 *catutthe vipallāse ṭhito attānaṃ kappiyaṃ upādiyati, idaṃ vuccati attavādupādānaṃ*, Nett 116.

208 *attavādūpādānena avijjāya saṃyujjati, ayaṃ vuccati avijjāyogo*, Nett 116.

209 The text later gives 'painful ways with sluggish and quick acquaintance and pleasant ways with sluggish and quick acquaintance' (*dukkhā ca paṭipadā dandhābhiññā dukkhā ca paṭipadā khippābhiññā, sukhā paṭipadā dandhābhiññā, sukhā paṭipadā khippābhiññā*, Nett 123).

210 Body, feeling, mind and *dhammas*. Explanations mainly drawn from Ñāṇamoli's translation of the *Nettippakaraṇa* (Ñāṇamoli, *The Guide*, pp. 160–1).

211 Heavenly, divine, noble and imperturbable.

212 The effort to prevent the arising of unwholesome states, to get rid of unwholesome states that have arisen, to arouse wholesome states, to increase wholesome states that have arisen.

213 Abandoning conceit, eliminating reliance, abandoning ignorance and pacification of being.

214 Truth, generosity, understanding and peace.

215 Will, energy, cognisance and enquiry.

216 Faculty-restraint, ardour, discovery and relinquishment of all essentials of existence.

217 Loving-kindness, compassion, gladness, onlooking equanimity, Nett, 119.

218 *dukkhā ca paṭipadā dandhābhiññā dukkhā ca paṭipadā khippābhiññā* [...] *kāye kāyānupassitā satipaṭṭhānaṃ ca vedanāsu vedanānupassitā satipaṭṭhānaṃ ca* [...] *paṭhamañ ca jhānaṃ dutiyaṃ ca jhānaṃ* [...] *paṭhamo ca vihāro dutiyo ca vihāro appaṇihitaṃ vimokkhamukhaṃ*, etc., Nett 123.

219 *sukhā paṭipadā dandhābhiññā* [...] *citte cittānupassitā* [...] *tatiyaṃ jhānaṃ* [...] *tatiyo sammappadhānaṃ suññataṃ vimokkhamukhaṃ*, Nett 123.

220 *sukhā paṭipadā khippābhiññā* [...] *dhammesu dhammānupassītā* [...] *catutthaṃ jhānaṃ* [...] *catutthaṃ sammappadhānaṃ animittaṃ vimokkhamukhaṃ*, Nett 123.

221 See also Nett 7.

222 A further discussion of the three gateways to liberation occurs at Nett 90. This states that a person of lusting-temperament finds outlet by the 'signless gateway to liberation' (*rāga-carito puggalo animittena vimokkhamukhena nīyāti*), and this is the concentration category (*animittavimokkhamukhaṃ samādhikkhandho*). A person of hating-temperament by means of the 'dispositionless gateway to liberation' (*dosa-*

carito puggalo appaṇihitena vimokkhamukhena nīyāti), and this is the virtue category (*appaṇihitavimokkhamukhaṃ sīlakkhandho*), and a person of 'deluded-temperament' (*mohacarito*) by means of the emptiness gateway to liberation (*mohacarito puggalo suññata-vimokkhamūkhena nīyāti*), and this is the understanding category (*suññatavimokkhamukhaṃ paññākkhandho*). These categories and passages have been discussed by Collins (*Selfless Persons*, p. 126).

223 Vism XXI 70, citing Paṭis II 58.

224 Paul Williams, *Mahāyāna Buddhism: The Doctrinal Foundations* (London, 1989), pp. 60–1.

225 S IV 400–1.

6 Views and non-attachment

1 Grace Burford, 'Theravāda Buddhist Soteriology' in *Paths to Liberation: The Mārga and its Transformations in Buddhist Thought*, Robert Buswell and Robert Gimello (eds) (Los Angeles, 1992), pp. 37–61 (p. 42).

2 Gómez, 'Proto-Mādhyamika in the Pāli Canon', p. 137.

3 Burford, 'Theravāda Buddhist Soteriology', p. 48. Burford compares this paradox to the paradox of desire in Buddhist thought. The paradox of desire states that desirelessness is ideal, yet one must desire the overcoming of desire. In a similar way, no-views is ideal, but this itself is an ideal, a position, and all positions are to be transcended; see Burford, ibid., pp. 48–9.

4 *atthi pana bhoto gotamassa kiñci diṭṭhi-gatan ti. diṭṭhi-gatan ti kho vaccha apanītam etaṃ tathāgatassa. diṭṭhaṃ h' etaṃ vaccha tathāgatena: iti rūpaṃ, iti rūpassa samudayo, iti rūpassa atthaṅgamo, iti vedanā, iti vedanāya samudayo, iti vedanāya atthaṅgamo, iti saññā, iti saññāya samudayo, iti saññāya atthaṅgamo, iti saṃkhārā, iti saṃkhārānaṃ samudayo, iti saṃkhārānaṃ atthaṃgamo, iti viññāṇaṃ, iti viññāṇassa samudayo, iti viññāṇassa atthaṅgamo ti. tasmā tathāgato sabbamaññitānaṃ sabbamathitānaṃ sabba-ahaṃkāramaṃkāramānānusayānaṃ khayā virāgā nirodhā cāgā paṭinissaggā anupādā vimutto ti vadāmī ti*, M I 486.

5 See Peter Harvey, *An Introduction to Buddhism* (Cambridge, 1990), pp. 96–7.

6 Although, as Richard Gombrich has argued, the simile of the raft was also misinterpreted by the later tradition:

> *Dhamma* in the plural can also mean the objects of thought, 'noeta', which correspond to the faculty of thought as sounds correspond to hearing. Lifting the last words out of context ['to abandon good *dhammas*, let alone bad *dhammas*'], Mahāyāna texts claimed that the Buddha prescribed the abandonment of all objects of thought; and by the same token that he also recommended the abandoning of the opposite, non-objects of thought – whatever they might be. The raft simile became a charter for paradox and irrationality (*How Buddhism Began*, p. 25).

7 See, for example, Steven Collins, *Selfless Persons*, pp. 128–9 and Richard Hayes, *Dignaga on the Interpretation of Signs*, pp. 45–8. David J. Kalupahana argues that Buddhism does have a view, expressed by the middle-way; Kalupahana, D.J., *The Philosophy of the Middle Way* (Albany, 1986), pp. 13–14.

8 *tad aniccaṃ, tam dukkham, yaṃ dukkhaṃ, tam n' etaṃ mama n' eso 'ham asmi na me so attā ti*, A V 188. This is the right-view that I discussed from the *Kiṃdiṭṭhika-sutta* in Chapters 3 and 4 (A V 185–90). It is the view of Anāthapiṇḍika.

9 See David F. Burton, *Emptiness Appraised*, p. 32, for a discussion of comparable passages in Nāgārjuna.

10 'When all *dhammas* have been removed, then all ways of speaking are also removed' (*sabbesu dhammesu samohatesu, samuhatā vādapathāpi sabbe ti*, Sn 1076); see Tilmann Vetter, 'Some remarks on the older parts of the Suttanipāta' in *Earliest Buddhism and Madhyamaka*, David Seyfort Ruegg and Lambert Schmithausen (eds) (Leiden, 1990), pp. 36–56.

11 *na diṭṭhiyā na sutiyā na ñāṇena (māgandiyā ti bhagavā)*
silabbatenāpi na suddhim āha,
adiṭṭhiyā asasutiyā añāṇā
asīlatā abbatā nopi tena, Sn 839.

12 *diṭṭhiñ ca nissāya anupucchamāno* [...]
samuggahītesu pamoham āgā
ito ca nāddakkhi aṇum pi saññaṃ
tasmā tuvaṃ momuhato dahāsi, Sn 841.

13 *na vedagū diṭṭhiyā na mutiyā*
sa mānam eti na hi tammayo so,
na kammunā nopi sutena neyyo
anupanito sa-nivesanesu.
saññā-virattassa na santi ganthā
paññā-vimuttassa na santi mohā,
saññañ ca diṭṭiñ ca ye aggahesuṃ
te ghaṭṭayantā vicaranti loke ti, Sn 846–7.

14 Gómez, 'Proto-Mādhyamika in the Pāli Canon', p. 155; see also Tilmann Vetter, 'Some remarks on the older parts of the Suttanipāta', pp. 36–56. Vetter also argues that there is a middle-way in the *Aṭṭhakavagga* which is not the same as that found elsewhere in the Pāli canon. He explains this in the following terms: '[N]ot only are all dogmas denied and all theories and knowledge – which could be interpreted as aiming at a peace of non-involvement – and all apperceptions [...] but this denying, too, is denied' (Vetter, 'Some remarks on the older parts of the Suttanipāta', p. 48). Vetter claims that this process points to a type of 'mysticism' being found in the *Aṭṭhakavagga*. He claims that certain passages in the *Aṭṭhakavagga* are 'contaminated'. By this, he means that certain passages are somehow corrupt. These are those passages that deny apperception (*saññā*), but praise knowledge (*paññā*), an example being Sn 792:

> A person undertaking vows himself, being attached to apperceptions, goes high and low. But the one who knows, the one of great wisdom, does not go high and low, having understood the *dhamma* by means of knowledge (*sayaṃ samādāya vatāni jantu, uccāvacaṃ gacchati saññasatto, vidvā ca vedehi samecca dhammaṃ, na uccāvacaṃ gacchati bhūripañño*).

Other passages, such as the last verse of the *Māgaṇḍiya-sutta* (Sn 847) cited above, Vetter interprets differently: 'There are no ties for one who is devoid of apperceptions. There are no illusions for one who is released through wisdom' (*saññā-virattassa na santi ganthā, paññā-vimuttassa na santi mohā*, Sn 847). This time, Vetter argues, *paññā* is 'wisdom' (p. 48) or 'real insight' (p. 49), not 'discriminating insight' as in the cited 'contaminated' verse. Vetter appears to understand one type of *paññā* (discriminating insight) to belong to the Buddhist tradition, and the other 'original' *paññā* of the *Aṭṭhakavagga* to belong to another trend, even another tradition. Vetter argues that there is an attempt to integrate the *paññā* of the Buddhists to that of the non-Buddhist, non-discriminating *paññā*. For Vetter, the no-views understanding in Buddhism is in fact non-Buddhist. The non-Buddhist group were not interested in rebirth and overcoming *saṃsāra*, but with the overcoming of all apperceptions (*saññā*, Vetter, 'Some remarks on the older parts of the Suttanipāta', pp. 42–3, 50–2). This leads him to some surprising conclusions. For example, the no-views understanding, as found expressed by the *avyākata*, is due to the usefulness of rejecting all views when certain questions are too difficult to answer (p. 51). Grace Burford argues in a similar way that the *Aṭṭhakavagga* represents an early pure type of Buddhism in which ontology and metaphysics were not important but finding purity in this life was. This original goal, that of finding purity, became corrupted by the Buddhist tradition, notably by the *Mahāniddesa* and *Paramatthajotikā*, which introduced 'new metaphysical values' into the original goal (Burford, *Desire, Death and Goodness: The Conflict of Ultimate Values in Theravāda Buddhism*, (New York, 1991), p. 188). This is in contrast to the *Aṭṭhakavagga and Pārāyanavagga* which had a 'non-metaphysical representation of the summum bonum' (ibid., p. 190). I will return to these ideas in my main argument.

15 Gómez, 'Proto-Mādhyamika in the Pāli Canon', pp. 146–7. As I noted in Chapter 1, Richard Gombrich holds that to state that the Buddha 'has no viewpoint [...] at all' is an 'extreme position', found only in the *Aṭṭhakavagga* and the *Pārāyanavagga* (Gombrich, *How Buddhism Began*, p. 16). I am not arguing that the Buddha has no viewpoint, but that right-view does not have the usual attributes of 'viewness', as the expression of some position. I am also arguing that the *Aṭṭhakavagga* and *Pārāyanavagga* are expressive of 'right-view' as 'no-view'.

16 Gómez, 'Proto-Mādhyamika in the Pāli Canon', p. 139.

17 Gómez cites the *Mahāviyūha-sutta's* criticisms of the terms 'I know, I see' (*jānāmi passāmi*, ibid., p. 140). However, what the *sutta* actually states, I think, is that there should not be attachment to knowledge:

> (Saying) 'I know, I see this is exactly so', some believe that purity is by means of view. (Even) if one has seen (it), what use is it for himself? Having transgressed (the noble path) they say that purity is by means of another (path) (*jānāmi passāmi tatheva etaṃ, diṭṭhiyā eke paccenti suddhiṃ, addakkhi ce kiñhi tumassa tena, atisitvā aññena vadanti suddhiṃ*, Sn 908).

As is stated throughout the Nikāyas, attachment to knowledge in the form of claiming 'only this is true' is condemned. Indeed, this phrase is found in the opening lines of the *Mahāviyūha-sutta* in which it is stated that those abiding in views dispute saying 'only this is true' (*ye kec 'me diṭṭhi-paribbasānā, idam eva saccanti vivādayan ti*, Sn 895). This phrase is also found in the *Pasūra-sutta* where it is stated that, 'if any have taken up a view, and say, "only this is true", say to them, "There will be no opponent for you here when a dispute has arisen"' (*ye diṭṭhimuggayha vivādayanti, idam eva saccan ti ca vādayanti, te tvaṃ vadassū na hi te 'dha atthi, vādamhi jāte paṭisenikattā*, Sn 832). Attachment destroys insight and knowledge.

18 *na brāhmaṇo kappam upeti saṅkhaṃ*
na diṭṭhisārī na pi ñāṇabandhu
ñatvā ca sa sammutiyo puthujjā
upekkhatī uggaṇhanti maññe, Sn 911.

19 *passāmi suddhaṃ paramaṃ arogaṃ*
diṭṭhena saṃsuddhi narassa hoti,
etābhijānaṃ paraman ti ñatvā
suddhānupassī ti pacceti ñāṇaṃ, Sn 788.

20 *idam eva saccaṃ, mogham aññan ti*, M II 170–1. In fact, in other places knowledge, understood as the *dhamma* (not truth as an object of attachment), is praised:

> Anger and lie-telling and doubt, and those mental states too (come into existence) when this very pair (pleasant and unpleasant) exist. A doubtful man should train himself in the path of knowledge. The ascetic spoke about mental states from knowledge (*kodho mosavajjañ ca kathaṃkathā ca, etepi dhammā dvayam eva sante, kathaṃkathī ñāṇapathāya sikkhe, ñatvā pavuttā samaṇena dhammā*, Sn 868.

The Pāli is in verse form in the original. The *Guhaṭṭhaka-sutta* states that one should understand apperception (*saññaṃ pariññā*, Sn 779), and the *Tuvaṭaka-sutta* the following. 'And knowing this *dhamma*, searching, a *bhikkhu* would train himself (in it), always being mindful. Knowing quenching as "peace", he would not be negligent in Gotama's teaching' (*etañ ca dhammam aññāya vicinaṃ bhikkhu sadā sato sikkhe, santī ti nibbutiṃ ñatvā, sāsane gotamassa na ppamajjeyya*, Sn 933). Vetter notes that this verse 'is in contention with the contention of Gómez' (Vetter, 'Some remarks on the older parts of the Suttanipāta', p. 45). The *Attadaṇḍa-sutta* states that: 'He truly knows, he has knowledge. Knowing the *dhamma*, he is not dependent' (*sa ve vidvā sa vedagū ñatvā dhammaṃ anissito*, Sn 947; see Vetter 'Some remarks on older parts of the Suttanipāta', p. 46; Gómez 'Proto-Mādhyamika in the Pāli Canon', p. 148). In the *Pārāyanavagga*, the sage is described as 'possessing wisdom' (*paññāṇavā*, Sn 1091). The *Posāla-sutta* also describes the cognitive process and the nature of knowledge. Posāla asks the Buddha about 'the knowledge of one whose apperception of forms has disappeared, who has abandoned all corporeality, who sees that nothing exists either internally or externally' (*vibhūtarūpasaññissa sabbakāyappahāyino, ajjhattañ ca bahiddhā ca n' atthi kiñcī ti passato, ñāṇaṃ sakkānupucchāmi kathaṃ neyyo tathāvidho*, Sn 1113). Part of the Buddha's reply states that:

> Knowing the origin of the state of nothingness (he thinks) 'Enjoyment is a fetter'. Knowing this thus, then he has insight therein. This is the true knowledge of the brahman who has lived the (perfect) life (*ākiñcañña-sambhavaṃ ñatvā nandī saṃyojanaṃ iti, evam etaṃ abhiññāya tato tattha vipassati: etaṃ ñāṇaṃ tathaṃ tassa brāhmaṇassa vusimato ti*, Sn 1115).

The *Māgandiya-sutta* states: 'There are no illusions for one who is released through wisdom' (*paññā-vimuttassa na santi mohā*, Sn 847 (cited above). Knowledge is knowledge of attachment. Knowledge consists of abandoning craving (*ācikkha dhammaṃ yam ahaṃ vijaññaṃ jāti-jarāya idha vippahānaṃ. taṇhādhipanne manuje pekkhamāno (piṅgiyā ti bhagavā) santāpajāte jarasā parete, tasmā tuvaṃ piṅgiya appamatto, jahassu taṇhaṃ apunabbhavāyā ti*, Sn 1122–3). Knowledge is given a positive evaluation, and it is defined as knowledge of non-attachment: 'He for whom there is no state of dependence, knowing the doctrine, is not dependent. For whom there exists no craving for existence or non-existence' (*yassa nissayatā n' atthi ñatvā dhammaṃ anissito, bhavāya vibhavāya vā taṇhā yassa na vijjati*, Sn 856; see Gómez, ibid., p. 146; Vetter, ibid., p. 46). Knowledge is criticized, as uniformly as in the Nikāyas as a whole, if it does not express the middle-way between the extremes of existence and non-existence. This is one of the aims of knowledge in early Buddhist thought. To fall into either extreme goes against the truth of dependent-origination.

21 An example of the teaching advising detachment from these means of knowledge in the *Aṭṭhakavagga* is the following:

> Giving up old corruptions, not forming new ones, he does not go according to his wishes, he is not a dogmatist. He is completely released from views (and) wise. He does not cling to the world, and does not reproach himself. He is without association in respect of all mental phenomena (*dhammas*), whatever is seen, or heard, or thought. That sage with burden laid down, completely freed, is without imaginings, unattached, not grasping (*pubbāsave hitvā nave akubbaṃ, na chandagū no pi nivissa-vādī, sa vippamutto diṭṭhigatehi dhīro, na lippati loke anattagarahī. sa sabbadhammesu visenibhūto, yaṃ kiñci diṭṭhaṃ va, sutaṃ mutaṃ vā, sa pannabhāro muni vippamutto, na kappiyo nūparato na patthiyo ti*, Sn 913–14; see also Sn 798, 803, 900; see Gómez, 'Proto-Mādhyamika', p 140.

22 *sīlabbataṃ vā pi pahāya sabbaṃ, kammañ ca sāvajjanavajjam etaṃ*, Sn 900.
23 *diṭṭhe sute khantim akubbamāno*, Sn 897.
24 *kathaṃdassī kathaṃsīlo upasanto ti vuccati*, Sn 848.
25 Sn 849. Cf., 'He for whom there is no state of dependence, knowing the *dhamma*, is not dependent' (*yassa nissayatā n' atthi ñatvā dhammaṃ anissito*, Sn 856). See also Sn 910: 'A dogmatist is indeed not easy to discipline, since he prefers a preconceived view. Saying that the good is there, in what he depends upon, he speaks of purity (saying) he saw reality there' (*nivissavādī na hi subbināyo, pakappitaṃ diṭṭhi purekkharāno, yaṃ nissito tattha subhaṃ vadāno, suddhiṃ-vado tattha tathaddasā so*, Sn 914).
26 *dhammesu ca na gacchati*, Sn 861.
27 Nett 65.
28 *diṭṭhaṃ, sutaṃ, mutaṃ, viññātaṃ, pattaṃ, pariyesitaṃ, anuvicaritaṃ manasā*, S III 203.
29 The *Alagaddūpama-sutta* gives the first four *khandhas*, as noted above.
30 *diṭṭhaṃ sutam mutam viññātaṃ pattaṃ pariyesitaṃ anuvicaritaṃ manasā tam pi: etaṃ mama eso'ham asmi, eso me attā ti samanupassati*, M I 135.
31 Indeed, I have compared this process to attachment to the *khandhas*.
32 S III 203.
33 Eric Fallick, 'Two Small Remnants of "Pre-Hīnayānist" Buddhism in the Pāli Nikāyas', *Buddhist Studies Review*, 17 (2000), 35–8.
34 *anupādinna-anupādāniyā*, Dhs 181 § 992.
35 Cf., 'By him not even a minute apperception has been formed here in respect of what is seen, heard, or thought' (*tass' idha diṭṭhe va sute mute vā, pakappitā n' atthi aṇū pi saññā*, Sn 802).
36 *ñāṇe pi so nissayaṃ*, Sn 800.
37 *diṭṭhim pi so na pacceti kiñci*, Sn 800. The term *pacceti* is translated as 'believe in'. The term literally means 'to come on to'; see PED s.v. *pacceti*.
38 Burford, *Desire, Death and Goodness*, p. 81.
39 Ibid., pp. 93–4. See also her comments elsewhere:

> If this commentary were to follow the example of the *Aṭṭhakavagga*, we would expect it to explain the latter [*diṭṭhi*] form of desire as the selfish attachment to any particular view. The *Mahāniddesa*, however, is very consistent in its interpretation of this form of desire as desire for specific wrong-views, as opposed to allegiance to the one correct teaching (i.e. of the Buddha). Burford, 'Theravāda Buddhist Soteriology', p. 50.

40 i.e. the *avyākata* against the true *dhamma*; see her discussion of Sn 837 (Burford, *Desire, Death and Goodness*, pp. 98–9).
41 Norman: 'than the noble path'; Norman, K.R., *The Group of Discourses* II, (London, 1995), p. 92.
42 *diṭṭhena ce suddhi narassa hoti*
ñāṇena vā so pajahāti dukkhaṃ,
aññena so sujjhati sopadhīko
diṭṭhi hi naṃ pāva tathā vadānaṃ.
na brāhmaṇo aññato suddhim āha
diṭṭhe sute sīlavate mute vā,
puññe ca pāpe ca anūpalitto
attañ jaho na-y-idha pakubbamāno, Sn 789–90.
43 Burford, 'Theravāda Buddhist Soteriology', p. 52.
44 Gómez 'Proto-Mādhyamika in the Pāli Canon', p. 141.
45 *aññena so sujjhati sopadhīko ti aññena asuddhimaggena micchā-paṭipadāya aniyyānikapathena aññatra satipaṭṭhānehi aññatra sammappadhānehi aññatra*

iddhipādehi aññatra indriyehi aññatra balehi aññatra bojjhaṅgehi aññatra ariyā aṭṭhaṅgikā maggā naro sujjhati visujjhati parisujjhati muccati (vimuccati) parimuccati; sopadhīko ti sarāgo sadoso samoho samāno sataṇho sadiṭṭhi sakileso saupādāno ti aññena so sujjhati sopadhīko, Nidd I 85–6.

Translation adapted from Burford, 'Theravāda Buddhist Soteriology', p. 51 (see Burford, p. 60, note 29).

46 See also the commentary on the phrase at Sn 792: 'having understood the doctrine by means of knowledge' (*vidvā ca vedehi samecca dhammaṃ*). The commentary, according to Burford, 'delineates the specific contents of this one true teaching.' (Burford, 'Theravāda Buddhist Soteriology', p. 52). The commentary explains that all *saṃkhāras* are impermanent, unsatisfactory and not-self. The sequence of dependent-origination is given in its *anuloma* and *paṭiloma* cycles. It is stated that there is *dukkha*, its arising, cessation and the way to its cessation. There are the corruptions, their arising, cessation and the way to their cessation, etc. This is the 'one true teaching' (***vidvā vedehi samecca dhamman ti****, sammeca abhisamecca dhammaṃ; sabbe saṃkhārā aniccā ti samecca abhisamecca dhammaṃ, sabbe saṃkhārā dukkhā ti samecca abhisamecca dhammaṃ, sabbe dhammā anattā ti samecca abhisamecca dhammaṃ; avijjā-paccayā saṅkharā ti samecca abhisamecca dhammaṃ; saṃkhārapaccayā viññāṇan ti samecca abhisamecca dhammaṃ; viññāṇapaccayā nāmarūpan ti–pe–nāmarūpapaccayā saḷāyatanan ti–pe–saḷāyatanapaccayā phasso ti–pe–phassapaccayā vedanā ti–pe–vedanāpaccayā taṇhā ti–pe–taṇhāpaccayā upādānan ti–pe–upādānapaccayā bhavo ti–pe–bhavapaccayā jātī ti–pe–jātipaccayā jarāmaraṇan ti samecca abhisamecca dhammaṃ; avijjānirodhā saṃkhāranirodho ti samecca abhisamecca dhammaṃ; saṃkhāranirodhā viññāṇanirodho ti samecca abhisamecca dhammaṃ; viññāṇanirodhā nāmarūpanirodho ti–pe–nāmarūpanirodhā saḷāyatananirodho ti–pe–saḷāyatananirodhā phassanirodho ti–pe–phassanirodhā vedanānirodho ti–pe–vedanānirodhā taṇhānirodho ti taṇhānirodhā upādānanirodho ti–pe–upādānanirodhā bhavanirodho ti–pe–bhavanirodhā jātinirodho ti–pe–jātinirodhā jarāmaraṇanirodho ti samecca abhisamecca dhammaṃ; idaṃ dukkhan ti samecca abhisamecca dhammaṃ; ayaṃ dukkhasamudayo ti–pe–ayaṃ dukkhanirodho ti–pe–ayaṃ dukkhanirodhagāminī paṭipadā ti samecca abhisamecca dhammaṃ; ime āsavā ti samecca abhisamecca dhammaṃ; ayaṃ āsavasamudayo ti–pe–ayaṃ āsavanirodho ti–pe–ayaṃ āsavanirodhagāminīpaṭi padā ti samecca abhisamecca dhammaṃ, ime dhammā abhiññeyyā ti samecca abhisamecca dhammaṃ, ime dhammā pariññeyyāti–pe–ime dhammā pahātabbā ti–pe–ime dhammā bhāvetabbā ti–pe–ime dhammā sacchikātabbā ti samecca abhisamecca dhammaṃ; channaṃ phassāyatanānaṃ samudayañ ca atthaṅgamañ ca assādañ ca ādīnavañ ca nissaraṇañ ca samecca abhisamecca dhammaṃ; pañcannaṃ upādānakkhandhānaṃ samudayañ ca atthaṅgamañ ca assādañ ca ādīnavañ ca nissaraṇañ ca samecca abhisamecca dhammaṃ; catunnaṃ mahābhūtānaṃ samudayañ ca atthaṅgamañ ca assādañ ca ādīnavañ ca nissaraṇañ ca samecca abhisamecca dhammaṃ; yaṃ kiñci samudayadhammaṃ, sabbaṃ taṃ nirodhadhammaṃ*, Nidd I 94–5).

47 Burford, 'Theravāda Buddhist Soteriology', p. 52.

48 Ibid., p. 53.

49 Cf. my discussion of the ten (sometimes five) means of knowledge in Chapter 2.

50 Griffiths, *On Being Mindless*, p. 157, note 63.

51 *sabbaṃ me khamati*, M I 497, *sabbaṃ me na khamatī ti*, M I 497, *ekaccaṃ me khamati, ekaccaṃ me na khamati*, M I 498.

52 Jayatilleke, *Early Buddhist Theory of Knowledge*, p. 213. Collins makes some slightly different comments on Dīghanakha's view (Collins, *Selfless Persons*, p. 122).

53 The text tells us that Dīghanakha was a 'wanderer' (*paribbājaka*, M I 497). Tradition tells us that he was the nephew of Sāriputta and that Sāriputta, before joining the

Buddha had been a student of Sañjaya Belaṭṭhiputta. He is then loosely associated with the sceptical tradition; see G.P. Malasekera, *Dictionary of Pāli Proper Names*, Volume I (New Delhi, 1995), pp. 1081–2.

54 *yā pi kho te esā Aggivessana diṭṭhi: sabbaṃ me na khamatī ti, esā pi te diṭṭhi na khamatī ti*, M I 497.

55 *esā ce me bho Gotama diṭṭhi khameyya taṃ p' assa tādisam eva, taṃ p' assa tādisam evā ti*, M I 497–98.

56 *te tañ c' eva diṭṭhiṃ na ppajahanti aññañ ca diṭṭhiṃ upādiyanti*, M I 498.

57 *te tañ c' eva diṭṭhiṃ pajahanti aññañ ca diṭṭhiṃ na upādiyanti*, M I 498. Of some interest is Jayatilleke's argument (Jayatilleke, *Early Buddhist Theory of Knowledge*, p. 92), that in the view of Dīghanakha we find a precursor of Jayarāśi. As is well known, Jayarāśi's *Tattvopaplavasiṃha* caused some excitement when it was first edited in the early part of the century, scholars at first believing it to be a 'lost Lokāyata text'. The text in fact rejects all means of knowledge, and so, in principle, can be compared to the view which agrees with no-view. For more on these ideas, see Eli Franco, *Perception, Knowledge and Disbelief: A Study of JayarāŚi's Scepticism* (Stuttgart, 1987).

58 *ye te samaṇabrāhmaṇā evaṃvādino evaṃdiṭṭhino: sabbaṃ me khamatī ti, tesam ayaṃ diṭṭhi sārāgāya santike saṃyogāya santike abhinandanāya santike ajjhosānāya santike upādānāya santike* [...] *ye te samaṇabrāhmaṇā evaṃvādino evaṃdiṭṭhino: sabbaṃ me na kkhamatī ti, tesam ayaṃ diṭṭhi asārāgāya santike asaṃyogāya santike anabhinandanāya santike anajjhosānāya santike anupādānāya santike*, M I 498.

59 *ukkaṃsati me bhavaṃ Gotamo diṭṭhi-gataṃ, samukkaṃseti me bhavaṃ Gotamo diṭṭhi-gatan ti*, M I 498.

60 *thāmasā parāmāsā abhinivissa*, M I 498, 499. The same terms we met in Chapter 4 and the discussion of the *Paṭisambhidāmagga*.

61 *idam eva saccaṃ, moggam aññan ti*, M I 498, 499.

62 *iti so viggahañ ca vivādañ ca vighātañ ca vihesañ ca attani sampassamāno tañ c' eva diṭṭhiṃ pajahati aññañ ca diṭṭhiṃ na upādiyati ; evam etāsaṃ diṭṭhīnaṃ pahānaṃ hoti, evam etāsaṃ diṭṭhīnaṃ paṭinissaggo hoti*, M I 499.

63 *yaṃ kiñci samudayadhammaṃ sabban taṃ nirodhadhamman ti*, M I 501.

64 *n' atthi sabbaso bhavananirodho ti*, M I 410, *atthi sabbaso bhavanirodho*, M I 410–11.

65 *ye kho te bhanto samaṇabrāhmaṇā evaṃvādino evaṃdiṭṭhino: n' atthi sabbaso bhavanirodho ti, tesam ayaṃ diṭṭhi sārāgāya santike saṃyogāya santike abhinandanāya santike ajjhosānāya santike. upādānāya santike ye pana te samaṇabrāhmaṇā evaṃvādino evaṃdiṭṭhino: atthi sabbaso bhavanirodho ti, tesam ayaṃ diṭṭhi asārāgāya santike asaṃyogāya santike anabhinandanāya santike anajjhosānāya santike anupādānāya santike.so iti paṭisaṇkhāya bhavānaṃ yeva nibbidāya virāgāya nirodhāya paṭipanno hoti*, M I 411.

66 *diṭṭhiṃ pajahati aññañ ca diṭṭhiṃ na upādiyati*, M I 499.

67 *so iti paṭisaṇkhāya bhavānaṃ yeva nibbidāya viragāya nirodhāya paṭipanno hoti*, M I 411.

68 *yathāvādī kho āvuso sadevake loke samārake sabrahmake, sassamaṇabrāhmaṇiyā pajāya sadevamanussāya na kenaci loke viggayha tiṭṭhati, yathā ca pana kāmehi visaṃyuttaṃ viharantaṃ taṃ brāhmaṇaṃ akathaṅkathiṃ chinnakukkuccaṃ bhavābhave vītataṇhaṃ saññā nānusenti, evaṃ vādī kho ahaṃ āvuso evam akkhāyī ti*, M I 108.

Conclusion

1 In the *Paccaya-sutta* (S II 42–3) at S II 42, the *Bhikkhu-sutta* (S II 43–5) at S II 45, the *Nāṇavatthu-sutta* (S II 56–9) at S II 58, the *Paṭhama ariyasāvaka-sutta* (S II 77–9) at S II 79 and the *Dutiya ariyasāvaka-sutta* (SII 79–80) at S II 80.

2 *yaṅ kiñci samudayadhammaṃ sabban taṃ nirodhadhamman ti*, M I 380.

Appendix

1 The first three views begin with:
idha bhikkhave ekacco samaṇo vā brāhmaṇo vā idaṃ kusalan ti yathābhūtaṃ na ppajānāti. idaṃ akusalan ti yathābhūtaṃ na ppajānāti. tassa evaṃ hoti: ahaṃ kho idaṃ kusalan ti yathābhūtaṃ na ppajānāmi. idaṃ akusalan ti yathābhūtaṃ na ppajānāmi. ahañ c' eva kho pana idaṃ kusalanti yathābhūtaṃ na appajānanto, idaṃ akusalan ti yathābhūtaṃ na appajānanto, idaṃ kusalan ti vā vyākareyyaṃ, idaṃ akusalan ti vā vyākareyyaṃ, tattha me assa chando vā rāgo vā doso vā paṭigho vā. yattha me assa chando vā rāgo vā doso vā paṭigho vā.
View 1: *taṃ mam' assa musā. yaṃ mam' assa musā, so mam' assa vighāto. yo mam' assa vighāto, so mam' assa antarāyo ti. iti so musāvādabhayā musāvādaparijegucchā n' ev' idaṃ kusalanti vyākaroti. na pan' idaṃ akusalan ti vyākaroti.*
View 2: *tattha me assa chando vā rāgo vā doso vā paṭigho vā. yattha me assa chando vā rāgo vā doso vā paṭigho vā, taṃ mam' assa upādānaṃ. yaṃ mam' assa upādānaṃ, so mam' assa vighāto. yo mam' assa vighāto, so mam' assa antarāyo ti. iti so upādānabhayā upādānaparijegucchā n' ev' idaṃ kusalan ti vyākaroti. na pan' idaṃ akusalan ti vyākaroti.*
View 3: *santi hi kho pana samaṇabrāhmaṇā paṇḍitā nipuṇā kataparappavādā vālavedhirūpā vobhindantā maññe caranti paññāgatena diṭṭhigatāni, te maṃ tattha samanuyuñjeyyuṃ samanugāheyyuṃ samanubhāseyyuṃ. ye maṃ tattha samanuyuñjeyyuṃ samanuyuñjeyyuṃ samanuyuñjeyyuṃ, tesāhaṃ na sampāyeyyaṃ. yesāhaṃ na sampāyeyyaṃ, so mam' assa vighāto. yo mam' assa vighāto, so mam' assa antarāyo ti. iti so anuyogabhayā anuyogaparijegucchā n' ev' idaṃ kusalan ti vyākaroti. na pan' idaṃ akusalan ti vyākaroti.*
All views (including the fourth view) conclude with: *tattha tattha pañhaṃ puṭṭho samāno vācāvikkhepaṃ āpajjati amarāvikkhepaṃ: evam pi me no. tathā ti pi me no. aññathā ti pi me no. no ti pi me no. no no ti pi me no ti.*

2 View 4: *idha bhikkhave ekacco samaṇo vā brāhmaṇo vā mando hoti momūho. so mandattā momūhattā tattha tattha pañhaṃ puṭṭho samāno vācāvikkhepaṃ āpajjati amarāvikkhepaṃ: atthi paro loko ti iti ce maṃ pucchasi, atthi paro loko ti iti ce me assa, atthi paro loko ti iti te naṃ vyākareyyaṃ. evam pi me no. tathā ti pi me no. aññathā ti pi me no. no ti pi me no. no no ti pi me no. n' atthi paro loko ti iti ce maṃ pucchasi, n' atthi paro loko ti iti ce me assa, n' atthi paro loko ti iti te naṃ vyākareyyaṃ. evam pi me no. tathā ti pi me no. aññathā ti pi me no. no ti pi me no. no no ti pi me no. atthi ca n' atthi ca paro loko ti iti ce maṃ pucchasi, atthi ca n' atthi ca paro loko ti iti ce me assa, atthi ca n' atthi ca paro loko ti iti te naṃ vyākareyyaṃ. evam pi me no. tathā ti pi me no. aññathā ti pi me no. no ti pi me no. no no ti pi me no. atthi sattā opapātikā ti iti ce maṃ pucchasi, atthi sattā opapātikā ti iti ce maṃ assa, atthi sattā opapātikā ti iti te naṃ vyākareyyaṃ. evam pi me no. tathā ti pi me no. aññathā ti pi me no. no ti pi me no. no no ti pi me no. n' atthi sattā opapātikā ti iti ce maṃ pucchasi, n' atthi sattā opapātikā ti iti ce me assa, n' atthi sattā opapātikā ti iti te naṃ vyākareyyaṃ. evam pi me no. tathā ti pi me no. aññathā ti pi me no. no ti pi me no. no no ti pi me no. atthi ca n' atthi ca sattā opapātikā ti iti ce maṃ pucchasi, atthi ca n' atthi ca sattā opapātikā ti iti ce me assa, atthi ca n' atthi ca sattā opapātikā ti iti te naṃ vyākareyyaṃ. evam pi me no. tathā ti pi me no. aññathā ti pi me no. no ti*

pi me no. no no ti pi me no. nevatthi na n' atthi sattā opapātikā ti iti ce maṃ pucchasi, n' ev' atthi na n' atthi sattā opapātikā ti iti ce me assa, n' ev' atthi na n' atthi sattā opapātikā ti iti ce naṃ vyākareyyaṃ. evam pi me no. tathā ti pi me no. aññathā ti pi me no. no ti pi me no. no no ti pi me no. atthi sukaṭadukkaṭānaṃ kammānaṃ phalaṃ vipāko ti iti ce maṃ pucchasi, atthi sukaṭadukkaṭānaṃ kammānaṃ phalaṃ vipāko ti iti ce me assa, atthi sukaṭadukkaṭānaṃ kammānaṃ phalaṃ vipāko ti iti te naṃ vyākareyyaṃ. evam pi me no. tathā ti pi me no. aññathā ti pi me no. no ti pi me no. no no ti pi me no. n' atthi sukaṭadukkaṭānaṃ kammānaṃ phalaṃ vipāko ti iti ce maṃ pucchasi, n' atthi sukaṭadukkaṭānaṃ kammānaṃ phalaṃ vipāko ti iti ce me assa, n' atthi sukaṭadukkaṭānaṃ kammānaṃ phalaṃ vipāko ti iti te naṃ vyākareyyaṃ. evam pi me no. tathā ti pi me no. aññathā ti pi me no. no ti pi me no. no no ti pi me no. atthi ca n' atthi ca sukaṭadukkaṭānaṃ kammānaṃ phalaṃ vipāko ti iti ce maṃ pucchasi, atthi ca n' atthi ca sukaṭadukkaṭānaṃ kammānaṃ phalaṃ vipāko iti ce me assa, atthi ca n' atthi ca sukaṭadukkaṭānaṃ kammānaṃ phalaṃ vipāko ti iti te naṃ vyākareyyaṃ. evam pi me no. tathā ti pi me no. aññathā ti pi me no. no ti pi me no. no no ti pi me no. n' ev' atthi na n' atthi sukaṭadukkaṭānaṃ kammānaṃ phalaṃ vipāko ti iti ce maṃ pucchasi, n' ev' atthi na n' atthi sukaṭadukkaṭānaṃ kammānaṃ phalaṃ vipāko ti iti ce me assa, n' ev' atthi na n' atthi sukaṭadukkaṭānaṃ kammānaṃ phalaṃ vipākoti iti te naṃ vyākareyyaṃ. evam pi me no. tathā ti pi me no. aññathā ti pi me no. no ti pi me no. no no ti pi me no. hoti tathāgato param maraṇā ti iti ce maṃ pucchasi, hoti tathāgato param maraṇā ti iti ce me assa, hoti tathāgato param maraṇā ti iti te naṃ vyākareyyaṃ. evam pi me no. tathā ti pi me no. aññathā pi me no. no ti pi me no. no no ti pi me no. na hoti tathāgato param maraṇā ti iti ce maṃ pucchasi, na hoti tathāgato param maraṇā ti iti ce me assa, na hoti tathāgato param maraṇā ti iti te naṃ vyākareyyaṃ. evam pi me no. tathā ti pi me no. aññathā ti pi me no. no ti pi me no. no no ti pi me no. hoti ca na hoti ca tathāgato param maraṇā ti iti ce maṃ pucchasi, hoti ca na hoti ca tathāgato param maraṇā ti iti ce me assa, hoti ca na hoti ca tathāgato param maraṇā ti iti te naṃ vyākareyyaṃ. evam pi me no. tathā ti pi me no. aññathā ti pi me no. no ti pi me no. no no ti pi me no. n' eva hoti na na hoti tathāgato param maraṇā ti iti ce maṃ pucchasi, n' eva hoti na na hoti tathāgato paraṃ maraṇā ti iti ce me assa, n' eva hoti na na hoti tathāgato param maraṇā ti iti te naṃ vyākareyyaṃ. evam pi me no. tathā ti pi me no. aññathā ti pi me no. no ti pi me no. no no ti pi me no, D I 24–8.

3 Jayatilleke, *Early Buddhist Theory of Knowledge*, p. 120, Dutt, *Early Monastic Buddhism*, pp. 51–2.
4 Jayatilleke, ibid., p. 127.
5 Jayatilleke, ibid., p. 128–9.
6 See Warder's discussion, *Outline of Indian Philosophy*, p. 45.
7 *evam pi me no. tathā ti pi me no. aññathā ti pi me no. no ti pi me no. no no ti pi me no*, D I 25.
8 Four clauses by not counting the first phrase *evam pi me no*. Watanabe, *Philosophy and its Development in the Nikāyas and Abhidhamma*, (Delhi, 1983), p. 89. Watanabe gives as his reference *Sumaṇgalavilāsinī*, 115–16.
9 *puna ca paraṃ* [...] *idh' ekacco satthā mando hoti momūho, so mandattā momūhattā tathā tathā pañhaṃ puṭṭho samāno vācāvikkhepaṃ āpajjati amarāvikkhepaṃ: evam pi me no. tathā ti pi me no. aññathā ti pi me no. no ti pi me no. no no ti pi no.* M I 520–1.
10 The other three are those who claim 'omniscience' (*sabbaññū*), the 'traditionalist' (*anussaviko*), and the third the 'reasoner' and 'enquirer' (*takkī, vīmaṃsī*). These can, of course, be compared to the four ways which 'negate the living of the holy life' cited in Chapter 2. These four kinds of holy life without consolation are evaluated in a more positive way than the previous group of four. Those who claim omniscience are most likely Jains – the *anussaviko* is surely an allusion to the Brahmanic tradition, the *takkī/vīmaṃsī* are familiar as a way of arriving at a viewpoint from the *Brahmajāla-sutta*.

11 View 1: *yato kho* [...] *ayaṃ attā rūpī cātummahābhūtiko mātāpettikasambhavo.*
View 2: *atthi kho* [...] *eso attā yaṃ tvaṃ vadesi n' eso n' atthī ti vadāmi. no ca kho bho ayaṃ attā ettāvatā sammā samucchinno hoti.*
atthi kho [...] *añño attā dibbo rūpī kāmāvacaro kabaliṅkārāhārabhakkho, taṃ tvaṃ na jānāsi na passasi. tam ahaṃ jānāmi passāmi.*
View 3: *atthi kho* [...] *añño attā dibbo rūpī manomayo sabbaṅgapaccaṅgī ahīnindriyo. taṃ tvaṃ na jānāsi na passasi. tam ahaṃ jānāmi passāmi.*
View 4: *atthi kho* [...] *añño attā sabbaso rūpasaññānaṃ samatikkamā paṭighasaññānaṃ atthaṅgamā nānāttasaññānaṃ amanasikārā ananto ākāso ti ākāsānañcāyatanūpago. taṃ tvaṃ na jānāsi na passasi. tam ahaṃ jānāmi passāmi.*
View 5: *atthi kho* [...] *añño attā sabbaso ākāsānañcāyatanaṃ samatikkamma anantaṃ viññāṇan ti viññaṇañcāyatanūpago. taṃ tvaṃ na jānāsi na passasi. tam ahaṃ jānāmi passāmi.*
View 6: *atthi kho* [...] *añño attā sabbaso viññāṇañcāyatanaṃ samatikkamma n' atthi kiñcī ti akiñcaññāyatanūpago taṃ tvaṃ na jānāsi na passasi. tam ahaṃ jānāmi passāmi.*
View 7: *atthi kho* [...] *añño attā sabbaso ākiñcaññāyatanaṃ samatikkamma santam etaṃ paṇītam etan ti nevasaññānāsaññāyatanūpago. taṃ tvaṃ na jānāsi na passasi. tam ahaṃ jānāmi passāmi.*
All views: *so kho* [...] *attā yato kāyassa bhedā ucchijjati vinassati na hoti param maraṇā. ettāvatā kho bho ayaṃ attā sammā samucchinno hotī ti*, D I 34–6.

12 *itth' eke sato sattassa ucchedaṃ vināsaṃ vibhavaṃ paññāpenti.*

13 See Bodhi, *The Discourse on the All-Embracing Net of Views*, p. 29.

14 *rūpi attā hoti arogo paraṃ maraṇā asaññī ti naṃ paññāpenti. arūpī* [...] *rūpī ca arūpī ca* [...] *n' eva rūpī nārūpī* [...] *anantavā* [...] *anantavā ca anantavā ca, n' ev' antavā nānantavā attā hoti arogo paraṃ maraṇā asaññī ti naṃ paññāpenti*, D I 32.

15 *rupī attā hoti arogo para maraṇā nevasaññīnāsaññī ti naṃ paññāpenti. ārūpī* [...] *rūpī ca ārūpī ca* [...] *n' eva rūpī nārūpī* [...] *anantavā* [...] *anantavā ca anantavā ca, n' ev' antavā nānantavā attā hoti arogo paraṃ maraṇā nevaassaññīnāsaññī ti naṃ paññāpenti*, D I 33.

16 View 1: *yato kho* [...] *ayaṃ attā pañcahi kāmaguṇehi samappito samaṅgibhūto paricāreti, ettāvatā kho bho ayaṃ attā paramadiṭṭhadhammanibbānaṃ patto hotī ti.*
View 2: *atthi kho* [...] *eso attā yaṃ tvaṃ vadesi. n' eso n' atthī ti vadāmi. no ca kho bho ayaṃ attā ettāvatā paramadiṭṭhadhammanibbānaṃ patto. hoti taṃ kissa hetu? kāmā hi bho aniccā dukkhā vipariṇāmadhammā tesaṃ vipariṇāmaññathābhāvā uppajjanti sokaparidevadukkhadomanassupāyāsā yato kho bho ayaṃ attā vivicc' eva kāmehi vivicca akusalehi dhammehi savitakkaṃ savicāraṃ vivekajaṃ pītisukhaṃ paṭhamaṃ jhānaṃ upasampajja viharati. ettāvatā kho bho ayaṃ attā paramadiṭṭhadhammanibbānaṃ patto hotī ti.*
View 3: *atthi kho* [...] *eso attā yaṃ tvaṃ vadesi. n' eso n' atthī ti vadāmi. no ca kho bho ayaṃ attā ettāvatā paramadiṭṭhadhammanibbānaṃ patto hoti. taṃ kissa hetu? yad eva tattha vitakkitaṃ vicāritaṃ eten' etaṃ oḷārikaṃ akkhāyati. yato kho bho ayaṃ attā vitakkavicārānaṃ vūpasamā ajjhattaṃ sampasādanaṃ cetaso ekodibhāvaṃ avitakkaṃ avicāraṃ samādhijaṃ pītisukhaṃ dutiyaṃ jhānaṃ upasampajja viharati. ettāvatā kho bho ayaṃ attā paramadiṭṭhadhammanibbānaṃ patto hotī ti. ettāvatā kho bho ayaṃ attā paramadiṭṭhadhammanibbānaṃ patto hotī ti.*
View 4: *atthi kho* [...] *eso attā yaṃ tvaṃ vadesi. n' eso n' atthī ti vadāmi. no ca kho bho ayaṃ attā ettāvatā paramadiṭṭhadhammanibbānaṃ patto hoti. taṃ kissa hetu? yad eva tattha pītigataṃ cetaso uppillāvitattaṃ eten' etaṃ oḷārikaṃ akkhāyati. yato kho bho ayaṃ attā pītiyā ca virāgā upekkhako ca viharati sato ca sampajāno sukhaṃ ca kāyena paṭisaṃvedeti, yaṃ taṃ ariyā ācikkhanti upekkhako satimā sukhavihārī ti tatiyaṃ jhānaṃ upasampajja viharati. ettāvatā kho bho ayaṃ attā paramadiṭṭhadhammanibbānaṃ patto hotī ti.*

View 5: *atthi kho* [...] *eso attā, yaṃ tvaṃ vadesi, n' eso n' atthī ti vadāmi. no ca kho bho ayaṃ attā ettāvatā paramadiṭṭhadhammanibbānaṃ patto hoti. taṃ kissa hetu? yad eva tattha sukham iti cetaso ābhogo eten' etaṃ oḷārikaṃ akkhāyati. yato kho bho ayaṃ attā sukhassa ca pahānā dukkhassa ca pahānā pubb' eva somanassadomanassānaṃ atthaṅgamā adukkhamasukhaṃ upekkhāsatipārisuddhiṃ catutthaṃ jhānaṃ upasampajja viharati, ettāvatā kho bho ayaṃ attā paramadiṭṭhadhammanibbānaṃ patto hotī ti*, D I 37–8.

17 Dutt, *Early Monastic Buddhism*, p. 61.

18 *adhicca-samuppano attā ca loko ca. taṃ kissa hetu? ahaṃ hi pubbe nāhosiṃ so 'mhi etarahi ahutvā santatāya pariṇato ti*, D I 29. Compare to D III 33–4, 138.

19 *adhicca-samuppano attā ca loko ca*, D I 29.

20 Dutt, *Early Monastic Buddhism*, pp. 53–4.

21 D I 12.

22 *so takka-pariyāhataṃ vīmaṇsānucaritaṃ sayaṃ paṭibhānaṃ evam āha*, D I 29.

23 *yo kho so bhavaṃ brahmā mahābrahmā abhibhū anabhibhūto aññadatthudaso vasavattī issaro kattā nimmātā seṭṭho sajitā vasī pitā bhūtabhavyānaṃ, yena mayaṃ bhotā brahmunā nimmitā, so nicco dhuvo sassato avipariṇāmadhammo sassatisamaṃ tath' eva ṭhassati. ye pana mayaṃ ahumhā tena bhotā brahmunā nimmitā, te mayaṃ aniccā addhuvā appāyukā cavanadhammā itthattaṃ āgatā ti*, D I 18–19.

24 *ye kho te bhonto devā na khiḍḍāpadosikā, te na ativelaṃ hassa-khiḍḍāratidhammasamāpannā viharanti. tesaṃ na ativelaṃ hassa-khiḍḍāratidhammasamāpannānaṃ viharataṃ sati na sammussati. satiyā asammosā te devā tamhā kāyā na cavanti, niccā dhuvā sassatā avipariṇāmadhammā sassatisamaṃ tath' eva ṭhassati. ye pana mayaṃ ahumhā khiḍḍāpadosikā, te mayaṃ ativelaṃ hassakhiḍḍāratidhammasamāpannā viharimbha. tesaṃ no ativelaṃ hassakhiḍḍāratidhammasamāpannānaṃ viharataṃ sati sammussati. satiyā sammosā evaṃ mayaṃ tamhā kāyā cutā aniccā addhuvā appāyukā cavanadhammā itthattaṃ āgatā ti*, D I 19–20.

25 *ye kho te bhonto devā na manopadosikā, te nātivelaṃ aññamaññaṃ upanijjhāyanti. te nātivelaṃ aññamaññaṃ upanijjhāyantā aññamaññamhi cittāni na ppadūsenti. te aññamaññaṃ appaduṭṭhacittā akilantakāyā akilantacittā. te devā tamhā kāyā na cavanti niccā dhuvā sassatā avipariṇāmadhammā sassatisamaṃ tath' eva ṭhassanti. ye pana mayaṃ ahumhā manopadosikā, te mayaṃ ativelaṃ aññamaññaṃ upanijjhāyimha. te mayaṃ ativelaṃ aññamaññaṃ upanijjhāyantā aññamaññamhi cittāni padūsimhā. te mayaṃ aññamaññamhi paduṭṭhacittā kilantakāyā kilantacittā evaṃ tamhā kāyā cutā aniccā addhuvā appāyukā cavanadhammā itthattaṃ āgatā ti*, D I 20–1.

26 *yaṃ kho idaṃ vuccati cakkhun ti pi sotan ti pi ghānaṃ ti pi jivhā ti pi kāyo ti pi, ayaṃ attā anicco addhuvo asassato vipariṇāmadhammo. yaṃ ca kho idaṃ vuccati cittan ti vā mano ti vā viññāṇan ti vā ayaṃ attā nicco dhuvo sassato avipariṇāmadhammo sassatisamaṃ tath' eva ṭhassatī ti*, D I 21. This view is described as being the view of a 'rationalist and investigator' (*takkī, vīmaṃsī*).

27 See A V 263 for the Brahmanical practices.

28 *ime cunda dasa kusalakammapathā suciyeva honti, sucikaraṇā ca. imesañ ca pana cunda dasannaṃ kusalānaṃ kammapathānaṃ samannāgamanahetu devā paññāyanti, manussā paññāyanti, yā vā pan' aññā pi kāci sugatiyo ti*, A V 268. See A V 266 where the opposite is said of the ten unwholesome courses of action.

29 *ko nu kho bho gotama hetu ko paccayo yena-m-idh' ekacce sattā kāyassa bhedā paraṃ maraṇā apāyaṃ duggatiṃ vinipātaṃ nirayaṃ upapajjanti? ko pana bho gotama hetu ko paccayo yena-m-idh' ekacce sattā kāyassa bhedā paraṃ maraṇā sugatiṃ saggaṃ lokaṃ upapajjantīti*, M I 285.

30 *adhammacariyā-visamacariyā-hetu kho gahapatayo evam idh' ekacce sattā kāyassa bhedā paraṃ maraṇā apāyaṃ duggatiṃ vinipātaṃ nirayaṃ upapajjanti.*

dhammacariyā-samacariyā-hetu kho gahapatayo evam idh' ekacce sattā kāyassa bhedā paraṃ maraṇā sugatiṃ saggaṃ lokaṃ upapajjantī ti, M I 285–6.

31 *tividhaṃ* [...] *kāye adhammacariyā-visamacariyā hoti*, M I 286.

32 *catubbidhaṃ vācāya adhammacariyā-visamacariyā hoti*, M I 286.

33 *tividhaṃ manasā adhammacariyā-visamacariyā hoti*, M I 286.

34 *atthi* [...] *dhammasamādānaṃ paccuppannadukkhañ c' eva āyatiñca dukkha-vipākaṃ*, M I 310.

35 *atthi* [...] *dhammasamādānaṃ paccuppannasukhaṃ āyatiṃ dukkhavipākaṃ*, M I 310–11.

36 *micchā-diṭṭhi-paccayā ca sukhaṃ somanassaṃ paṭisaṃvedeti*, M I 314.

37 *atthi bhikkhave dhammasamādānaṃ paccuppannadukkhaṃ āyatiṃ sukhavipākaṃ*, M I 312.

38 *sahāpi dukkhena sahāpi domanassena sammā-diṭṭhi hoti. sammā-diṭṭhi-paccayā ca dukkhaṃ domanassaṃ paṭisaṃvedeti*, M I 314–15.

39 *atthi bhikkhave dhammasamādānaṃ paccuppannasukhañ c' eva āyatiñ ca sukhavipākaṃ*, M I 311.

40 *sahāpi sukhena sahāpi somanassena sammā-diṭṭhi hoti. sammā-diṭṭhi-paccayā ca sukhaṃ somanassaṃ paṭisaṃvedeti*, M I 315.

41 *puthusamaṇabrāhmaṇaparappavāde abhivihacca bhāsate ca tāpate ca virocate*, M I 317.

42 *yathā kathaṃ pana bho gotama ariyassa vinaye paccorohaṇī hotī ti*, A V 250.

43 *idha brāhmaṇa ariyasāvako iti paṭisaṃcikkhati: pāṇātipātassa kho pāpako vipāko diṭṭhe c' eva dhamme abhisamparāyañ cā ti. so iti paṭisaṅkhāya pāṇātipātaṃ pajahati, pāṇātipātā paccorohati*, A V 250. This is similar to the *Apaṇṇaka-sutta*.

44 *micchā-diṭṭhiyā kho pāpako vipāko diṭṭhe c' eva dhamme abhisamparāyañ cā ti, so iti paṭisaṅkhāya micchā-diṭṭhiṃ pajahati, micchā-diṭṭhiyā paccorohati*, A V 251.

45 *kāyasamācāram p' ahaṃ* [...] *duvidhena vadāmi: sevitabbam pi asevitabbam pi. tañ ca aññamaññaṃ kāyasamācāraṃ*, M III 45.

46 *vacīsamācāram p' ahaṃ bhikkhave, duvidhena vadāmi: sevitabbam pi asevitabbam pi. tañ ca aññamaññaṃ vacīsamācāraṃ. manosamācāram p' ahaṃ bhikkhave, duvidhena vadāmi:sevitabbam pi asevitabbam pi. tañ ca aññamaññaṃ manosamācāraṃ. cittuppādam p' ahaṃ bhikkhave, duvidhena vadāmi: sevitabbam pi asevitabbam pi. tañ ca aññamaññaṃ cittuppādaṃ. saññāpaṭilābham p' ahaṃ bhikkhave, duvidhena vadāmi: sevitabbam pi asevitabbam pi. tañ ca aññamaññaṃ saññāpaṭilābhaṃ. diṭṭhipaṭilābham p' ahaṃ bhikkhave duvidhena vadāmi: sevitabbam pi asevitabbam pi. tañ ca aññamaññaṃ diṭṭhipaṭilābhaṃ. attabhāvapaṭilābham p' ahaṃ bhikkhave, duvidhena vadāmi: sevitabbam pi asevitabbam pi. tañ ca aññamaññaṃ attabhāvapaṭilābhan ti*, M III 45–6.

47 *kāyasamācāraṃ sevato akusalā dhammā abhivaḍḍhanti kusalā dhammā parihāyanti. evarūpo kāyasamācāro na sevitabbo*, M III 46.

48 *yathārūpañ ca* [...] *kāyasamācāraṃ sevato akusalā dhammā parihāyanti kusalā dhammā abhivaḍḍhanti. evarūpo kāyasamācāro sevitabbo*, M III 46.

49 This term has a technical meaning in Abhidhamma: 'the arising of consciousness'.

50 *idha* [...] *ekacco abhijjhālu hoti, abhijjhāsahagatena cetasā viharati*, M III 49.

51 *idha bhante ekacco anabhijjhālu hoti, abhijjhāsahagatena cetasā viharati. avyāpādavā hoti, avyādapādasahagatena cetasā viharati. avihesavā hoti, avihesāsahagatena cetasā viharati. evarūpaṃ bhante cittuppādaṃ sevato akusalā dhammā parihāyanti. kusalā dhammā abhivaḍḍhanti*, M III 51.

52 The *sutta* also discusses two types of 'acquisition of personality' (*attabhāva-paṭilābhaṃ*). The type which should not be cultivated is that which is 'subject to affliction' (*sabyāpajjhaṃ*), preventing the holder to 'put an end to being' (*apariniṭṭhitabhāvāya*). The acquisition of personality which should be cultivated is 'free from affliction' (*abyāpajjhaṃ*), enabling the holder to 'put an end to being'

(*pariniṭṭhitabhāvāya*, M III 53). The text goes on to discuss a large number of other things which should and should not be cultivated, such as sense objects (M III 56–7), almsfood, villages and people (M III 59).

53 *diṭṭhi-paṭilābhaṃ sevato akusalā dhammā abhivaḍḍhanti, kusalā dhammā parihāyanti. evarūpo diṭṭhi-paṭilābho na sevitabbo, yathārūpañ ca* [...] *diṭṭhi-paṭilābhaṃ sevato akusalā dhammā parihāyanti, kusalā dhammā abhivaḍḍhanti, evarūpo diṭṭhi-paṭilābho sevitabbo*, M III 52.

54 *somanassasahagataṃ diṭṭhi-gatasampayuttaṃ asankhārikam ekaṃ. somanassa-sahagataṃ diṭṭhi-gatasampayuttaṃ sankhārikam ekaṃ. somanassasahagataṃ diṭṭhi-gatavippayuttaṃ asankhārikam ekaṃ. somanassasahagataṃ diṭṭhi-gatavippayuttaṃ sankhārikam ekaṃ. upekkhāsahagataṃ diṭṭhisamapayuttaṃ asankhārikam ekaṃ. upekkhāsahagataṃ diṭṭhi-samapayuttaṃ sankhārikam ekaṃ.*

upekkhāsahagataṃ diṭṭhi-gatavippayuttaṃ asankhārikam ekaṃ. upekkhāsahagataṃ diṭṭhi-gatavippayuttaṃ sankhārikam ekaṃ. dhomanassa-sahagataṃ paṭighasampayuttaṃ asankhārikam ekaṃ. dhomanassa-sahagataṃ paṭighasampayuttaṃ sasankhārikam ekaṃ. upekkhāsahagataṃ vicikicchāsampayuttam ekaṃ. upekkhā-sahagataṃ uddhacca-sampayuttam ekaṃ.

This is from the *Abhidhammatthasaṃgaha*. Translation by Bhikkhu Bodhi, *A Comprehensive Manual of Abhidhamma*, pp. 32–7.

BIBLIOGRAPHY

PĀLI TEXTS

Aṅguttara-nikāya I–V, Morris, R. and Hardy, E. (eds) (PTS, London, 1885–1900).
Atthasālinī, Muller, E. (ed.) (1897), revised edn (PTS, London, 1979).
Dhammapada: *Dhammapadaṭṭhakathā*, Norman, H.C. (ed.) (PTS, London, 1906–14).
Dhammasaṅgaṇi, Muller, E. (ed.) (PTS, London, 1885).
Dīgha-nikāya I–III, Rhys Davids, T.W., Carpenter, J.E. and Stede, W. (eds) (PTS, London, 1890–1911).
Jātaka I–VI, Fausboll, V. (ed.) (London, 1877–96).
Katthāvatthu I–II, Taylor, A.C. (ed.) (PTS, London, 1894–7).
Mahāniddesa I–II, de La Vallé Poussin, L. and Thomas, E.J. (eds) (PTS, London, 1916–17).
Mahāvaṃsa, Geiger, W. (ed.) (PTS, London, 1908).
Majjhima-nikāya I–III, Trenckner, V. and Chalmers, R. (eds) (PTS, London, 1888–1902).
Manorathapūraṇī I–V, Walleser, M. and Kopp, H. (PTS, London, 1924–57).
Milindapañha, Trenckner, V. (ed.) (PTS, London, 1880).
Nettippakaraṇa, Hardy, E. (ed.) (PTS, London, 1902).
Papañcasūdanī I–V, Woods, J.H., Kośambi, D. and Horner, I.B. (eds) (PTS, London, 1922–38).
Paṭisambhidāmagga I–II, Taylor, A.C. (ed.) (PTS, London, 1905–7).
Paṭṭhāna, Rhys Davids, C.A.F. (ed.) (PTS, London, 1906).
Peṭakopadesa, Barua, A. (ed.) (PTS, London, 1949).
Puggalapaññatti, Morris, R. (ed.) (PTS, London, 1883).
Sammohavinodanī, Buddhadatta, A.P. (ed.) (PTS, London, 1923).
Saṃyutta-nikāya I–V, Feer, L. (ed.) (PTS, London, 1884–98).
Sāratthappakāsinī I–II, Woodward, F.L. (ed.) (PTS, London, 1921–37).
Sumaṅgalavilāsinī I–III, Rhys Davids, T.W., Carpenter, J.E. and Stede, W. (eds) (PTS, London, 1886–1932).
Suttanipāta, Anderson, D. and Smith, H. (eds) (PTS, London, 2nd ed. 1968).
Tikapaṭṭhāna I–III, (with commentary) Rhys Davids, C.A.F (ed.) (PTS, London, 1921–3).
Udāna, Stenthal, P. (ed.) (PTS, London, 1885).
Udānaaṭṭakathā, Woodward, F.L. (ed.) (PTS. London, 1926).
Vibhaṅga, Rhys Davids, C.A.F. (ed.) (PTS, London, 1904).
Vinayapiṭaka I–V, Oldenberg, H. (ed.) (PTS, London, 1879–83).
Visuddhimagga, Warren, H.C. (ed.) revised Kosambi, D. (Harvard, 1950).

TRANSLATIONS INTO ENGLISH

Aung, S.Z. and Rhys Davids, C.A.F., *Points of Controversy* (PTS, London, 1915).
Bhikkhu Bodhi, *The Discourse on the All-Embracing Net of Views: The Brahmajāla Sutta and its Commentaries* (Kandy, 1978).
—— *A Comprehensive Manual of Abhidhamma: The Abhidhammattha Sangaha of Ācariya Anuruddha* (Kandy, 1993).
—— *The Middle Length Discourses of the Buddha: A New Translation of the Majjhima Nikāya* (Boston, MA, 1995).
—— *Connected Discourses of the Buddha*, Volumes I–II (PTS, Oxford, 2000).
Horner, I.B., *The Book of the Discipline* I–VI (London, 1938–60).
—— *Middle Length Sayings* I–III (PTS, London, 1954–9).
—— *Milinda's Questions* I–II (London, 1963–4).
Jacobi, H., *Jaina Sutras,* Part II (Oxford, 1884).
Jones, J.J., *The Mahāvastu*, 3 Volumes (London, 1949–56).
Maung Tin, *The Expositor* I–II (PTS, London, 1920).
Ñāṇamoli, Bhikkhu, *The Path of Purification* (Colombo, 1956).
—— *The Guide* (PTS, London, 1962).
—— *Piṭaka Disclosure* (PTS, London, 1964).
—— *The Path of Discrimination* (PTS, London, 1982).
—— *The Dispeller of Delusion*, Part I (PTS, London, 1987).
—— *The Dispeller of Delusion,* Part II (PTS, Oxford, 1991).
Norman, K.R., *Elders' Verses* I–II (PTS, London, 1969–71).
—— *The Group of Discourses* II (PTS, London, 1995).
—— *The Pātimokkha* (PTS, London, 2001).
Rhys Davids, C.A.F., *A Buddhist Manual of Psychological Ethics* (PTS, London, 1900).
Rhys Davids, T.W. and Rhys Davids, C.A.F., *Dialogues of the Buddha* I–III (London, 1899–1921).
U Thiṭṭila, *The Book of Analysis* (PTS, London, 1969).
U Nārada, *Conditional Relations* I–II (PTS, London, 1969–81).
Walshe, M., *The Long Discourses of the Buddha: A Translation of the Dīgha Nikāya* (Boston, MA, 1995).
Woodward, F.L. and Hare, E.M., *The Book of Gradual Sayings* I–V (PTS, London, 1923–6).

SECONDARY SOURCES

Anderson, C.S., *Pain and its Ending: The Four Noble Truths in the Theravāda Buddhist Canon* (Richmond, 1999).
Barua, B.M., *Pre-Buddhistic Indian Philosophy* (Calcutta, 1921).
Basham, A.L., *History and Doctrines of the Ājīvikas* (London, 1951).
—— *The Wonder that was India* (London, 1967).
Bhattacharya, C., 'Can there be Empirical Evidence for General Truth', *Journal of Indian Philosophy*, 15 (1987), pp. 333–47.
Bhattacharya, K., 'Diṭṭhaṃ, sutaṃ, mutaṃ, viññātaṃ', in *Buddhist Studies in Honour of Walpola Rahula*, S. Balasooriya, A. Barau, R. Gombrich, Siri Gunasingha, U. Mallwarachchi and E. Perry (eds) (London, 1980).

Bilmoria, P., 'Jñāna and Pramā: The Logic of Knowing. A Critical Appraisal', *Journal of Indian Philosophy*, 13 (1985), pp. 73–102.

Bhikkhu Bodhi, 'The Buddha's Survey of Views', in *Recent Researches in Buddhist Studies: Essays in Honour of Professor Y. Karunadasa*, Kuala Lumpar Dhammajoti, Asanga Tilakaratne and Kapila Abhayawansa (eds) (Colombo, 1997), pp. 51–69.

—— 'Transcendental Dependent Arising', *The Wheel Publication*, 277/278 (Kandy, 1980).

Braithwaite, R.B., *An Empiricist's View of Religious Belief* (Cambridge, 1955).

Brockington, J.L., *The Sacred Thread: Hinduism in its Continuity and Diversity* (Edinburgh, 1981).

Bronkhorst, J., *The Two Traditions of Meditation in Ancient India* (Stuttgart, 1986).

—— 'Dharma and Abhidharma', *Bulletin of the School of Oriental and African Studies*, 48 (1985), pp. 305–20.

Burford, G., *Desire, Death and Goodness; The Conflict of Ultimate Values in Theravāda Buddhism* (New York, 1991).

—— 'Theravāda Buddhist Soteriology', in *Paths to Liberation: The Mārga and its Transformations in Buddhist Thought*, R. Buswell and R. Gimello (eds) (Honolulu, 1992), pp. 37–61.

Burton, D.F., *Emptiness Appraised* (Richmond, 1999).

Buswell, R.E. and Gimello, R.M. (eds), *Paths to Liberation: The Mārga and its Transformations in Buddhist Thought* (Honolulu, 1992).

Carter, J.R., *Dhamma: Western Academic Approaches and Sinhalese Buddhist Interpretations. A Study of a Religious Concept* (Tokyo, 1978).

—— *On Understanding Buddhists: Essays on the Theravāda Tradition in Sri Lanka* (New York, 1993).

Chakrabarti, K.K., 'Some Remarks on Indian Theories of Truth', *Journal of Indian Philosophy*, 12 (1984), pp. 339–55.

Chatalian, G., 'Jayatilleke on the Concept of Meaningfulness in the Pāli Nikāyas', *Philosophy East and West*, 18 (1968), pp. 67–76.

Chattopadhyaya, D. (ed.), *Cārvāka/Lokāyata: An Anthology of Source Materials and Some Recent Studies* (New Delhi, 1990).

Christian, W.A., *Meaning and Truth in Religion* (Princeton, 1964).

—— *Oppositions of Religious Doctrines* (London, 1972).

Collins, S., *Selfless Persons: Imagery and Thought in Theravāda Buddhism* (Cambridge, 1982).

—— *Nirvana and Other Buddhist Felicities: Utopias of the Pali Imaginaire* (Cambridge, 1998).

Cousins, L.S., 'Good or Skilful? *Kusala* in Canon and Commentary', *Journal of Buddhist Ethics*, 3 (1996), pp. 136–64.

—— Review of Carol Anderson, *Journal of Buddhist Ethics*, 8 (2001), pp. 36–41.

Denwood, P. and Piatigorsky, A. (eds), *Buddhist Studies Ancient and Modern* (London, 1983).

Dharmasena, C.B., 'Purification of view', *The Wheel Publication*, 39–40 (Kandy, 1979), 26–53.

Douglas, M., *Purity and Danger: An Analysis of Concepts of Pollution and Taboo* (London, 1966).

Dundas, P., *The Jains* (London, 1992).

Dutt, N., *Early Monastic Buddhism*, 2nd edn (Calcutta, 1971).

Eliade, M., *The Encyclopaedia of Religion* (New York, 1987).

Fallick, E., 'Two Small Remnants of "Pre-Hīnayānist" Buddhism in the Pāli Nikāyas', *Buddhist Studies Review*, 17 (2000), pp. 35–8.

Franco, E., *Perception, Knowledge and Disbelief: A Study of Jayarāśi's Scepticism* (Stuttgart, 1987).

Gethin, R.M.L., 'The Five Khandhas: Their Treatment in the Nikāyas and Early Abhidhamma', *Journal of Indian Philosophy*, 14 (1986), pp. 35–53.

—— *The Buddhist Path to Awakening: A Study of the Bodhi-Pakkhiyā Dhammā* (Leiden, 1992).

—— 'Wrong View (micchā-diṭṭhi) and Right View (sammā-diṭṭhi) in the Theravāda Abhidhamma', in *Recent Researches in Buddhist Studies: Essays in Honour of Professor Y. Karunadasa*, Kuala Lumpar Dhammajoti, Asanga Tilakaratne and Kapila Abhayawansa (eds) (Colombo 1997), pp. 211–29.

—— *The Foundations of Buddhism* (Oxford, 1998).

Gettier, E., 'Is Justified True Belief Knowledge', *Analysis*, 23 (1963), pp. 121–3.

Gombrich, R.F., *Precept and Practice* (Oxford, 1971).

—— *Theravāda Buddhism* (London, 1988).

—— 'Recovering the Buddha's Message', in *The Buddhist Forum, Volume 1 Seminar Papers 1987–1988*, School of Oriental and African Studies (London, 1990), pp. 5–20.

—— *How Buddhism Began: The Conditioned Genesis of the Early Teachings* (London, 1996).

Gómez, L.O., 'Emptiness and Moral Perfection', *Philosophy East and West*, 23 (1973), pp. 361–73.

—— 'Some Aspects of the Free-Will Question in the Nikāyas', *Philosophy East and West*, 25 (1975), pp. 81–90.

—— 'Proto-Mādhyamika in the Pāli Canon', *Philosophy East and West*, 26 (1976), pp. 137–65.

Griffiths, P.J., 'Concentration or Insight: The Problematic of Theravāda Meditation Theory', *Journal of the American Academy of Religion*, 49 (1981), pp. 605–24.

—— *On Being Mindless: Buddhist Meditation and the Mind–Body Problem* (La Salle, 1986).

—— *On Being Buddha: The Classical Doctrine of Buddhahood* (New York, 1994).

Halbfass, W., *India and Europe: An Essay in Understanding* (Albany, 1988).

Hamilton, S., *Identity and Experience: The Constitution of the Human Being According to Early Buddhism* (London, 1996).

—— *Early Buddhism: A New Approach. The I of the Beholder* (Richmond, 2000).

Harvey, P., *An Introduction to Buddhism* (Cambridge, 1990).

Hayes, R., *Dignaga on the Interpretation of Signs* (Dordrecht, 1988).

Hoffman, F., 'Early Buddhist Fourfold Logic', *Journal of Indian Philosophy*, 12 (1982), pp. 309–37.

—— 'The Pragmatic Efficacy of Saddhā', *Journal of Indian Philosophy*, 15 (1987), pp. 399–412.

Horner, I.B., *The Early Buddhist Theory of Man Perfected* (London, 1936).

Hudson, W.D. (ed.), *The Is–Ought Question: A Collection of Papers on the Central Problem in Moral Philosophy* (London, 1969).

Hume, David, *A Treatise of Human Nature: Books Two and Three*, Páll Árdal (ed.) (London, 1972).

Huntington, C.W., *The Emptiness of Emptiness: An Introduction to Early Indian Mādhyamika* (Honolulu, 1989).

Jackson, R., *Is Enlightenment Possible? Dharmakīrti and rGyal tshab rje on Knowledge, Rebirth, No-Self and Liberation* (New York, 1993).

Jaini, P.S., 'Prajñā and dṛṣṭi in the Vaibhāṣika Abhidharma', in *Prajñāpāramitā and Related Systems: Studies in Honour of Edward Conze*, L. Lancaster (ed.) (Berkeley, 1977), pp. 403–15.

Jayatilleke, K.N., *Early Buddhist Theory of Knowledge* (London, 1963).

Johnson, L.E., *Focusing on Truth* (London, 1992).

Kalupahana, D.J., *The Philosophy of the Middle Way* (Albany, 1986).

Katz, N., *Buddhist Images of Human Perfection: The Arahant of the Sutta Piṭaka Compared to the Bodhisattva and the Mahāsiddha* (Delhi, 1982).

Katz, S.T. (ed.), *Mysticism and Philosophical Analysis* (London, 1978).

Lindbeck, G.A., *The Nature of Doctrine: Religion and Theology in a Post-Liberal Age* (London, 1984).

Lindtner, C., *Nagārjuniana: Studies in the Writings and Philosophy of Nāgārjuna* (Copenhagen, 1982).

Lopez, D. (ed.), *Buddhist Hermeneutics* (Honolulu, 1988).

—— 'Belief', in *Critical Terms for Religious Studies*, M.C. Taylor (ed.) (Chicago, 1998).

MacIntyre, A., *After Virtue* (South Bend, 1981).

Malasekera, G.P., *Dictionary of Pāli Proper Names*, Volume I (New Delhi, 1995).

Masefield, P., *Divine Revelation in Pali Buddhism* (Colombo/London, 1986).

Matilal, B.K., 'Ignorance or Misconception? – A Note on Avidyā in Buddhism', in *Buddhist Studies in Honour of Walpola Rahula*, S. Balasooriya, A Baeau, R. Gombrich, Siri Gunasingha, U. Mallwarachchi and E. Perry (eds) (London, 1980).

—— 'Error and Truth – Classical Indian Theories', *Philosophy East and West*, 31 (1981), pp. 215–24.

—— *Logical and Ethical Issues of Religious Belief* (Calcutta, 1982).

—— *Perception: An Essay on Classical Indian Theories of Knowledge* (Oxford, 1986).

Mohanty, J.N., 'Prāmaṇya and Workability: Response to Potter', *Journal of Indian Philosophy*, 12 (1984), pp. 329–38.

—— *Reason and Tradition in Indian Thought* (Oxford, 1992).

Muir, J., 'Verses Illustrating the Cārvāka Tenets', in *Cārvāka/Lokāyata: An Anthology of Source Materials and Some Recent Studies* (New Delhi, 1990), pp. 351–68.

Ñāṇananda, Bhikkhu, *Concept and Reality in Early Buddhist Thought* (Ceylon, 1971).

Ñāṇārāma, Mahāthera, *The Seven Stages of Purification and The Insight Knowledges* (Kandy, 1983).

Norman, K.R., 'Pāli and the Language of the Heretics', *Collected Papers*, Volume I (PTS, Oxford, 1990), pp. 238–46.

—— 'Māgadhisms in the Kathāvatthu', in K.R. Norman, *Collected Papers*, Volume II (Oxford, 1991), pp. 59–70.

—— 'A Note on *attā* in the *Alagaddūpama-sutta*', in K.R. Norman, *Collected Papers*, Volume II (Oxford, 1991), pp. 200–9.

—— *A Philological Approach to Buddhism* (London, 1997).

O'Conner, D.J., *The Correspondence Theory of Truth* (London, 1975).

Olivelle, P., *Upaniṣads* (Oxford, 1996).

Pajin, D., 'The Legitimacy of the Term "Philosophy" in an Indian Context: The Beginnings of Indian Philosophy', *Journal of Indian Philosophy*, 15 (1987), pp. 349–62.

Pande, G.C., *Studies in the Origins of Buddhism* (Allahabad, 1957).

Potter, K.H., *Presuppositions of Indian Philosophies* (Englewood Cliffs, 1963).

—— 'The Background of Skepticism, East and West', *Journal of Indian Philosophy*, 3 (1975), pp. 299–313.

—— 'Does Indian Epistemology Concern Justified True Belief', *Journal of Indian Philosophy*, 12 (1984), pp. 307–27.

Premasiri, P.D., 'The Philosophy of the Aṭṭhakavagga', *The Wheel Publication*, 182 (Kandy, 1972), pp. 1–30.

Proudfoot, W., *Religious Experience* (Berkeley, 1985).

Pye, M., *Skilful Means: A Concept in Mahāyāna Buddhism* (London, 1978).

Rahula, W., *What the Buddha Taught*, 2nd edn (London, 1967).

Richardson, A. and Bowden, J., *A New Dictionary of Christian Theology* (London, 1983).

Robinson, R.H., *The Buddhist Religion* (Belmont, 1970).

Sayādaw, L., 'Some Points in Buddhist Doctrine', *Journal of the Pāli Text Society* (1913), pp. 115–64.

Schleiermacher, F., *On Religion: Speeches to its Cultured Despisers* (New York, 1958).

Schmithausen, L., 'On Some Aspects of Descriptions or Theories of "Liberating Insight" and "Enlightenment" in Early Buddhism', *Studien Zum Jainismus und Buddhismus (Gedenkschrift für Ludwig Alsdorf)* (K. Bruhn und A. Wezler, Wiesbaden, 1981), pp. 199–250.

Sharpe, R.K., *The Analysis of Knowing: A Decade of Research* (Princeton, 1983).

Shastri, D.R., 'A Short History of Indian Materialism, Sensationalism and Hedonism', in *Cārvaāka/Lokāyata: An Anthology of Source Materials and Some Recent Studies*, D. Chattopadhyaya (ed.) (New Delhi, 1990), pp. 396–431.

Siderits, M., 'A Note on the Early Buddhist Theory of Truth', *Philosophy East and West*, 29 (1979), pp. 491–9.

—— 'The Madhyamaka Critique of Epistemology', *Journal of Indian Philosophy*, 9 (1980), pp. 307–35.

Smart, N., *The Religious Experience of Mankind* (London, 1971).

Smith, W.C., *The Meaning and End of Religion: A New Approach to the Religious Traditions of Mankind* (New York, 1963).

Southwold, M., *Buddhism in Life: The Anthropological Study of Religion and the Sinhalese Practice of Buddhism* (Manchester, 1983).

Streng, F., 'The Buddhist Doctrine of Two Truths as Religious Philosophy', *Journal of Indian Philosophy*, I (1970–2), pp. 262–71.

Swearer, D.K., 'Two Types of Saving Knowledge in the Pāli Suttas', *Philosophy East and West*, 22 (1972), pp. 355–71.

Syrkin, A., 'On the first work of the Sutta Piṭaka: The Brahmajāla-Sutta', in *Buddhist Studies Ancient and Modern*, P. Denwood and A. Piatigorsky (eds) (London, 1983), pp. 153–66.

Taylor, M.C. (ed.), *Critical Terms for Religious Studies* (Chicago, 1998).

Thomas, E.J., *History of Buddhist Thought* (London, 1933).

Tucci, G., 'A Sketch of Indian Materialism', in *Cārvāka/Lokāyata: An Anthology of Source Materials and Some Recent Studies*, D. Chattopadhyaya (ed.) (New Delhi, 1990), pp. 384–93.

Vetter, T., 'Some Remarks on the Older Parts of the Suttanipāta', in *Earliest Buddhism and Madhyamaka*, D. Seyfort Ruegg and L. Schmithausen (eds) (Leiden, 1990), pp. 36–56.

Vogel, C., *The Teachings of the Six Heretics* (Wiesbaden, 1970).

Warder, A.K., 'On the Relationship Between Early Buddhism and Other Contemporary Systems', *Bulletin of the School of Oriental and African Studies*, 18 (1956), pp. 43–63.

—— *Outline of Indian Philosophy* (Delhi, 1971).

—— 'Is Nāgārjuna a Mahāyānist?', in *The Problem of Two Truths in Buddhism and Vedānta*, M. Sprung (ed.) (Dordecht, 1973), pp. 78–88.

—— *Indian Buddhism*, 2nd edn (Delhi, 1980).

Watanabe, F., *Philosophy and its Development in the Nikāyas and Abhidhamma* (Delhi, 1983).

Wayman, A., 'The Meaning of Unwisdom (Avidya)', *Philosophy East and West*, 7 (1957), pp. 21–6.

—— 'The Twenty Reifying Views (*sakkāyadiṭṭhi*)', in *Buddhist Insight: Essays by Alex Wayman*, G. Elder (ed.) (Delhi, 1984).

Whaling, F., *Contemporary Approaches to the Study of Religion*, Volume I, The Humanities (Berlin, 1984).

White, A.R., *Truth* (London, 1971).

Williams, P., *Mahāyāna Buddhism: The Doctrinal Foundations* (London, 1989).

—— *Buddhist Thought: A Complete Introduction to the Indian Tradition* (London, 2000).

Wittgenstein, L., *Tractatus logico-philosophicus*, D.F. Pears and B.F. McGuiness (trans.) (London, 1961).

—— *Lectures and Conversations on Aesthetics, Psychology and Religious Belief*, C. Barrett (ed.) (Berkeley, 1966).

INDEX